TEXTUAL STUDIES IN THE BOOK OF JOSHUA

HARVARD SEMITIC MUSEUM

HARVARD SEMITIC MONOGRAPHS

edited by
Frank Moore Cross

Number 28

TEXTUAL STUDIES IN THE BOOK OF JOSHUA

by
Leonard J. Greenspoon

Leonard J. Greenspoon

TEXTUAL STUDIES IN THE BOOK OF JOSHUA

Scholars Press
Chico, California

TEXTUAL STUDIES IN THE BOOK OF JOSHUA

Leonard J. Greenspoon

Library of Congress Cataloging in Publication Data

Greenspoon, Leonard Jay
  Textual studies in the Book of Joshua.

  (Harvard Semitic monographs ; no. 28)
  1. Bible. O.T. Joshua—Criticism, Textual. I. Title.
II. Series.
BS1295.2.G73 1983 222'.2044   83–3434
ISBN 0–89130–622–6

Printed in the United States of America

To

Rose

Magda, Sigi

Ellie, Gallit, Talya

CONTENTS

Preface   ix

Abbreviations   xi

INTRODUCTION AND EXPLANATION OF SIGLA   1

    Notes to Introduction   5

1. THE READINGS OF THEODOTION IN JOSHUA   7

    Charts: 10
    The Readings of Theodotion in Joshua
    Statistical Summary of Th.-readings

    Category 1:   Th. = OG = MT   33
      1.1
      1.2
    Category 2:   Th. = OG ≠ MT   57
    Cateogry 3:   Th. ≠ OG, but both = MT   83
    Category 4:   Th. = MT ≠ OG   115
      4.1
      4.2
      4.3
    Category 5:   Th. ≠ MT and Th. ≠ OG   159
    Category 6:   עגלול   170
    Notes to Chapter 1   173

    Appendix: The Siglum οι ο′   207
    Notes to Appendix   217

2. THEODOTION AND AQUILA, THEODOTION AND
    SYMMACHUS IN JOSHUA   219

    Charts: 221
    Statistical Summary of Th.-Aq. and Th.-Sym.
      Equivalents
    Agreements between Aquila and Theodotion
    Agreements between Symmachus and Theodotion

    Aquila   235
    Symmachus   255
    Notes to Chapter 2   265

3. THE καιγε RECENSION IN JOSHUA   269

    Chart:
    Characteristics Identified with the καιγε
      Recension   270

Charts: 339
καιγε and non-καιγε readings in Th.
καιγε and non-καιγε readings in Aq.
καιγε and non-καιγε readings in the
    additions of Origen and in other,
    'qualitative' changes made by Origen
καιγε and non-καιγε readings in Sym.
καιγε readings in other witnesses to the text

Notes to Chapter 3   357

CONCLUSION   379

BIBLIOGRAPHY   383

INDEX OF PASSAGES TREATED   391

/

PREFACE

I was first introduced to the scholarly study of Joshua by G. Ernest Wright, who at the time was in the process of writing his introduction to the Anchor Bible commentary on the book of Joshua. It was from him that I first heard of Max L. Margolis. While working on my dissertation at Harvard, I benefited in countless ways from having the opportunity to work with Frank M. Cross. Not only in his particular suggestions, but also in the rigor and integrity of his scholarship as a whole he set an impressive example for me. Paul Hanson and John Strugnell were also very helpful during that time.

Over the past few years, during which I have been re-vising my dissertation for publication in the Harvard Semitic Monographs series, it has been a rare privilege to have gotten to know Harry M. Orlinsky. On several occasions in person, and on many others via the mail, he has guided me through the numerous pitfalls that may entrap the text critic. If, as I fear, I have fallen into some, I can only reply that such lapses would have been both more frequent and more serious had it not been for him.

The phrase the New South has many meanings. For me it has meant the opportunity to work in pleasant surroundings with interested colleagues at Clemson University in South Carolina and to come to know others engaged in Biblical Studies through the Southeast. I especially want to thank my Department head, Alan Schaffer, whose methods of encouragement--although not always appreciated at the time--have borne results. Clemson University, through its program of Faculty Research Grants, has generously helped to defray the cost of publication of this volume. A special thanks goes to Betty Barrett, who learned Greek and Hebrew in order to type this manuscript. She may well be one of the few people who read this book through from beginning to end; perseverance of that sort deserves a reward far greater than I can bestow.

I count it as no small victory that as I finish this work, I still have a warm and loving family--my wife, Ellie, and my daughters, Gallit and Talya--with whom to enjoy it. In a way, the growth of my family has paralleled the growth of my interest in Joshua, for my first daughter was born shortly before I completed the dissertation and my second, just before I finished this book.

Two important commentaries on the book of Joshua have appeared over the last two years: M. H. Woudstra's in the New International Commentary on the Old Testament and Robert C. Boling - G. Ernest Wright's in the Anchor Bible. I was unable to use either in this book, but do plan to discuss them, especially their handling of the text, in reviews and review articles.

Barthélemy

Dominique Barthélemy, *Les Devanciers d'Aquila*, Supplements to *Vetus Testamentum*, 10 (Leiden: E. J. Brill, 1963).

BDB

Francis Brown, S. R. Driver, and Charles A. Briggs, eds., *A Hebrew and English Lexicon of the Old Testament with an Appendix Containing the Biblical Aramaic*, corrected reprint of 1907 ed. (Oxford: Clarendon Press, 1968).

Benjamin

Charles Dow Benjamin, *The Variations between the Hebrew and Greek Texts of Joshua: Chapters 1 - 12* (University of Pennsylvania, 1921).

B-F

F. Blass and A. Debrunner, *A Greek Grammar of the New Testament and Other Early Christian Literature*, translated and revised by Robert W. Funk (Chicago: The University of Chicago Press, 1961).

BH^3

Rud. Kittel *et al.*, eds., *Biblica Hebraica*, 14th ed., emended printing of 7th ed., a revised and expanded version of 3rd ed. (Stuttgart, 1966) [Joshua prepared by M. Noth].

BH^4

K. Elliger, W. Rudolph, *et al.*, eds., *Biblia Hebraica Stuttgartensia* (Stuttgart, 1977) [Joshua prepared by R. Meyer].

B-McL

Alan England Brooke and Norman McLean, with Henry St. John Thackeray for Vols. II and III, eds., *The Old Testament in Greek:* Vol. I, *The Octateuch*; Vol. II, *The Later Historical Books*; Vol. III, Part 1, *Esther, Judith, Tobit* (Cambridge, 1906-1940).

Bodine

Walter Ray Bodine, *The Greek Text of Judges: Recensional Developments*, Harvard Semitic Monographs, 23 (Chico: Scholars Press, 1980).

Bodine, "*KAIGE* in Judges"

Walter Ray Bodine, "*KAIGE* and other Recensional Developments in the Greek Text of Judges," *Bulletin of the International Organization for Septuagint and Cognate Studies* 13 (1980), 45-57.

Field	Frederick Field, ed., *Origenis Hexaplorum quae supersunt sive veterum interpretum Graecorum in totum Vetus Testamentum fragmenta*, 2 vols. (Oxford, 1875).
GKC	W. Gesenius, *Hebrew Grammar*, ed. E. Kautzsch, 2nd Eng. ed., revised in accordance with 28th German edition by A. E. Cowley (Oxford: Clarendon Press, 1966).
Holmes	Samuel Holmes, *Joshua: The Hebrew and Greek Texts* (Cambridge: University Press, 1914).
H-R	Edwin Hatch and Henry A. Redpath, *A Concordance to the Septuagint and the Other Greek Versions of the Old Testament (Including the Apocryphal Books)*, photomechanical reprint of the 1897 Oxford ed., 3 vols. in 2 (Graz, Austria, 1954).
Lagarde	Paul de Lagarde, *Bibliothecae Syriacae a Paulo de Lagarde collectae quae ad philologiam sacram pertinent*, ed. Alfred Rahlfs (Göttingen, 1892).
L-S	H. G. Liddell and R. Scott, *A Greek-English Lexicon* (New York, 1878).
Margolis	Max L. Margolis, *The Book of Joshua in Greek* (Paris: Librairie Orientaliste Paul Guethner, 1931).
Margolis "Specimen"	Max L. Margolis, "Specimen of a New Edition of the Greek Joshua," *Jewish Studies in Memory of Israel Abrahams* (New York: Jewish Institute of Religion, 1927), pp. 307-323; reprinted in Sidney Jellicoe, ed., *Studies in the Septuagint: Origins, Recensions, and Interpretations* (New York: KTAV, 1974), pp. 434-450.
Margolis "ΧΩΡΙΣ"	Max L. Margolis, ΧΩΡΙΣ," *Oriental Studies published in Commemoration of the Fortieth Anniversary of Paul Haupt as Director of the Oriental Seminary of the Johns Hopkins University* (Baltimore: The Johns Hopkins University Press, 1926), pp. 84-92.
Noth	Martin Noth, *Das Buch Josua*, 3rd ed., HAT 7 (Tübingen: J. C. B. Mohr [Paul Siebeck], 1971).

O'Connell   Kevin G. O'Connell, *The Theodotionic Revision of the Book of Exodus*, Harvard Semitic Monographs, 3 (Cambridge: Harvard University Press, 1972).

Orlinsky, "Joshua"   Harry M. Orlinsky, "The Hebrew *Vorlage* of the Septuagint of the Book of Joshua," *Supplements to Vetus Testamentum*, 17 (Rome, 1968) (Leiden: E. J. Brill, 1969), 187-195.

Pretzl   Otto Pretzl, "Die griechischen Handscriften-gruppen im Buche Josue untersucht nach ihrer Eigenart und ihrem Verhältnis zueinander," *Biblica* 9 (1928), 377-427.

R-T   Joseph Reider, *An Index to Aquila*, completed and revised by Nigel Turner, Supplements to *Vetus Testamentum*, 12 (Leiden: E. J. Brill, 1966).

Shenkel   James Donald Shenkel, *Chronology and Recensional Development in the Greek Text of Kings*, Harvard Semitic Monographs, 1 (Cambridge: Harvard University Press, 1968).

Smyth   Herbert Weir Smyth, *Greek Grammar*, revised by Gordon M. Messing (Cambridge: Harvard University Press, 1966).

Soggin   J. Alberto Soggin, *Joshua*, tr. R. A. Wilson, The Old Testament Library (Philadelphia: Westminster Press, 1972).

Thackeray   H. St. John Thackeray, *A Grammar of the Old Testament in Greek*, vol. 1 (Introduction, Orthography and Accidence) (Cambridge: University Press, 1909).

Tov   Emanuel Tov, "Transliterations of Hebrew Words in the Greek Versions of the Old Testament: A Further Characteristic of the *kaige*-Th. Revision?" *Textus* 8. Annual of the Hebrew University Bible Project, ed. S. Talmon (Jerusalem: Magnes Press, 1973), 78-92.

Note: We have not included in the above list abbreviations for books of the Bible or for journals.

INTRODUCTION AND EXPLANATION OF SIGLA

We have undertaken this study as an effort to advance the discipline of text criticism in general and Joshua studies in particular. Taking our cue from a line of research that has been especially productive in recent years, we focus our attention on the Theodotionic recension in the book of Joshua.

Over the past century several text critics have turned to the book of Joshua on occasion; one towering figure made this book the center of his scholarly research--Max L. Margolis. A scholar firmly convinced of the correctness of the Lagardian approach, he produced a masterful edition, in which he sought to present a text as close as possible to the original form of the Old Greek translation of Joshua. Four parts of this edition (covering 1:1 - 19:38) were available to us.[1] Margolis' critical judgments concerning the OG of Joshua are excellent, so that even when we are unable to accept some of his conclusions we admire the process by which he arrived at them. The complete corpus of Margolis' work on the Septuagint has never been published, but what is available remains of inestimable value for those working in the field.[2]

Margolis' methodology for arriving at the form of the OG was sound and the results he reached in this respect have stood the test of time remarkably well. In another, related area this has not been the case; Margolis' judgment that the OG translator had before him a text almost identical to the MT, which he then modified generally in the direction of curtailment, cannot be sustained.[3] The evidence--which makes it clear that the OG translator of Joshua made every attempt to represent what he read or misread in his Hebrew text--simply does not support such negative opinions concerning this translator's fidelity to the Hebrew he rendered. For Joshua no one has argued this point more forcefully and cogently than Harry M. Orlinsky.[4]

The following quotation from Kevin O'Connell sums up well
the way in which we have organized the material presented in
this book:

> The best way to identify ΚΑΙΓΕ material is to show
> its intermediary position between the OG and Aquila,
> its tendency to revise the OG toward the Hebrew text
> (whether MT or proto-MT) and its sharing of known[5]
> ΚΑΙΓΕ stylistic or translational characteristics.

Chapter one of our work relates to the second member of
O'Connell's proposed triad. A detailed study of the 171
readings ascribed to Th. in Joshua shows that he did revise
(a form of) the OG to a Hebrew identical in almost every respect to the MT. This chapter ends with an appendix concerning the text tradition designated as οι ο'.

Chapter two establishes the "intermediary" position that
Th. occupies between the OG and Aq.; he occupies a similar
position with respect to the OG and Sym. Both Aq. and Sym.
knew and used Th., the former as *the* basis and the later as *a*
basis for their own further activity.

In Chapter three we take up 96 characteristics that can be
identified with the καιγε recension. Th. shares many of these
characteristics, and especially the tendency to establish
standard Greek renderings for certain Hebrew words and phrases.
We also discuss other witnesses to this recension.

In citing manuscripts, we make use of the letter designa-
tions found in B-McL. For the principal versions these
include:

Ꭺ	=	Armenian
Ꮯ	=	Sahidic
Ꮛ	=	Ethiopic
Ꮮ	=	Old Latin
Ꮪ	=	Syro-hexapla (from Lagarde's edition)
Ꮪ^m	=	readings from Andreas Masius, who had access to a Syriac manuscript now lost.

For Aquila, Theodotion, and Symmachus we use either the Greek
α', θ', σ', or the abbreviations Aq., Th., Sym., respectively.

For the grouping of manuscripts we follow Margolis, who divides most manuscripts into four recensions:

Egyptian (abbreviation: E̲)

Lucianic (S̲)

Palestinian (P̲)

Constantinople (C̲).

The main representatives of E̲ are LXX^B and r, also the Coptic and Ethiopic versions. This recension, especially Codex Vaticanus (B), is our best witness to the OG in Joshua.[6] The Lucianic recension (S̲) may be divided into two subgroups:

S̲$_a$ = Kgnwℓ

S̲$_b$ = tpd. Up until 2:18(middle) b is also Lucianic.

These manuscripts are held together by a number of unique readings. We discuss the Palestinian and Constantinople recensions in some detail in the appendix to chapter one. Here we simply list the major representatives of each recension:

P̲   Gbb'cx∮ On

C̲   AMNϴlouyb$_2$.[7] The N̲-group, while not a recension proper, does form a cohesive unit in Joshua. The major manuscripts in this group are efjsvz. v is of particular importance in that in its margin, and occasionally in its text, are found most of the readings ascribed to Theodotion for Joshua.

We list all readings of Theodotion in Greek, providing a translation in that language for those readings preserved only in Syriac. This is also true for Aquila and Symmachus. When it is necessary to write a word or phrase in Syriac, we generally use Hebrew characters and underline them.

Note: The MT is cited from *BH*[4].

Notes to Introduction

1. Emanuel Tov recently reported his discovery of the
missing fifth part of this work, which covers the remainder of
Joshua in pp. 385-475. Tov also reported his plans to publish
this material, which he located in the archives of Dropsie
University in Philadelphia. On this see Emanuel Tov, "The
Discovery of the Missing Part of Margolis' Edition of Joshua,"
*Bulletin of the International Organization for Septuagint and
Cognate Studies* 14 (1981), 17-21.

2. On Margolis' contributions as a text critic of the Old
Testament, see especially Harry M. Orlinsky, "Margolis' Work
in the Septuagint," *Max Leopold Margolis: Scholar and Teacher*
(Philadelphia, 1952), pp. 34-44 (chapter IV). Jacob Reider
prepared an annotated bibliography of all of Margolis' work for
the same volume. We have made use of Margolis' unpublished
work in the following articles: Leonard Greenspoon, "Max L.
Margolis on the Complutensian Text of Joshua," *Bulletin of the
International Organization for Septuagint and Cognate Studies*
12 (1979), 43-56; *idem*, "Ars Scribendi: Max Margolis' Paper
'Preparing Scribe's Copy in the Age of Manuscripts,'" *Jewish
Quarterly Review* NS 71 (1981), 133-150; *idem*, "Ars Scribendi;
Pars Reperta," *JQR* 72 (1982), 43f. Our sincerest thanks go to
Professor Harry M. Orlinsky and to the staff at Dropsie
University for allowing us access to this material. We are
presently preparing a volume on Margolis for the Society of
Biblical Literature's "Biblical Scholarship in North America"
series.

3. Typical of Margolis' opinion in this regard is the
following statement (from "Textual Criticism of the Greek
Old Testament," *Proceedings of the American Philosophical
Society* 67 [1928], p. 196): On the whole the Old Greek
translator "handled his Hebrew freely, repeatedly curtailing
the text . . . . While here and there the translator read a
slightly different Hebrew compared with the received Hebrew,
substantially the Hebrew and the Greek. . .do tally." It is
worth pointing out that by and large the Old Greek text of
Joshua is shorter than the MT; witness the preponderance of
asterisked passages in Origen's Hexapla.

4. See especially Orlinsky, "Joshua," and the literature
cited there.

5. O'Connell, p. 291. Bodine (p. 42) remarks that "the
second half of the third of these is the most objective,
especially now that so many translational characteristics
have been isolated and made known through publication." He
rightly cautions that "although the others are useful. . .they
are subject to complicating factors."

6. For Margolis' comments on LXX^B and other manuscripts, see Margolis, "Specimen." There (pp. 315f) he writes, for example, that "the road to the original text of the Old Greek leads across the common, unrevised text. . . . Ultimately we must operate with $\underline{E}$, but not without taking into account the residue of the common text imbedded elsewhere."

7. Margolis divided the manuscripts of the $\underline{P}$ recension into two subgroups:

$\underline{P}_1$ (which for him represents the Hexapla) = G♭b'c;

$\underline{P}_2$ (for him the Tetrapla)   = x𝕤 On.

The Readings of Theodotion in Joshua

At 171 places in the book of Joshua a reading has been attributed to Th. in one or more sources. These readings range in length from a single word to two verses. In this chapter our primary interest is the relationship of Th. to the OG and to the MT. In order to investigate these relationships and draw from the mass of evidence some general conclusions, we have divided the readings ascribed to Th. into 6 categories. The organizing principles of the first 5 can be viewed through the following formulae:

category 1   where Th. = OG = MT
category 2   where Th. = OG ≠ MT
category 3   where Th. ≠ OG, but both = MT
category 4   where Th. = MT ≠ OC
category 5   where Th. ≠ MT and Th. ≠ OG

category 6 brings together 4 readings that preserve Th.'s representations of the Hebrew place name עגלון.

Categories 1 and 4 are further divided into two and three sub-categories, respectively. The Th.-OG relationship is more prominent in categories 2 and 3, while the relationship of Th. to the MT receives greater emphasis in categories 4 and 5. We are fair neither to the complexity of relationships nor to the diverse nature of the material if we attempt to force the evidence to fit too neatly into these formulae; nevertheless, such formulae do retain their usefulness as organizing principles, without which an orderly presentation of material is impossible.

As we noted above, the two points of greatest interest in this part of our study are the text from which and the text to which Th. made his revision. Through the evidence gathered in this chapter we are able to identify the text Th. revised: (a form of) the OG. It also becomes clear that Th. corrected this form of the OG to a Hebrew text identical in almost every reading to the MT. LXX^B is far and away our surest guide to the OG, although this manuscript is not immune to corruption through scribal error or hexaplaric influence. The possibility of scribal error must be taken into account in determining the correct form of the readings for ϑ', α', σ', and ο' as well. It stands to reason that conclusions concerning relationships can be no sounder than our prior determinations concerning the texts of the OG and Th.

Since this chapter is both a study in itself and the basis for the studies we conduct in the following chapters, the presentation of evidence is as full as possible. The numbers we assign to the readings of Th. in this chapter are employed throughout this book, and the division into categories and sub-categories is followed in chapter 2 as well as here.

Each of the first 5 categories has its own introduction, which begins with an explanation of the formula underlying the inclusion of readings within it. The next section of these introductions contains a brief discussion of the major conclusions reached on the basis of the evidence included in that category. A statement on the pattern for presentation of evidence also forms part of each introduction.

The chart that follows is divided into 8 columns: (1) the number assigned to each reading of Th.; (2) the category or sub-category into which the reading is placed; (3) the location of the reading within the book of Joshua (where there is a difference in the numbering of verses or arrangement of material between the MT and the LXX, the chapter and verse of the latter are placed within parenthesis); (4) the reading itself, in Greek; (5) the source or sources that contain the reading ascribed to Th.; (6-8) an x in the α', σ', or ο' column indicates that a partial or complete equivalent for the reading of Th. is attributed to that text in one or more sources.

Columns 4-8 require further comment. What we present in these columns are the results of our research. At times there are contradictions or other difficulties in ascriptions that make it difficult to determine the exact wording of Th. Difficulties also arise when two different forms are attributed to Th. or when the sole form ascribed to him is corrupt. The same holds true when attempting to arrive at the authentic texts for α', σ', and ο'. We have had to make judgments in these cases, and substantiation for our judgements is supplied in our discussion of each reading. Since Th. wrote in Greek, we have given all his readings in that language. We give support for translations from the Syriac at appropriate places in the discussion of such readings.

The Readings of Theodotion in Joshua

					α'	σ'	ο'
1.	(4.1)	1:1	δουλου κυριου	𝔊(txt)			x
2.	(4.1)	1:2(a)	τουτον	𝔊(txt)			
3.	(4.1)	1:2(b)	τοις υιοις ισραηλ	𝔤^m			
4.	(4.1)	1:3	επ αυτου (or: επ αυτον)	Mv			
5.	(4.3)	1:5	ουθεις κατα προσωπον σου	vz(sine nom)	x	x	
6.	(1.2)	1:6	διελεις	vz			
7.	(1.2)	1:7(a)	ουδε	M		x	x
8.	(4.3)	1:7(b)	πορευη	Mvz			

11

#		Ref.	Greek	Source	α'	σ'	ο'
9.	(3)	1:8	ινα φυλασσης ποιειν παντα τα γεγραμμενα	v	x	x	x
10.	(1.2)	1:11	διαβαινετε	v			x
11.	(2)	1:13	κυριου	v			x
12.	(3)	1:18	πλην	v	x		
13.	(4.1)	2:1	κρυβη	Mvz(sine nom)	x		
14.	(4.1)	2:2	ιδου	g^m			x
15.	(2)	2:4(a)	εκρυψεν αυτους και ειπεν αυτοις	v	x	x	x
16.	(4.1)	2:4(b)	και ουκ εγνων ποθεν εισιν	vz			

				Mv(txt)	α'	σ'	ο
17.	(3)	2:6	τοις ξυλοις της λιθοκολλησεως της οικοδομης	Mv(txt)	X	X	X
18.	(1.1)	2:7	οπισω αυτων	ν	X	X	X
19.	(4.1)	2:9	και οτι τετηκασιν παντες οι κατοικουντες την γην απο προσωπου υμων	M	X		X
20.	(3)	2:12	μετα του οικου	Mν	X		
21.	(4.3)	2:14	και εσται ως αν παραβη κυριος ημιν την πολιν ποιησομεν μετα σου	ν	X		X
22.	(1.2)	3:4	ινα επιστρεψη	ν	X	X	X
23.	(1.2)	3:6	επορευοντο	ν(txt)	X	X	X

		verse			α'	σ'	ο'
24.	(2)	3:8	της μερος του υδατος	v	x	x	x
25.	(1.2)	3:10	εν τουτω	v			x
26.	(2)	3:12	ενα αφ εκαστης φυλης	v	x	x	x
27.	(4.1)	3:13	δυο δρομος	Mgv	x	x	
28.	(4.3)	3:14	και εγενετο ως απηριθμησε ο λαος	Mv	x	x	x
29.	(3)	3:15(a)	δυο	M	x		
30.	(3)	3:15(b)	το [επληρουν]	v			
31.	(4.3)	3:16	μερος σφοδρα	v	x	x	x
32.	(3)	3:17	διεβησαν	v		x	

No.		Verse	Greek	v(txt)	α'	σ'	ο'
33.	(3)	4:1	τω ιησου	ϧ	x	x	x
34.	(4.3)	4:5	εις προσωπον κιβωτου κυριου		x		
35.	(3)	4:10(a)	εμμεσω	M	x		
36.	(1.2)	4:10(b), 4:11	διεβησαν	v / M			x
37.	(2)	4:12	ο ηπισατε	v	x	x	x
38.	(1.2)	4:14	ωσπερ	v			x
39.	(3)	4:19	το	v			x
40.	(3)	4:22	αναγγελειτε	v		x	x
41.	(1.2)	4:23	παρηλθομεν	v	x		x

				α'	σ'	ο'
42.	(2)	5:2	Σιωνοτομακα Σραιδιαι Σραιαχα / επιτιδαι Σραιαχα και	V	x	x	x
43.	(3)	5:12	και εφαγον απο των καρπων της γης χανααν	MVz	x	x	
44.	(2)	6:2	Σοντο	MV			x
45.	(2)	6:17	(τω κυριω) των δυναμεων	V			x
46.	(3)	6:24(a)	ενεπυρισθη εν πυρι	V	x	x	x
47.	(5)	6:24(b)	και παντος χαλκου	V			x
48.	(4.3)	7:1	αχαν	V	x	x	x
49.	(1.2)	7:3	μη αναβητω	V	x	x	x

#		verse	reading	source	α'	σ'	ο'
50.	(3)	7:15	αφροσυνην	g^m			
51.	(3)	7:21(a)	ιματιον	vz (om θ')	x	x	
52.	(3)	7:21(b)	και επεθυμησα	bg	x		
53.	(3)	7:24	κοιλαδα αχωρ	M		x	
54.	(3)	7:26	κοιλας αχωρ	v	x	x	
55.	(4.3)	8:5	και πας ο λαος ιση πομ	v	x	x	x
56.	(5)	8:12-13	Key words: βηθαυν (v 12); θαλασσαν της γαι (v 12 end)	g^m		x	
57.	(1.1)	8:19	εκ του τοπου αυτων	v	x	x	x
58.	(5)	9:4(9:10)	ιωπωπ	v (txt)	x	x	x

17

No.		Ref.	Greek		α'	σ'	ο'
59.	(2)	9:5(9:11)	και οι αρτοι αυτων ο επισιτισμος αυτων ξηρος και βεβρωμενος	v	x	x	x
60.	(4.3)	9:9(9:15)	την ακοην	ὁϐ	x	x	
61.	(4.1)	9:21(9:27)	και ειπαν αυτοις οι αρχοντες	ϐ(txt)			
62.	(4.3)	10:1	αδωνισεδεκ	vz	x	x	x
63.	(2)	10:3	φειδων	v(txt)	x	x	x
64.	(4.3)	10:5(a)	των αμορραιων	vg^m	x	x	x
65.	(6)	10:5(b)	αιγλωμ/εγλωμ	vz	x	x	x
66.	(4.2)	10:10(a)	απο προσωπου ισραηλ	v			x
67.	(4.3)	10:10(b)	βαιθωρων	v	x	x	x

					α'	σ'	ο'
68.	(1.2)	10:10(c)	μακηδα	v	x	x	x
69.	(4.3)	10:11(a)	βαιθωρων	v	x	x	x
70.	(2)	10:11(b)	λιθους χαλαζης	v(txt)	x	x	x
71.	(1.2)	10:11(c)	[απο] θανοντες	v	x		x
72.	(1.1)	10:11(d)	μαχαιρα	v	x	x	x
73.	(4.1)	10:13	ουχι τουτο γεγραμμενον επι βιβλιου του ευθους	g(txt)			
74.	(3)	10:19	υμεις δε μη στηκετε καταδιωκοντες οπισω	v	x	x	x
75.	(2)	10:20(a)	παντες οι υιοι ισραηλ	v	x	x	x

					α´	σ´	ο´
76.	(1.1)	10:20(b)	ϲωϲ	v	x	x	x
77.	(6)	10:23	αιγλωμ	v	x	x	x
78.	(4.1)	10:27	λιθους μεγαλους	v	x	x	x
79.	(3)	10:28	ξιφους	v	x	x	x
80.	(1.1)	10:30	εν αυτη	.v	x	x	x
81.	(5)	10:33	τοτε εξηλθεν αιλαμ βασιλευς γαζειρ βοηθησων τη λαχεις	vv(txt) z	x	x	x
82.	(6)	10:34	οδολλαμ	v(txt)	x	x	x
83.	(1.2)	10:40(a)	ναγεβ	v	x	x	x
84.	(1.1)	10:40(b)	τους βασιλεις	v	x	x	x

	ο'	σ'	σ'				
85.	(3)	10:41	πασαν γην γοσομ	ν	x	x	x
86.	(1.2)	11:1(a)	ιωβαβ	νz	x	x	x
87.	(4.3)	11:1(b)	μαδων	ν	x	x	x
88.	(4.3)	11:1(c)	συμοων	ν	x	x	x
89.	(1.2)	11:8(a)	μασρεφωθμαιμ	ν	x	x	x
90.	(2)	11:8(b)	μασφα	ν	x	x	x
91.	(3)	11:10	επεστραψεν	ν	x	x	x
92.	(2)	11:13	(τας)κεχωματισμενας	ß	x	x	x
93.	(4.3)	11:19	την γαβαων τοις υιοις ιηλ	ν	x		

					α̇	σ̇	ο̇
94.	(2)	11:21(a)	ανωβ		x	x	x
95.	(1.1)	11:21(b)	ιησους	∨	x	x	x
96.	(1.1)	11:23	(φυλας) αυτων	∨	x	x	x
97.	(1.2)	12:1	δυο ανειλον υιοι ισραηλ	∨	x	x	x
98.	(1.2)	12:2(a)	αρουρ	∨	x	x	x
99.	(1.1)	12:2(b)	ορια υιων αμμων	∨	x	x	x
100.	(1.2)	12:4-5	και εν εδραει αρχων	∨	x		x
101.	(4.3)	12:5	γεσουρε (-ει)	∨	x	x	x
102.	(3)	12:7	(εις) σεειρα	∨	x	x	x

					α'	σ'	o'
103.	(6)	12:12	αιλωμ	v	x		x
104.	(1.2)	12:14	αραδ	v(txt)	x		x
105.	(1.2)	13:5	βααλγα(δ)	vz	x	x	x
106.	(4.3)	13:8	δεδωκεν αυτοις	v	x	x	x
107.	(4.3)	13:11	γεσουρει	v	x	x	x
108.	(3)	13:13	μαχαθι	v	x		x
109.	(1.1)	13:16	και η	v	x	x	x
110.	(4.3)	13:21	αρχοντας σηων	v	x	x	x
111.	(1.1)	13:23	υιων ρουβην	v	x	x	x

					α'	σ'	ο'
112.	(2)	13:26	δεβεια	v	x		x
113.	(3)	13:27(a)	βηθναμρα	v			x
114.	(1.2)	13:27(b)	μερους της θαλασσης	v	x	x	x
115.	(3)	14:6	εν γαλγαλοις	v		x	x
116.	(1.2)	14:7	και απεκριθην	v(txt) ƃ	x	x	x
117.	(1.1)	14:8	(αδελφοι) μου	v	x	x	x
118.	(4.3)	14:9	θεου μου	v	x	x	x
119.	(3)	14:12	εν τη ημερα εκεινη	v	x	x	x
120.	(4.3)	15:3	σ(ε)ινα	v	x	x	x

					α'	σ'	ο'
121.	(4.3)	15:6(a)	επι βαιθαγλα	v	x	x	x
122.	(4.3)	15:6(b)	βοεν	vz	x	x	x
123.	(2)	15:9	και διεκβαλλει εις γα(ε)ι ορος εφρων	vz	x	x	x
124.	(4.3)	15:14	οπσαι	v	x	x	x
125.	(3)	15:17	αδελφος	v	x	x	x
126.	(1.2)	15:19(a)	ναγεβ	v(txt)	x	x	x
127.	(2)	15:19(b)	γωλαθμαιμ	v	x	x	x
128.	(4.3)	15:21	πολεις αυτων απο τελους φυλης	vz	x	x	x

				α'	σ'	θ'	
129.	(4.3)	15:23	και ασωρ	v	x	x	x
130.	(4.3)	15:25 (15:24)	και ασωρ την καινην	v	x	x	x
131.	(3)	15:46	αζωτου	g			x
132.	(5)	16:2	δ'ης	v(txt)	x	x	x
133.	(3)	16:10	εν μεθερ φαραω	v	x	x	x
134.	(4.3)	17:2	και τοχεκ και τοις υιοις αοωρ και	v	x	x	x
135.	(4.1)	17:4	υιου ναυη	v	x	x	x
136.	(4.3)	17:16	σιδηρος	g^m			x
137.	(3)	18:8	διαγραψαι	vg^m	x	x	

					α΄	σ΄	ο΄
138.	(4.3)	18:15	ορια θαλασσης	v	x	x	x
139.	(4.3)	18:28	καριαθ πολεις	ℊ	x		
140.	(4.1)	19:34	(τω) ιουδα	ℊ(txt)		x	x
141.	(1.2)	20:9	εν χειρι	v	x	x	x
142.	(4.3)	21:3	εκ της κληρονομιας αυτων	ℊ	x		
143.	(1.2)	21:13	την πολιν	v			x
144.	(5)	21:20	η πολις των ιερεων αυτων	z	x	x	x
145.	(5)	21:26	πασαι αι πολεις	v	x	x	x
146.	(1.2)	21:44(a)	αυτους	v		x	x

					α'	σ'	ο'
147.	(1.2)	21:44(b)	ανεστη	v	x	x	x
148.	(1.2)	21:44(c)	κυριος ειπε τας χειρας αυτων	v			x
149.	(4.3)	22:1	ρουβηνιτας	v(txt)	x	x	x
150.	(3)	22:5(a)	και κολλασθαι	℘	x	x	x
151.	(3)	22:5(b)	καρδιας	v	x	x	
152.	(4.3)	22:8	επιστρεφετε	v	x	x	x
153.	(3)	22:10(a)	θυσιαστηριον	v	x	x	x
154.	(3)	22:10(b)	τω	v	x	x	x
155.	(4.3)	22:18(a)	υμεις	v	x		x

					α'	σ'	ο'
156.	(1.2)	22:18(b)	[παντ] α	v			x
157.	(4.1)	22:25	ανα μεσον ημων και υμων (οι) υιοι ρουβην και (οι) υιοι γαδ τον ιορδανην	v	x	x	x
158.	(4.3)	22:28	και εροθμεν	v	x	x	x
159.	(2)	22:34	και τω γαδ και ειπαν	v	x	x	x
160.	(3)	23:4(a)	(υπ) εβαλα	n	x	x	
161.	(4.3)	23:4(b)	εθνη α εξωλοθρευσα	v	x	x	x
162.	(4.3)	23:10	[ουτος] εξεπολεμει μεθ υμων	vz(sine nom)	x		x
163.	(1.2)	23:13	πλευραις	v(txt)	x	x	x

					α'	σ'	ο
164.	(2)	24:1	σηλω	v(txt)	x	x	o
165.	(4.3)	24:10	και ευλογιαις ευλογησεν σαιη	v	x	x	x
166.	(3)	24:15	εκλεξασθε	v(txt)	x	x	x
167.	(2)	24:25	σηλω	v(txt)	x	x	x
168.	(4.3)	24:26(a)	εκει	v	x	x	
169.	(3)	24:26(b)	υποκατω της δρυος	ὁv	x	x	x
170.	(3)	24:27	ουτος	v(txt)			x
171.	(2)	(24:33b)	και εκυριευσεν	v			x

Statistical Summary of Th.-readings

1. Number of readings (total):   171

2. By chapter:

1.	12	13.	10
2.	9	14.	5
3.	11	15.	12
4.	9	16.	2
5.	2	17.	3
6.	4	18.	3
7.	7	19.	1
8.	3	20.	1
9.	4	21.	7
10.	24	22.	11
11.	11	23.	4
12.	8	24.	8

3. 1:1 - 13:25 is one half of the book of Joshua in Hebrew by verses; 13:25 also represents the approximate middle point in the Greek and in other versions. 111 of the Th.-readings fall in the first half, with (only) 60 in the second half.

Category 1: Introduction

Th. = OG = MT. This formula is self-explanatory. Most of
these readings are preserved in the margin of manuscript v
and form a contrast with v(txt); occasionally, v(txt) is
attributed to Th., and a marginal reading, if present, contrasts with this. In each of these readings Th. retained the
OG as a satisfactory representation of the Hebrew to which he
was revising (here clearly = MT). They provide us with
examples of the material Th. took up unchanged into his
recension.

        v is a member of Margolis' N-group, along with efjsz.
Taking this opportunity to investigate that group as well as
the OG and Th., we have organized the material in category 1
around the readings of v and the N-group. At the beginning
of our discussion of each example the reading of the MT, Th.,
and v (or other N-group manuscript) is given. There follow
(1) whenever the reading of Th. also appears in o´, Aq., or
Sym., this is noted, with the word "none" indicating that
the reading of Th. is not found in any of these three texts;
(2) manuscripts outside of the N-group that share the reading
of v or at least the characteristic feature of that reading;
(3) all non-OG, non-N readings, usually listing evidence from
Aq., Sym., o´, and οι λ first.
                            o
        The outline given above represents the general pattern
for presentation and choice of evidence; however, we do not
hesitate to modify this pattern when such flexibility results
in greater clarity. This is true for all sections of this
chapter. The remarks that follow the presentation of evidence
vary in length and scope and are not limited to specific
questions about the text of Th. This also holds true throughout chapter 1.
        The readings we include in 1.1, the first sub-category in
this section, meet the following criteria: (1) the reading of
Th. is also found in o´α´σ´; (2) there is no difficulty in

determining the OG, which is retained in the text of Th.; (3)
the OG clearly translates a Hebrew identical to the MT; (4)
the reading of v(txt) is characteristic of the N-group; (5)
the reading of the N-group is not widely attested outside of
the group. In general these are straightforward, uncomplicated,
and perhaps unexciting readings. The readings contained in 1.2
present more complex data in one or more respects.

1.1

18. (2:7) MT: אחריהם; Th.: οπισω αυτων; N-group: αυτους
οπισω (fvz[txt]), αυτων οπισω (jsz[mg])
(1) o´α´σ´; (2) none; (3) none

57. (8:19) MT: ממקומו; Th.: εκ του τοπου αυτων; N-group:
οπισω αυτων
(1) o´α´σ´; (2) none; (3) Ɫ reads *de locis illis*. x omits
του, and b'n replace εκ with απο. For αυτων ₵ has *ubi absconsi
sunt* (so B-McL).
In the MT the pronominal suffix is singular:
והאורב קם ממקומו. The Greek και τα ενεδρα εξανεστησαν leads to
the plural αυτων.

72. (10:11[d]) MT: בחרב; Th.: μαχαιρα; N-group: εν
μαχαιρα
(1) o´α´σ´; (2) hoq; (3) *gladiis* appears in Ɫ Spec and
μαχαιρας in c.
The use of εν in manuscripts of the N-group results in a
more literal representation of the MT (בחרב) than that found
in the OG and Aq.-Sym.-Th. Where there is a reading characteristic of the N-group, it is not usually the most literal
rendering of the MT.[1]

76. (10:20[b]) MT: עד; Th.: εως; v(txt) and other manuscripts of the N-group omit εως
(1) o´α´σ´; (2) u; (3) none
The text of the N-group at this point is the result of
haplography: OG εως εις τελος. The pronominal suffix עד תמם
is reflected neither in the OG nor in any other extant witness
to the text.

80. (10:30) MT: (2°) בה; Th.: εν αυτη; N-group: εξ
αυτων
(1) o´α´σ´; (2) none; (3) εξ αυτης is found in houЖ-ed.
No. 80 refers to the second εν αυτη in the OG of this
verse.

84. (10:40[b]) MT: מלכיהם; Th.: τους βασιλεις; N-group:
τας βασιλειας

(1) o'a'σ'; (2) u; (3) none

Our main concern here is the noun itself and not the number of the pronominal suffix: MT מלכיהם; OG (τους βασιλεις)
αυτης. The feminine singular of the Greek may be in agreement
with the preceding noun[2] or perhaps go back to την γην. The
reading of the N-group is best explained as the result of
inner-Greek corruption.

95. (11:21[b]) MT: (2°) יהושע; Th.: ιησους; N-group:
κυριος

(1) o'a'σ'; (2) none; (3) u omits ιησους

No. 95 refers to the second ιησους in the OG of this verse.

96. (11:23) MT: לשבטיהם; Th.: (φυλας) αυτων; N-group:
(φυλας) αυτου

(1) o'a'σ'; (2) none: (3) none

The reading characteristic of the N-group here has the
pronominal suffix in the singular. This may well be in agreement with "Israel." This suggestion is rendered more probable
when we consider that the OG did not express the plural suffix
in the preceding word כמחלקם (εν μερισμω; cf. the addition of
the suffix, to agree with the MT, in manuscripts of the P
recension). The lack of the first plural suffix (after
μερισμω) would serve to facilitate the change of the second
from plural to singular.

99. (12:2[b]) MT: גבול בני עמון; Th.: ορια υιων αμμων;
N-group: οριων αμμων

(1) o'a'σ'; (2) u; (3) Manuscripts of the Lucianic recension read οριον instead of ορια and have the proper name in
the form αμμαν.

In the reading of the N-group the two words ορια υιων have
fallen together into the single word οριων.

109. (13:16) MT: והעיר; Th.: και η; N-group: η
(1) ο'α'σ'; (2) f omits η rather than και with the rest of
the N-group; (3) u has η and the following words in the
accusative: (και) την πολιν την.

111. (13:23) MT: (2°) בני ראובן; Th.: υιων ρουβην; N-
group: ρουβην
(1) ο'α'σ'; (2) u; (3) npa$_2$ have των before υιων.

This omission of υιων in the N-group is probably related
to the lack of υιων in the OG of a similar phrase at the beginning of this verse.[3] The text that results in the N-
group exhibits a certain consistency in this regard, as does
the MT (+ = contains the בני/υιων element; - = lacks this
element):

MT + +
OG - +
N   - - .

117. (14:8) MT: ראחי; Th.: (αδελφοι) μου; v(txt) and
other manuscripts of the N-group omit μου after αδελφοι.
(1) ο'α'σ'; (2) Aiy; (3) kmqu replace μου with ημων.

The reading of the N-group here is probably the result of
a simple haplography, the pronoun being lost in the Greek
between -οι and the definite article οι.

1.2

6. (1:6) MT: תנחיל; Th.: διελεις; N-group: αποδιαστελεις
(1) (z has the same marginal notation as v at this point)
none; (2) here v(txt) has the most widely attested reading
(see below at [3]); (3) διελεις, the reading of Th., is
found in B*cmr. αποδιελεις appears in B^{ab}bik and διαστελεις
in h. The reading of v(txt) occurs in AFMNθrell Eus. k(mg)
has αποδιαστελεις διαμειριεις.
The determination of the OG reading here is not easy.
The verb of the most widely attested reading (αποδιαστελλω) is
found only here and at 2 Mac 6:5. αποδιαιρω, the verb in
B^{ab}bik, is found nowhere else in the material covered by H-R.
διαιρω (in B* and Th.) occurs over 40 times in the LXX, including three other times in Joshua (18:4, 5; 22:8).[4] Our
consideration of the evidence leads us to conclude that the
reading in B* and Th. is the OG. In this we are supported by
Margolis.[5] In addition to a comparison with such passages
as Joshua 18:4 and Prv 28:10, 23, it is instructive to note
that one can best explain the variants here if the OG did
indeed contain the form διελεις.

7. (1:7[a]) MT: (שמאול)ו; Th. ουδε; M(txt): η
(1) (The source for this reading of Th. is M[mg]) none;
(2) η, the reading of M(txt), is also found in AFNθafhiklo
quxya₂b₂Аₓℤβ Luc. η appeared in the text of o' and Sym.
according to the following notation in v(mg): o'σ' η εις;
(3) ουδε and η are the only conjunctions that occur in the
extant witnesses to this text.
The appearance of ουδε in the E recension is decisive for
our inclusion of this form in the text of the OG. Margolis
also places ουδε in the OG.[6]

10. (1:11) MT: עברים; Th.: διαβαινετε; N-group:
διαβησεσθε
In our explanation of this reading, we follow for the most part
the interpretation proposed by Margolis.[7] With reference to
the notation in v(mg), οι o' χω θ' βαινετε, he states that
οι o' χω has been misplaced and belongs to και which precedes

the pronoun υμεις.[8] In our opinion the second part of
the notation in v(mg) (ϑ' βαινετε) must mean that Th. had the
compound διαβαινετε found in LXX[B] and elsewhere. There is no
support for simple βαινω or for any verb other than διαβαινω.
(1) As recorded in M(mg), οι λ̥ read διαβαινετε; (2) the future
tense reading of M(txt) and v(txt) also appears in ANϑaefgj-
oqsuxyz(txt)a₂b₂⫲-codd(vid)₵₤; (3) z(mg)(sine nom) also reads
διαβαινετε.[9]

The variant διαβησεσϑε was present in pre-Origenic copies,
according to Margolis, who notes that the Greek translator
sometimes employed the present and at other times the future
to render the Hebrew participle in the sense of the future.

22. (3:4) MT: למען חדעו אשר ; Th.: ινα επιστησϑε; N-group:
ινα επιστησεσϑε (fsvz), ινα επιστησησϑε (ej)
(1) o'; (2) all variants (except for the readings of Aq.
and Sym.; see below) involve forms of επισταμαι, the verb
found in LXX[B] and Th.: -σεσϑε (fsvz) in lpruw and -σησϑε (ej)
in F[b]dkm; (3) from v(mg) we also obtain the following readings:
οπως γνωτε in Aq.; αλλα ινα ειδητε in Sym.
   There is no doubt that the reading of Th., LXX[B], and almost
all other witnesses is the OG.[10] Further, this reading does
equal the MT. The shift from ινα to οπως on the part of Aq.
is paralleled at 1:8.[11]

23. (3:6) MT: וילכו; Th.: επορευοντο; N-group: επορευοντο
(1) (the ascription of this reading to Th. is preserved in
v[txt]) none; (2) the reading of v(txt) is found in all witnesses except those listed in (3) below; (3) variants fall
into two groups: (a) προεπορευοντο in gnptw (manuscripts of
the Lucianic recension); επορευϑησαν in abx₵₤₤ (basically,
manuscripts of Margolis' Palestinian recension). πορευομαι
in the aorist tense is also the reading of o' and Aq., as
noted in v(mg). v(mg) attributes the following to Sym.: και
απηλϑον προ του λαου.[12]
   In our opinion the reading of Th., LXX[B], and others presents the original OG. There are several arguments to support
this position. First, προεπορευοντο of the Lucianic family
is apparently an expansion of επορευοντο with an eye toward the

following prepositional phrase and also with προπορευεσθε
(earlier in v 6) in mind. Secondly, the aorist tense of the P̲
recension and Aq. can be viewed as a revision of the imperfect
tense found in LXX[B] and Th., with the aim of arriving at
greater consistency (cf. the preceding verb in the aorist).
Thus the major variants to the reading of LXX[B]-Th. are best
explained if επορευοντο is indeed the OG. Margolis does include this form in his text of the Old Greek.[13]

25. (3:10) MT: בזאת; Th.: εν τουτω; N̲-group: εν τω νυν
(svz[txt]), εν τουτω νυν (ej)
(1) o'; (2) f has τουτο και; (3) εν τουτο appears in gu
and εν τουτοις in b$_2$. In 𝓛 this phrase is followed by *enim*.
   νυν in manuscripts of the N̲-group is most likely a free
addition. From this notation (which contrasts [only] εν τουτω
of Th. with εν τω νυν found in v[txt]) we are unable to say
whether or not Th. included in his text the equivalent for
ויאמר יהושע which is lacking in the OG.[14]

36. (4:10[b], 11) MT: ויעברו; Th.: διεβησαν; N̲-group:
διεβησαν
The justification for combining what appear to be two separate
readings of Th. (verse 10 v[mg]: διεβησαν] ϑ' οι o᾽ χω;
verse 11 M[mg]: διεβη] ϑ' [διεβη]σαν) is provided by Margolis.
He states that "M[m] substantiates v[m] 4, 10 (ϑ'. . . σαν, the
note clearly belongs in this verse and not in the next where
it is meaningless)."[15] In v 11, to which M(mg) attached its
notation, there is no support for reading the plural of the
verb.[16] Further, v(mg) attributes the plural διεβησαν to Th.
at v 10. Surely, as Margolis argues, the notation in M(mg)
should be attached to the earlier verse.[17] In what follows we
accept Margolis' argument that v(mg) and M(mg) are both to
be connected with 4:10(b) and that both preserved the same
plural form for Th.
(1) none; (2) v(txt) contains the plural διεβησαν, as do all
witnesses except those listed in (3) below; (3) the singular
διεβη is found in AMNϑabhklmouxyb$_2$𝓐𝓛𝓢.

Margolis includes the plural διεβησαν (that is, the reading of Th., LXX[B], and others) in his text of the OG.[18] He notes that διεβη in the singular reflects an adjustment to the preceding εσπευσεν, while the MT has both verbs in the plural. Apparently because of the proximity of the first verb (σπευδω) to the singular subject ο λαος, even the most literal translator of the Hebrew balked at reproducing the plural form found in the MT. With the latter verb (διαβαινω), the OG translator, it would appear, felt no such restraint. Thus, the reading with the verb in the plural, which precisely renders the MT, is original to the OG, while the variant is a later attempt to harmonize the forms of the two verbs in the last part of v 10.

There is still one question to be answered with respect to the notation in v(mg), which reads in full "ϑ' οι ο' χω." Margolis states that χωρις in this case implies omission.[19] He does not, however, specify what οι ο' omitted. There is no evidence for the omission of the entire word διεβησαν. Therefore, we conclude that the "omission" here refers to the plural ending -σαν.[20]

38. (4:14) MT: כאשר; Th.: ωσπερ; N-group: ον τροπον (1) ο'; (2) F; (3) d has ως. For OG ωσπερ μωυσην m has ος και μωυση.

The reading of the N-group presents a distinctive rendering of Hebrew כאשר. The text of v, unlike the OG, does not lack an explicit equivalent for ייראו.[21] (A second) εφοβουντο appeared also in the text of Th., although this fact is not noted in v(txt or mg).

41. (4:23) MT: עברנו; Th.: παρηλθομεν; N-group: παρελθωμεν (vz only) (1) ο'α'σ'; (2) Cyp (pr αν); (3) παρηλθαμεν occurs in bhn. z(mg) (sine nom) reads παρηλθον.

Margolis suggests that the form in z(mg) be read παρηλθομεν, as in v(mg).[22]

49. (7:3) MT: יעל אל; Th.: μη αναβητω; N-group: μη
αναβη

(1) ο'α'; (2) none; (3) <ανα>βαινετω[23] is attributed to σ΄
in v(mg). αναβαινετω is also found in AFMNϴdghik-ptwyz(mg)
a₂b₂ Cyr. αναβατω is the reading of a.

There is no reason to doubt that the reading of Th.,
which is also that of LXX[B], is the OG. This is also the judgment of Margolis.

68. (10:10[c]) MT: מקדה; Th.: μακηδα; N-group: μαδηκα
(jvz[txt]), μαδικα (ef)

(1) ο'α'σ'; (2) only one other reading shows the transposition of k and d that is characteristic of the N-group here:
μαδαικα in Cyr; (3) only minor variation is recorded elsewhere: μακιδα (n), Maceta (𝔄), μακηλα (F[b]la₂), Mageda (𝔏).

The reading of LXX[B] is that of the OG, and there is little
variation among the different traditions. μακηδα (OG, Th., and
others) comes quite close to the form of the proper name preserved in the MT, while the reading with consonants transposed
is characteristic of manuscripts of the N-group.

71. (10:11[c]) MT: מחו; Th.: [απο] ϑανοντες; N-group:
αποϑνησκοντες

(1) ο'α'; (2) Δ₈ u𝔏 Cyr; (3) (οι) αποϑανοντες is omitted in
F[b]n Spec.

The reading of Th. is that of the OG. For this section of
10:11 as a whole, there is some uncertainty as to whether or
not the Hebrew *Vorlage* of the OG was the same as the MT.[24]
However, for the one word specifically covered by the reading
of Th. (here equal to the OG), there is no doubt that we are
dealing with a translation of the same Hebrew as that found
in the MT.

83. (10:40[a]) MT: והנגב; Th.: ναγεβ; N-group: ναβαι
(1) ο'; (2) v(txt) has και την ναβαι, the reading of LXX[B]
(the E recension) and the N-group; (3) the OG transliteration
ναγεβ, which Th. retained in his text, is also found in
AFGNϴa-dfhimptuxyz(mg)b₂𝔄𝔅. The following translation for

Hebrew והגגב is attributed to α'σ' in vz(sine nom)ᴢ: και τον
νοτον (ולחימנא). In Kgn (usually among the best witnesses to
the S recension) the elements representing Hebrew גגב and שפלה
have been transposed. These manuscripts, as well as others of
the S recension, place και τον νοτον (και τον νοτον in Kgpt,
και τον νωτον in n, και νοτον in d), the translation found in
α'σ', after και την πεδινην.

We agree with Margolis' inclusion of the form την ναγεβ
in his text of the OG.[25] As charted by Margolis, the path
from ναβαι (=LXX[B]) to ναγεβ (=OG) is to be traced as follows:
ναβαι followed by κ(αι)=ναβαικ=ναβεκ=νακεβ=ναγεβ.

126. (15:19[a]) MT: הנגב; Th.: ναγεβ; N-group: ναγεβ
(1) (The ascription of this reading to Th. is preserved in
v[txt]) none; (2) the OG transliteration ναγεβ is the
reading of v (see above); it is the underlying form for the
E and C recensions and for the subgroup designated by Margolis
as P₁; (3) as in no. 83 above, v(mg) attributes the translation νοτου to α'σ'. At 15:19 this reading is attributed to o'
also. νοτου is also found in agnxz(mg)ᴢᶜᴢ(txt).

In both of these examples Th. retained the transliteration
of Hebrew נגב that he found in the OG. On the other hand,
Aq.-Sym. supplied a translation in each case.[26] The translation also appears in manuscripts of the S recension (but not
Ł, which reads Nazeb) in both passages and in those of P₂ at
15:19.

נגב occurs 26 times in the Hebrew of Joshua.[27] The OG
translator placed the transliteration ναγεβ in his text four
times (10:40; 11:16; 12:8; 15:19).[28] There is every reason
to believe that in these four passages the translator understood נגב (preceded in each case by the definite article) as
a proper name. Our examination of 10:40 and 15:19 indicated
that the OG procedure was not followed by α'σ' and (under
their influence?) by Greek manuscripts of the S recension. A
similar pattern is found at 11:16 and 12:8. At 11:16 ᴢ preserves the following reading for Aq.-Sym.: וכלה חימנא
(και πασαν την νοτον).[29] νοτος appears in a plus in manuscripts
of the S recension. At 12:8 ᴢ again preserves a reading for

Aq.-Sym. in which the translation νοτος occurs: בחימנא
(εν τω νοτω).[30] Manuscripts of the S̲ recension have νοτος in
their text before εν ναγεβ. Here Margolis indicates that νοτω
in S̲ is a duplicate rendering from Aq.-Sym.[31]

The OG translator used λιψ to render נגב in almost all
other cases in which he read a form of this word in his Hebrew
Vorlage.[32] In every one of these passages manuscripts in
Margolis' P̲₁ subgroup have νοτος. Manuscripts of the S̲ recension retain the OG. In one of his earliest articles on Joshua,
Margolis already drew attention to the distinctive pattern of
usage for νοτος in manuscripts of (what he later was to term)
S̲ and P̲₁: "In the middle part of the book there is a remarkable agreement between Lucian (=19.108. Compl.) and Hexapla
(G for instance), even if the points of difference which are
constant (comp. the Greek for "south") are had in mind."[33]
Manuscripts of the C̲ recension also have νοτος (for OG λιψ) in
chapter 15, but not in later chapters.

From the examples discussed above (in which the OG contained ναγεβ) it is likely that Aq.-Sym. are the source for
the "remarkable agreement" among various manuscript traditions
on the use of νοτος for Hebrew נגב. This suggestion is confirmed by the evidence in those passages in which νοτος
replaces OG λιψ. Four times (all in chapter 15) v(mg)
attributes νοτος to ο' λ and once to λ. At 15:2 𝄢 attributes
to Sym. the reading לוח תימנא (προς νοτον; OG: επι λιβα).[34]
In 18:13, where the OG reads προς λιβα, separate readings have
been preserved for Aq. and Sym. in 𝄢: Aq. לוח תימנא
(προς νοτον); Sym. לתימנא (εις νοτον). In 18:14
חימנא...אנבה, apparently attributed to Aq. in 𝄢, contains
νοτος twice (OG: απο λιβος ... λιβα). Finally, at 18:15 νοτος
is again attributed to Sym. in 𝄢: דתימנא (του νοτου; OG:
προς λιβα).

Aq. and Sym. were apparently consistent in their rendering
of נגב; at least in Joshua there is no clear evidence that
their texts contained a transliteration or a translation other
than νοτος.[35] The use or non-use of νοτος in the various
manuscript traditions seems to have been dependent on the OG.
Where the OG transliterated, the S̲ recension either substituted
translation with νοτος or included νοτος in addition to ναγεβ.

For the subgroup $\underline{P}_1$ there was no need to alter the transliteration of the OG. However, the translation of Aq.-Sym.
replaced the OG translation (λιψ) in manuscripts of $\underline{P}_1$ (and
$\underline{C}$, for chapter 15). We know from 10:40 and 15:19 that Th.
differed from Aq.-Sym. where the OG transliterated. We have
no evidence for the procedure of Th. where the OG translated
with λιψ; however, we would be surprised if the text of Th.
did not contain OG λιψ in every case.[36]

86. (11:1[a]) MT: יורב; Th.: ιωβαβ; $\underline{N}$-group: ιωαβ
(1) (z has the same marginal notation as v at this point)
o'a'σ'; (2) only one other reading shows the loss of medial b:
ιοαβ in u; (3) other variants are ιωβαμ (k), ιωβαθ (a$_2$),
ιωραμ (h), $Iroban$ (℣).

See remarks at 68 above. The reading without medial b is
clearly characteristic of the $\underline{N}$-group.

89. (11:8[a]) MT: משרפות מים; Th.: μασρεφωθμαειμ; $\underline{N}$-
group: μασερων
The reading of Aq. here has been preserved in at least two
forms: μασρεφωθμαειμ in v(mg), where the same reading is also
ascribed to Th. and o', and ועדמא למאצרפות דמיא in ℣ (presumably,
και εως μασρεφωθ υδατων). Field records the following:
"Euseb. in Onomastico, p. 282: μαστραιφωθ μαιμ. Akulas·
μαστραιφωθ υδατος. Symmaxos· μαστραιφωθ θαλασσης [Margolis:
μασρ- On$_1$]."[37] In all probability και εως μασρεφωθ υδατων is
the authentic reading of Aq. (ad aquam appears in Or-lat); at
15:19 Aq. also translated מים (גלה) where the OG and Th.
transliterated.[38]
(1) o' (see above); (2) the underlying form for manuscripts
of the $\underline{N}$-group is μασερων, the reading of LXX^B (see below);
(3) we listed above the reading attributed to Sym. in the
Onomasticon of Eusebius. From the reading preserved in ℣
(דהי דמן ימא) and απο θαλασσης found in manuscripts of $\underline{S}$
(and drawn from Sym.),[39] it is almost certain that the preposition απο was part of the original text of Sym.
    Margolis places μασερεφωθ μαιν in his text of the OG.
According to him, "μασερων $\underline{E}$ goes back to μασερ<εβ>ων and that
to μασερεφωθ (comp. μαζερωθ ℣ and $mas[s]ephoth$ Or$_1$), μαιν

(i.e. μαῑ) was lost before και." In our opinion this conjectured OG reflects MT מַשְׂרֵפוֹת מִיִם, as does the underlying form
for the P and C recensions, μασρεφωθ μαειμ (=Th.ο', as recorded
in v[mg]). Margolis lists the underlying form for the S recension as μασερημωθ απο θαλασσης.[40] Margolis states that
μασερημωθ represents מַשְׂרֵפוֹת in st. absol. He adds that απο
θαλασσης reflects מִיָם, rather than מַיִם of the MT.[41] In light
of other readings in Joshua involving translation-transliteration, it is interesting to note that there is no attempt here
to translate מַשְׂרֵפוֹת, even though מַשְׂרֵפוֹת (from the root שׂרף)
occurs with the meaning of "(a) burning" in Jer 34:5 and Is
33:12.[42]

מַשְׂרֵפוֹת מִיִם occurs in the MT again at 13:6. LXX[B] there
reads μασερεθμεμφωνμαιμ, which, as Holmes notes, "assumes" the
MT.[43] Margolis includes μασερεφωθ μαειμ in his text of the OG
for this passage. The translation υδατων is preserved for Sym.
in b(mg). Soggin notes that this locality is generally
identified with ḵẖirbet el muśrῑfe, south of ras en-nāqūrah
(in modern Hebrew rō's hanniqrā).

97. (12:1) MT: אֲשֶׁר הִכּוּ בְנֵי יִשְׂרָאֵל; Th.: ους ανειλον υιοι
ισραηλ; N-group: ους ανειλεν μωυσης και οι υιοι ισραηλ
(1) ο'α'; (2) only Bbchqux𝕽 present a text without the
plus μωυσης και (and the change of the verb to the singular).
Thus the reading of the N-group is found in AFNθrell 𝔸𝔼(but
see [3] below); (3) 𝕾 marks μωυσης και as additional and contains the verb in the plural in its text. For ανειλον-ισραηλ
r reads ανειλεν ιησους. Abn omit οι before υιοι (as in the
reading of Th.). v(mg) preserves the following reading for
σ': ους επληξαν υιοι ισραηλ.

The original text at this point is that of the MT and
LXX[B] (=Th.). The widespread plus material has been incorporated into the text at this point for at least two reasons:
(1) Moses was involved in the Transjordanian campaigns (cf.
Nu 21:21-35); (2) the filling out of the verse in the above
manner forms a very nice parallel with v 7 (thus in the LXX:
ους ανειλεν ιησους και οι υιοι ισραηλ).[44]

The question then arises as to whether or not this plus material was already in the Hebrew *Vorlage* of the OG, in which case LXX[B] has been hexaplarically corrected (in Joshua, a rare, but demonstrable occurrence) and Th. represents a correction of the OG in the direction of the MT. While we cannot be absolutely sure in such a matter, our feeling is that the extra material was introduced into various Greek traditions (CS) later than the OG, probably traveling the well-worn path from marginal (explanatory) gloss to text. We are influenced in this judgment by our observation that the Hebew *Vorlage* of the OG is not characterized by the insertion or introduction of material or epithets dealing with Moses.[45]

The omission of οι in the reading attributed to Th. does not seem to be text critically important: (1) It could have dropped out accidentally in the text of Th. or in the source used for the material in v(mg) (thus οι υιοι).[46] (2) Sporadically, the definite article is omitted when translating construct constructions, but in no tradition is this carried through systematically. Thus we conclude that Th. here = OG = MT, with the additional material being later than the OG and with some uncertainty as to whether or not the text of Th. had the article.

98. (12:2[a]) MT: מֵעֲרוֹעֵר; Th.: αροηρ; N-group: αρνων (1) o'α'σ'; (2) Bhqru; (3) all other manuscripts and traditions read αροηρ.[47] z(mg) records αριηρ (sine nom).

Margolis includes αροηρ in his text of the OG.[48] He states that LXX[B] has αρνων as an error for αροηρ (or αρωηρ) through αρηορ (αρηωρ). This leads to the omission of αρνων later in this verse.[49] Holmes makes essentially the same point and further makes reference to 13:9, where LXX[B], in translating the same phrase, exhibits a text free from the error found here.[50] Thus, the OG here = MT, and this is also the reading of Th.

100. (12:4-5) MT: ובאדרעי ומשל; Th.: και εν εδραει αρχων;
N-group: και εν εδραειν εκ των ραφαειν αρχων
(1) o' (for a', see [3] below); (2) none; (3) manuscripts
of the E, S, and C recensions contain the form εδραειν, which
in manuscripts of the N-group is followed by the plus εκ των
ραφαειν αρχων. v(mg) attributes the following reading to a':
και εν εδραει εξουσιαζων.⁵¹

The unique feature in the reading of the N-group is the
plus, which was evidently derived from the earlier part of
v 4. ⁵² As indicated above, the most widely attested spelling
of the proper name is εδραειν̱ (so LXXᴮ). However, Margolis
concludes that the OG form was εδραει (without the final -ν).
He explains that "the ending -ν was tacked on by analogy of
other names ending in -ειν."⁵³ We agree with the conclusions
of Margolis at this point. The result is that the reading of
the OG, which was retained by Th., does equal the MT.

104. (12:14) MT: ערד: Th.: αραδ; N-group: αραδ
(1) (The ascription of this reading to Th. is preserved in v
[txt]) none; (2) αραδ, the reading of v(txt), is also found
in Kdegjnptwz (txt); ααραδ is found in s𝓏; (3) other readings
with αρ- are (βασιλεα) αιραθ (βασιλεα)αραθ in B, αραθ in ru,
(βασιλεα) αιραε(βασιλεα) αραθι in h. v(mg) records the
following: o', αδερ; a', αεδερ. Other readings with e/ad-
are εδα (m), αδερ (AGNθz[mg] rell 𝒳-codd[αβερ, 𝒳-ed] 𝒮 On).

The underlying forms for the various recensions are as
follows: εραθ (Egyptian), αραδ (Lucianic), αδερ (Palestinian
and Constantinople).⁵⁴ According to Margolis, the OG is εραδ
(with slight corruption εραθ) or αραδ (the reading of the
Lucianic recension). Both of these equal ערד of the MT. The
doublet in LXXᴮ and h is not original to the OG. αδερ reflects
עדר or is an error for αρεδ (so Margolis). We attach no great
significance to the first vowel (a/e), since a shift from α to
ε before ρ is not uncommon in the Greek of this period.⁵⁵
Confusion between resh and dalet, always a problem, has produced the variation in the order of consonants.

It seems almost by chance that the Egyptian and Lucianic
recensions have retained the sequence r-d. In 15:21, where
the MT reads עדר, manuscripts of the Lucianic and Egyptian

recensions have the sequence *r-(d)* (as here), while the order
d-p (= MT at 15:21) is found in most manuscripts of the
Palestinian and Constantinople recensions.[56]

105. (13:5) MT: מבעל גד; Th.: βααλγα(δ); <u>N</u>-group: γαλγαλ
While both v(mg) and z(mg) preserve the reading of Th. as
βααλγα, we agree with Margolis that the correct (underlying)
form for Th. is Βααλγαδ.[57] The same is true for o'σ',
listed jointly with Th. in the margin of the two <u>N</u>-group manuscripts. See below.

(1) o'σ' (see preceding note); (2) the reading of the <u>N</u>-
group, γαλγαλ, is also the underlying form for the E(gyptian)
and C(constantinople) recensions (LXX[B] has γαλγαα); (3)
among other readings are γααλβαϑ g and γααλμαϑ n (γααλβαϑ is
the underlying form for the Lucianic recension); also βααλγαδ
c²dptx and βαελγαδ Gbc²k(mg--see below) (the underlying form
for the Palestinian recension is βααλγαδ).[58] v(mg) z(mg)
record for Aq. the reading βαεγγα, but the correct form for Aq.
is βαελγαδ (see above and note this form in several manuscripts
listed previously).

This proper name occurs three times in Joshua and nowhere
else in the Old Testament. In all three places, Margolis includes the form βααλγαδ in his text of the OG. Here (in 13:5)
he notes that the forms γαλγαλ and γααλβαϑ are corrupted from
βααλγαδ. One might suggest that the 'corrupting' influence of
גלגל was also at work. In 11:17, as Margolis points out,
βαλαγαδ (of LXX[B]) is easily corrected into βααλγαδ.[59] At
12:7, Margolis reads βααλγαδ as OG (LXX[B]: βαλαγαδα). We
agree with Margolis as to the form of the OG for the proper
name.

We indicated above that there is some difficulty in determining the original form of the reading to be attributed to
Th. In the writing of the marginal variations, it is possible
that a scribe, wanting to preserve accurately the differences
at the beginning of the proper name, failed to exercise adequate care at its conclusion.[60] While some degree of uncertainty remains, it does not seem unreasonable to include no.
105 as an example of the formula Th. = OG = MT.[61]

114. (13:27[b]) MT: ם־ הꞀꜱ; Th.: μερους της θαλασσης;
N-group: (εως) της θαλασσης
(1) o'; (2) u; (3) v(mg) also records the following
readings: for Aq., εως τελευταιου θα<λασσης>;[62] for Sym.,
εως ακρου θαλασσης. The reading of Th. here is certainly that of the OG. The
N-group has suffered an haplography, probably due to the sequence of Greek words ending in -ς. With reference to the
words recorded here for Th., there is no doubt that μερους
της θαλασσης reflects a Hebrew *Vorlage* identical to the MT.
Aq. and Sym. are unique in their rejection of (OG) μερος in
favor of more "precise" translations[63] and in their omission
of the definite article before θαλασσης (in agreement with the
Hebrew construction).

116. (14:7) MT: וꜱ⻓וꜱꜱꜱ; Th.: και απεκριθην; N-group: και
απεκριθην
Some doubt may be attached to the ascription of και απεκριθην
to Th. We feel, however, that such doubt can be adequately
cleared up. The reading with the verb in the first person
singular is ascribed to θ' and a' in 𝔊.[64] However, this same
reading is attributed in 𝔊^m to a' and σ' (not θ'). The key
to the determination of the correct reading of Th. (and Sym.)
is provided here, as in several examples elsewhere, by manuscript v. v(txt) ascribes the first person reading to θ' and
a', exactly as found in 𝔊. Further, it lists in its margin
a separate reading for σ' (as well as o'). The agreement
between 𝔊 and v(txt) in this matter is decisive, especially
since v(mg) does provide a(nother) reading for Sym. The
notation contained in 𝔊^m is to be corrected accordingly.
(1) a'; (2) the reading of v(txt) is found in all witnesses
except those listed in (3) below; (3) the most widely
attested variant, απεκριθησαν (verb in the third person plural),
appears in AGNθabciloqwxyz(mg)b₂𝔊𝔊 and is ascribed to o' in
v(mg). The reading of Sym., απεκριναμεν (preserved in v[mg];
see above), casts the verb in the first person plural, a form
also found in 𝔄. The third person singular appears in a₂𝔏.

αποκρινω in the first person singular is included in
Margolis' text of the OG.[65]   This does reflect MT ויאשב.   One
might argue that another reading (e.g., one with the verb in
the third person plural) was original to the OG, with a
correction effected in those manuscriptions which exhibit the
first person singular. However, we note that precisely those
manuscripts in which an MT(-type) correction is most likely
show the non-MT reading, whereas it is not characteristic of
LXX^B and manuscripts related to it to correct toward the MT.

The reading with the third person plural apparently looks
ahead to οι αδελφοι at the beginning of v 8 for the subject
of this verb. Indications that this explanation is correct
come from the following two observations: (1) those manuscripts which have απεκριθησαν in general omit the conjunction
at the beginning of v 8, thus facilitating the process which
linked this verb with οι αδελφοι. (2) At least some of
these manuscripts alter the pronominal suffix of τον νουν
from third singular to third plural.[66]   Taking into account
all of the factors outlined above, we feel certain that the
formula Th. = OG = MT can be justly applied to this example.

141. (20:9) MT: ביד; Th.: εν χειρι; N-group: εκ χειρος
(1) o'α'; (2) the reading εκ χειρος, found in the manuscripts
of the N-group, also appears in ANθdiklmoptuwya$_2$b$_2$; (3) v(mg)
also records the following reading for σ': δια των χειρων.
𝄐𝄐 have *a manibus*.

The reading of Th. is the same as LXX^B. It is a literal
translation of the Hebrew of the MT and is the OG. Thus, εν
χειρι of Th. is an example of the formula Th. = OG = MT. The
reading with εκ may perhaps be a bit clearer Greek, but is a
less literal representation of the Hebrew preposition. The
plural translation is interpretive.

143. (21:13) MT: את עיר; Th.: την πολιν; v(txt) and the
other manuscripts of the N-group omit την πολιν.
(1) o' (see below); (2) none; (3) 𝄐𝄐-ed have the noun in
the plural.

At first glance, no. 143 appears to present nothing out of
the ordinary. v contains a text unique to the manuscripts of
the N-group and records in its margin a different reading, in
this case one ascribed to Th. την πολιν is clearly the OG,
and this reading equals the MT as well. The omission of την
πολιν in the N-group is apparently the result of haplography.[67]

One difficulty, however, still remains. The full notation
in v(mg) is recorded by B-McL as follows: "οι ο' χω θ' (?)
ου την πολιν." Since the omission of την πολιν occurs only
in manuscripts of the N-group, which are not part of the tradition indicated by the siglum οι ο', Margolis concludes that
at this point χω means *addunt*. With some reluctance, we
agree with Margolis' conclusions here.[68]

146. (21:44[a]) MT: להם; Th.: αυτους; N-group: αυτοις
The principal variation at the first part of v 44 involves (a)
the order of the subject and object and (b) the case used to
express the object of the verb. (a) From the one word preserved for Th. here, it is not possible to determine whether
he retained the word order of the OG (verb-object-subject) or
corrected to that of the MT (verb-subject-object). We note
that manuscripts of the N-group exhibit the MT word order.
For (b) see below.
(1) o'σ'; (2) θiluyb$_2$ (αυτοις and change of word order, as
in N-group), Acdgnpt (αυτοις, but with OG word order detained);
(3) αυτην in m; om in k.

It is difficult to be certain which form (αυτους or αυτοις)
appeared in the OG here. The presence of the accusative in
LXX[B] lends support to its being original in the OG. The
reading with the object in the accusative conforms to the
pattern of usage with the verb καταπαυω elsewhere in the LXX
and is also consistent with the usage outside of the Septuagint. [69] The reading with the dative, it may be argued, is a
somewhat more literal rendering of the Hebrew להם and may in
fact be an effort in that direction. However, one cannot rule
out the possibility that either one of these forms may have
been generated accidentally in a given tradition, since a
change of but one letter would produce αυτοις out of αυτους
or vice versa. In short, we cannot be sure that αυτους is

the form of the OG, but our observations tend to support this
conclusion. In either case, the one word ascribed to Th. equals
the MT. Thus, with some reservations, we can state that the
formula Th. = OG = MT does hold true for no. 146.

147. (21:44[b]) MT: עמד; Th.: ανεστη; N-group: αντεστη
(1) o'; (2) NΘaghkmnptua$_2$b$_2$Ɇ(vid)Ɫ; (3) ουκ εστη ανηρ, α';
και ουκ απεστη ουδεις, σ'.[70]

There is no reason to doubt that the reading of Th., LXX^B,
and others is the OG. The use of the verb ανιστημι to translate a form of עמד is comparatively rare, though by no means
unparalleled.[71] In addition, this reading equals the MT.[72]

148. (21:44[c]) MT: יהוה בידם; Th.: κυριος εις τας χειρας
αυτων; N-group: κυριος αυτοις εις τας χειρας αυτων
(1) o'; (2) ANΘdikptuwa$_2$b$_2$; (3) the additional element
αυτοις is also found in the following readings: αυτοις κυριος
in gly; κυριος > αυτοις in n; κυριος + αυτους in Ɫ (so B-McL).

It is apparent that the reading of Th. here is that of the
OG. It is equally clear that this reading translates a Hebrew
Vorlage identical to the MT. We note that the plus αυτοις is
fairly widespread. It gives every indication of being a marginal gloss (i.e., an alternate translation to the [more]
literal εις τας χειρας αυτων), which has entered various Greek
traditions at different points in the text.

156. (22:18[b]) MT: כל; Th.: [παντ]α; N-group: παντι
(1) o'; (2) none; (3) none

The N-group alone used the dative, rather than the accusative, with the preposition. The reading of the OG has been
preserved in LXX^B, Th., and the manuscripts outside of the N-
group, all of which (as well as z) follow the preposition επι
with the accusative. A possible explanation for the use of the
dative in the N-group is provided by manuscript f, where the
preposition επι is replaced by εν.

One is not able, however, simply to equate the OG with the
MT. This becomes apparent when one compares the translation
of the Hebrew phrase here with that of the similar (same?)
phrase in v 20. Thus επι παντα ισραηλ occurs in v 18

(MT: ‏אל כל עדת ישראל‏), while the Greek in v 20 reads επι
(την) πασαν συναγωγην ισραηλ (MT: ‏על כל עדת ישראל‏). No
attempt is recored at v 18 to achieve a more literal translation of the MT. It may be that the OG was deemed a satisfactory rendering of a Hebrew *Vorlage* identical to the MT.
Alternately, one might suggest that the Hebrew text was glossed
at a later date on the basis of v 20, such an action being induced by the similar wording of the two verses. Thus, while
it cannot be stated with certainty that the formula Th. = OG =
MT obtains here, it does seem best to classify no. 156 in this
category.[73]

163. (23:13) MT: ‏בצדיכם‏; Th.: πλευραις; N-group: πλευραις
(1) (The ascription of this reading to Th. is preserved in
v [txt]) α'σ'; (2) πλευραις, the reading of v(txt), is found
in gmnwⱫ Thdt in addition to fsz of the N-group. It also
appears in a plus in dpt after σκανδαλα; (3) (εν ταις)
πτερναις is the reading of all other manuscripts including
LXX[B]; as recorded in v(mg), it is also the reading of o'.[74]

πτερνα, found in manuscripts of the E, P, and C recensions,
always translates the Hebrew root ‏עקב‏ in the OG (elsewhere).[75]
Hence its use here to translate ‏צד‏ would be unique. However,
given the fact that ‏בצדיכם‏ follows the *hapax legomenon*
‏(ול)שטט‏, the argument could be made that πτερνα is an interpretive rendering of MT ‏צד‏, which did indeed form part of the
OG.[76] In this case, the reading of Th. (and others) would be
seen not as a preservation of the OG, but as a correction in
the direction of a literal translation of Hebrew ‏צד‏ (πλευρ-α/ον
is a not uncommon translation of ‏צד‏).[77]

A comparison of this passage in Joshua with Nu 33:55 leads
us to reject the above argument. The relevant sections are
as follows:

MT
Nu   33:55   ‏לשכים בעיניכם ולצנינם בצדיכם‏
Josh 23:13   ‏ולשטט בצדיכם ולצננים בעיניכם‏
OG
Nu   σκολοπες εν τοις οφθαλμοις υμων και βολιδες εν
               ταις πλευραις υμων
Josh   και εις ηλους εν ταις πλευραις υμων και εις
               βολιδας εν τοις οφθαλμοις υμων

Hebrew ‏צנינם/צנינים‎ occurs only in these two passages in the MT. Thus it is almost certainly not mere coincidence that the OG translator at Josh 23:13 employed the same word (βολις) that appears in the OG at Nu 33:55. It appears that he had knowledge of the OG rendering of the Numbers passage. Since this is so, there is good reason to believe that the translator of Joshua would also have followed the OG of Numbers in his rendering of ‏בצדיכם‎. We noted above that πλευρα and πλευρον are both found as translations of Hebrew ‏צד‎. While it is true that πλευρα appears more frequently than πλευρον in all uses, it is the latter which more often translates ‏צד‎ (with πλευρα more often rendering ‏צלע‎).[78] Thus the appearance here of πλευραις (rather than πλευροις) gains added significance.

An inner-Greek corruption led to the following change: ΠΛΕΥΡΑΙΣ>ΠΤΕΡΝΑΙΣ. The corrupt form, found in LXX[B] and elsewhere, surely occurred before Origen, who left it (uncorrected) in his fifth column.[79] The widespread retention of the corrupt πτερναις was aided by the somewhat obscure context in which it appears and by the fact that, although corrupt, πτερναις is a real word and not jarringly out-of-place here.

Category 2: Introduction

Th. = OG ≠ MT. Both the = and the ≠ signs should be understood in a very general way. In many readings included here
Th. retained the exact wording of the OG. In other cases he
changed that wording, but retained a distinctive feature,
frequently one we categorize as non-MT, of the OG. It is
Th.'s retention of the OG against (a) a more literal rendering
of the MT or (b) a correction to the MT that interests us here.
The OG reflects a Hebrew *Vorlage* different from the MT in some,
but not in all places; however, in each case the OG does
contain wording that is either not a fully literal representation of the MT or is a translation of a different Hebrew.

These are among the most important examples for demon-
strating the close relationship between Th. and the OG.
As Th. revised the OG, on occasion he retained non-MT elements
he found there, even as he changed and corrected its wording
in other respects. There is no doubt that Th. was a careful
revisor, but also a human one, whose high regard for the Greek
text with which he worked is evident in his attempts to incor-
porate its wording or style in the examples presented in this
section and elsewhere. Do examples drawn from category 2 lead
to the conclusion that Th. was revising to a Hebrew different
from the MT? We think not. While such an explanation may
seem attractive at first glance, it is not in line with the
picture of Th. that emerges in the other sections of this
chapter. Our understanding of Th. as a careful, but human
revisor is.

The general pattern for presentation of evidence in this
category is as follows: First we give the readings of the OG,
Th., and the MT. When Th. retained the exact wording of the
OG, we list this OG-Th. reading only once. Then (1) whenver
the reading of Th. also appears in o´, Aq., or Sym., this is
noted, with the word "none" indicating that the reading of Th.
is not found in any of these three texts; (2) additional

readings, including (a) those that support Th. and the OG,
(b) those that show corrections or accomodations to the MT,
(c) others. As in the first chapter the discussions that
follow take their form from the evidence presented. We do
place emphasis on the differences between Th. and the OG and
between distinctive aspects of the Th.-OG reading and the MT.

2

11. (1:13)

OG: το ρημα κυριου

Th.:   κυριου

MT: הדבר

(1) o'; (2) the reading of Th. is found in AFMNϑa-df-iln-rtxya₂b₂𝓐𝓒𝓩𝓼ᵐ (sub ÷). m has των ρηματων κυριου. κυριου is not found in LXXᴮ, most of the manuscripts of the N-group, kuw, and 𝓔.

Margolis includes κυριου in his text of the OG and makes the following observations: the omission of κυριου in k attests indirectly the obelus. The word must have been present in Origen's exemplar.[80] We agree with Margolis' inclusion of this word in the text of the OG. This is to be counted as one of the relatively few places in Joshua in which LXXᴮ has been hexaplarically corrected (unless one wishes to argue that κυριου was dropped accidentically from LXXᴮ). יהוה appeared in the Hebrew *Vorlage* of the OG, a plus induced by the several other occurrences of this word in v 13. It may also have been influenced by a text which lacked משה בעבר הירדן in the following verse.[81] The shorter MT (without יהוה) is original.

15. (2:4[a])

OG-Th.: εκρυψεν αυτους και ειπεν αυτοις

MT: ותצפנו ותאמר

(1) o'α'σ'; (2) no tradition outside of the MT has the object of the verb κρυπτω/צפן in the singular. αυτοις, for which there is no corresponding element in the MT, is omitted in k 𝓔 and placed sub ÷ in 𝓼.[82] In FNefgijnrsvza₂ a plus, derived from v 6, appears after αυτους.[83] The manuscripts of the N-group (efjsvz) contain this plus in its fullest form: εν τη λινοκαλαμη τη εστοιβασμενη αυτη επι του δωματος.

Margolis suggests that the plural αυτους is a tacit correction of Hebrew ו-.[84] Perhaps the original text of this passage lacked an explicit object for the verb at this point. In any case, the context calls for the plural object, whether understood or expressed. αυτοις, found after ειπεν in the Greek, is both superfluous and somewhat confusing. However,

it was in the OG, as the evidence demonstrates, and probably
reflects the presence of an additional לחם in its Hebrew
Vorlage. Thus, Th. retained the OG, which differs at two
points from the MT, while correction to the MT (through the
elimination of αυτοις) is found in at least a few witnesses
to the text.

24. (3:8)

OG: επι μερους του υδατος[85]
Th.:   επι μερος του υδατος
MT: עד קצה מי

(1) o'; (2) the reading of Th., which retains the preposition επι but places its object in the accusative, is found
in MNahklua$_2$b$_2$. εις μερος του υδατος, ascribed to Sym. in
v(mg), is the reading of dptz(mg) ℓ. Except for Bv(mg) (see
below), all remaining Greek manuscripts show the OG επι μερους
(in m του μερους). v(mg) attributes to Aq. the reading εως
μερους υδατων.

The use of επι in the OG here and in the parallel passage
at v 15 may indicate that the OG translator read (misread ?)
על, instead of MT עד, in his Hebrew *Vorlage*. Th.'s retention
of the OG preposition here stands in contrast to the more
literal renderings with εις (εως in Aq.).[86] It is this contrast which places no. 24 in category 2, regardless of whether
the *Vorlage* of the OG was different from or identical to the
MT.

26. (3:12)

OG-Th.: ενα αφ εκαστης θυλης
MT: איש אחד איש אחד לשבט

The reading attributed in v(mg) to Th. and o' is ενα αφ
εκαστης φυλης. These words (or their equivalents, cf. Aq.
and Sym. below) are found everywhere else as well (including
v[txt]). Since one expects a contrast between the reading
cited in v(mg) and that of v(txt), this is somewhat puzzling.
A clue to the correct interpretation of the reading attributed
to Th. is provided by v(txt) itself, where we find the
following distinctive N-group reading: ενα ενα αφ εκαστης
φυλης. Thus the contrast to be drawn is between Th. (and o'),

where the phrase is simply ενα . . . φυλης, and v(txt), in
which the phrase appears in a somewhat expanded form. The
other citations in v(mg), to the extent that they also contain
a longer form of this phrase, confirm this analysis.
(1) o'; (2) the fullest correction to the MT is supplied by
Aq. as preserved in v(mg): (ισραηλ) ανδρα ενα ανδρα ενα του
σκηπτρου (και εσται).[87] For Sym., v(mg) preserves the
following: (ισραηλ) ανδρα ενα καθ εκαστην φυλην (και ως αν
αναπαυσηται). ανδρα preceding ενα αφ εκαστης φυλης is
attributed to οι ⅄ in M(mg)v(mg sub ※) and is also found in
FNbcdpqtAⱬ^m(※). As noted above, ενα ενα. . .φυλης is
characteristic of the N-group, appearing in manuscripts fsvz.
B-McL also records *unum unum virum ab una una tribu* (Ɇ) and
virum secundum tribum (ᵬ₵).

A similar phrase is found at 4:2, 4: איש אחד איש אחד משבט.
In both places the OG reads as here. At 4:2 ανδρα (ενα) appears
in Fbcdkpqtv(mg)x Aⱬ(sub ※) (ενα > ανδρας in M[mg]) and at 4:4
in bcdkptxⱬ(sub ※).

Margolis states that the OG contracted איש אחד איש אחד
to ενα.[88] Rather than using such terms as "contraction" to
characterize the OG here (and at 4:2,4), we would emphasize
that the OG has translated this phrase in an intelligent and
fully intelligible manner. Thus the usual English translation
is "from/for each tribe a man" (but it could also be "one
from/for each tribe"). Manuscripts of the P recension and a
few others represent literally one איש with ανδρα, as does Sym.
The full literal translation is found only in Aq.[89] Th.
recognized OG ενα αφ εκαστης φυλης as a perfectly acceptable
rendering of Hebrew איש אחד איש אחד לשבט and thus accepted it
into his text, while others effected a more literal representation of the same Hebrew phrase. Therefore, although we are
not dealing here with divergent Hebrew *Vorlagen*, we have
placed no. 26 in category 2.[90]

37. (4:12)

OG-Th.: οι ημισεις

MT: וחצי

(1) o'σ'; (2) singular το ημισυ, ascribed to Aq. in v(txt),
is the reading of the N-group and kmqℓ(vid)ℒ (also ημισου in
Δ₈b and οι ημισου in 1pr). The OG translator of Joshua generally used a form in the
singular to render חצי, which does however resemble a plural
construct. Here the rarer plural of the OG was retained by Th.
The revision to the singular is a more literal reflection of
the Hebrew.[91]

42. (5:2)

OG: μαχαιρας εκ πετρας ακροτομου και καθισας περιτεμε[92]

Th.: μαχαιρας πετρινας ακροτομους και καθισας περιτεμε

MT: חרבות צרים ושוב מל

(1) none; (2) v(mg) records the following other readings:

α' μαχαιρας πετρινας και επιστρεψας περιτεμε[93]

σ' μαχαιραν εξ ακροτομου και παλιν περιτεμε

οι ο' μαχαιρας εκ πετρας ακροτομου.

The reading of LXX^B is μαχαιρας πετρινας εκ πετρας ακροτομου
και καθισας περιτεμε. πετρινας is omitted in Aboxyb₂ℱℒ.
εκ πετρας ακροτομου appears sub ∸ in ℒ; dm Cyp omit εκ
πετρας. ακροτομους is found in bdmxℒ Cyp.

According to Margolis, the reading of LXX^B is the underlying form for the E, S, and C recensions.[94] The procedure
of Origen, who apparently did not find πετρινας in the κοινη
text with which he was working, was as follows (so Margolis):
∸εκ πετρας: ακροτομους.[95] The phrase חרבות צרים occurs again
in v 3, where the OG reads μαχαιρας πετρινας ακροτομους (so
LXX^B[E], S, and C).[96]

That the OG translator of Joshua rendered the same phrase
differently even in neighboring verses should occasion no
surprise, for numerous examples of the same or similar phenomena
can be listed.[97] Often Th.'s aim in revising the OG was to
standardize the translation of various words or phrases.[98]
We suggest that Th. had before him a text which contained the
OG for v 2. Noticing that the same phrase occurred in the
(Hebrew of the) next verse and perhaps not feeling completely

satisfied with the OG at v 2, Th. may have read ahead to the
Greek of v 3. He apparently preferred the OG rendering of
חרבות צרים there and introduced that into his text for v 2.
In this manner Th. revised one passage in the OG through the
use of another OG passage. It is likely that this reading of
Th. is the source both for the introduction of the doublet
πετρινας into the text of the E̲, S̲, and C̲ recensions (also
for πετρινας in Aq.) at v 2 and for the form ακροτομους in P̲.[99]

If μαχαιρας πετρινας ακροτομους were the entire reading
preserved for Th. at this point, then no. 42 would have been
placed in category 3. However, it is our feeling that the
"dominant" character of this reading is to be seen in the
latter part, where Th. admitted into his text OG και κα̲θ̲ι̲σ̲α̲ς̲
περιτεμε. As has been widely noted, καθισας points to a Hebrew
Vorlage which contained ושב (וְשֵׁב) rather than ושוב of the MT.
It is not impossible that in the Hebrew *Vorlage* of the OG
(and Th.?) שוב was written without *scriptio plena*, thus
producing a form that could be from either ישב or שוב.[100]
Thus we cannot be sure that divergent Hebrew *Vorlagen* have
accounted for the different readings here. However, we do have
in Aq. and Sym. (see also i[mg]. . .και επιστρεψας περιτεμε)
renderings which point unmistakably to MT שוב. It is for
this reason that we have included no. 42 in category 2.[101]

44. (6:2)

OG: δυνατους οντας εν ισχυι

Th.:   οντας

MT: _____

(1) (The reading of Th. is preserved in both M[mg]: θ' οντας
and v[mg]: οντας] θ' ο' χω)[102] none; (2) οντας is omitted in ο'
(see above) and in AMNθabloxyb₂ℱ(vid).

There is no doubt that the reading with οντας reflects a
Hebrew *Vorlage* identical to the MT. οντας was introduced,
apparently at the time the Hebrew was first translated into
Greek, in order to integrate this concluding phrase more
smoothly into the grammatical structure of the verse. Margolis,
who includes οντας in his text of the OG, gives the word a

64

concessive force.[103] The more literal rendering of this
phrase omits οντας, since it does not represent a specific
element present in the Hebrew. Thus, Th.'s retention of OG
οντας stands in contrast to the correction to the MT found in
several witnesses to the text.[104]

45. (6:17)

OG: κυριω σαβαωθ[105]

Th.:   (τω κυριω) των δυναμεων

MT: ליהוה

(1) o'; (2) κυριω σαβαωθ is the reading of Bqru (thus,
this is the reading of Margolis' Egyptian recension); τω
κυριω σαβαωθ is found in M(mg)cefjsvz(txt). gndptw have
τω κυριω των δυναμεων κυριω σαβαωθ (for κυριω 2° d has κυριου
and w reads κυριος); ∉ Cyr read τω κυριω των δυναμεων σαβαωθ.[106]
k has τω κυριω (see below). AF*M(txt)NϑZ(mg) rell 𝔸ℊᵐ(των
δυναμεων sub ⟶) read τω κυριω των δυναμεων (F²b' lack the
article τω); thus the reading of the manuscripts of the
Palestinian and Constantinople recensions is τω κυριω των
δυναμεων. m omits this phrase entirely.

We agree with Margolis that the OG had in its Hebrew
Vorlage יהוה צבאות.[107] Margolis places the phrase κυριω
σαβαωθ in his text of the OG, and the observation that this is
the reading of the manuscripts which most often preserve the
(unrevised) OG tends to support his judgment here. We note
that the phrase יהוה צבאות does not occur in the MT of Joshua,
nor does it occur elsewhere in the Greek for this book. Thus,
one cannot speak of the "usual practice" for representing
this phrase in the Greek for Joshua.

Margolis also formulates the following explanation for the
difference in the handling of this phrase between the OG(E)
and P (and C): P marks the increment with the ⟶, but writes
in the place of σαβαωθ its Greek equivalent (των δυναμεων),
apparently because readers of LXX were wont to read (*kere!*)
των δυναμεων for the textual (*kethib!*) σαβαωθ. Possibly the
kere was noted in the margin. We cannot support Margolis in
his ingenious suggestion, but point instead to the fact that
των δυναμεων has been established as the καιγε recension's
standard representation of the Hebrew צבאות (יהוה).[108]

Thus, it is likely that Origin had before him a (common) text in which the καιγε reading had replaced that of the OG. Since Th. has such a reading, it is attractive to suggest that the phrase (τω κυριω) των δυναμεων in this passage originated with him and spread from there into the common text. The shorter text of the MT (represented in the Greek only by manuscript k) is original here; the longer text introduces into Joshua a phrase which is without parallel elsewhere in the book (see above).

59. (9:5[9:11])

OG: και ο αρτος αυτων του επισιτισμου ξηρος και
ευρωτιων109

Th.: και οι αρτοι αυτων ο επισιτισμος αυτων ξηρος και
βεβρωμενος

MT: וכל לחם צידם יבש היה נקדים

The authentic reading of Th. has been preserved only in v(mg). In z(mg) there appears another reading attributed to Th., which is the same as the reading attributed to o' in v(mg). z(mg) records nothing for o'. Both v and z have the same marginal readings for Aq. and Sym. Here greater weight should be placed on the citations in v(mg), where separate and distinct readings are found for Th., Aq., Sym., and o'. z(mg) correctly transmitted the readings of Aq. and Sym., but mistakenly attributed that of o' to Th.[110] Margolis states that o' should be read in place of θ' in z(mg); in his comments it is clear that he regards the reading of v(mg) as that of Th.[111]

(1) none; (2) v(mg)z(mg) record the following readings (for o' see above):

α' και πας ο αρτος ο επισιτισμος αυτων ξηρος εγενηθη και
εψαθυρωμενος[112]

σ' και πας ο αρτος του επισιτισμου αυτων ξηρος εγενετο καπυρος

o' και οι αρτοι του επισιτισμου αυτων ξηροι και βεβρωμενοι.[113]

𝔖 preserves two readings for α'σ': לחמא (αρτος) and דמנגב בנורא.[114] M has two marginal readings: εγενοντο ξηροι (for ξηρος) and ευρωτιωντες (for βεβρωμενος).

We have not listed separately the numerous variants that occur in this passage. Instead, we give the underlying forms for the various recensions as determined by Margolis and confirmed by us:

E   και ο αρτος αυτων του επισιτισμου ξηρος και ευρωτιων και βεβρωμενος

S   και οι αρτοι αυτων ο επισιτισμος αυτων ξηρος και βεβρωμενος και ευρωτιων

C   και οι αρτοι του επισιτισμου αυτων ξηροι και βεβρωμενοι

P   και οι αρτοι του ερισιτισμου αυτων ξηροι ⁒ εγενηθησαν ⵼ και: βεβρωμενοι.

Margolis includes extensive comments on this passage. He felt that כל, attested by Aq.-Sym., was ignored by the OG translator who nevertheless kept to the singular. Of particular interest to us here are his remarks about the procedure of Th. According to Margolis, Th. ignores כל with the OG, but implies it by the use of the plural: οι αρτοι. This is followed by αυτων as in the OG (αυτων του επισιτισμου, inverted order). Then Th. continued appositionally as in Aq.: ο επισιτισμος αυτων, so as to conform again to the OG: ξηρος. The OG will have written και ευρωτιων; the plus και βεβρωμενος comes from Th., who replaced ευρωτιων by βεβρωμενος with a view to OG v 12.

We cannot agree with Margolis' conclusions about the procedure of the OG translator or Th. for the first part of this passage. The lack of πας in the OG shows that in all probability the translator did not find כל in his Hebrew *Vorlage*. Th. followed the OG to the extent that he did not include in his text a translation for כל. His change to the plural in no way implies כל, but rather gives us a first indication of his use of the OG of v 12 (where the plural οι αρτοι is found) to render the Hebrew here.[115] With this and other examples such as no. 42 in mind, we have no difficulty with Margolis' explanation of the various phrases found at the end of this passage.

Soggin, Holmes, and Benjamin present alternate under-
standings of what stood in the OG and its *Vorlage* here. For
Soggin and Benjamin, E (LXX^B) presents the OG.[116] According
to Soggin, LXX read ευρωτιων, i.e. *wbl(h)* 'mouldy, spoilt'
instead of *kl* (probably a confusion between *kap* and *bēt*).[117]
Holmes, like Margolis, recognizes that ευρωτιων and βεβρωμενος
are doublets. However, unlike Margolis, he judges βεβρωμενος
as the original: "v 12 . . . shows that ευρωτιων, which
twelve mss and the Lyons Heptateuch omit, is a doublet of
βεβρωμενος." In response to Soggin-Benjamin, we note that the
position of ευρωτιων (. . . ξηρος και ευρωτιων και βεβρωμενος)
is rather odd if it is meant to render a word which stood at
the head of the clause before לחם (ο αρτος). Moreover, for
chapter 9 the OG translator consistently used παλαι- to translate forms of the root בלה. The MT and LXX at v 12 read as
follows:

MT: זה לחמנו . . . ועתה הנה יבש׳ והיה נקדים
LXX (9:18) ουτοι οι αρτοι . . . νυν δε εξηρανθησαν και γεγονασιν
βεβρωμενοι. נקדים is a rare word, and we are not surprised
that the OG translator made use of different words to translate
it even in parallel passages.[118] Surely this variation is
original to the OG, and the comparison with v 12 confirms that
ευρωτιων (and not βεβρωμενος, with Holmes) stood in the OG at
v 5.

The strongest argument in favor of Margolis' view concerning και ευρωτιων (alone) is that it allows for a relationship between the OG and Th. that is in line with what is found
elsewhere. It is characteristic of Th. to have sought to
standardize the Greek rendering of a Hebrew word or expression.
It is also characteristic of Th. that, when he placed βεβρωμεν-
into his text at v 5, he used the singular in agreement with
the OG (and not the plural with the MT). This need not show
divergent *Vorlagen*, but rather the degree to which Th. followed
the OG even when revising it.[119] The widespread introduction
of Th.'s reading into the text of the various recensions is
paralleled at no. 42.

We note further that Th. has both retained αυτων in its
OG position and included a second αυτων after επισιτισμος in
agreement with the Hebrew צידם.[120] For the rest, Th. and the

OG both read ξηρος και βεβρω/ευρω- for the MT יבש היה נקדים. This suggests a Hebrew text in which the conjunction appeared, rather than היה of the MT. Here corrections toward a text like that of the MT are found in Aq.-Sym. and the P̲ recension, but not in Th.[121] Since Th. has retained several features of the OG (no translation for כל, αυτων in inverted order, και rather than a translation for Hebrew היה, the last element [βεβρω/ευρω-] in the singular), where elsewhere corrections *toward* the MT are found, we have placed this reading in category 2. Such placement expresses our judgment concerning the "dominant" character of this reading,[122] but does not overlook the fact that Th. also revised the OG in accordance with his practice elsewhere.

63. (10:3)
    OG: φεδων[123]
    Th.:   φειδων
    MT: פְּרָאם

(1) (The ascription of this reading to Th. is preserved in v[txt]) none; (2) among other readings with *d* are φιδον in u, φιδωθ in gh*n (dpt have φιλ̲ωθ), φεδαμ (b'*b**). v(mg) records the following readings, which contain *r* (as in the MT): ο'α' φερααμ, σ' φορον. φερααμ is also found in AGθach[b]kmxy. Other readings containing *r* include φεραν (q), φεραμ (M[txt] Niow), φερεαμ (b₂). φεδραμ of *b*[a?] is a conflation of the OG and MT. Ƚ reads *Cheldeon* (Margolis: χελδεων). LXX[B] and most other manuscripts have φειδων.[124]

As determined by Margolis, the underlying forms for the various recensions are as follows: φειδων (E̲), φιδωθ (S̲), φεραμμ (P̲C̲).[125] Margolis conjectures φεδων as the OG on the basis of φειδων (E̲) and χελδεων (Ƚ) (from φεδδεων). Hence original *e* was corrupted into *ei*. φειδων, Margolis continues, leads to no satisfactory Hebrew form, while φε̲δων is reducible to פדאן or פדאם.

Margolis closes his discussion of this reading by noting the "temptation" to restore δερων or φερ̲ωμ = פְּרָאם, since δ may have been corrupted from ρ. While inner-Greek corruption

(ρ > δ) is certainly a possible explanation for the readings
with δ, we prefer to resist the "temptation" and see behind
φεδων a Hebrew *Vorlage* in which ד appeared rather than ר of
the MT. ד and ר, of course, were frequently confused.[126]
There exists the additional possibility that the OG translator
(mis)read פדאם in his Hebrew text, when MT פראם actually
appeared. In either case φ-δων is the reading of the OG, and
Th. included it (or a form very close to it) in his text,
while elsewhere φερααμ (and closely related spellings) represent MT פראם. The name *Piram*, as king of Jarmuth or in any
other context, does not occur again in the Old Testament.

70. (10:11[b])
    OG-Th.: λιθους χαλαζης [127]
    MT: אבנים גדלות
As recorded in B-McL and Margolis, only the word λιθους is
attributed to Th. in v(txt). However, the extent of the
reading attributed there to Th. should be expanded to include
the following χαλαζης. When v(txt) ascribes its reading to
ϑ', α', σ', and/or o', there is always a contrast to be made
between this and the citations in v(mg). If the only word
sub ϑ' here is λιθους, then the anticipated contrast is
lacking, for the reading preserved for o'α'σ' in v(mg)
includes λιθους exactly as in v(txt).[128]   Therefore, we conclude that the notation in v(txt) for Th. is meant to include
at least the following word (χαλαζης), thereby bringing into
contrast the reading of v(txt)-Th. and that of o'α'σ'.
(1)   none;   (2)   v(mg) records the following for o'α'σ':
λιθους μεγαλους χαλαζης εκ του ουρανου; $\mathcal{g}^{m}$ attributes
λιθους μεγαλους to Aq. μεγαλους also follows λιθους in akoqx;
of these x alone omits (OG) χαλαζης
    Margolis includes λιθους χαλαζης in his text of the OG.[129]
According to him, χαλαζης (OG) is for גדלות (MT) by interpretation from what follows. It is unlikely, however, that the
OG translator would have failed to translate גדלות had it been
present in his Hebrew *Vorlage*.

It is probable that in the text underlying both the OG and MT traditions "stones" stood unmodified at this point. In the *Vorlage* of the OG these "stones" became "hailstones." Margolis correctly perceived that χαλαζης (ברד) was drawn from a clause later in this same verse. A scribe, noting its use there, included it as a marginal gloss on the earlier occurrence of (simple) "stones." The journey from margin to text is a familiar one. In the tradition behind the MT, another marginal gloss ("great"), easily supplied from the context, entered the text at the same point. Most corrections here took the form of a conflation of these two readings. Th. retained the OG and thus lacks this correction, which does at least bring in the גדלות of the MT.[130]

Our suggested reconstruction receives considerable support from one of the Joshua fragments found at Qumran. There we read אבנים מן השמים.[131]

75. (10:20[a])

> OG: πας ισραηλ[132]
> Th.: παντες οι υιοι ισραηλ
> MT: בני ישראל

(1) ο'α'σ'; (2) παντες οι υιοι, the reading of Th., is found in Af^bNθdik(om οι)lmptwya₂b₂Ӿ; οι υιοι appears in Gabx(om οι x*)∅ℊ. πας is the reading of e-hjnoqsuvz∅ℤ. Bcr (=OG, so Margolis) have πας υιος.

As determined by Margolis, the underlying forms for the various recensions are as follows: πας υιος (Egyptian), πας (Lucianic), παντες οι υιοι (Constantinople), οι υιοι (Palestinian). Margolis speaks of πας υιος, which he includes in his text of the OG, as "free for בני."[133] We are not comfortable with such a formulation, nor are we convinced that πας υιος represents the OG. In our opinion πας, the reading of the manuscripts of the Lucianic recension, is the OG here.[134] In its original form, the text read simply ישראל(ו) יהושע). While ישראל alone is not common in the Hebrew of the book of Joshua in such a construction (i.e., as subject), its use here is paralleled in 8:24.[135] In the Hebrew *Vorlage* of the OG, this was expanded by the addition of כל (πας; כל/πας ισραηλ, a phrase found quite often). The

tradition that lies behind the MT clothed the naked ישראל
with בני. If this is correct, then readings such as πας υιος
and παντες οι υιοι are conflations of the OG and the MT.
The reading with the singular (Br) is unusual; it may well
represent a very early correction toward the MT, retaining
πας (in the singular) of the OG.

Th. worked with either a text of the OG or one that
already contained the reading of LXX^B. In either case his
reading is not the full correction to the MT found in manuscripts of the Palestinian recension. In his effort to
correct toward a Hebrew identical with the MT (either by
adding υιοι [if that was lacking in the text with which he
worked] or changing the expression to the plural [if πας
υιος was present in the text before him]), Th. included παντες
(πας) in his text. Th.'s reading here is to be understood as
the result of this retention of OG παντες (πας).

90. (11:8[b])
    OG: μασεφα136
    Th.:   μασφα
    MT: מַצֵּפָה

(1) σ'; (2) v(mg) ascribes the reading μασσηφα to ο'α'.
μασσωχ, the reading of LXX^B, is also found in r; related
readings are μασωχ (hq), μασσωκ (u), μασωκ (efjsvz[txt]). x
has μασφα, the form attributed to Th.-Sym. in v(mg). Other
readings are Mosfa (μοσφα) in 乙, Masfe (so Margolis; B-McL:
masfre) in Or-lat, μασιφα in b, μασηφα in moℵ, μασσηφα(=ο'α') in
ANϑaciklwyz(mg)b₂, μασφαν in Kn, μασφαμ in g, μασφοαμ in dpt,
μασσηφαϑ in G, μασηκαφατ in F, μαναοση in a₂, Lon in ¢.

Although the reading of LXX^B ends in -χ, Margolis lists
μασ(σ)ωκ as the underlying form for the E recension (note
final -κ in u and manuscripts of the N-group). Margolis con-
structs the following bridge to span the distance between this
form and his conjectured OG: "μασσωκ with κ duplicated from κατ,
hence μασσω from μασφω=μασφα=μασεφα."137 The underlying forms
for the remaining recensions are μασφαν (S), μασφα (P₂),
μασσηφα (P₁C).

Our chief interest here is the final vowel. With the possible exception of Or-lat (*masfe*), -*a* appears as the final vowel in all readings or their underlying forms. This suggests the vocalization מִצְפָּה, rather than מִצְפֶּה of the MT. A comparison with verse 3 is most instructive in this regard. There Hebew מִצְפֶּה (ה אֶרֶץ) is vocalized מצפה in the MT. Margolis includes μασεφα, as at v 8, in his text of the OG "on the basis of μασεφαν which underlies μασεμαν E (μ for β from φ). . . . The ending -ν induced by γην (την)."[138]

At v 3 μασσηφα is the underlying form for the P̲ and C̲ recensions. μασσαν, the underlying form of the S̲ recension, "easily leads to μασφαν," the underlying form of the same recension at v 8. It appears that the OG translator standardized the vocalization of this proper name on the basis of v 3, where apparently the tradition lying behind the OG and that of the MT preserved the same pronunciation. The two locations (מצפה of v 3 and מִצְפֶּה of v 8) are almost certainly the same place.[139] It is generally suggested that one or the other vocalization is original in both verses.[140]

It is not impossible that the -*pah/peh* variation is original (and not limited to this location).[141] In any case, at v 8 Th. retained the final vowel of the OG and thus included in his text a reading that does not clearly represent the vocalization preserved in the MT.

The standardization of the -*pah* vocalization extended in the OG to three other localities vocalized מִצְפֶּה in the MT:

	MT	OG (so Margolis)	
13:26	מִצְפֵּה (רמת ה)	μασσηφα	(=ES) to the tribe of Gad
15:38	מִצְפֶּה (וה)	μασφα	(=ESC) to the tribe of Judah
18:26	מִצְפֶּה (וה)	μασσηφα	(=P₁) to the tribe of Benjamin

In none of these passages do we find any indication of a correction to the -*peh* vocalization preserved in the MT.

92. (11:13)

OG: τας κεχωματισμενας
Th.:   (τας) ωχυρωμενας[142]
MT: הֶעֹמְדוֹת עַל תִּלָּם

Our first concern here is to establish, if possible, a secure equivalent in Greek for the reading attributed to Th. in $\mathcal{S}$: לדחממסנן. According to B-McL, this is equal to the Latin *firmatas*. Field translates the Syriac as τας υφισταμενας (s. υπομενουσας). He rates as less satisfactory the translation of Masius: οχυρας. Margolis suggests that the reading ωχυρωμενας, attributed to o' in v(mg), belongs instead to Th.[143] In support of his suggestion, with which we agree, we can offer two considerations:

(1) the reading in v(mg) contains the same verbal root (οχυρ-οω) as the translation suggested by Masius (as recorded in Field).

(2) no manuscript usually designated by the siglum o' in v(mg) and elsewhere has a reading anything like that attributed to this tradition in v(mg).[144] Thus, we accept (τας) ωχυρωμενας as the probable reading of Th.

(1) none; (2) $\mathcal{S}$ records for Aq. the following reading: דקימן על חללא. In Greek there are preserved readings for Aq. in two sources: τας εστηκυιας επι χωματος in v(mg)z(mg) and εστηκυιας εκ χωματος in g.[145] Margolis suggests that the Syriac חֵעלָא be emended to חֵעלָא singular, as in the Greek citations. Thus, Aq. read (τας) εστηκυιας επι χωματος. $\mathcal{S}$ records for Sym. the following reading: דממחתן. Again in Greek there are preserved readings in two sources: v(mg)z(mg) ιδρυμενας εκαστην επι υψους and ιδρυμενας εκαστην επι υψους και εστωσας επι των θηνων αυτων in g. The second part of this citation (και εστωσας επι των θηνων αυτων) is a doublet and appears as a plus (with the correct form θ̲ι̲νων) in the remaining manuscripts of the Lucianic recension (F$^{a\ mg}$)K(vid) dhptw. G(sub ※)bcxÅ follow κεχωματισμενας with αυτων.

The representation of the Hebrew phrase in the OG is rather free, suggesting that here the translator was aiming to get the point across, rather than give a literal translation. As Holmes notes, "the translator seems to have coined a word. Perhaps the assonance with חומה had something to do with it."[146] That this is a coined word is true, since this root occurs only here in Greek with the meaning "to fortify with mounds."[147] Still, its meaning would be quite clear. The

explanation offered by Holmes for the use of this root here
cannot be accepted. Rather, its occurrence here is linked to
the use of the noun χωμα to translate חל at 8:28, the only
time חל or χωμα occurs in the Hebrew or Greek of Joshua,
respectively. The root utilized by Th. was suggested by its sporadic
usage elsewhere in the OG of Joshua, where it generally translates a form of the root בצר.[148]   Th.'s rejection of the OG
in favor of an admittedly more free representation may have
been occasioned by the strangeness of the OG. It certainly
need not represent any difference of *Vorlage*.

At first glance, the use of the χωμα-root in Aq.'s reading
would suggest direct knowledge of the OG's coined verb.
However, while such knowledge is not to be discounted out of
hand, the usage in 8:28 that influenced the Greek translator
could have done so also for Aq.--and independently of any
direct knowledge of the OG.[149]

It is unclear whether Th., Aq., or Sym. included αυτων
with several manuscripts of the P recension and the doublet
in the Lucianic tradition. It is also not clear whether the
OG read a plural and no suffix or just did not include the
suffix of its *Vorlage* because of the free construction adopted.
However, since the suffix of the Hebrew חלם is explicitly
translated in certain Greek traditions and since the possibility
exists that the OG and Th. (as well as Aq. and Sym.) read the
plural instead of the suffixed form of the MT, we have included this reading in category 2. Finally, we note that Th.
remains closest to the OG in his use of a similar (free)
construction to represent the Hebrew.

94. (11:21[a])
     OG.-Th.: ανωβ

     MT: עֲנָב
(1) ο'α'σ'; (2) the Old Greek form also appears in AFGϑ
abciklxyb₂ℳℒℬ On (thus it is characteristic of manuscripts in
the P and C recensions). gnptw read εναк; d has αναк (εναк
is characteristic of the S recension). In N αναλωβ is found;
in a₂ ανωϑ. (Also αναβωβ [71], αναβαωϑ [236], αναϑωβ [18].)

Elsewhere, including LXX^B, αναβωθ is found; this form is
characteristic of the E recension.[150]

$_{αβ}$ Explaining the form in LXX^B, Margolis writes: αναβωθ =
αvωθ?[151]He makes reference to 15:50, where עֲנָב again appears
in the Hebrew. There also Margolis includes αvωβ (the
reading of the C recension) in his text of the OG.[152] The
underlying forms for the other recensions are αvων (E), αvωχ
(S), αvαβ (P=On). He remarks that αvωβ (the OG both at 11:21
and 15:50) represents עֲנָב, while αvαβ (the reading of P at
15:50) = MT עֲנָב.

There is the possibility that the reading of S at 11:21
is but a corruption of this same ε/αvαβ, with the final consonant corrupted by the following και.[153] Alternately, εvακ
could represent a Hebrew *Vorlage* in which 'עֲנב' appeared or
at least was read by some translator.[154] When we take these
two occurrences of the place name together (it is found
nowhere else in the Old Testament), we are able to say that
at 11:21 Th. retained the OG, where elsewhere a correction to
the vocalization preserved in the MT appears.[155]

112. (13:26)

OG: εως των οριων δεβωρ[156]

Th.:   δεβειρ

MT: עַד גְּבוּל לִדְבִר

(1) α'o'; (2) Readings ending in -ρ (as in θ'α'o', the OG,
and the MT) are *Debor* (δεβωρ = OG) in 𝕃, δαβειρ in ΑΝθi*yz
(mg)a$_2$b$_2$𝕏 On, δαβηρ in kmo, δεβειρ in Gabx, δεβηρ in b'l,
δαιβειρ in i^a, δαιβηρ in c. δαιβων, the reading of LXX^B, is
also found in dprtu𝕔𝕫; gn have δεβων (thus δαιβων is the
underlying form for the E and S recensions).[157] Other forms
ending in -ων are δαβων (efjsvz[txt]) and δαιμων (q).

δεβειρ (the underlying form for the P recension and the
reading of θ'α'o') and δαβειρ (the underlying form of the C
recension) both represent דְּבִר, the vocalization preserved in
the MT.[158] δε(/αι)βωρ, the reading of the OG, represents
דְּבֹר.[159] To this extent the reading of Th. (δεβειρ) is a
correction to (the vocalization preserved in) the MT.
Th., however, did not include an explicit representation for
the first letter (ל) of the proper name as found in the MT,

a letter commentators generally agree is original (even though many do not accept the vocalization preserved in the MT.)[160]
There is no reason why the OG translator would have failed to reproduce ל had he found it in his Hebrew *Vorlage*. We are therefore led to conclude that ל (after גבול) had dropped out of the Hebrew text with which this translator was working. We need not have recourse to the same explanation to account for the "lack" of λ (ל) in Th. Margolis offers the following alternatives to explain the OG here: "the OG may not have found the ל (p. גבול) or taken it as *nota dativi*." The first alternative does account for the OG (see above), while the second explains the procedure of Th. We believe that the Hebrew to which Th. was correcting contained ל (as in the MT), which was interpreted by him as the *nota dativi*. The "failure" by Th. to supply an explicit translation for this element is due to his tendency to remain as close as possible to the OG when fashioning his revision.[161] It is a measure of the influence that the work of Th. exerted that his procedure was considered adequate by Aq., Origen, and others.[162]

123 (15:9)

OG.-Th.: και διεκβαλλει εις γα(ε)ι ορος εφρων[163]

MT: ויצא אל ערי הר עפרון

In Joshua 15:5b-11 the northern boundary/frontier of the tribe of Judah is drawn. The listing of boundary points and frontier towns runs from east to west. In a parallel passage the southern boundary/frontier of Benjamin is described (18:15-19b). There the listing moves from west to east. In 15:9 the fixed points are (1) ראש ההר (see the preceding verse), (2) מעין מי נפתוח, (3) ערי הר עפרון, and (4) בעלה היא קרית יערים. We expect to find the same points (although in the opposite order) in the parallel passage at 18:15, and for the most part we do: (1) קרית יערים (LXX: καριαθ βααλ, another name for the same place),[164] (2) ימה, (3) מעין מי נפתוח, (4) ההר (mentioned in v 16). (3) ערי הר עפרון of 15:9 and (2) ימה of 18:14 are each placed between מעין מי נפתוח and קרית יערים in their respective lists. The Hebrew in both verses is usually considered unsatisfactory at this point. Margolis, when selected to head the Palestine Oriental Society, devoted his presidential address to this topic.[165]   He notes that 'westward' of 18:15 is "clearly impossible" (since the list there runs from west to east) and terms 'cities' of Mount Ephron "equally puzzling."[166]   Margolis determined that in the OG of both passages a form of γαι appeared at this point. Thus the OG translator must have read a form of עי in his Hebrew *Vorlage* at both 15:9 and 18:15. This does present a smoother text, although not necessarily the original one.[167]

(1) none; (2) v(mg) and z(mg) record the following other readings:

ο'α' και διεκβαλλει επι κωμας ορους
σ' και εξηλθεν εις πολεις ορους.

εις γαι ορος (εφρων) (= OG and Th.) is found in dgnptA (thus it is the reading of the S̲ recension). επι κωμας ορους (= ο'α') appears in Gbckxȝ (επι κωμας sub ※ Gȝ); thus Margolis lists ※ επι κωμας: ορους as the reading of the P̲ recension. εις το ορος is the reading of LXX^B and the E̲ recension in general; manuscripts of the C̲ recension have only ορους.

In explaining the reading of LXX^B, Margolis states that "γαι is apparently the prototype of το through γε."[168]   The OG translator read עי, and not MT ערי, in his Hebrew *Vorlage*; Aq. (επι = על instead of MT אל?) and Sym. correct to the MT. Confusion between עי and ערי/עיר was not uncommon in the transmission of a Hebrew text, since only one letter is involved.[169]   Th. retained the OG either because (1) he read עי in the Hebrew text to which he was correcting or (2) he failed to notice that ערי, rather than עי, appeared in his Hebrew text. When we consider the similarity of עי and ערי and the tendency on the part of Th. to remain as close as possible to the text of the OG, the second alternative is quite possible.

It is most likely that neither ערי nor עי stood here originally. Many commentators see in ערי of the MT a dittograph of הר. This is reasonable. However, the detailed exposition of Margolis shows that they err in making such statements as "ערי. Omitted by LXX" and "LXX has only 'towards the mountain.'"[170]   The Hebrew *Vorlage* of the OG did not "omit" ערי, but read instead עי. עי is probably also the result of dittography. These observations lead to the

conclusion that in the original text there was nothing between
אל and הר (thus ויצא אל הר עפרון). While others (Soggin, for
example) seem to have reached the same conclusion, they failed
to take into account both the MT and the probable OG.

127. (15:19[b])

OG: γωλαθ μαειν171

Th.: γωλαθμαιμ

MT: גֻּלֹּת מים

(1) oʹ; (2) Aq. and Sym. translated the Hebrew (their
readings are preserved in v[mg]):

αʹ (δωσεις μοι) λυτρωσιν υδατος (και εδωκεν)
σʹ (και δος μοι) κτησιν υδατος (και εδωκεν).

βοθθανεις is the reading of LXX^B; it is also found in qr乙.
Elsewhere the following forms appear: Beththianis (∅^{t}),
Bethanis (∅^{c}), Golathmaim (𝕏), Golath meam (乙), לגולאת מאים (∅);
also βαθθανεις (h*), γολαθμαιμ (bʹdp On), γολαθμεμ (m),
γολοθμαιμ (77), γωλαλμαιμ (b$_2$), γαλαθμαιμ (j), χωλαμαιμ (a$_2$),
λωγαδμαιμ (1), γωλαθαειμ (k), γολαθαιμ (h^b), γοθλαμεκα (fsvz
[txt]), γωλαθ (Ng), γολαθ (n), γωλαθμαιμ AGθz(mg) rell.

Later in this verse גלת (without מים) occurs twice again
in the MT. From the form preserved in LXX^B (γοναιθλαν in both
places) it appears that the Hebrew Vorlage of the OG contained
מים in these two places as well.172   βοθθανεις in LXX^B is a
difficult form.173   According to Margolis, this "considerable
corruption" might be explained as follows: "Perhaps ις (at
the end) < κ (comp. γοθλαμεκα [fsvz(txt)]) dittographed from
και, νε<μαι<μαιν, βοθθα<γολαθ."174

Our main reason for including no. 127 in category 2 is the
-a- vowel in the second syllable. This vowel appeared in the
OG and apparently in all other transliterated forms as well.175
The -a- vowel suggests that the OG translator understood
Hebrew גלת (vocalized גֻּלֹּת in the MT) as a construct singular.
This suggestion is confirmed by the definite article (την)
placed before γωλαθ μαειν and by the way in which the adjectives
עליות and תחתיות are rendered (την ανω and την κατω respectively). The singular is retained not only in the transliteration of Th., but also in the translation of both Aq. and Sym.
κτησις, the 'translation' of Sym. (both here and at Judges 1:15),

is little more than a guess.[176] λυτρωσιν, attributed to

Aq. here and in Ec 12:6, seems to go back to a Hebrew text in

which גאלה (גְּאֻלָּח) appeared or at least was read.[177] Less

likely, λυτρωσιν may represent an interpretive rendering of

Hebrew גלה. Nowhere is there any clear indication of a

correction to the plural (גֹלֹת) of the MT.

In the parallel passage of Judges 1:15 גלה is again

vocalized גֻּלֹּת in the MT. There, however, the adjectives appear

in the singular (עלית and תחתית). It is probable that in

Joshua the OG translator and others were influenced by this

passage from Judges.[178]

At 15:19 Aq. and Sym. translated; Th., following the pro-

cedure of the OG, employed transliteration to represent the

Hebrew. Emanuel Tov has brought the practice of translitera-

tion into the discussion of the καιγε recension. The signifi-

cance of no. 127 in this regard is discussed, together with

related examples, under no. 94 in chapter 3.[179]

159. (22:34)

    OG: και επωνομασεν ιησους τον βωμον των ρουβην και των

          γαδ και του ημισους φυλης μανασση και ειπεν (οτι)[180]

    Th.:   και τω

          γαδ και ειπαν

    MT: (כי) ויקראו בני ראובן ובני גד למזבח

(1) ο'α'σ'; (2) plural επωνομασαν is found in bcdgnptv(mg)

x𝕏ℤ; b-egjnpstv(mg)xz(txt)ℤℨ omit ιησους. bxℨ place τον

βωμον after γαδ. των (twice) is found only in Bch*o. In

general, τω appears elsewhere. bxℨ omit και του ημισους φθλης

μαωασση. του ημισους is the reading of Bh*mo; in general, τω

ημισει appears elsewhere. ℨ has דואמרו=(και ειπαν). The

plural also appears in bcejoqsvxz (ειπαν), dpt (ειπον),

ℰ(dixerunt, so B-McL). και ειπεν/-ον is omitted in gnℤ.[181]

    LXX[B] (the Egyptian recension) has preserved the OG for

v 34a. The underlying forms for the other recensions are as

follows:

P και επωνομασαν τω ρουβην και τω γαδ τον βωμον ÷ και ειπαν

C και επωνομασεν ιησους τον βωμον τω ρουβην και τω γαδ και τω
    ημισει φυλης μανασση και ειπεν

S και επωνομασαν τον βωμον τω ρουβην και τω γαδ και τω ημισει
    φυλης μανασση.

The form of v 34a in the Hebrew *Vorlage* of the OG varied
considerably from that preserved in the Hebrew of the MT. In
the OG Joshua becomes the subject of קרא/επονομαζω (necessi-
tating a singular verb), למזבח/τον βωμον is placed directly
after this verb, the half-tribe of Manasseh appears along
with Reuben and Gad (as in the Greek of the preceding two
verses and elsewhere), and ויאמר/και ειπεν comes before כי/οτι.

It is generally felt that something has been omitted after
למזבח.[182] Robert Gordis argued that this verse is complete as
it stands in the MT and may be translated: "The sons of
Reuben and the sons of Gad called the altar: A-witness-that-
the-Lord-God-is-between-us."[183] Even if one accepts
Gordis' suggestion, he would have to admit that this is a
difficult verse, which has produced a considerable number of
different readings in the versions.

As we saw above, one attempt to improve or clarify was
found in the Hebrew *Vorlage* of the OG. The fullest correction
to the MT is found in the manuscripts of the Palestinian
recension. Their reading permits us to reconstruct the entire
text of Th. for v 34a: και επωνομασαν τω ρουβην και τω γαδ
και ειπαν. Th.'s main concern in this passage was apparently
to eliminate ιησους and και του ημισους μανασση and to make
the verb plural (as in the MT). Thus he neglected to restore
βωμον to its position after "Gad." Having a plural verb at
the beginning of the verse, Th. changed ειπεν to ειπαν,
without realizing that this clause was "additional" in the
Greek text that he was revising. As on other occasions, Th.
in his effort to translate a Hebrew text identical to the MT
allowed certain (non-MT) elements and constructions from the
OG to slip into his text.[184]

164. (24:1)

    OG: εις σηλω

    Th.:   σηλω

    MT: שכמה

(1) (The ascription of this reading to Th. is preserved in
v[txt]) none; (2) v(mg) attributes συχεμ to α'ο'σ'; συχεμ
also appears in abcxz(mg)ℊ.[185] Other readings are σιλω in
n and σηλωμ in hiqwℰℤ.

167. (24:25)

OG: εν σηλω

Th.:   σηλω

MT: בשכם

(1) (The ascription of this reading to Th. is preserved in v[txt]) none; (2) as noted in B-McL, v(mg) contains the following readings: ο'α'...συχεμ, σ' εν σικιμοις. συχεμ is also found in a*bcxz(mg)a₂* (txt) (συχεν in b'). Other readings are σιλω in fn, σηλωμ in hl^bq*κ* and σιλωμ in l*w.

Harry M. Orlinsky, after studying this problem from a text critical point of view at the request of the late G. Ernest Wright, wrote the following:

> I believe that the original LXX read 'Shiloh' in its Hebrew *Vorlage* and that the Palestinian Recension substituted 'Shechem' for it...Thus the Palestinian Recension simply adjusted original 'Shiloh' to 'Shechem' to accord with the reading in the current Hebrew text. In other words, I regard these as authentic variants in different Hebrew text-traditions. While I assume that Masoretic 'Shechem' is original, and that a supposed original 'Shiloh' leads us nowhere, the case must be solved by other data than text criticism.[186]

After his examination of all the data, Wright concludes that Masoretic 'Shechem' is indeed original in these passages. We are unable to go beyond the previous discussion of this matter. For our purposes it is sufficient to note that in these two passages Th. retained the text of the OG, which contained a reading different from that found in the MT.

171. (24:33b)

OG-Th.: και εκυριευσεν

MT: _____

At the end of the book of Joshua material appears in the OG that is not found in the MT. This additional material is designated 24:33a-b.

(1) ο'; (2) κατεκυριευσεν is found in AMθad(-σαν)efhjklopstu (κατακ-) vy-b₂.

In the absence of any contrary indication, the reading of LXX^B, which is also that of Th., S̲ and P̲₁, is to be accepted as the OG here. This material appeared in the Hebrew *Vorlage*

of the OG,[187]   and apparently Th. also found these verses
in the Hebrew to which he was correcting. On the other hand,
in an effort to preserve as much as possible of the OG, he may
have retained these verses and somehow indicated in his text
that they were not contained in the Hebrew.

Category 3: Introduction

Th. ≠ OG, but both = MT. Already in category 2, revision of
the OG on the part of Th. was visible. In category 3 such
revision becomes the chief concern. In these examples Th.
substituted a rendering of his own for the one he found in
the OG; both texts, Th. and the OG, reflect a Hebrew identical
to the MT.

Th.'s revising in these cases shows an attempt to arrive
at more precise, more literal reflections of the MT. In many
cases his concern is to standardize Greek equivalents for
certain Hebrew words or phrases. Some of these standard
equivalents are identified as characteristics of the καιγε
recension and as such are discussed in chapter 3. This effort
to standardize often shows Th.'s affinity to the OG even as he
revises it. In some cases we are unable to determine what led
Th. to reject the OG; however, there is little to suggest whim
or caprice. The pattern that we trace leads unmistakably to
the conclusion that there was method, although not pursued
with the utmost rigor (cf. Aq.), in Th.'s practice.

In many of these readings there is no agreement between
Th. and the OG; that is, Th.'s substitution is complete inso-
far as the extant evidence is concerned. There is, however,
sufficient evidence of Th.'s partial or complete agreement
with the OG elsewhere to make it clear that Th. had the OG
before him even in those examples not susceptible to proof
(see also the prefatory note at 1:18 [no. 12] below).

The general pattern for presentation of evidence in this
category is as follows: First we give the readings of the
OG, Th., and the MT. Then (1) whenever the reading of Th.
also appears in o´, Aq., or Sym, this is noted, with the word
"none" indicating that the reading of Th. is not found in
any of these three texts; (2) additional readings, including
(a) those that support Th., (b) those containing the OG,
(c) others.

3
9. (1:8)

OG: ινα ειδης ποιειν παντα τα γεγραμμενα

Th.:   ινα φυλασσης ποιειν παντα τα γεγραμμενα

MT: למען תשמר לעשות ככל הכתוב

(1) none; (2) v(mg) also records the following: for o', ινα
συνης ποιειν παντα τα γεγραμμενα; for σ', ινα φυλασσης ποιειν
κατα παντα τα γεγραμμενα; for α', οπως φυλασσης του ποιειν κατα
παν το γεγραμμενον. 𝔊ᵐ ascribes the reading דתטר (ινα φυλασσης)
to οι λ.¹⁸⁸ φυλασσης is found in degnpt (-ση gn)ℤ Cyp Luc. OG
ειδης is found only in BM(mg)z(mg). Among other readings for
the verb are συνειδης (r),¹⁸⁹ συνιης (k), συνηεις (a₂),
συνηση (o), intelligas (𝔄). fjsvz(txt) have συνης εν πασιν οις
εαν ποιης οπως φυλασσης. συνης is the reading of AFM(txt)
N𝔗 rell 𝔊.

Margolis includes ειδης in his text of the OG.¹⁹⁰ Its
preservation in LXXᴮ and its relation to the readings of the
other traditions tend to confirm Margolis' decision here.
According to Margolis, the OG reflects תשמע. In other words,
the Greek translator read תשמע in his Hebrew Vorlage, rather
than MT תשמר. Such a mistake could easily have occurred in
the transmission of the Hebrew text.

To support his retroversion of the OG, Margolis can point
to only one passage (1 K 20 [21]:31) in which the Greek
rendered Hebrew שמע in this manner. שמע, moreover, is no
more likely an equivalent for ειδεναι than is שמר. Both
Hebrew שמר and Greek ειδεναι have a wide range of meanings,
and it is not difficult to imagine an interpretation of these
verbs that would permit ειδεναι to render שמר. In a similar
expression in the preceding verse the OG translated the infinitive לשמר as φυλασσεσθαι. Here (v 8) the OG translator
varied his rendering, and in so doing chose to translate
Hebrew שמר in an admittedly unusual manner.

Less probable than the explanation of Margolis is that
of Holmes, seconded by Benjamin.¹⁹¹ He suggests that the
translator misread the Hebrew as תשכל and "as this had been
translated by συνης just before, varied with ειδης." We
note that (1) תשמר and תשכל are not that similar in their
spelling and (2) ειδεναι is never used (outside of this

example, if Holmes is correct) to represent Hebrew שכל.

Since there is no persuasive argument in favor of a
Vorlage other than the Hebrew of the MT and since we offer
an explanation for the unusual rendering of Hebrew שמר (the
desire to vary, see above), we believe that the simplest
solution is to accept חשמר(=MT) as the form that appeared in
the Hebrew *Vorlage* of the OG. φυλασσω, the verb found in the
reading of Th. (so also Aq.-Sym., the manuscripts of the
Lucianic recension, and those of the N-group [in a plus]), is
the standard translation of Hebrew שמר (so v 7) and thus re-
moves any ambiguity or lack of precision found in the rendering
of the OG.[192]

With the exception of the readings of Aq. and Sym., there
are no attempts recorded to render the words ככל הכתוב more
literally. As Margolis notes, the OG does not translate
(כל)כ,[193] which is translated by the expected κατα in Aq. and
Sym. The suggestion that the *Vorlage* of the OG lacked -כ at
this point is strengthened by a comparison with 1:7, where
κατα appears in most of the manuscripts which reflect the MT,
and 8:34(9:7), where LXX has κατα παντα τα γεγραμμενα for MT
ככל הכתוב. In this regard, Th. reads with the OG, which
probably reflects a Hebrew *Vorlage* different from the MT. No
difference in *Vorlage* is suggested by the plural of the OG
and Th. (παντα τα γεγραμμενα), as can be seen by a comparison
with the Greek at 8:34 cited above. Aq. alone uses the
singular to achieve a more literal translation (cf. the
correctors in v 7) and uniquely places the definite article
του in front of the infinitive to represent the Hebrew
ל(עשות).

12. (1:18)
OG: αλλα
Th.: πλην
MT: רק

Prefatory note: No. 12 is one of the examples in which the
preserved reading of Th. and that of the OG have little or
nothing in common, and yet both, it is apparent, represent a
Hebrew *Vorlage* identical to the MT. (See further the

introduction to this category.) These examples are entirely
different from those found in category 4, where the Hebrew
Vorlage of the OG differs from the MT.
(1) α'; (2) outside of Th. and Aq., πλην alone is found only
in c; πλην αλλα is the reading of F. B-McL translates the
reading of Ӿ as *sed tantum*.
Since both αλλα and πλην are acceptable translations of
Hebrew רק in this usage, there is no question of different
Vorlagen here. αλλα is the reading of the OG at this point,
as the lack of any widespread variants confirms. Th. substituted another word (πλην), which is practically synonymous
with what he found in the OG.[194] Aq. also included πλην in
his text. In chapter 3 we present evidence to suggest that
the רק = πλην equivalence represents a tendency, if not a
characteristic, of the καιγε recension.[195]

17. (2:6)

> OG: (αυτους εν) τη λινοκαλαμη τη εστοιβασμενη
> Th.:   τοις ξυλοις της λινοκαλαμης της
>   εστοιβασμενης
> MT: (ב)פשׁתי העץ הערכות

The reading recorded for Th. in M(mg), τοις ξυλοις, is part
of the fuller phrase attributed to Th. in v(txt): τοις ξυλοις
της λινοκαλαμης της εστοιβασμενης.
(1) none; (2) v(mg) records for α'σ'ο' the following reading,
which is the same as the OG: αυτους εν τη λινοκαλαμη. The
text of Th. is found, with minor variation, in F^bNbefgjhsv
(sub ϑ') z(txt): τοις ξυλοις της λινοκαλαμης (τοις gj*)
εστοιβασμενης (-νοις j*n). Other readings include τοις
ξυλοις τοις ληνοκαλαμοις τοις εστιβασμενοις (c) and τη
ληνωκαλαμην η εστυβασμενη (m).

λινοκαλαμη is a *hapax legomenon* in the Greek translation
of the Hebrew Bible.[196] Margolis states that this word
"answers to" פשׁתי העץ of the MT.[197] We agree that the Hebrew
Vorlage of the OG at this point was identical with the MT.
Elsewhere in Greek λινοκαλαμη means "(fine) flax, flax-straw."
The Hebrew phrase is usually translated into English as
"the stalks of flax."[198]

While Th., followed by the manuscripts of the Lucianic
recension (see above and Margolis), aims at a more literal
representation than the OG, we note that, to a certain extent
at least, his is a translation *ad sensum*:

MT (1) פשתי (pl.) (2) העץ (sing.)
Th.(1) ξυλοις (pl.) (2) λινοκαλαμης (sing.)

(that is, the corresponding elements in the Greek of Th. are
reversed when compared with the Hebrew of the MT; also, the
Greek for פשתי is singular, while the Greek for עץ is plural).
In both the MT and Th. the participle agrees with the word
meaning "flax."[199]

20. (2:12)

OG: εν τω οικω (του πατρος μου)
Th.:   μετα του οικου
MT: עם בית

(1) α'; (2) μετα του οικου is also found in Ncz(mg); B-McL
gives the reading of 𝕷 as *et cum domo*. g𝕬 omit εν.

There should be no doubt that the OG (preserved in LXX[B]
and elsewhere) equals the MT at this point. A certain lack of
precision is discernible in that earlier in this verse the OG
translated Hebrew עמכם by υμιν, whereas here it used a preposition to render a similar construction.[200] Such lack of precision does not point to a different *Vorlage*.[201] The reading
of Th. brings the OG closer to its Hebrew *Vorlage*, for the
preposition μετα is a more literal rendering of MT עם.

29. (3:15[a])

OG: επι (τον ιορδανην)
Th.:   εις
MT: עד

See the prefatory note at 1:18 (no. 12).
(1) α'; (2) εις is also the reading of the N-group
(efjsv[txt]z) and cgnpqtd₂𝕬(vid)𝕮(vid)𝕷(vid)𝕷(vid). d omits
the entire prepositional phrase; u, only the preposition.

In our discussion of no. 24 (3:8) in the previous category, we noted that there Th. retained OG επι, while Aq.
employed εως to reflect the Hebrew preposition עד. Here, in a
context which is parallel to 3:8, the reading of both Th.

and Aq. is ειϛ, which means that neither has the same reading recorded for him in both places. For whatever reason Th. did not alter OG επι at v 8 (he may have overlooked it), while he did at v 15. In the latter case it seems that Aq. accepted the rendering of Th. into his text.[202]

At 3:8 we also raised the possibility that the preposition of the OG there and at v 15 reflects a Hebrew *Vorlage* in which על, and not עד of the MT, was read. If that is true, then this example more properly belongs in the following category (where Th. = MT ≠ OG).[203]

30. (3:15[b])

   OG: επληρου
   Th.:   [επληρου] το[204]
   MT: מָלְאָ

(1) none; (2) the reading of the OG appears in BAF*MNahlv zb₂. επληρουτο is found in all other witnesses (B-McL: F[b] rell Eus Cyr), except a₂ (επληρουν) and o (επιπληρουτο). See also Ł: *Iordanis inpletus esset.*

Margolis includes the reading of LXX[B] (επληρου) in his text of the OG. At the same time he indicates that perhaps the "rival reading" επληρουτο (as in Th.) should be preferred.[205] If this latter view is accepted, then this example more properly belongs in category 1 (where Th. = OG = MT). If the OG is επληρου and this was the form that Th. had before him, then we assume that he effected the change ascribed to him in order to reflect with more precision his understanding of the Hebrew text.[206]

32. (3:17)

   OG: διεβαινον
   Th.(?): διεβησαν
   MT: עברים

(1) none; (2) the reading attributed to Th. (?) in v(mg) is also found in abdkptxyd₂A/β(vid)₵ℰ/β Eus Cyr; q reads διαβαινοντεϛ. The OG reading διεβαινον is found in v(txt) sub σ'.

According to both Margolis and B-McL, there is some
doubt concerning the ascription of this reading to Th. The
notation is presumably not clear in v(mg). We raise the
possibility that this reading was ascribed in v(mg) to o',
since several manuscripts usually designated by the siglum o'
do contain διεβησαν.[207]

33. (4:1)

OG: τω ιησοι

Th.: τω ιησου

MT: אל יהושע

(1) none; (2) The OG is found only in Bv(mg). τω ιησου is
the reading of NΔ₈ cefhjlqrsuv[txt](sub θ')z(txt). Among other
readings are *ad Iesu* (𝕃) and προς ισραηλ(w). προς ιησουν
appears in AFMz(mg) rell 𝔖. v(mg) records the following:
o' ου προς ιησουν.

The clause ויאמר יהוה אל יהושע occurs 11 other times in
the Hebrew of Joshua (אמר-יהושע [ההיא בעת] at 5:2). In seven
cases LXX[B] has προς ιησουν, which is the OG for those
passages.[208] In the other four occurrences LXX[B] has τω
ιησοι.[209]In these four cases the number of manuscripts reading
τω ιησοι is small: 1:1:Bv(mg); τω ιησου is found elsewhere,
except for a reading ascribed to Aq.-Sym. in which the
prepositional phrase appears; 4:15: BAv(mg); τω ιησου is
found in manuscripts of the Palestinian and Constantinople
recensions; προς ιησουν appears in those of the Lucianic
recension; 5:2:BAv(mg); τω ιησου appears in almost all other
manuscripts; 5:9:BAF*v(mg); τω ιησου is found in manuscripts
of the P and C recensions; προς ιησουν appears in those of
the Lucianic recension.

Margolis accepts τω ιησοι as the OG in those five places,
including here at 4:1, where it appears in LXX[B]. This
spelling of the dative may be an orthographic peculiarity of B.
In our opinion, however, it indicates that B is the sole
witness [along with v(mg)] that consistently escaped the
process by which -σου entered into the other traditions.[210]
If this is so, then LXX[B] is the OG in these cases also and the
reading of Th. is representative of the standardizing process.[211]

35. (4:10[a])

    OG: εν τω ιορδανη

    Th.:   εμμεσω

    MT: בתוך

(1) α'; (2) bv(mg)xz(mg)𝕬𝕾(μεσω sub ※) have εν μεσω τω ιορδανη; b'cq𝕰(vid), εν μεσω του ιορδανου. A form of μεσον appears elsewhere only in μεσον εν τω ιορδανη (k). The reading of Th. with εμμεσω is a more literal rendering of Hebrew בתוך. Both this and the reading of the OG (εν) reflect a Hebrew *Vorlage* identical to the MT. The use of εν μεσω to translate בתוך is to be connected in Joshua with the use of the same phrase to translate more literally Hebrew בקרב. The latter represents a characteristic identified elsewhere with the καιγε recension, and the former fits into the same pattern.[212]

39. (4:19)

    OG: κατα   μερος

    Th.:   το

    MT: _____

As accorded in B-McL and Margolis, the reading in v(mg) is as follows: ϑ(?) το οι ο' χω. χω here means *omittunt*, and this marginal note is meant to contrast the inclusion of το (before μερος) in Th. with the lack of the article in οι ο'.[213]

(1) none; (2) Fadginpa₂ also place the article το before μερος (in t το μεσον appears).

Manuscripts with το μερος are for the most part in the Lucianic recension. The inclusion of the article results in a more commonly-utilized grammatical construction: το...το (where the article and the attributive follow the noun preceded by the article, rather than following a noun with no article before it).[214] Thus the reading of Th. yields κατα το μερος το προς ηλιου ανατολας. The OG reproduces the situation of the MT, where no article is found in the construct chain.

40. (4:22)

OG: αναγγειλατε

Th.:   αναγγελειτε

MT: והודעתם

(1) o'; (2) αναγγελειτε is also found in FMϴdhilptuxyb₂.
Other readings are αναγγελειται (bo), απαγγειλατε (m),
απαγγελειτε (k). B-McL also records *referitis* for Ɫ and
nuntiabitis for Ᵹ (תודעון).
The form of LXX^B, which has preserved the OG here (see
below), is aorist imperative. The form of Th. (and of the
Palestinian and Constantinople recensions) is future indicative second plural. Both of these reflect a Hebrew *Vorlage*
identical to the MT. Here one need not be concerned primarily
with the question of closeness to the Hebrew text. The OG,
as is its wont, handled parallel constructions in diverse ways:

v 7   ואמרתם -- και συ δηλωσεις

v 22   והודעתם -- αναγγειλατε.215

Th. attempted to impose a pattern, by making the verbal form of
the second construction (v 22) conform to the first (v 7).216

43. (5:12)

OG: εκαρπισαντο δε την χωραν των φοινικων

Th.:   και εφαγον απο των καρπων της γης χαναατν217

MT: ויאכלו מתבואת ארץ כנען

There is some uncertainty about   the precise form of the
reading to be attributed to Th. The clause is preserved as
follows in v(mg)z(mg): και εφαγον απο των καρπωματων της γης
χανααν. For των καρπωματων M(mg) has των καρπων (or τον
καρπον).218 It is most likely that Th. did have the noun in
the plural. Was that noun καρπωμα or καρπος? Field, who had
collated M and z (but not v), appears to favor των καρπων as
the authentic reading for Th.219   καρπος represents תבואה
six times in the Old Greek, and the other Hebrew words it
translates have meanings not too dissimilar from תבואה.220
In the Greek of the LXX καρπωμα translates עלה/אשה; elsewhere,
however, καρπωμα can mean fruit(s) (from which came idea of
offering [of fruits]?).221

On the basis of the above, it does not seem possible for one to be sure what Th. wrote. This is especially so for two other reasons: (1) the choice of Th.'s Greek here is conditioned on what he found in the Greek in front of him: εκαρπισαντο (from καρπ-ιζω). In his efforts to represent the Hebrew more literally (see below), he apparently desired to utilize this same root, which is the root of both words recorded for Th.; (2) καρπων and καρπωματων are so similar that either one of them could have generated the other in the course of transmission. While one might argue that καρπων is the result of the shortening of an original καρπωματων, there is another line of argumentation that leads us to conclude that here M(mg) preserved the authentic reading for Th. and for Aq.-Sym. For Aq.-Sym., v(mg)z(mg) have και εφαγον απο γενηματος της χανααν, while M(mg) accurately presents the reading as και...γενηματος της γης χανααν.²²² In addition, v lacks the ascription of this reading to Aq.-Sym. Since M(mg) correctly preserved the reading and ascription for Aq.-Sym., it is likely that the same is true for Th. Taking into account all of these considerations, we have determined that the original reading of Th. was και εφαγον απο των καρπων της γης χανααν.

(1) none; (2) the reading of α'σ', και εφαγον απο γενηματος της γης χανααν, was discussed above. For εκαρπισαντο, Ꝋcdghnpt Thdt have εκαρπωσαντο and F^b(mg)(sine nom) reads εφαγον. g places the following plus before this clause: και εφαγον επι (read απο)²²³ γενηματος της γης χανααναιου. LXX^B has κουραν for χωραν. Thdt has γην for χωραν.

As Margolis points out, κουραν of LXX^B is a "singular reading." He includes χωραν in his text of the OG.²²⁴ We agree with Margolis and others that χωραν was the reading of the OG. Since καρπιζω in the middle may mean "to enjoy the fruits of," there is no reason to suggest that the Hebrew *Vorlage* of the OG was anything other than the Hebrew of the MT: ויאכלו מתבואת.²²⁵ Th. produced a more literal translation of the same Hebrew, influenced in his choice of noun by the OG (see above). Aq.-Sym. use γενημα, which is the the usual OG equivalent for תבואה, and they place that noun in the singular (cf. Th.).²²⁶ They do not place a definite article before the noun, as does Th. In this respect also they are closer to the Hebrew, which has no article in this position because of the construct chain.[227] The use of των φοινικων for כנען in the OG is paralleled at Joshua 5:1:

MT   מלכי הכנעני

OG   βασιλεις της φοινικης.[228]

Although such usage is not the norm in Joshua or elsewhere, there is no reason to suspect that a different Hebrew *Vorlage* underlies its occurrence here.

In summary, the Hebrew that the OG represents is in no way different from that of the MT. The efforts of Th. were in the direction of producing a more literal translation of this same Hebrew by using (1) a separate verb to translate Hebrew ויאכלו, (2) the preposition απο (=Hebrew -מ), (3) a noun for the Hebrew תבואה, (4) της γης χανααν (note γης for OG χωραν).

46. (6:24[a])

> OG: ενεπρησθη ενπυρισμω[229]
>
> Th.: ενεπυρισθη εν πυρι
>
> MT: שרפו באש

See the prefatory note at 1:18 (no. 12).

(1) α'σ'ο'; (2) the complete reading of Th. is also found in AF[b]MNϑabdhiklmopxya₂b₂ (om εν dm). The verb alone of Th., ενεπυρισθη, appears in gnt. cqu have εν πυρι in common with Th.; e*j read ενπρησωμ. 𝒵 and Luc have *igni*, as do 𝒜𝒞𝜠 according to B-McL.

Margolis lists ενεπρησθη εμπυρισμω as the reading of the OG, and Field terms εμπυρισμω "potior scriptura."[230] If the form εμπυρισμω is the OG, then this is the sole use of the noun εμπυρισμος to translate אש.[231] In that case, the OG does not contain an element corresponding to the preposition -ב that stood in its Hebrew *Vorlage*. If the OG translator wrote ενπυρισμω, it is probably correct to understand this form as εν + πυρισμω.[232] πυρισμος would then be a *hapax legomenon*; εν, an explicit translation of the Hebrew preposition.[233]

Since the reading with εμπ- or **ενπ**- is the *lectio diffici-lior* and is found in those manuscripts that generally preserve the Greek text in its earliest form, there is little doubt that it is the OG. Furthermore, since it contains a rare word (εμπυρισμος), if not a *hapax legomenon* (πυρισμος), we are not surprised that it was replaced in some traditions by a form of the common πυρ.[234]

The two verbs used, εμπιπρημι/εμπρηθω (for the OG) and εμπυριζω (for Th.), are virtually synonymous. The OG transla-tor of Joshua used εμπιπρημι/εμπρηθω six times (outside of this passage) and εμπυριζω once.[235] It is not easy to determine the motivation for substituting a synonymous verb for one already in the text.[236] If, however, we are correct to argue that the more common rendering of the prepositional phrase represents a first change in wording from the OG, then we are able to connect this development with the subsequent substitution of verbs: (1) the reading of the OG is that of LXX[B] (see above); (2) the more difficult rendering of Hebrew באש stimulated its replacement by a common one, yielding ενεπρησθη εν πυρι; (3) in order to achieve a more 'elegant' Greek, a verbal root was introduced which also contained the πυρ- element.[237]

50. (7:15)

OG: ανομημα
Th.:   αφροσυνην
MT: נבלה

See the prefatory note at 1:18 (no. 12).

(1) (The reading of Th. is preserved in g^m) none; (2) ανομιμα in bchlns*, ανομιαν in q.

ανομημα, the reading of the OG, translates נבלה only here. Elsewhere it represents a number of different words.[238] αφροσυνη, the reading which Th. placed in his text, appears seven times in the OG from Dtn to 2 Sam. In each case it translates נבלה.[239] In its uses after 2 Sam αφροσυνη never translates נבלה.[240] Through his choice of that word here, Th. sought to effect a consistent pattern of translation for נבלה. In addition, Th. eliminated some of the imprecision in the OG of Joshua, where ανομημα renders two different Hebrew words.[241]

51. (7:21[a])

OG: ψιλην

Th.: ιματιον

MT: אדרת

See the prefatory note at 1:18 (no. 12).

(1) none; (2) only in M(mg)(sine nom) is there another
reading with ιματιον: εν τοις λαφοιροις ιματιον. As part of
more extensive citations preserved in Greek, Aq. reads στολην
(so v[mg]z[mg]) and Sym. has υφασμα (v[mg] alone).[242] Readings
that cover this word are preserved for both in 𝔖 as well: α'
אסטלא, σ' נחתא. The Syriac attributed to Aq. can be translated
with confidence as στολην.[243] On the basis of the Greek in
v(mg), it appears that μφασμα underlies the Syriac ascribed to
Sym., although some doubt may be cast on this equivalence.[244]
Among other readings στολην is found in gln (in g, as part of
a plus preceding OG ψιλην), vestem in Luc (and 𝔈𝔖, according
to B-McL), and vestram in 𝔏.

There is no generally accepted Greek equivalent for אדרת
in the Septuagint. Outside of the Elijah cycle, where the
word occurs five times, אדרת is rendered by a different Greek
word each time it appears.[245] ψιλος, a hapax legomenon in
the LXX and the lectio difficilior here, is the OG. The
reading of Sym. does not occur elsewhere as a translation of
אדרת. The reading of Aq., στολη, is not used in the OG
translation of Joshua.[246] In Jonah 3:6 it does translate
אדרת; elsewhere it most often renders בגד.

The reading of Th. here is ιματιον. In the OG of Joshua
ιματιον is found three times, twice translating שלמה and once
שמלה. Like στολη, it generally represents Hebrew בגד. The
very obscurity of OG ψιλος in this context, as well as the
relative infrequency of Hebrew אדרת itself, led Th. to substitute a word of his own choice, presumably in order to bring
the Greek closer to his conception of what the Hebrew meant.
It is somewhat surprising that he selected ιματιον (rather
than, for example, στολη as found in Aq.), inasmuch as in its
other three occurrences in the book of Joshua this word carries
no suggestion at all of luxury.[247] There is, perhaps, a touch
of irony in the word chosen here by Th. to render the Hebrew.

52. (7:21[b])

    OG: και ενθυμηθεις (αυτων)

    Th.:   και επεθυμησα [248]

    MT: ואחמדם

(1) α'; (2) other readings are ερασθεις in M(mg)(sine nom) and λιμβισθεις in k(mg)(sine nom).

και ενθυμηθεις, found in LXX[B] and in the text of every other Greek manuscript, is the OG. We do not attach primary importance to Th.'s substitution of an aorist for a participle, since και ενθυμηθεις...ελαβον is a perfectly normal way for the Greek translator to represent a Hebrew construction such as ואחמדם ואקחם. More significance is to be placed on the verb used by the OG and that found in Th. ενθυμεομαι, the verbal root of the OG reading, does not render MT חמד elsewhere. At 6:18, where MT reads יחרימו, LXX has ενθυμηθεντες (that is, the same verb found here at 7:21). This has led many to suggest that the OG read יחמדו, and the further suggestion is sometimes made that the latter reading is original in this context.[249] The appearance of the חרם root three (other) times in v 18 could well have led a scribe astray. If the חמד root were original to the Hebrew of v 18, then it would be joined there with לקח, as in 7:21. This would in effect aid in forming a prelude to the events of chapter 7 (see Soggin). However, the range of meanings of ενθυμεομαι is probably broad enough to cover יחרימו, and, as Soggin states, this "correction is useful but not essential." It may be that the OG's choice at 7:21 was influenced by its rendering at 6:18, whatever the Hebrew there.

The verb used by Th. is from the root επιθυμεω, which is used six times in the OG to translate the qal of חמד. If Th. found יחרימו in his Hebrew text of 6:18, he may have chosen to alter the OG here so as to avoid having the same Greek translate two different Hebrew roots. If he found יחמדו at 6:18, he may well have changed the OG there to the same root utilized by him here.[250] His choice of the verb επιθυμεω at 7:21(b) was conditioned on at least three factors: (1) this is the most widely used translation of the qal of Hebrew חמד; (2) this is closely associated with the verb used by the OG;

(3) this is the verb used by the OG to translate חמד at Dtn 7:25 (where לקח is also found), a passage that anticipates this incident.

53. (7:24)

OG: (εις) εμεκαχωρ

Th.:   κοιλαδα αχωρ[251]

MT: עמק עכור

As recorded in B-McL, the reading preserved in M(mg) for ϑ'σ' is κοιλαδα....[252] Field records the reading as κοιλαδα αχωρ, drawing on the evidence not only of M, but also "Procop. in Cat. Niceph. T. II, p. 47." There is little doubt that M(mg) attributed the full κοιλαδα αχωρ to ϑ'σ' at v 24. First, we note that κοιλαδα αχωρ is the reading attributed to σ' (in M[mg]j[mg]v[mg]) and Th. (v[mg]) at v 26. Also, v(mg) reads κοιλαδα αχωρ at v 24. Although the ascription has been dropped in v(mg), the close connection between the margins of v and M allows us to fill out the marginal reading in M on the basis of that in v.[253]

(1) σ'; (2) κοιλαδα αχωρ is also found in gv(mg; see above) Ϗ-codℤ.[254] In k εμεκαχωρ is preceded by φαραγγα.[255] The following reading has been preserved in F^b(mg)(sine nom): κοιλαδα ταραχης.

Earlier in this verse the OG translator apparently found ויעל אחר עמק עכור in his Hebrew *Vorlage*, which he rendered και ανηγαγεν αυτον εις φαραγγα αχωρ.[256]

54. (7:26)

OG: εμεκαχωρ

Th.:   κοιλας αχωρ

MT: עמק עכור

κοιλας αχωρ is attributed to ϑ' in (v[mg]) and σ' (in v[mg]M [mg]j[mg]), as at v 24. While the same reading is attributed to α' in j(mg), v(mg) ascribes κοιλας ταραχου to α'. We place greater weight on the fuller material contained in v(mg), where separate readings are recorded for σ'ϑ' and α'. Thus we believe that κοιλας ταραχου is the authentic reading of α'. We should perhaps read ϑ' in place of α' in j(mg). z(mg) (sine nom) has κοιλας αχωρ. Field and Margolis also note that κοιλας αχωρ is an anonymous reading in Cat. Niceph. (see at 7:24). Field includes the following additional notation: "Euseb. in Onomastico, p. 118: ενεμεκ [nusquam legitur in LXX]: α'σ' εν τη κοιλαδι."

(1) σ'; (2) α' wrote κοιλας ταραχου (see above); as at 7:24, κοιλας ταραχης is found in F^b(mg)(sine nom). In g εμεκαχωρ is preceded by κοιλας αχωρ.

At 7:24, 26 Th. supplied a translation for Hebrew עמק, which he included in his text in place of the transliteration εμεκ that he found in the Greek with which he was working.[257] He then retained the OG's transliteration of עכור. It is possible that the procedure of the OG translator stems from a lack of knowledge as to the precise meaning of the root עכר.[258] It is far more likely that the OG translator employed trans- literation to represent עכור simply because he interpreted it as part of a place name.[259]

α', apparently rejecting this transliteration, replaced it with the translation ταραχου. This same word in its feminine form appears twice as an anonymous reading in F^b(mg). At v 25 the verb ταρασσω appears as a translation of the root עכר in a reading attributed to Sym. in b(mg): τι εταραξας ημας (OG: τι ωλεθρευσας ημας; MT מה עכרתנו). In g this same reading appears: למנא דלחת לך (Field: τι εταραξας ημας). This is preceded in g by οι λ ερμηνευται (הנון דשרכא מפשׂקנא) and, according to Margolis, in Masius by α'σ'θ' or α'σ' και οι λ ερμηνευται.

Emanuel Tov has brought the practice of transliteration into the discussion of the καιγε recension. The significance of nos. 53 and 54 in this regard is discussed, together with related examples, under no. 94 in chapter 3.

74. (10:19)

OG: υμεις δε μη εστηκατε καταδιωκοντες οπισω
Th.: υμεις δε μη στηκετε καταδιωκοντες οπισω[260]
MT: ואתם אל תעמדו רדפו אחרי

v(mg) has separate and distinct readings recorded for θ', α', σ', and ο'. z has only two marginal notations: one for σ' (which is identical with that attributed to σ' in v[mg]) and one for α'θ' (which is identical with that attributed to α' alone in v[mg]). Placing greater weight on the fuller material contained in v(mg), we believe that the authentic reading of Th. has been preserved there: υμεις δε μη στηκετε καταδιωκοντες οπισω.²⁶¹

(1) none; (2) v(mg)z(mg) record the following readings for Aq. and Sym.:

α' και υμεις μη στηκετε διωξατε οπισω

σ' υμεις δε μη αποστητε διωξατε κατοπιν. As preserved in v(mg), the reading of ο' is υμεις δε μη εστηκετε καταδιωκοντες οπισω. x reads εστηκετε (= ο'), and ab have στηκετε (as in Th. and Aq.). στητε, characteristic of the S recension, appears in dgnptw. The additional element ωδε appears in o (στηκατε ωδε) and efjqsvz (εστηκατε ωδε). Thus it is characteristic of the N-group, as is the reading αλλα καταδιωκετε, which is found in efjoqsvz(txt)ℤ(om αλλα). 77 has αλλα διωκετε.

Margolis terms OG καταδιωκοντες "free (as if מרדף)," and he contrasts it with the readings of Aq.-Sym. (and, we might add, the N-group).²⁶² It is clear, however, that here the Hebrew *Vorlage* of the OG differed in no respect from the MT. Th. limited his revision of the OG to the substitution of the form στηκετε for OG εστηκατε. Thackeray notes that εστηκα was used in the present sense "I stand."²⁶³ στηκω (as in the reading of Th. and Aq.) is a new present that was beginning to replace it: "the present meaning regularly attaching to certain perfects caused the evolution in the later language of new present forms out of the perfect forms."²⁶⁴ The concurrent use of both στηκω and εστηκα helps to explain those readings recorded above in which elements of the perfect and present combine to produce mixed formations.²⁶⁵

στηκετε also appears in the text of Aq., who carried out the further revision necessary to make the Greek more closely correspond to the Hebrew. In this process Aq. (and also Sym.) employed διωκω, rather than καταδιωκω as in the OG and Th. The use of διωκω to translate Hebrew רדף represents a characteristic identified elsewhere with the καιγε recension. As such, it is discussed, together with related examples, in chapter 3.²⁶⁶

79. (10:28)

    OG: εν στοματι μαχαιρας

    Th.:   ξιφους

    MT: חרב

(1) ο'

No. 79 involves a characteristic identified elsewhere
with the καιγε recension. As such, it is discussed fully,
together with related examples, under no. 50 in chapter 3.
There we also bring in the readings of other witnesses to the
text and determine their significance.

85. (10:41)

    OG: πασαν την γην γοσον[267]

    Th.:   πασαν γην γοσομ

    MT: כל ארץ גשן

(1) ο'α'σ'; (2) LXX^B contains πασαν την γοσομ.

The following readings are considered in relation to the
text of LXX^B. For πασαν την xb'b*$\not{g}$(και sub ※) read και την
πασαν γην. και precedes πασαν in Kb^adgknptwa$_2$$\not{A}\not{L}$. πασαν is
preceded by και την in G (sub ※)c. For την Ga have γην ($\not{L}$
terram). την + γην is found in AFKNΘb^adegi-ptwya$_2$b$_2$$\not{A}\not{L}$. Other
spellings for the proper name are γοσωμ (k), γοσον (Gcux$\not{L}^c$ On),
γοσην (w), Gasom ($\not{L}$), γο̣ζομ (gz[txt]), γο̣ζωμ (ej), γο̣ζον (K),
γομο̣ζ (n), σομ (m). According to Margolis, the following are
the underlying forms of those recensions that differ from
LXX^B at the beginning of this phrase: και την: πασαν (P̲) ;
και πασαν (the Lucianic recension).[268] From the reading preserved for Th. we cannot be sure that he included some
representation of MT ואת before his translation of
כל ארץ גשן, but it is likely that he did. For the remainder
of the phrase, πασαν την γην γο̣ζον is the underlying form of
S̲; πασαν την γην γοσομ, of C̲; πασαν την γοσομ, of E̲; πασαν
γην γοσον, of P̲.

Margolis states that "P̲ writes γην (without the article)
for ארץ (in statu constructo), merely correcting την of E̲
(if the error was present before Origen). The OG will have
read as SC."[269] We agree with Margolis that the OG was
πασαν την γην (with γην dropping out of the tradition behind
LXX^B by haplography). Thus the Hebrew Vorlage of the OG was

identical to the Hebrew of the MT, and the variant reading
without γην is the result of a corruption in the transmission
of the Greek text.

Th. probably did have before him a text like that of LXX[B]
in which γην had already dropped out.[270] Th. would then have
performed the task of changing την to γην. There are several
examples indicating that Th. was not strict in the matter of
excluding the article in a construct chain.[271] Had he a text
in front of him like that of the OG, we doubt that he would
have troubled himself about an extra την.[272]

The OG read נגשׁן in its *Vorlage*. It is not surprising
to find *n-m* interchange at the end of a proper name, and we do
not attach any significance to the variation occurring here.
At 11:16 Margolis also holds γοσου to be OG, and at 15:51 he
conjectures the same form for the OG.

91. (11:10)

    OG: απεστραφη

    Th.:   επεστρεψεν

    MT: וישׁב

(1) o'α'σ'; (2) επεστρεψεν is also found in AFGNϑacikmxyz
(mg)a₂b₂. Other readings are επεστραφη (K), απεστρεψεν (bl),
ανεστραφη (s).

Margolis correctly includes απεστραφη in his text of the
OG.[273] The change from this to a reading with the verb
επιστρεφω illustrates a characteristic identified elsewhere
with the καιγε recension. Its significance in this regard is
discussed, together with related examples, under no. 82 in
chapter 3.

102. (12:7)

    OG: εις σηειρ

    Th.:   (εις) σεειρα

    MT: שׂעירה

(1) o'α'σ'; (2) σεειρα is also found in AFGNϑbgixya₂b₂.
Other readings are ασσεειρα (for εις σηειρ) (b'), σιειρ (u),
σηειρα (aklo), σιηρα (m), σεηρα (n), σειρ (q), σειρα (dpt),
σεσει. (c), ση...(K), σηειρ (𝕃). h omits εις.

According to Margolis, the underlying forms for the various recensions are as follows: σηειρ (E = OG), σηειρα (S), σεειρα (PC).[274]   Margolis states that σεειρα is an inferior reading here. At 11:17, where the MT reads שעיר, the OG (= LXX[B], so Margolis) is εις σηειρ (as at 12:7). There, however, the initial vowel of the other recensions is reversed: σεειρα, S; σηειρα (PC = On).[275]

There is no consistent pattern in the various traditions with respect to the handling of directive -$\bar{a}h$.[276]   The tendency to reproduce -$\bar{a}h$ does, however, seem to be more pronounced in manuscripts of the P(alestinian) and C(onstantinople) recensions.

108. (13:13)
    OG: (τον) μαχατει (1°)
    Th.:   μαχαθι
    MT: המעכתי
(1) o'α'; (2) the OG is preserved only in Bh*r𝐸𝐿. μαχειτι is found in fsvz(txt). Among other readings are μαχητει (ej), μαχαθη (m), μαχαθε (d), μαχθει (q), μαχθη (l), *Machatiim* (𝐶). AGNθh[b]z(mg)rell𝐴 on have μαχαθι, the reading of Th.

The form מעכה occurs later in v 13 (and only there). Elsewhere in Joshua מעכתי occurs at 12:5, 13:11. At 12:5 Margolis reads μαχατει as OG (with C). He states that μαχει of LXX[B] is accordingly an error. [277]   The remaining underlying forms at 12:5 are του μαχαθι και της ναχι for S, την μαχαθ(ε)ι for P(=On). At 13:11 μαχατει of E (Br𝐶𝐿) is again taken by Margolis as the OG. μαχαθ(ε)ι is the reading of the other recensions (=On). Later in v 13 OG (LXX[B]) reads μαχατει, with μαχαθ(ε)ι the reading of the other recensions (PCS).[278] The general pattern that emerges from these four occurrences of the proper name is μαχατει = OG (usually LXX[B] [E]), with μαχαθ(ε)ι appearing in most or all other recensions.

In this case, either one or the other of the consonants τ-θ is used with consistency in the various recensions.[279] The decision that LXX[B], and thus the consonant -τ-, represents the OG is correct. Fairly often in the book of Joshua only members of the E(gyptian) recension have retained the OG. Here the reading of LXX[B] (E), presenting as it does a contrast with the practice in all other recensions, appears to stand apart from the process by which -ϑ- entered into the other traditions and to be earlier than these traditions.

113. (13:27[a])

OG: βαιϑναμρα [280]

Th.:   βηϑναμρα

MT: רבית נמרה

(1) o'; (2) LXX[B] has βαινϑαναβρα. Rather than list the 22 other spellings preserved for this proper name (see B-McL), we give here the underlying forms for the various recensions as determined by Margolis: βαιϑναβρα (Lucianic), βαιϑαναβρα (Egyptian), βηϑναμρα (Palestinian, Constantinople = On). [281]

This place name does not occur again in Joshua. Elsewhere in the Old Testament it is found at Nu 32:36. [282] Margolis consistently accepts or conjectures βαιϑ as the form for the OG in proper names that reflect Hebrew ------ + בית. βηϑ predominates in P(C), although the pattern there is not so consistent as that of the OG. For the second part of this proper name, we note that the letter b appears in the underlying form of both E and S. We find no reason to suspect that the m>b change occurred already in the Hebrew Vorlage of the OG and therefore consider it an inner-Greek development (so also m>mb found in scattered manuscripts), although it may have been present in the Greek text revised by Th. [283]

115. (14:6)

OG: εν γαλγαλ

Th.:   εν γαλγαλοις

MT: בגלגל

(1) o'σ'; (2) γαλγαλ is found in Bmu; ojsvz(txt) have γαλγαδ. γαλγαγα appears in ₵₦₦; γαλγαλοις is the reading of AGNϑz(mg) rell.

Margolis states that OG will have written γαλγαλοις, which is the reading of Th. [284] His choice here may have been based on the general pattern one finds elsewhere in the Greek of Joshua. In chapters 1-10 this place name occurs seven times in the OG, always with the plural ending. In three other places in these chapters the OG lacks the sentence in which

גלגל appears in the MT. In each of these cases the plural ending is found where a correction to the MT is made. For the other three occurrences of this proper name, the Greek does not present so consistent a pattern. In 12:23, where LXX^B has της γαλειλαιας, Margolis accepts γαλγαλ as the OG (PC have γελγελ).[285] At 15:7, where LXX^B has τααγαδ, Margolis again reads γαλγαλ as the OG (with PC).[286]

In these last two examples there was good reason not to regard the reading of LXX^B as the authentic reading of the OG. Here, at 14:6, there seems to be no compelling reason for our not accepting the reading of LXX^B(E) as the OG, especially when we recall that often in Joshua the Egyptian recension alone has preserved the OG. The observation that γαλγαλ-α(-ων, -οις) is far more common in the Greek of Joshua provides us with all the more reason for seeing γαλγαλ of LXX^B as original, for the addition of the plural ending has the effect of bringing this reading into line with the usual practice. The argument that -οις has been lost in the tradition behind LXX^B would have more force if the immediate context provided the opportunity for omission by homoeoteleuton, but it does not. Therefore, we believe that the OG at 14:6 read γαλγαλ, with the change to γαλγαλοις a later, standardizing development.[287]

119. (14:12)

OG: τη ημερα εκεινη (1°)
Th.:   εν τη ημερα εκεινη
MT: ביום ההוא (1°)

(1) o'α'σ'; (2) the following manuscripts also place the preposition εν at the beginning of this phrase: AGNθabdegiptxyz(mg)a$_2$b$_2$. In efjsvz(txt) ταυτη appears instead of εκεινη.

At its second occurrence in v 21 this phrase again appears in the OG as τη ημερα εκεινη. There the following manuscripts are listed with the preposition εν at the beginning: AG^{b}Nθabcdikmprtv(mg)xya$_2$b$_2$. The addition of εν to what is surely the reading of the OG yields a more literal rendering of the MT, for it supplies an explicit element in Greek corresponding to the Hebrew preposition -ב. There need be no question of divergent Hebrew texts here.

One might ask why a reading for ϑ′ (and o′α′σ′) has been
preserved at the first occurrence of this phrase, and not also
at the second. Did not Th. include εν there as well? We can
perhaps read the notation *sine nom* in v(mg) at the second
occurrence as a reference to the fuller notation just above.
It may also be that the distinctive reading of v(txt),
characteristic of the N-group as a whole, at the first occurrence led to the preservation of a marginal notation there
primarily for the εκεινη-ταυτη contrast.

125. (15:17)

    OG: αδελφου

    Th.:   αδελφος

    MT: אֲחִי

(1) o′α′; (2) nominative αδελφος, as in Th., is found in
ϑbcdglnpq (pr o)tux𝐴𝐿; it is characteristic of the P and S
recensions. Genitive αδελφου is found in manuscripts of the
E and C recensions. v(txt) attributes αδελφου to σ′.

The construct form אחי appears in the context of a proper
name:

MT   עתניאל בן קנז אחי כלב

LXX γοϑονιηλ υιος κενεζ αδελφ-ου/ος χαλεβ. Margolis includes
αδελφος in his OG text and speaks of αδελφου as "harmonistic
and taken from Ju 1:13."[288]   In the Judges passage (cf. 3:9)
the same phrase appears in the MT. αδελφος is the reading of
Agnqwx𝐴𝐿; the remaining manuscripts, including LXX[B], have the
genitive. Commenting on this variation in Judges and on the
significance of the use of the term אח, Robert Boling makes
the following observations: "'brother' that is, military
confederate, as in well-known Mari usage of *aḫu*. In the
course of traditionary differentiation, Othniel was regarded
as either Caleb's brother (LXX[A]) or nephew (LXX[B]). Intricate
Calebite genealogies in 1 Chron 2 and 4 imply complex tribal
histories."[289]   That the Judges passage influenced the OG
translator of Joshua or his Hebrew *Vorlage* is clear from
o νεωτερος, which followed χαλεβ in the OG at Joshua 15:17.[290]

When Margolis spoke of αδελφου as "harmonistic," he was
referring to the change from "OG" αδελφος to αδελφου on the
basis of the genitive in the B text of Judges, which he felt

contained the OG. We now know that for Judges the B text
represents not the OG, but the pre-Origenic καιγε recension.[291]
The OG of Judges is most consistently found in the Lucianic
manuscripts and Ƚ, which are the witnesses for the nominative
αδελφος here. Thus it is probable that the OG at Judges 1:13
read αδελφος. If this is so, then we are able to turn around
Margolis' argument and view αδελφος as harmonistic. It may
well be that Th. did have in mind the (old) Greek of Judges
1:13 when he changed the genitive to the nominative, for we
know that Th. often strove to standardize divergent Greek
renderings of the same words or phrases.[292]   The fact that
αδελφου is the reading of manuscripts (especially B and the E̲
recension in general) in which the OG most frequently appears
for Joshua gives added support to our acceptance of the
genitive as original to the OG.

131. (15:46)
      OG: ασεδωδ [293]
      Th.:   αζωτου [294]
      MT: אשדוד

𝔖 ascribes the reading אזוטוס to Th. at this point. This can
be rendered with confidence as αζωτου, the same reading
attributed to ο' in v(mg).[295] αζωτου also appears in z(mg)(sine
nom).
(1) ο' (see above); (2) the reading attributed to ϑ' and ο'
appears in no other extant witness to the text. As determined
by Margolis, the underlying forms for the various recensions
are as follows: αοηδωϑ (E̲S̲), αοδωδ (C̲), εοδωδ (P̲).[296]

     The place name אשדוד occurs two other times in the MT of
Joshua (11:22, 15:47). There also Margolis conjectures ασεδωδ
as the OG.[297]   Outside of Joshua αζωτος appears as the representation for אשדוד and various forms developed from it. Once
in Joshua the OG translator did make use of a form of αζωτος,
αζωτειω, to represent אשדודי. Elsewhere, however, as we noted
above, a transliteration of the place name appears. The
choice of αζωτου by Th. introduced into this passage the
standard representation of אשדוד. This procedure is in line
with his practice elsewhere, as numerous examples show.

133. (16:10)

OG: εν τω εφραιμ

Th.:   εν μεσω εφραιμ

MT: בקרב אפרים

(1) α'σ'; (2) as recorded in v(mg), o' has εν τω εφραιμ
(=OG). Other readings include εν τοις υιοις εφραιμ in dnptv
(mg)ℤ, εν γαζερ εν τοις υιοις εφραιμ in g, and εν τω ορει
εφραιμ in efjsv(txt)z.

εν τω εφραιμ is the reading of the OG and reflects a
Hebrew *Vorlage* identical to the MT.[298]   The reading of Th.
with εν μεσω is a more literal rendering of Hebrew בקרב and
as such represents a characteristic identified elsewhere with
the καιγε recension.[299]

137. (18:8)

OG: χωροβατησαι

Th.:   διαγραψαι

MT: לכתב

See the prefatory note at 1:18 (no. 12). διαγραψαι is
attributed to θ'σ'α' in v(mg), to σ'α' in *b*(mg), to οι λ in
z(mg). Margolis notes that 𝔊ᵐ attributes this reading to θ'σ'.
(1) σ'α' (see above); (2) v(mg)z(mg)(both sine nom) record
χωρογραφησαι. There are no other variants.

כתב is used in a rather specialized sense five times in
Joshua 18 (vv 4, 6, 8, 8, 9): "describe in writing, write a
description (with reference to the land)." In v 4 OG
διαγραψατωσαν is from the same verb, διαγραφω, as that
attributed to Th. in v 8. In v 6 the use of the root μερ-ιζω
to represent Hebrew כתב is unique.[300]   Twice in v 8 the OG
settles on χωροβατω as its translation of כתב in this
specialized sense, while in v 9 it uses the same verb to
represent עבר.[301] Later in v 9 the OG uses γραφω to translate
כתב. It appears that the use of διαγραφω by Th. in v 8 was
an effort to standardize the translation adopted by the OG in
v 4 and thus arrive at a consistent pattern with respect to
כתב in this section of chapter 18, where the OG employs three
or four different verbs.[302]

108

150. (22:5[a])

    OG: και προσκεισθαι

    Th.:   και κολλασθαι[303]

    MT: ולדבקה

See the prefatory note at 1:18 (no. 12). 𝔊 ascribes the
reading ולמהנקפו to Aq.-Th. We accept Field's determination
that this is to be translated και κολλασθαι.

(1) α'; (2) other readings are προσκεισθε in km, προκεισθαι
in f, προσκυνεισθαι in lw, προσκυνειν in d, and προστιθεσθαι
in b.

προσκειμαι translates a form of the root דבק only here
and at Dtn 4:4. Its range of meanings includes the idea
expressed here, "to cleave." Both the lack of widespread
variants and the application of the principle of *lectio
difficilior* lead us to conclude that προσκεισθαι does represent the OG here. The verb κολλαω, which Th. included in his
text at this point, often translates דבק in the LXX.[304]
In addition to introducing a standard translation for דבק,
Th. may also have desired to restrict the Hebrew equivalents
of προσκειμαι to the usual גור.[305]

151. (22:5[b])

    OG: της διανοιας υμων

    Th.:   καρδιας

    MT: לבבכם

See the prefatory note at 1:18 (no. 12).
(1) σ'α'; (2) the reading of Th. is also found in ANθgik-
nptuwyz(mg)a₂b₂𝔄𝔏.

There are three translations of (ב)לב found in the OG
of Joshua: καρδια (five times), διανοια (three times),[306]
νους (once). No consistent pattern emerges.[307] Our determination of the OG here is based chiefly on the inclusion of
διανοιας in the text of those manuscripts that generally
exhibit the OG. The reason for the change by Th. is not clear;
there is no question of differing Hebrew texts. In the LXX
as a whole καρδια does appear considerably more often than
διανοια as a translation for לב(ב), but the degree to which
such statistics have relevance here is uncertain.[308]

153. (22:10[a])
    OG: βωμον (1°)
    Th.:   θυσιαστηριον
    MT: מזבח (1°)

See the prefatory note at 1:18 (no. 12).

(1) α'σ'; (2) for o' see below.

As listed in B-McL, the ascriptions here are not certain:
βωμον (1°) sub θ' (vid) v(txt); βωμον (1°)] o' (?) σ' (?)
α' (?) θυσιαστηριον v(mg). We suggest that the reading in
v(txt) should be attributed to o' and that Th. read θυσιαστηριον
along with Sym. and Aq. No manuscript tradition, including
that indicated by the siglum o', reads θυσιαστηριον here.[309]
At this point θυσιαστηριον is not found outside of the citation
in v(mg).

In the OG a lexical distinction was made between the altar
built by the two and one-half tribes (βωμος) and the altar "of
the Lord our God" (θυσιαστηριον). The reading recorded here
in v(mg) appears to be part of an effort to eliminate this
distinction through the systematic use of θυσιαστηριον. If
we have correctly reinterpreted the sigla, Th. can be identified with this effort. In our opinion the systematic use of
θυσιαστηριον in this context is related to a characteristic
identified elsewhere with the καιγε recension. As such, it is
discussed, together with other examples, under no. 28 in chapter 3.

154. (22:10[b])
    OG: μεγαν του ιδειν
    Th.:   τω
    MT: גדול למראה

(1) o'α'σ'; (2) τω is also found in Kcgx (το in a).

The reading του is that of the OG. The reading ascribed
to Th. represents more literally -ל of the Hebrew and to
this degree brings the OG closer to the MT.

110

160. (23:4[a])

OG: επερ(ρ)ιφα

Th.: (υπ) εβαλα[310]

MT: הפלתי

See the prefatory note at 1:18 (no. 12). The correct reading
for Th., Aq., and Sym. is uncertain due to different ascriptions in v(mg) and z(mg): ϑ' εβαλα, z(mg); σ' εβαλα, v(mg);
σ' υπεβαλον, z(mg); α' υπεβαλον, v(mg). Further confusion
is introduced by the following note that appears in Field:
"Parsonsii amanuensis ex eodem [z(mg)] exscripsit: Ō.
υπεβαλον. ϑ. υπεβαλα." Under the circumstances we think it
prudent to list the reading of Th. as (υπ) εβαλα. The only
reading ascribed to Aq. is υπεβαλον, while the text of Sym.
cannot be determined with certainty.

(1) none; (2) for the readings of Aq. and Sym. see above.
οπερ ειπα appears in Bm. Among other readings are οπερ ειπον
(dnpt), ωσπερ ειπων (g), sicut dixi (₵), sicut dixit (𝕃).
Also, απερριφα (aa₂), επεριψα (ϑck), οπερ ειπα επεριφα (b),
reliqui (𝔸𝕃), ecce dedi (𝔹). επερ(ρ)ιφα is found in AMN rell 𝖘.

We reconstruct the following underlying forms for the
various recensions: οπερ ειπα (Egyptian), ωσπερ ειπον
Lucianic), επερ(ρ)ιφα (Palestinian, Constantinople).
επερ(ρ)ιφα most likely represents the OG.[311] It is not difficult to explain the readings of manuscripts in the Egyptian
and Lucianic recensions as the result of inner-Greek corruption
of this form (ΕΠΕΡΡΙΦΑ>ΟΠΕΡ ΕΙΠΑ). If επερριφα is the OG,
then its Vorlage at this point need be nothing other than the
Hebrew of the MT. Elsewhere in the LXX the root επιρριπτω
generally translates a form of שלך, as at Josh 10:11, the
only other occurrence of this verb in the Greek of Joshua.

In Jer 15:8 this root renders the causative of נפל
(as here), but there the Hebrew does not have the specialized
meaning "assign, apportion, by lot." Approximately a dozen
times in the LXX βαλλω translates the causative of נפל in the
sense of casting lots and/or apportioning by lot.[312] Thus,
the reading εβαλα, which may well be that of Th., extends to
the Greek of Josh 23:4 what is the usual representation of the
Hebrew here. It also serves to distinguish between the

"casting, throwing" action here and that of 10:11, both
translated in the OG by the same verb. [313]

166.   (24:15)

   OG: ελεσθε
   Th.:   εκλεξασθε
   MT: בחרו

See the prefatory note at 1:18 (no. 12).

(1) (The ascription of this reading to Th. is preserved in
v[txt]) α'; (2) OG ελεσθε, found in AM(εδ-)Νθabchik(txt)lu
xyz(mg)a₂b₂, is characteristic of the P and C recensions; in
addition, this form is attributed to o' and σ' in v(mg).
εκλεξασθε, the reading of Th., appears in manuscripts of the
Lucianic and Egyptian recensions and also those of the N-
group.

   αιρεω, the verbal root employed by the OG translation
here, occurs only sporadically throughout the Septuagint; it
is, however, fully comprehensible as a representation of
Hebrew בחר. Th., through his use of εκλεγω, introduced into
this passage the standard equivalent for the verb found in
OG.[314]This substitution is consistent with the activity recorded for Th. in a number of other examples.

   An unusual feature of no. 166 is that Th.'s εκλεξασθε
managed to enter LXX^B and other manuscripts of the E recension,
where we generally find the OG.[315] Th.'s influence on the S
recension is, however, paralleled elsewhere.[316]It is also not
usual to locate the OG in manuscripts of the P recension alone
(or joined, as in this case, only by C). Thus no. 166 cautions
us against making facile identifications through a mechanical
application of the formula LXX^B = OG, even when proper names,
frequently subject to corruption, are not involved.

169. (24:26[b])

OG: υπο την τερεμινθον

Th.:   υποκατω της δρυος

MT: תחת הָאֵלָה

The reading υποκατω της δρυος is attributed to θ' in both
b(mg) and v(mg). The same reading is preserved for α' in
these two sources and z(mg). v(mg)z(mg) ascribe the following
to σ': υπο δρυν. $ records לתחת מן בלוטא for α'σ'. Field
translates this as υποκατω της δρυος. While such a retroversion is not absolutely secure, it does raise the possibility
that the attribution in $ is mistaken and should read α'θ'.
Further support for this change is drawn from the observation
that there is occasionally in Joshua agreement between the
marginal notations in *b* and those in $. Whether this connec-
tion can be used to correct one or the other is unclear.
Here *b* has the support of v.

(1) α' (see above); (2) the readings of Aq. and Sym. are
discussed above. τερεμινθον is found sub o' in v(txt);
τερεβινθον is the reading of AMNc-hlmnpqtwya₂ℰℤ. [317]

In a difficult passage at 17:9 the OG has η τερεμινθος
(הָאֵלָה [יערים]) for MT הָאֵלֶה (ערים).[318] The pointing of the
Masoretes has produced a *hapax legomenon* at 24:26:
אַלָּה (cf. אַלּוֹן) "oak," rather than the expected אֵלָה (cf. אֵלוֹן)
"terebinth." While the OG used δρυς to represent both -אֵל
and -אֵל, it generally restricted τερεμινθος to -אֵל. Thus, we
might speculate that the Greek translator read האלה in the
expected way (cf. 17:9), while Th. knew of the tradition that
later led the Masoretes to produce a unique pointing here.
Additionally, Th. may have wanted to distinguish the reading
here from what he found at 17:9. We cannot be sure, however,
that the reading of Th. exhibits knowledge of the tradition
later used by the Masoretes, or that the OG did not know of
such an understanding. Therefore, we prefer to include no.
169 in category 3, since both readings may well equal MT
(even to the unique pointing preserved there).

170. (24:27)

OG: αυτος [319]

Th.:   ουτος

MT: הׁיא

(1) none; (2) ουτος is found in AMNϑd-jlmnpr-uv (sub ϑ')
wy-b₂א(vid)Ⴑ Thdt Cyp. v(mg) has the following notation:
ο' ⅄ (οτι) αυτος.

Arguments can be advanced to support the originality of
either of these two readings. Confusion because of the similar
spelling of αυτος and ουτος cannot be excluded. Since the
Vorlage is in either case identical to the Hebrew of the MT,
we have included 24:27 in category 3.

Category 4: Introduction

Th. = MT ≠ OG. In the last category we saw examples of Th.'s
substitution of his rendering of the MT for the OG's rendering
of the MT. We may also speak of substitution in category 4,
but here such substitutions are in the nature of corrections.
The OG in these cases does not reflect the Hebrew of the MT;
in most cases, however, the OG does accurately reflect the
Hebrew that the translator read in his *Vorlage*.

Whereas category 2 provided us with evidence that on
occasion Th. retained non-MT elements from the OG, category
4 makes it clear that such retentions were the exception and
not the rule. Although it cannot always be shown that Th. was
correcting (a form of) the OG, the numerous clear examples of
the close relationship between Th. and the OG point in that
direction for all cases. At the least, our interpretation
provides a coherent picture of the text from which Th. made
his revision. Of equal, if not greater significance is the
observation that in every example we present in this category
Th. is correcting to a Hebrew text identical to the MT.

This section is divided into three sub-categories: 4.1,
4.2, 4.3. In 4.1 Th. adds material lacking in the OG (and
its *Vorlage*). In the presentation of material we first give
the readings of Th. and the MT. Then (1) whenever the reading
of Th. also appears in o', Aq., or Sym., this is noted, with
the word "none" indicating that the reading of Th. is not
found in any of these three texts; (2) other witnesses for
this additional material or a form of this material. Category
4.2 contains the one reading that involves solely the elimination of words from the OG that are not found in the MT.
The number of readings in category 4.3 is far larger. As
in previous categories, there are examples of both partial
and no agreement with the OG. The general pattern for presentation of material in 4.3 is as follows: First we give the
readings of the OG, Th., and the MT. Then (1) see (1) above;
(2) additional readings, including (a) those that support Th.,

(b) those containing the OG, (c) others. As is true throughout chapter 1, the discussions that follow do not conform to any set pattern.

4.1

1. (1:1)

  Th.: δουλου κυριου

  MT: עֶבֶד יהוה

(1) ο';[320] (2) δουλου κυριου also appears in FMϑ[b]abcghinqr xz(mg)A̶C̶E̶L̶S̶(sub ※ M sub ※ ϑ'S̶) Thdt. Other readings with δουλος are δουλου του ϑεου in m and δουλου ϑεου κυριου in a₂. The use of δουλος to translate עבד represents a characteristic identified elsewhere with the καιγε recension. The significance of no. 1 in this regard is discussed, together with related examples, under no. 61 in chapter 3.

2. (1:2[a])

  Th.: τουτον

  MT: הזה

(2) οι $\frac{\lambda}{o}$; (2) Fcdkptxa₂A̶-ed(vid)E̶S̶(sub ※ ϑ') Or-lat

3. (1:2[b])

  Th.: τοις υιοις ισραηλ[321]

  MT: לבני ישראל

(1) none; (2) cdkptxA̶E̶S̶ (sub ※)

4. (1:3)

  Th.: επ αυτου (or: επ αυτον)

  MT: בו

The reading of Th. is preserved in two forms: επ αυτου in v(mg) and επ αυτον in M(mg).

(1) none; (2) επ αυτου, as in v(mg), appears in cgxS̶(sub ※); επ αυτον, the form ascribed to Th. in M(mg), is found in pta₂. Other readings are επ αυτω (n) and επ αυτην (d).

13. (2:1)

  Th.: κρυβη

  MT: חֶרֶשׁ

(1) α'; (2) κρυβη appears in F. With the spelling κρυφη this reading is found in Nc(κρυφα)dkptxS̶[m](sub ※). Tract reads *absconse*, so also A̶C̶E̶ as interpreted by B-McL.[322]

118

14. (2:2)

    Th.:   ιδου

    MT: הנה

(1) οι ⅄ o'; (2) ιδου appears as part of a variety of
longer readings in AFM(txt and mg)Nϑabcdhiklmopqtuxya₂b₂λ̷ε̷ς̷
(ιδου sub ※ ϑ').

16. (2:4[b])

    Th.:   και ουκ εγνων ποϑεν εισιν

    MT: ולא ידעתי מאין המה

(1) none; (2) FM(mg)Ncdhkpstxε̷ς̷(sub ※) have this clause
in the form ascribed to Th. Slight differences are found in n
(και ουκ εγνω ποϑεν εισην) and g (και ουκ εγνωσαν ποϑεν
εισιν).[323] The text of λ̷ at this point is translated by
B-McL as *et ego non noueram unde sint*.

19. (2:9)

    Th.:   και οτι τετηκασιν παντες οι κατοικουντες την γην
            απο προσωπου υμων

    MT: וכי נמגו כל ישבי הארץ מפניכם

(1) οι ⅄; (2) the clause beginning και οτι τετηκασιν παντες
(see below) is found in Ncdkptxλ̷ε̷ς̷(sub ※ λ̷ς̷) (dptε̷ omit οτι).
ς̷, according to B-McL, reads *quia soluti sunt qui habitant in
terra ante faciem vestram*.

The ascription of this reading to Th. is found only in
M(mg): ϑ' και οι ⅄. Similar wording is ascribed to o' and
οι ⅄ in v(mg) and to οι ⅄ alone in z(mg). As recorded in M(mg)
and attributed there to Th., this clause begins και οτι
τετηκασιν παντες, which is a literal rendering of וכי נמגו כל.
By contrast, και εκτετηκασιν παντες, the beginning of the
clause as preserved in v(mg) z(mg), lacks οτι, and in this form
the reading is not found elsewhere.[324] In our judgment both
the form of the clause as recorded in M(mg) and its ascription
to Th. are authentic.

27. (3:13)

> Th.: σωρος εις
>
> MT: גַּד אֶחָד

(1) α'; (2) σωρος εις also occurs in Fcdhkptx ℊ^m(sub ※);
b reads ως ορος. In addition, B-McL lists the following:
sicut aceruus unus (𝐀-ed), *aceruus*... (ℊ-ap-Barh), *sicut nouus*
aceruus columnae (𝐀-cod). The readings and ascriptions for Th.-Aq.-Sym.
have been preserved in several different forms: ϑ'α' σωρος εις σ' ασκωμα
εν in M(mg); ϑ'α' σωρος εις σ' ασκωμα in v(mg); α' σωρος σ'
ασκωμα in z(mg); ϑ' ασκομα εν α'σ' σωρος εις in g. Margolis,
who also lists ασκωμα εν as the reading ascribed to σ' in ℊ,
indicates that in g we are to read ϑ' for σ' and σ' for ϑ',
thus yielding σ' ασκωμα εν α'ϑ'σωρος εις.[325] Margolis'
suggestion is to be followed, for it brings the citations in
g into line with the rest of the evidence. Further support
for the inclusion of ασκωμα in the text of Sym. here is provided at v 16. There, where the OG and almost all Greek
manuscripts employ πηγμα εν to render נַד אֶחד, b(mg) records
ασκωμα εν as the reading of Sym.[326]   σωρος can thus be
ascribed with confidence to Th. as well as Aq. at v 13. This
word does not translate נַד elsewhere. The readings of all
three also contained a form of εις, as noted only in M(mg),
where in this instance readings and ascriptions have been
preserved most accurately.

61. (9:21[9:27])

> Th.: και ειπαν αυτοις οι αρχοντες
>
> MT: וַיֹּאמרוּ אליהם הנשיאים

(1) none; (2) M(mg)ϑabcqv^mg(sub ※)xy^a?z(mg)𝐀ℰℊ(sub ※ ϑ')
read και ειπαν (-ον c) αυτοις οι αρχοντες. m has only και
ειπον; dpt, και.

73. (10:13)

> Th.: ουχι τουτο γεγραμμενον επι βιβλιου του ευθους
>
> MT: הלא היא כתובה על ספר הישר

(1) none; (2) the reading of Th. is found in Gϑbcejmoqv(mg)
xz(mg)𝐀ℰℊ(sub ※ Gv[mg] sub ※ϑ' ℊ). This clause appears in a
somewhat different form in gn Thdt, witnesses to the Lucianic

recension: ουχι αυτο γεγραπται επι βιβλιον το ευρεθεν.³²⁷

In the text of Th., from which Origen drew his material
at this point, του ευθους translates הישר. This use of ευθυς
to render a form of the root ישר illustrates a characteristic
identified elsewhere with the καιγε recension. The significance of 10:13 in this regard is discussed, together with
related examples, under no. 79 in chapter 3.

78. (10:27)

    OG: λιθους

    Th.:   λιθους μεγαλους

    MT: אבנים גדלות

(1) o'α'σ'; (2) λιθους μεγαλους, as in the text of Th., is
the reading of Gθa-dghkm-qtxz(mg)𝔄𝔼𝔅(μεγαλους sub ÷ G𝔅); Fᵇ
has λιθους μεγιστους. For λιθους of the OG, efjsvᵃ̇²z(txt)
read λιθον.

135. (17:4)

    Th.:   υιου ναυη

    MT: בן נון

(1) o'α'; (2) AGNθabciklotuxyb₂𝔄𝔅 have υιου ναυη, as in
Th.-Aq. v(mg) ascribes (ιησου) υιου νουν to Sym. Other
readings are του ναυη (a₂), υιω ναυη (f), υιου ναυι (m), and
υιου ναβι (p).

140. (19:34)

    Th.:   (τω) ιουδα

    MT: וביהודה

Field records the following notation of Masius: "Cum porro
deinceps est in libris vulgatis και ο ιορδανης etc., suppletur
locus ex Theodotione in mixta sic: και ÷ τω ιουδα ⨯ ο
ιορδανης etc."

(1) 𝔅 preserves the following reading for σ': מן מערבא ליהודה
(Field: απο δυσμων τω ιουδα); (2) as noted in B-McL,
bckx𝔅(sub ÷ θ') have ιουδα.

According to B-McL, 𝔄 reads *Iuda* and 𝔼ᶜ *et in Juda* (both before
the conjunction), and τω ιουδα replaces ο ιορδανης in On(vid).

157. (22:25)

OG: ανα μεσον ημων και υμων τον ιορδανην
Th.: ανα μεσον ημων και υμων (οι) υιοι ρουβην και (οι)
υιοι γαδ τον ιορδαηνην
MT: ביננו וביניכם בני ראובן ובני גד את הירדן

(1) o'σ'; (2) οι υιοι ρουβην και οι υιοι γαδ (the reading
of Th., see below) appears in bcoqxΑß (sub ※ ß); the definite
article is omitted in both places in cox. As recorded in
B-McL, v(mg) attributes ...και υιοις γαδ... to α'. efjsvzℇ
(sub ※ v) read υιων ρουβην και υιων γαδ και ημιοσυ φυλης
μανασση.

The following reading is ascribed in v(mg) to ϑ'o'σ':
ανα μεσον ημων και υμων και υιοι γαδ τον ιορδανην. z(mg)
(sine nom) records the same reading, with the addition of the
article οι before υιοι. In neither of these forms does this
expression represent the fullest correction to the MT. The OG
apparently lacked בני ובני גד בני ראובן in its Hebrew *Vorlage*,
and the correction found in manuscripts of the Palestinian
recension restores both "Reuben" and "Gad": οι υιοι ρουβην
και οι υιοι γαδ. We feel certain that this full correction
appeared in the text of Th. and that the shorter phrase
preserved in v(mg)z(mg) is the result of haplography. Thus,
the text of Th. at this point read as follows: ανα μεσον
ημων και υμων (οι)υιοι ρουβην και (οι) υιοι γαδ τον ιορδανην.
The reading of Th. is superior to that in the genitive,
characteristic of the N-group, in that it correctly understands
this phrase as a vocative (thus the English translation:
"between us and you, *you* sons of Reuben and sons of Gad").

In ANϑafgilnoqtuyb₂ℂℇℒ, manuscripts of the Constantinople
and Lucianic recensions, the order of pronouns has been reversed: υμων και ημων. Such confusion is common in Greek
texts.[328]

4.2

66. (10:10[a])

    OG: απο προσωπου των υιων ισραηλ

    Th.:   απο προσωπου ισραηλ

    MT: לפני ישראל

(1) ο′ ; (2) AGNΔ₈ϑabdlmptwxyb₂ℵℰℤ omit των υιων; ju, των.

4.3

5. (1:5)

OG: ουκ αντιστησεται ανθρωπος κατενωπιον υμων

Th.: ουθεις κατα προσωπον σου

MT: לא יחיצב איש לפניך

(1) σ'; (2) v(mg) preserves the following reading for α':
ου στηλωθησεται ανηρ εις προσωπον σου. Elsewhere only manuscript 30 and Luc show the pronominal suffix in the singular.
The OG reflects the plural suffix -כם in its Hebrew
Vorlage, while the pronominal suffix of the MT is singular.
Since this clause occurs in a divine address to Joshua, the
latter is more appropriate. This is especially so in v 5.
Alternation in number and person is fairly frequent, however,
and thus it is not surprising that the OG translator found
the plural suffix in his *Vorlage*.[329] Dtn 11:25, which is in
a parallel context, provides an additional source for textual
corruption: MT: לא יחיצב איש בפניכם; LXX: ουκ αντιστησεται
ουδεις κατα προσωπον υμων.

In his choice of words Th. also appears to have been
influenced by the Dtn passage, although at the same time he
corrected the number of the pronominal suffix in the OG of
Joshua. The reading of Aq. in particular exhibits several
characteristics identified elsewhere with the καιγε recension.
As such, it is discussed, with related examples, in chapter 3.
There we also point out another influence on Th.'s wording
here.[330]

8. (1:7[b])

OG: πρασσης

Th.: πορευη

MT: חלך

(1) none; (2) a form of the verb ποιεω, the usual Greek
equivalent for עשה in Joshua, is found in depta₂ and in
manuscripts of the N-group (in a conflate reading at v 8).

Only in Th. is there a reading preserved that clearly
translates the MT. As Margolis notes, the OG reflects
(את) כל אשר תעשה in its Hebrew *Vorlage*. He calls attention to
Dtn 29:8 (29:9 in LXX), where the MT has את כל אשר תעשון
(LXX: παντα οσα ποιησετε).[331]

It is probable that the text of the MT at 1:7 was
corrupted by the parallel expression in v 9. Through application of the principle of maximal variation we judge the
reading of the *Vorlage* of the OG to be original in v 7. This
is the sole use of the verb πρασσω in the OG of Joshua. Is it
possible that other revisors of the OG felt that somehow
πρασσω was an adequate reflection of Hebrew הלך?

21. (2:14)

OG: και αυτη ειπεν ως αν παραδοι κυριος υμιν την
πολιν ποιησετε εις εμε

Th.: και εσται ως αν παραδω κυριος ημιν την πολιν
ποιησωμεν μετα σου

MT: אם לא תגידו את דברנו זה והיה בתת יהוה
לנו את הארץ ועשינו עמך

(1) o'α'; (2) M(mg) attributes the following reading to
οι λ: εαν μη αναγγειλης το ρημα τουτο και εσται ως αν παραδω
κυριος ημιν την πολιν ποιησθε μετα σου. v(mg) also attributes
to οι λ the first part of this reading in the following form:
εαν μη αναγγειλης το ρημα ημων τουτο. The reading of 𝕃 is
*si non indicaveritis haec verba nostra et erit cum tradiderit
nobis Dominus civitatem faciemus tecum.* ως is also preceded
by και εσται, as in Th., in ackxz(mg)𝕃^m. παραδοι is found
only in Br; elsewhere παραδω appears. cz(mg) have ημιν,
(και c) ποιησομεν, and μετα σου. την γην, rather than την
πολιν, is the reading of kx𝕃^m(mg).

The OG lacked אם לא תגידו את דברנו זה in its Hebrew
Vorlage. Margolis states that the OG "seems to have found in
the place of והיה [of the MT] the corrupt והיא which the
translator read as two words: א (א)והי = והיא אמרה; the
change of person followed of necessity."[332] The systematic
change of person referred to by Margolis must already have
occurred in the Hebrew *Vorlage*.

We are certain that Th. included in his text a translation
of Hebrew אם לא תגידו/-די את דברנו זה[333] and omitted OG
και αυτη ειπεν. In his effort to correct the pronoun υμιν
and verb ποιησετε to the first person, so as to conform to
Hebrew לנו and (ו)עשינו), Th. neglected to correct την πολιν
of the OG to την γην (=MT הארץ) (see kx𝕃^m).[334]

28. (3:14)

OG: και απηρεν ο λαος

Th.: και εγενετο ως απηρεν ο λαος [335]

MT: ריהי בנסע העם

(1) α' (see below); (2) v(mg) preserves the following other readings: ο' και ως απηρεν ο λαος, σ' ως δε απηρεν ο λαος. εγενετο ως is also found in FNabcdikpqtxa₂ʌ̸ʓ̸ʓ̸ᵐ.[336] πας ο λαος appears in efjsvzℤ.

Margolis calls into question the ascription of readings to θ' and ο' as preserved in v(mg). According to him, the ascriptions are to be reversed, so that α'ο' read και εγενετο ως απηρεν ο λαος and θ' has και ως απηρεν ο λαος.[337] Support for this change in ascriptions can perhaps be found in the observation that those manuscripts usually designated by the siglum (οι) ο' contain the reading και εγενετο ως .... [338] This change in ascription is, however, at variance with M(mg): θ'α' εγενετο, and here Margolis does not make any change. In the absence of any clear evidence to the contrary, we accept as authentic the notation in v(mg) that Th. did include και εγενετο ως απηρεν ο λαος in his text.[339]

Margolis states that in this passage the Old Greek translator simplified "the unwieldy construction" of the MT. We feel, on the other hand, that the OG here accurately reflects ויהסע in its Hebrew *Vorlage*. That the OG translator did reproduce his *Vorlage* quite closely in such constructions is seen from both the preceding and following verses:

v 13 MT והיה כנוח

OG και εσται ως αν καταπαυσωσιν

v 15 MT וכבוא

OG ως δε εισεπορευοντο.

Thus the reading of Th. represents a correction to a Hebrew identical to the MT.[340]

31.　(3:16)

OG:　　εως μερους καριαθαιν[341]

Th.:　　μερους σαρθαμ

MT:　　(מ)צד צרתן

According to B-McL, σαρθαμ is the reading attributed to
θ'ο'α'σ' in v(mg). Margolis lists the form as σαρθαν.[342]
This difference is not significant, inasmuch as interchange
between final *m* and *n* is frequent.

(1) ο'α'σ'; (2) LXX[B] has εως μερους καθιαιρειν. Among other
readings are *Cariatharim* in 𝕏, καριαθιμ in gn, σαρθαν in kx𝒔[m],
and צרתם in 𝒔. καριαθιαρειμ is found in A (-ριμ)FMN rell 𝑩𝑪𝑬.

καριαθαιν is a conjecture on the part of Margolis.[343]
According to him, the Greek translator appears to have read
קִרְ°תַ֯ן and "wrote καριαθαιν (cf. καριαθιμ in gn), which later
was resolved into καριαθ ιαρειμ; καθιαιρειν (B) is a corruption of καριαθειν." Holmes suggests that the Greek translator
read כערתן, while Benjamin takes the Hebrew to have been
קריתים. [344] The reading of Th., σαρθαμ/ν, is equivalent to
the form of the proper name preserved in the MT.

　　Commentators generally agree that OG εως μερους reflects
the reading/misreading (for the latter, see especially Holmes)
of קצה (אשר) עד in its Hebrew *Vorlage*. While that may be so
for the OG, it need not follow that μερους in the reading of
Th. also reflects קצה, rather than צד of the MT. We note
that only manuscript x, with απο in place of OG εως, supplies
a clear translation for Hebrew מ(צד). In the case of this
manuscript, we may be sure that the phrase απο μερους is
reflecting מצד of the MT.[345] The preposition of Th.'s text
is not preserved here, but in all probability it also was απο,
producing the reading απο μερους σαρθαμ. In fashioning a
phrase to translate Hebrew מצד צרתן (=MT), Th. thus retained
μερους of the OG, even if μερους reflected something other
than צד in the OG. [346]

34. (4:5)

OG: εμπροσθεν μου προ προσωπου κυριου

Th.: εις προσωπον κιβωτου κυριου

MT: לפני ארון יהוה

(1) α'σ' (see [2] below); (2) *b* attributes εις προσωπον κιβωτου κυριου to α'σ'θ'. 𝔊 records the following reading for α'σ', which apparently covers εμπροσθεν-προσωπου: קדם פרצופא. 𝔊 follows with a reading attributed only to σ': קבוחה דמריא (κιβωτου κυριου). We can be sure that the text of α' also included κιβωτου κυριου, and this not only from the phrase preserved in *b*(mg). In the first reading recorded in Syriac, for both α' and σ', the form פרצופא appears. This stands in contrast to 𝔊(txt), where we find פרצופה, which is then followed directly by דמריא. Elsewhere, only manuscript q has a text with κιβωτου: (μου +) και εμπροσθεν κιβωτου κυριου του θεου ημων.

As Margolis indicates, the OG reflects a Hebrew *Vorlage* in which לפני was written twice; hence לְפָנַי לִפְנֵי.347   Also, it appears that this *Vorlage* did not contain ארון , which is supplied in the correction of θ'α'σ'. We are inclined to believe that the OG did contain κιβωτου, which was early lost by homoioteleuton: προ προσωπου κιβωτου κυριου.348   Since, however, no manuscript that usually contains the OG has such a reading, our suggestion must remain tentative. Thus we are led to include no. 34 in this category, where the text of Th. represents a correction of the OG toward a Hebrew identical to the MT. 349

48. (7:1)

    OG: αχαρ

    Th.:   αχαν

    MT: עכן

(1) o'a'σ'; (2) αχαν is also the reading of AϑbfxyΧb₂.

    The different spellings of this proper name, here and elsewhere, have been the subject of considerable scholarly discussion. A contributing factor in this regard is the confusion between *r* and *n* at the end of the word.[350]

55. (8:5)

    OG: και παντες οι μετ εμου

    Th.:   και πας ο λαος ο μετ εμου

    MT: וכל העם אשר אתי

(1) α'σ'o'; (2) the reading of Th. is also found in AFMNϑ cdghilmoptwyz(mg)a₂b₂ΑΖ(om o 2° F*y). Other readings are και πας ο μετ εμου λαος (k) and και πας ο λαος (n).

    The OG translator apparently did not find העם in his Hebrew *Vorlage* and therefore employed the plural παντες to render כל.[351] If this is so, העם must have dropped out accidentally in this Hebrew text, for וכל אשר אתי is not original here. Although it is possible that the *Vorlage* of the OG was identical to the MT and that the translator considered παντες a satisfactory rendering of כל העם, our study of the OG translation of Joshua leads us to conclude that the OG would have represented העם more explicitly had it been in its *Vorlage*. Thus the text of Th. is a correction of the OG to the MT.

60. (9:9[9:15])

    OG: το ονομα αυτου

    Th.:   την ακοην

    MT: שמעו

The reading of Th. here is preserved in both Greek, την ακοην in *b* and Syriac, שמעה in ʂ.

(1) α'σ'; (2) none

    The noun שמע is extremely rare in the MT. It occurs but four times (Joshua 6:27, 9:9; Jeremiah 6:24; Esther 9:4), always with a pronominal suffix. At Jer 6:24 the LXX

accurately reflects the Hebrew: ηκουσαμεν την ακοην αυτων
(MT: שמעו את שמענו).352At Joshua 6:27 the OG has το ονομα αυτου
(as at 9:15), where the MT reads שמעו. For the passage in
chapter 6 bϫ ascribe the reading ακοη αυτου to α'σ', but not
also to ϑ' as at 9:9. In both verses ϑ'α'σ' are the sole
witnesses to this reading.

At both 6:27 and 9:9 the OG apparently reflects שמו in its
Hebrew *Vorlage* rather than שמעו of the MT.353 It is possible,
on the other hand, that the OG translator had before him a
Hebrew text identical to the MT. His rendering in these
passages would then be explained by (1) his misreading of the
rare noun as the far more common one354 or (2) his feeling
that ονομα was a suitable translation for שמע. In our opinion
the text of the OG in these two passages accurately reflects
a *Vorlage* different from the MT, so that την ακοην of Th.
is a correction of that OG to a Hebrew identical to the MT.
At the very least, we have in Th. a more literal rendering of
Hebrew שמע.

62. (10:1)

    OG: αδωνιβεζεκ

    Th.: αδωνισεδεκ

    MT: אדני צדק

(1) ο'α'σ'; (2) αδωνισεδεκ is also the reading of F^ckx.355

As Margolis and others have noted, the OG here and at
v 3 reflects אדני בזק in its Hebrew *Vorlage*.356 This is
also the spelling found in the MT and LXX at Judges 1:5-7.
Noth regards אדני בזק, the OG here and in v 3, as original
in the Joshua passages, while G.E. Wright advanced arguments
that the original form of this name may well be preserved in
the MT of Joshua.357 For our purposes it is sufficient to
affirm that אדני בזק did stand in the Hebrew *Vorlage* of
Joshua and that this form was accurately represented by the OG
translator. Th., who at this point had before him a Hebrew
text identical to the MT, corrected this OG through his use
of αδωνισεδεκ.

64. (10:5[a])

OG: βασιλεις των ιεβουσαιων

Th.:   των αμορραιων

MT: מלכי האמרי

In $\mathcal{S}^m$ plural των αμορραιων is attributed to ϑ'α'σ'. In v(mg) the plural is similarly ascribed to ϑ', while a reading with the proper name in the singular is recorded for α'σ' and ο': βασιλεις του αμορραιου. More weight is to be attached to the fuller evidence cited in v(mg), since there a distinction is made that is not noted in $\mathcal{S}^m$. Moreover, the use of the singular to reflect precisely Hebrew האמרי is in line with the practice of Aq.[358]

(1) none (see above); (2) plural αμορραιων, as in Th., is also found in F$^{c?}$ckoq$\mathcal{E}^c\mathcal{Z}$. Gx have singular του αμορραιου.

There is little doubt that the reading of the MT is original in this context. In the Hebrew *Vorlage* of the OG היבוסי was found, which the translator rendered in the plural (see below). היבוסי may have supplanted an original האמרי in this Hebrew text under the influence of the following ירושלם.

The reading of Th. is a correction of the OG to a Hebrew identical to the MT. In fashioning his correction, Th. retained the plural number of the OG, which was employed there in accordance with the usual practice of this translator in such constructions. An examination of relevant passages shows that the OG translator of Joshua tended to represent proper names in the plural in expressions such as "king of..." (even though these names appeared in the singular in his *Vorlage*), and to limit the singular to the various lists of people. As in other examples, Th. retained a distinctive feature or practice of the OG translation, one that in this case was not "retained" in α', σ', or ο'.

67. (10:10[b])

OG: ωρωνειμ [359]

Th.:   βαιϑωρων

MT: בית חורן

(1) none (but see [2] below); (2) v(mg) preserves the following reading for σ'ο'α': βηϑωρων. Br have ωρωνειν. Other readings that equal or approximate the OG are ωρωνειμ

in efjsv(txt)z(txt) Cyr, ορωνιμ in h*u, ορωνεμ in q. βαιθωρων,
with ϑ', is found in F^bNdoptv(mg)z(mg). Other readings include
βηθορων (h^bk), βεθωρων (mwa₂, w places εν before the proper
name), *Bethoron* (𝔸-ed), *Bethron* (𝔸-cod), *Baetheron* (𝕃), εν
βαιθορων (gn). AGϑv(mg)rell ∅ On read βηθωρων, with σ'ο'α'.

The OG reflects חורנם (חוֹרֻנַם) or a similar form in its
Hebrew *Vorlage*.360   According to Soggin, who terms such a
reading "improbable," the *Vorlage* of the OG perhaps "had a
mem enclitic which was no longer understood as such." 361

69. (10:11[a])

OG: ωρωνειμ
Th.:   βαιθωρων
MT: בית חורן

(1) none (but see [2] below);   (2) v(mg) preserves the
following reading for o'α'σ': βηθωρων. LXX^B has ωρωνειν.
Other readings that equal or approximate the OG are ωρωνειμ
in efjsvz(txt) Cyr, ορωνιμ in h*u, βαιθωρωνειν in r. Gabqxϕ
read βηθωρων, with o'α'σ'.
Other readings include βηθορων (h^bk), βη.θωρων (o), βεθωρων
(Almwa₂), βεθορων (i), *Bethoron* (𝔸-ed Spec-ed), *Bethron*
(𝔸-cod), *Bitoron* (Spec-cod), βαιθωρ (n). Reading βαιθωρων,
with ϑ', are F^bNϑz(mg)rell 𝕃.

For the reading of the OG and its *Vorlage* see no. 67
above. In comparing the representations for the first part
of this proper name at vv 10 and 11, we note that at 10:10
βαιθ- is found primarily in the Lucianic manuscripts and
βηθ- in those of the P(alestinian) and C(onstantinople)
recensions. At v 11 βαιθ- is found in manuscripts of the
Lucianic and C recensions, while βηθ- continues to be
characteristic of the Palestinian recension.362

87. (11:1[b])

OG: μαρρων

Th.: μαδων

MT: מדון

(1) o'α'σ'; (2) only Bu preserve the OG. Readings that approximate this are μαρρω. (F*), μαρρωμ (ia₂), μαρρωα (F^{b?c?}), μαρων (gnⱧ-ed), *Meron* (Ⱨ-codd). Other readings include μαρδων in efjkrvz, *Amarron* in Ᵽ, αμαρρω in o, αμορρων in q, *Amorraeorum* in Or-lat, αμμορραιων in h. AF^{b?c?}GNϑrell ɴ On-ed have μαδων, with ϑ'.

According to Margolis, the OG reflects (מָרוֹן, מֶרוֹן, מָרוֹן) מרון in its Hebrew *Vorlage*.[363] Some support for a reading with *r* is supplied by the text at 12:20: MT: מראון (שמרון מלך); OG (so Margolis) βασιλεα μαρρων.[364] מדון, however, also appears in the MT at 12:19 in a phrase apparently lacking in the Hebrew *Vorlage* of the OG.[365] Another place name, מי מרום at 11:5, 7, should also be brought into this discussion. Although Margolis includes the form το υδωρ μαρρωμ (with the same consonants as the MT) in his text of the OG for vv 5, 7, Soggin may be correct when he states that μαρρων, found in LXX^B, points to an identification of these two places (מדון and מי מרום in the MT) in the OG.[366] Finally, we cannot exclude the possibility that the common ר/ד confusion played some part in the forms of the proper name found in v 1 and elsewhere.

We conclude that the Hebrew *Vorlage* of the OG did contain מרון at this point, which was accurately reflected by the translator. We are not sure whether this form is original or, as is more likely, the result of change, either conscious or accidental, from an original מדון (the form the MT preserves).[367] In either case it is clear that Th. corrected this OG to a Hebrew identical to the MT, and for this reason no. 87 is included in category 4.

88. (11:1[c])

    OG: συμοων

    Th.:   συμερων[368]

    MT: שִׁמְרוֹן

(1) ο'α'σ' (but see below); (2) συμοων, the reading of LXX[B]
(=OG), is also found in hquℓ; σομεων (but Margolis reads
σομερων) in k is the only other form of the proper name pre-
served in Greek without -ρ- (Or-lat: *Simeon*; ℒ: *Samoan*).
Other readings are συμερων (as in ϑ'ο'α'σ') in sz(mg), συμορων
(= OG, so Margolis) in or, σομορων in F[b]KNcdgipt, σωμορων in n,
Somorron in ℒ, *Semeron* in 𝔸, σομερσειν in a₂, υμερων in
efjvz(txt), μαρρων in 236, μαιρων in y, σομερων in AF*Gϑablmxb₂.

    Margolis interprets the form in LXX[B] as "a corruption
from συμορων (ρ dropped after ο)."[369] He also makes the
following observations: "The statement in v(mg) cannot be
correct as it stands, since υ is found in E and satellites
only; the main point is the initial σ and the glossator meant
to write σομερων (and for one or the other of οι λ possibly
σεμερων, cf. V[ulgate: *Semeron*]). As the readings of S
[σομορων] and PC [σομερων] stand, there is accomodation to
שִׁמְרוֹן."

    שִׁמְרוֹן appears as a place name twice again in the Hebrew
of Joshua (and nowhere outside of Joshua in this usage).[370]
In both places, 12:20 and 19:15, LXX[B] reads συμοων, as at 11:1.
This consistent rendering strongly suggests that here, as
often elsewhere, LXX[B] (and the E recension in general) alone
has preserved the OG. In these three passages the translator
read a form without -r- (BH[4] suggests שמעון) in his Hebrew
Vorlage, rather than שמרון of the MT. Soggin amassed a number
of extra-Biblical sources to support συμοων.[371] While this
evidence does not prove that the form rendered by LXX[B] is
original in this context, as Soggin apparently feels,[372] it
does allow us to see in συμοων the accurate representation of
a legitimate place name (cf. Margolis' judgment that συμοων
is but a corruption from συμορων).

    We also note that the OG translator kept this place name
separate from the tribal name Simeon (שִׁמְעוֹן, found in 19:1-9;
21:4,9), which he wrote συμεων. While the *o-e* distinction may

be artificial, it does indicate care on the part of the OG translator to hold the two names apart.

It is clear that Th. corrected the OG to the extent that he represented the *consonants* of the MT reading: שמרון. As the reading of Th. has been preserved in v(mg), it does not show the accomodation to שָׁמְרוֹן that forms with σομ- seem to represent. Although Margolis casts doubt on the authenticity of the *u*-vowel in the first syllable of the word attributed to Th., it is only by circular reasoning that we can exclude this vowel from the text of Th. on the grounds that it is fround "in E and satellites only." While it is almost certain that "one or the other of οι λ" did write σομ-/σεμ-, [373] there is no compelling reason to trace this reading back to Th., who tended to remain as close as possible to the Greek text he revised (here: σο̤-).

The change from -o- (OG) to -ε(ρ)- (Th.) may be of no particular significance.[374] On the other hand, this change may be the result of the desire by Th. to represent more closely the vocalization preserved in the MT.[375] Giving appropriate weight to all of the evidence, we feel justified in attributing to Th. the *full* correction to the reading שָׁמְרוֹן.

93. (11:19)

OG: ην ουκ ελαβεν ισραηλ

Th.: ητις ου παρεδωκεν τοις υιοις ισραηλ

MT: אשר השלימה אל בני ישראל

(1) none; (2) v(mg) also records the following readings:

α' η ου παρεδοθη τοις υιοις ισραηλ

σ' ητις ειρηνευσε προς τους υιους ισραηλ.

We present below the MT and the underlying forms of the various recensions for the entire verse:

MT   לא היתה עיר אשר השלימה אל בני ישראל בלתי החוי

ישבי גבעון את הכל לקחו במלחמה

E   (=LXX[B]) ουκ ην πολις ην ουκ ελαβεν ισραηλ παντα ελαβοσαν εν πολεμω

S   ουκ εγενετο πολις ητις ειρηνευσεν τοις υιοις ισραηλ πλην ο ευαιος ο κατοικων εν γαβαων και ουκ ην πολις ητις ου παρεδοθη τοις υιοις ισραηλ πασας ελαβον εν πολεμω

P ÷ και: ουκ ην πολις ητις ου παρεδωκεν τοις υιοις ισραηλ ※·
πλην ο ευαιος ο κατοικων εν γαβαων: παντας ελαβεν εν πολεμω
C και ουκ ην πολις ητις ου παρεδωκεν τοις υιοις ισραηλ παντας
ελαβεν εν πολεμω

Notes: In the plus at the beginning of the verse S used the
verb (ειρηνευσεν) attributed to Sym.; later in the verse S
borrowed from Aq. (ου παρεδοθη). Since Origen apparently
took the reading ητις ου παρεδωκεν τοις υιοις ισραηλ from Th.,
it is likely that Th. is also the source for the ※ material
immediately following (πλην-γαβαων). An interesting reading
is found here in x: ητις ου παρεδωκεν κυριος τοις υιοις
ισραηλ; cf. F^bb (both read ην and omit κυριος) ΑΣ (vid).

Commenting on ουκ ελαβεν in the OG, Holmes states the
following: "The meaning of השלים 'to make peace with' was
not known to LXX. In x.1 and 4 it is rendered by αυτομολεω,
here by ου λαμβανω." [376] For several reasons this explanation
strikes us as unsatisfactory. First, we are not convinced
that the OG translator was unaware of the meaning "to make
peace with." A form of αυτομολεω [377] is found everywhere at
10:1, 4, except for the marginal notation ειρηνευσαν (F^b)
recorded at v 4. This Greek verb has meanings such as "desert,
keep changing sides, rat, come of one's own accord." When
one considers this fairly wide range of meanings for αυτομολεω,
there is no reason to doubt that it is at least an adequate
representation of Hebrew השלים with the meaning "to make peace
with."[378] In fact, with its connotation of "desertion, ratting,"
this Greek verb is quite appropriate in the context of chapter
10. From the point of view of Adonizedek (OG: αδωνιβεζεκ)
and his confederates, Gibeon's action in "making peace with"
or "going over to" Israel was indeed an act of desertion and
changing sides.

Returning to the comments of Holmes, we do not believe
that the OG translator found אשר השלימה אל בני ישראל in his
Hebrew *Vorlage* at 11:19. Accordingly, we cannot agree with
the last part of Holmes' comments. Holmes failed to mention
that the entire structure of this clause is different in the
MT and the OG and that the OG has no translation for
בלתי החוי ישבי גבעון, which comes immediately after this
clause in the MT. The OG, in our opinion, accurately reflected

its Hebrew *Vorlage* both in the structure of the first clause
and the absence of the second. We reconstruct the original
of this verse as follows:

לא היתה עיר אשר השלימה אל בני ישראל את הכל לקחו במלחמה .

This sentence is inaccurate as it stands, and the differences
between the OG and the MT are the result of two different
attempts at correction. In the tradition underlying the MT
the clause בלתי-גבעון was added; in the Hebrew *Vorlage* of the
OG the rather blank אשר לא לקח/לכד ישראל (or something close
to that) was substituted for the original אשר השלימה אל בני
ישראל .

While Sym. offers the most literal translation of the MT,
the readings of Th. and Aq. are also efforts to correct the
OG to a Hebrew identical to the MT. [379] We are not sure that
Th. had a clear understanding of this clause;[380] however, we
find nothing to indicate that Th. corrected the OG to a
Hebrew different from that of the MT. Origen, we note, saw
in the text of Th. a representation of Hebrew אשר השלימה אל
בני ישראל, and Aq. is dependent on Th. for his rendering of
this material. [381]

101.   (12:5)

OG: γεσειρει [382]

Th.:   γεσουρε (-ει) [383]

MT: הגשורי

(1) o'α'σ'; (2) LXX[B] has γεργεσει. Readings that approximate this are των γεργεσει in n, των γεργεσιν in pt, γεργεσιν
in d¢, *Gargasi* in ₤, εργεσε in u. Readings that equal or
approximate the form of the proper name attributed to Th. are
γεσουρε in b, γεσουρι in AF*Nϑack[a]oxz(mg)a₂b₂, γεσουρη in
k*l, γεσσουρε in G, γερουρι in y, γειουρι in i, βεσουρι in m.
ϸ has גשור .

According to Margolis, the reading of LXX[B], also found
in Lucianic manuscripts and those of the N-group, is an
"error induced by the gentilic = גרגשי."[384] He goes on to
state that the OG reflects גשירי in its Hebrew *Vorlage*. At
13:2, 11 (see no. 107 below), and 13 the MT again reads גשורי.
In each case the OG is γεσειρει. The OG translator employed
the same form later in v 13, where the MT has גשור.[385] With

respect to this proper name the OG translator consistently
found, or at least read, a -י- in his Hebrew *Vorlage* where the
MT, with equal consistency, has a -ו-. [386]

107. (13:11)

OG: γεσειρει

Th.: γεσουρει

MT: הגשורי

(1) o'α'; (2) v(mg) attributes the following form to σ'
(in z[mg] it appears sine nom): γεσουριτου. The reading of
the OG is found in Bfrvz∅∅. dgnpt, manuscripts of the
Lucianic recension, have γεργεσι.[387] Other readings include
γεσηρι (u), γεσσιρι (s), γεσερι (o), *Geseri* (Ľ), *Gesar*
(Ӿ-codd[vid]), γασιρι (h), σερι (q). Readings that equal or
approximate the form of the proper name ascribed to Th. are
γεσορει in c, γεσουρη in l, γαισουρι in y, γεσσουρει in Gk,
Gesur (Ӿ-ed[vid]), *Gesgur* (Ӿ-codd[vid]), γεσουρι in Anϑrell On.
Ϩ has גשור.

For the reading of the OG and its *Vorlage* see no. 101
above. Only at 12:5 is the consistent reading of the OG,
γεσειρει, not preserved in LXX[B]. At 12:5, 13:2, 11, the
Lucianic manuscripts read γεργεσι. In 13:13 (twice) they
read γεσειρει with the OG. In all the passages in which MT
גשורי or גשור appears, the underlying form for the Palestinian
and Constantinople recensions is γεσουρει. This is also the
form attributed to Th. at 12:5 and 13:11. Since in both
places it represents a correction of the OG to a Hebrew
identical to the MT, nos. 101 and 107 are placed together
in category 4.

106. (13:8)

OG: δεδωκεν αυτω

Th.: δεδωκεν αυτοις

MT: נתן להם (2°)

(1) o'α'σ'; (2) the reading of Th. is also found in Gabcgmx
Ӿ∅Ľ∅. Only Br. preserve the OG. αυτην is the reading of ANϑ
and the remaining cursive manuscripts except l, which has αυτη,
and hnz₂, which omit either this word or the entire clause.

Margolis includes the reading of LXX^B in his text of
the OG. As he explains, αυτω has reference to τω ημισει
earlier in the verse.[388]αυτην shows the influence of corrections with (κληρονομιαν) ην earlier in v 8. Th.'s correction
translates plural להם found in the MT.[389]

110. (13:21)

    OG: εναρα σειων [390]

    Th.:   αρχοντας σηων

    MT: נסיכי סיחון

(1) o'α'σ'; (2) αρχοντα is found in B*^{b}AG*Nalmrb$_2$∅; αρχοντας
is the reading of B$^?$(vid)G$^{a?}$θ rell ∄∄∄ (pr et ∄∄^{c}∄). Only
LXX^B has εναρα. egjnps-vz∄ read παρα; AGNθh$^{b?}$ rell ∄ omit.
For σειων, Nabcfi$^{a?}$j-msu-b$_2$∄ read σηων (σηωρ in A). Other
readings are τον σειων (n), τω σηων (g), τω ων (t), το ων (p).

As determined by Margolis, the underlying forms for the
various recensions are as follows: αρχοντας παρα σειων
(Egyptian), αρχοντας σηων (Palestinian and Constantinople),
αρχοντας παρα τω σηων (Lucianic).[391] According to Margolis,
αρχοντα εναρα of LXX^B is an error for αρχοντας παρα, which
Margolis includes in his text of the OG. Just how easy such
an error would be, particularly in uncial manuscripts, is
indicated by Schleusner: ΑΡΧΟΝΤΑΣΠΑΡΑ > ΑΡΧΟΝΤΑΕΝΑΡΑ.[392]
As attractive as this conjecture is, we, along with Holmes,
reject it in favor of another explanation. As Holmes writes:
"Hollenberg is probably right in regarding αρχοντα and εναρα
as doublets; εναρα being the original word. נסיך is very
rare; it occurs only four times in O.T. LXX no doubt guessed.
εναρα is found nowhere else in the Greek Bible." [393] While
we agree with Holmes and Hollenberg on the originality of εναρα,
we feel that far more precision is desirable in determining
the factors influencing the OG "guess."

In Ezek 32:30 and Ps 82(83):12 a form of αρχων is used
to translate נסיך, and in the present context one might well
expect that the connection of נשיאי מדין with נסיכי סיחון
(so the MT) would have led the translator to the proper
meaning of this word. We note, however, that in the Greek
it is precisely this connection that is broken by the
appearance of και(ו) between και τους ηγουμενους μαδιαν

and τον ευει, the name of the first "prince or vassal of
Sihon." [394]   Furthermore, נסיכי סיחון is dissociated from
what follows by the appearance of και (ו) between σειων and
τους κατοικουντας.[395]   The appearance of these two conjunctions
in (the Hebrew *Vorlage* of) the OG, with the resultant
dissociating of τον ευει--σειων from what precedes and follows,
created a difficulty in interpretation for the Greek translator. He may have used εναρα, found elsewhere in Greek only in
the plural and with the meaning "booty, spoil," to render נסיך
with the meaning of "molten image" (so Daniel 11:8).[396]
Alternately, the translator may have read or misread נכסי in
his *Vorlage*, a word meaning "riches, treasures" and found, for
example, in Josh 22:8. The "guess" on the part of the translator was surely an "educated" one, aimed at making some sense
out of these four or five names, which appear together elsewhere only at Numbers 31:8 (and with but one exception, צור,
are not found again in the Hebrew Bible).[397]   Thus, we have
raised the possibility that the translator interpreted the
names of these "princes, vassals" as names of deities or
types of riches (treasures).

It is not surprising that εναρα, a *hapax legomenon* in
the LXX, occasioned the marginal notation αρχοντας, which
was eventually incorporated into the text. [398] At this point
it is appropriate to recall the observations of Schleusner,
but to reverse the process (ΑΡΧΟΝΤΑΕΝΑΡΑ > ΑΡΧΟΝΤΑΣΠΑΡΑ).
According to this reconstruction, the reading of LXX[B] alone has
preserved a stage on the way to αρχοντας παρα. If Th. found
this παρα in the text with which he worked, he omitted it,
since it did not correspond to a specific element in the Hebrew
and was to that degree extra vis-à-vis that text.

Commenting on the spelling of the proper name, Margolis
says: "Difficult is the reading σειων [of LXX[B], accepted by
us, but not Margolis, as the OG] against the usual orthography; perhaps taken as a place name ...." The very difficulty of this orthography points to its originality here.

It is not clear whether or not the Greek translator had
before him a text exactly like that of the MT. Nor can we
be sure of all the factors that led him to render this passage
as he did. Since, however, the reading of Th. is a clear

translation of the Hebrew preserved in the MT, we have put
no. 110 in category 4.

118. (14:9)

    OG: κυριου του θεου ημων
    Th.:   θεου μου
    MT: יהוה אלהי

(1) o'α'σ'; (2) the correction to the MT is also found in
AGabcxa$_2$ℵℤℤ. σου is found in defgjnptsuv(txt)wz(txt) $ℊ^m$(mg).

    According to Margolis, ημων equals "thine and mine.
The OG nevertheless will have read אלהי as in the MT." [399]
We prefer to see in OG του θεου ημων a translation of אלהינו.
θεου μου of Th. then is a correction of this OG to a Hebrew
identical to the MT.

    In our opinion the reading of the OG is original at v 9,
while the MT was corrupted by the phrase יהוה אלהי found in
both the MT and OG at the end of v 8. σου of the Lucianic
manuscripts and those of the N-group shows the influence of
the second person singular of the preceding verb מלאת.[400]This
may be on analogy with v8:

v 8

προσετεθην ... κυριω τω θεω μου
v 9, Lucianic and N-group manuscripts
προσετεθης ... κυριου του θεου σου.
Further evidence of the considerable influence exerted by the
last clause of v 8 on the parallel formulation in v 9 is
afforded by the change in the person of the verb (προσετεθης >
προσετεθην) in manuscripts of the P and C recensions at v 9.

120. (15:3)

    OG: σεννα [401]
    Th.:   σ(ε)ινα
    MT: צְנֶה

(1) o'α'; (2) v(mg) ascribes the reading σιν to σ'. B* has
εννακ. Other readings include εννααρ(ej), σεννακ (B^{ab}hq),
σεννα (=OG) (θmoℤ On), σενα (Analyb$_2$), σενναα (r), σενναθ (a$_2$),
σεννααρ (suvz), σενααρ (i), σεννεαρ (f), Sinach (ℵ),
Acsenachim (ℤ). Gbcx have σεινα, with Th. A preposition
appears in εως ενακ (n), εως σεννα (t), super Senac (ℤ),
εως εννα rell. ℵ has לצינן.

Margolis lists these underlying forms for the readings of the various recensions: E and C, σεννα (=OG); S, εως σεννα; P, σεινα (=Th.). [402] The -κ that appears at the end of some readings is the result of corruption from the following κ(αι). Margolis observes that צִנָּה is reflected in OG σεννα, which Th. changes to σ(ε)ινα to represent צִנָּה, the form preserved in the MT.[403] Those forms with -νν- perhaps reflect a tradition in which the proper name was derived from a צנן root.[404]

It is difficult to assess the degree to which the directive -āh was understood by the various traditions here. Examples such as 12:7 (no. 102, included in category 3) show that the OG could recognize and correctly interpret such a construction.

121. (15:6[a])

    OG: επι βαιθαγλαν

    Th.: επι βαιθαγλα [405]

    MT: בית חגלה

v(mg) has preserved a reading attributed to θ'ο'α'σ': βιθαγλα. In the transmission of this reading a mistake occurred; the original form is recorded (sine nom) in z(mg): βαιθαγλα.[406] The relation between the marginal readings in these two manuscripts of the N-group is close, as Margolis notes: "z shares with v a substantial number of marginal readings, but often drops the ascriptions and similar by-work. But sometimes the reverse is the case."[407] Thus, there is validity to our correcting a marginal reading in one by reference to the other, even when the ascriptions are not preserved in both. (1) ο'α'σ'; (2) Rather than list the 20 spellings preserved for this proper name (see B-McL), we give here the underlying forms for the various recensions, as determined by Margolis: βαιθαγλααμ (=LXX[B]) (Egyptian), βαιθγααν (Lucianic), βαιθαγλα (Constantinople), βηθ/βαιθαγλα (Palestinian).[408]

-αγλαν is a conjecture on the part of Margolis. We feel that he is correct and that the appearance of a final n or m in the Hebrew Vorlage of the OG would help to explain the numerous Greek forms ending in a consonant. 15:6 is the first occurrence of this place name in the Old Testament. It appears twice again in the book of Joshua (18:19, 18:21) and nowhere outside of Joshua.[409] At 18:19 Margolis accepts βαιθ αγλα as the OG; at 18:21, βαιθ εγλα. The lack of a final consonant in the *Vorlage* of the OG in these two passages may be due to the mention of εγλα (חגלה daughter of צלפחד) in 17:3.

122. (15:6[b])

OG: βαιων

Th.: βοεν

MT: בֹּהַן

(1) o'α'; (2) v(mg) attributes the spelling βοον to σ'. x On-ed have βοεν, with Th. Other readings are βαιον (km), βονθου (On-cod). ʃ has באור.

According to Margolis, OG βαιων equals בֹּהָן, while the reading of Th. (as well as that of Sym.) represents בֹּהַן, the vocalization preserved in the MT.[410]

124. (15:14)

OG: σουσει

Th.: σησαι

MT: שֵׁשַׁי

(1) o'α'σ'; (2) akx have σησαι (σησαιον in 64), with Th. Other readings include σουσαι in A, *Susui* in Or-lat, σουει in c, *Tusi* in ʃ. Also σεσι in dgnpt.

Commenting on the OG here, Margolis states that σουσει "may go back to σωσει or (through σοσει) to σεσει."[411] He sees in σεσ(ε)ι of the Lucianic manuscripts an adjustment to Nu 13:22 (not v 23, as Margolis notes), where for Hebrew ששי the OG has σεσσ(ε)ι. Elsewhere, this proper name occurs in Ju 1:10, where A reads σεσι and B, σεσσι. The reading of Th. at Josh 15:14 represents a correction of the OG to the vocalization preserved in the MT.

128.   (15:21)

OG: πολεις αυτων πολεις προς τη φυλη

Th.:   πολεις αυτων απο τελους φυλης[412]

MT: הערים מקצה למטה

(1)   none;   (2)   v(mg)z(mg) also record the following readings:

ο' πολεις προς τη φυλη

α' αι πολεις απο τελευταιου της φυλης

σ' αι πολεις απ ακρου τη φυλη (φυγη z).[413]

Rather than list separately the numerous variants that occur in this passage, we give the underlying forms of the various recensions as determined by Margolis and confirmed by us:[414]

E (LXX^B=OG) πολεις αυτων πολεις προς τη φυλη

S   αι πολεις φυλης υιων ιουδα αυται πολις πρωτη

C   αι πολεις αυτων πολις πρωτη φυλης

P   πολεις αυτων ÷πολεις: προς τη φυλη (so x; cf. 𝔖).

Margolis explains the difference between the MT and OG in the following manner: "πολεις αυτων (MT הערים) is the general heading for verses 21b-62, πολεις 2° -ερημου the special heading for the cities of the Negeb 21b-32. In the MT the two headings are merged into one." He adds that "προς τη answers to מקצה ל, altered into πρωτη SC by error (then, of course, πολις in the singular)." Holmes offers a different explanation for πολεις αυτων πολεις προς: "The translation of מקצה would be απο μερους, when the α of απο was lost ΠΟΜΕΡΟΥΣ became ΠΟΛΙΣΠΡΟΣ."[415] According to this interpretation, the reading of LXX^B does not represent the OG rendering of a Hebrew *Vorlage* different from the MT, but is instead a corruption of the OG translation of a text almost identical to the MT. We accept Margolis' determination of the OG here, even though we do have doubts about his explanation for the difference between the Hebrew *Vorlage* of the OG and the MT.

Th. revised the OG to the extent that he eliminated the πολεις that he took to be additional and included a far more literal rendering of Hebrew מקצה.[416] His text does not, however, represent a full correction to the MT of the type that is found in Aq. and Sym. The OG translator read עריהם as well as (ה)ערים in his *Vorlage*, and Th. retained this form (πολεις αυτων) in the process of making his corrections.

Placing greater emphasis here on this element of correction, we have included no. 128 in category 4.

129. (15:23)

     OG: και ασερ ιθναιν [417]

     Th.:   και ασωρ [418]

     MT: וחצור ויתנן

(1) ο'α'σ'; (2) readings with the conjunction (thus with two separate proper names, as in the MT) are ασωρ και εθναν in x On (-μαν cod), ασσωρ και ιαθναν in G, ασωρ και ιωναν in b', ασωρ και ιοναν in *b*, ασωρ και ιθνα in c. 𝔖 has וחצור ואתנן. Readings without the conjunction (so the OG) are ασοριωναιν in Bgr^{a?}, ασωριωναιν in r*, *Esorionaim* in ℭ^t, *Aserionem* in 𝔏, *Aserionam* in 𝔏, ασωριναιμ in h, ασερωναν in t, αεριωναν in g, αεριοναν in n, *Asthronem* in ℭ^c. Reflecting only the second (part of the) proper name are the following: εθναν in k, ιθναν in lob₂Ӿ-ed, ιεθναν in fv, ιθνα in ANӾ-codd, εθηνα in a, ιοναν in im, ιονα in ya₂, θνα in θ, ιεθνα rell.

    Margolis lists these underlying forms for the readings of the various recensions: E(gyptian), και ασοριοναιν; Lucianic, και ασεριοναν; C(onstantinople), και ιθναν; P(alestinian), ❊ και ασωρ: και ιεθναν (=On). According to Margolis, "the correction of ασοριοναιν into ασερ ιθναιν or ασερ ιθναν is easy. Hence [the OG] = חָצֹר יתנן. [see also Margolis' recon- structions at the beginning of vv 27, 28]. P supplies και ασωρ = וחצור and then replaces ασοριθ̮ναιν by ιεθναν ...." [419] In the MT the place name "Ithnan" occurs only here. In the Hebrew *Vorlage* of the OG what are two places ("Hazor" and "Ithnan") in the MT appeared as one, "Hazar-ithnan."[420]

    We can see in the reading of Th. at this point a full correction to the two place names listed in the MT, and this in spite of the fact that what is preserved for Th. does not cover both names. v(txt) has και ιεθναν alone (see above), and it is in v(mg) that Th. is cited. The most likely inter- pretation is that by this notation v(mg) indicates that Th. placed και ασωρ before what appeared in its text, και ιεθναν.[421] Thus the text of Th. read και ασωρ και ι(ε)θναν, two separate place names as in the MT (and with the vocalization preserved there).[422]

130. (15:25[15:24])

OG: και αι κωμαι αυτης[423]

Th.: και ασωρ την καινην

MT: וחצור חדתה

(1) o'α'σ'; (2) q is the only manuscript in which the OG,
as determined by Margolis, appears. και αι κωμαι αυτων is
the reading of manuscripts in the Egyptian recension, including LXX[B]; και αι κωμαι αυτων και αι επαυλεις αυτων is the
underlying form for the Lucianic recension. Manuscripts of
the Constantinople recension lack any equivalent for the
Hebrew here. και ασωρ την καινην is found, with some minor
variation, in Gbck𝔰 On. x has και ασωρ και αδαθα.

If Margolis is correct that και αι κωμαι αυτης is the OG,
then the translator apparently read וחצרתה (וְחֲצֻרֹתֶהָ) in his
Hebrew _Vorlage_.[424] It is not clear whether this represents
the actual text of the _Vorlage_ or the manner in which a care-
lessly written or poorly preserved וחצור חדתה was understood.[425]

Hebrew חצור חדתה is generally translated "Hazor-hadattah."
Th. apparently interpreted חדתה as the adjective "new" with
Aramaic ה-.[426] While this interpretation may be erroneous,
there is no reason to suggest that και ασωρ την καινην renders
anything other than the Hebrew preserved in the MT. x
transliterated חדתה and took it as a separate place name (note
the additional και).[427]

134. (17:2)

OG: και τοις υιοις συχεμ και τοις υιοις συμαρε και τοις
     υιοις ε/ο-φερ[428]

Th.:   σεχεμ και τοις υιοις οφερ και

MT: ולבני שֶׁכֶם ולבני חֵפֶר ולבני שְׁמִידָע

(1) σ' (ras vid); (2) v(mg) records the following reading
for α'ο': σεχεμ και τοις υιοις εφερ και τοις υιοις σεμιδαε
ουτοι κατα δημους αυτων. As noted in B-McL, v(mg) attributes
[σ]ε[χεμ] to o' ⅃. σεχεμ is found in A[1]GNkmuv(mg)xyb₂₵𝔜
(εχεμ in A*acioqa₂𝔄-ed). εφερ is the underlying form of the
Palestinian recension; οφερ of other recensions.

In the MT "Hepher" appears before "Shemida," while in the OG the order is reversed. It is probable that the Greek translator rendered these names in the order in which they appeared in his Hebrew *Vorlage*. The readings attributed to ϑ'σ'-α'ο' restore the Hebrew order, as do manuscripts of the Palestinian recension. Although Margolis places εφερ in his OG text both here and in v 3,[429] the manuscript evidence supports the originality of οφερ. If οφερ, preserved in those traditions where we expect to find the OG, is the earlier spelling of this proper name, then εφερ can be seen as a correction toward the vocalization preserved by the Masoretes. Th., primarily concerned with word order at this point, retained the OG spelling of this name.[430]

136. (17:16)

OG: και ιππος επιλεκτος [431]

Th.:   σιδηρεος [432]

MT: ורכב ברזל

The ascription of a reading to Th. here is contained in the following comment by Masius: "pro, σιδηρος, legit Syrus, σιδηρεος....debet tamen asterisco hoc vocabulum notari... additum ex Theodotione est ferri vocabulum.... (Instead of σιδηρος, 𝔖 reads σιδηρεος....however, this word is to be marked with an ⁎ ....the word 'of iron' is added from Theodotion....)."[433]

(1) οι ⅄ (see below); (2) LXX[B] has και ιππος επιλεκτος και σιδηρος. 𝔖 records the following reading for οι ⅄: ומרכבתא דפרזלא (Field: και αρματα σιδηρα).[434] επιλεκτος (מגביא) appears sub ÷ in 𝔖; it is ascribed to ο' in v(mg), the text of which contains the characteristic N-group reading εκλεκτος. και σιδηρος is omitted in gnℤ; thus the S recension represents the OG, as determined by Margolis.

Margolis states that "και σιδηρος [which appears in manuscripts of the E, P, and C recensions] is apparently an addition. επιλεκτος = בחור or ברור for [MT] ברזל."[435] In v 18 רכב ברזל occurs again. The appearance there of ιππος επιλεκτος alone in the OG confirms Margolis' analysis at v 16.[436] It is not clear whether επιλεκτος points to בחור or ברור in the Hebrew *Vorlage* of the OG or is the result of a misreading

on the part of the translator. It is less likely that
επιλεκτος represents an interpretive rendering on the part
of a translator who read ברזל in the Hebrew he was translating.

The reading of Th. is a clear translation of a Hebrew
identical to the MT. A correction to the MT in the form και
σιδηρος has entered as a doublet into all traditions except S.[437]
Is Th. the source for the introduction of σιδηρ-, however
interpreted, into the text of the E, P, and C recensions?
Origin, we note, did make use of Th. here to supply a translation for ברזל. Our understanding of Th.'s procedure leads
us to suggest that Th. retained OG ιππος in his text; Aq.
and/or Sym. wrote αρματα, attributed to οι λ in ȝ (see above).

138. (18:15)

OG: τα ορια εις γα(ε)ιν[438]
Th.:   ορια θαλασσης
MT: הגבול ימה ויצא

For preliminary remarks on this passage and its relation to
15:9 see no. 123 under category 2.
(1) o'; (2) according to ȝ^m, σ' read εις θαλασσαν. z(mg)
(sine nom) records γασσειν. ορια is preceded by the definite
article τα in manuscripts of the Lucianic and Constantinople
recensions. OG εις γα(ε)ιν, found in ANϑ(om εις)efjmoqsuv(txt)
yzb₂ȝƉ, is the reading of the Constantinople recension; εις
εκλειμ appears in dgnpt, manuscripts of the Lucianic recension.
Manuscripts of the Egyptian recension, including LXX^B, and
some of those of the Palestinian recension have εις γασειν.
aȝ have τα ορια θαλασσης;[439] x reads οκαρια θαλασσης. A
translation for ויצא appears in the following manuscripts:
GbcȝƉ (sub ※ GƉ), και εξελευσεται; x, και διελευσεται.

Dissatisfaction with the MT here is almost universal. The
basic difficulty is that ימה is out of place in a listing that
runs from west to east.[440] The RSV, with reference to 15:9,
translates, "and the boundary goes from there to Ephron."
While a reference to 15:9 may be in order,[441] there is no
evidence for a reading of "Ephron" at 18:15. Soggin offers
the following: "and the boundary goes from there to Gasin."
He notes that the transcription is conjectural.[442] BH^3 proposed
the deletion of Hebrew ימה ויצא.[443] Margolis, who includes

εις γαειν in his text of the OG, states that this = עֲיָמָה.[444]
This is in line with his determination of the OG in the
parallel passage at 15:9.

The reading of Sym., as recorded in ß[m], does render ימה
in a fashion that is usual in the book of Joshua; that is,
with a preposition and θαλασσα, with or without the article.
The expression of Th., ορια θαλασσης, which lies behind the
reading of ß, is also a rendering of the Hebrew preserved in
the MT.[445] We feel certain that the complete text of Th.
(only ορια θαλασσης has been preserved) contained both the
definite article before ορια (= MT [גבול]ה), with the OG,[446]
and a translation of the following ויצא, with manuscripts of
the Palestinian recension.

Th. corrected the OG here; at 15:9 he retained it. In
seeking to account for the difference in Th.'s handling of
parallel passages, it is worth pointing out that at 18:15 his
change of εις γα(ε)ιν (עימה) to θαλασσης (ימה) was part of
the larger correction outlined above.

139. (18:28)

OG: και γαβααθ και πολις ιαρειμ πολεις (τρεις και δεκα)[447]
Th.:   καριαθ πολεις [448]
MT: גבעת קרית ערים

ß ascribes the following Syriac to α'θ': קורית מדינא.
As Margolis notes, this = καριαθ πολις. We agree with
Margolis' determination that this is to be read καριαθ πολεις,
which reflects קרית ערים. [449]
(1) α' (2) LXX[B] has και πολεις και γαβαωθιαρειμ πολεις
(τρεις και δεκα). Here the elements representing Hebrew גבעה
and קרית have been transposed; additionally, the conjunction
appears before each of these elements. As Holmes notes,
this would yield Hebrew וקרית וגבעה.[450] Margolis does not
accept this transposition as original to the OG (or, we would
add, to its Hebrew *Vorlage*), and we are inclined to agree with
him. We generally associate such transposition with the
Lucianic recension; however, no tradition was entirely immune
to this phenomenon.[451] Margolis lists the following as the
underlying forms for the various recensions:

E   και πολις και γαβαωθιαρειμ πολεις

S   και γαβαωθ και ερεθ πολεις

C   και γαβααθ και πολις αρειμ πολεις

P   ╤και: γαβααθ ╤και $\frac{\text{πολις ιαρειμ}}{\text{πολις αρειμ}}$ $\underline{P}_1$ $\underline{P}_2$.[452]

     It is clear that the OG translator read ערים יערים (קרית)
in his Hebrew *Vorlage*. Thus he wrote πολις ιαρειμ
πολεις. According to Margolis, "P omits πολεις; $\underline{P}_1$ retains
ιαρειμ, but $\underline{P}_2$C αρειμ = MT." [453] The text that results,
especially in subgroup $\underline{P}_2$, is a correction to the MT, for
πολις αρειμ = ערים קרית. Such a correction, however, shows
little appreciation for the meaning of the Hebrew; it would
be extremely difficult for a reader to make any sense out of
αρειμ followed by numbers.

     On the other hand, the correction attributed to Th. and
Aq., especially as interpreted by Margolis, is an effort not
merely to represent the Hebrew, but to render it intelligently
and intelligibly. This is the only correction which trans-
literates קרית, thereby showing an understanding of this
word as a proper name, and translates the following ערים.
This procedure is far more satisfactory than the mechanical
representation found in some manuscripts of the P recension.[454]

     Holmes seems to accept πολις ιαρειμ (πολεις) as the
original reading of this passage. He speaks of omission by
haplography in the MT. Soggin also feels that K.-Jearim is
probably right here. Although this view has gained wide
acceptance and is certainly reasonable, it is possible that the
shorter, more difficult reading of the MT is to be preferred.
At 15:9 the MT reads ערים יערים קרית היא בעלה ("Baalah; that is,
Kiriath-jearim"). At 15:60 and 18:14 the following equivalence
appears: ערים יערים קרית היא בעל קרית ("Kiriath-baal; that is,
Kiriath-jearim"). At 18:15 the Hebrew *Vorlage* pf the OG read
בעל קרית, where the MT has ערים קרית. A place that is
referred to as Baalah, Kiriath-jearim, and Kiriath-baal can
perhaps also be identified in a text as simply Kiriath. In
the context of 18:28 the "correction" to Kiriath-jearim might
easily suggest itself. [455]

142. (21:3)

    OG: εν τω κατακληρονομειν

    Th.:   εκ της κληρονομιας αυτων

    MT: מִנַּחֲלָתָם

∅ ascribes the reading מן ירתותא דילהון to Aq.-Th. Field's
translation, with which we agree, is εκ της κληρονομιας αυτων.
(1) α΄; (2) Bghnr preserve the reading of the OG; AῙ have
in possessionem. εν τω κατακληρονομειν αυτους is found in
ANϑrell.

εν τω κατακληρονομειν alone is found in those manuscripts
that generally preserve the OG. An addition to reflect the
pronominal suffix is made in all other Greek manuscripts.
Outside of Th. and Aq., however, there is no attempt to render
with more precision the preposition מן. This, plus the
observation that the OG translator used a verb form here, leads
us to conclude that he probably read a participle in his
Vorlage at this point.[456]   In all likelihood such a form did
appear in the Hebrew *Vorlage* of the OG, the result of scribal
error. Of the corrections recorded here, only that of Th.
brings the translation of the whole phrase into line with a
Hebrew identical to the MT.

149. (22:1)

    OG: (τους) υιους ρουβην

    Th.:   ρουβηνιτας

    MT: (ל)ראובני

(1) α΄σ΄; (2) the reading of Th. is also found in ANϑisuv
(sub ϑ΄α΄σ΄)yz(txt)a₂b₂ (ρουβινιτας in ejl, ροβηνιτας in m).
v(mg) ascribes υιους ρουβην to ο΄.

ראובני, always followed by גדי, occurs three other times
in the book of Joshua (1:12; 12:6; 13:8). In each of these
places the OG translates the Hebrew with ρουβην alone.[457]
Thus it is likely that τους υιους ρουβην at 22:1 reflects the
presence of לבני ראובן in the Hebrew *Vorlage* of the OG.
ראובני (ρουβηνιτας) of the MT is original in this context, but
it is not difficult to explain the appearance of בני ראובן
here: this is the first verse of a chapter in which the
phrase בני ראובן/(οι) υιοι ρουβην appears very often,[458]
and it was in anticipation of this frequent usage throughout

chapter 22 that this phrase supplanted the rarer ראובני here.
The form used by Th. to translate the Hebrew does not appear
elsewhere, although we might speculate that it occurred in
other portions of the Theodotionic revision that have not been
preserved.

152. (22:8)
    OG: απηλθοσαν
    Th.: επιστρεφετε
    MT: שׁוּבוּ

In the MT this verse is cast in the form of a command, with
imperative plural verbs and pronominal suffixes in the second
plural. In the OG v 8 appears with verbs and pronominal
suffixes in the third plural. The OG also reflects a Hebrew
Vorlage in which the first clause of v 8, ויאמר אליהם לאמר,
and the first verb of v 9, וישבו, were not present. Holmes
makes a strong case for the superiority of the OG here; he
also outlines a process by which the MT may have developed
out of a text identical to the *Vorlage* of the OG.[459]
Our concern here is limited to the one verb for which a
reading of Th. is preserved. The marginal citations in v
contrast with the following plus which appears in v(txt)
and the N-group in general: αναλυετε εις τους οικους υμων
και.[460]

(1) none (but see α' below); (2) v(mg) also records these
readings: ο' απελθετε (in z[mg][sine nom]); σ' αποστρεψετε;[461]
α' επιστραφητε.[462] aefijsvz place αναλυετε (ai: απελθατε)
εις τους οικους υμων και before απηλθοσαν (see above). Other
readings are απηλθον (θrx), εισηλθον (h), απελθατε (m), *ite*
(Ł), αναλυετε (Kdgkntw), ανελυετε(p), אזלו (ﺵ).[463]

    In the one word preserved the reading of Th. is a clear
correction to a Hebrew text identical to the MT. We feel
certain that Th. also made the other changes necessary to
bring the OG closer to the MT. The use of the verb επιστρεφω
by Th. and Aq. to translate שוב illustrates a characteristic
identified elsewhere with the καιγε recension. The significance
of no. 152 in this regard is discussed, together with related
examples, under no. 82 in chapter 3.[464]

155. (22:18[a])

    OG: και εσται εαν   αποστητε
    Th.:   υμεις 465
    MT: והיה אתם תמרדו

In our explanation of the reading to be ascribed to Th. here,
we follow the interpretation proposed by Margolis. The full
citation of v(mg), as recorded in B-McL, is οι ο' χω θ' (?) α'
υμεις αποστητε. Margolis states that χωρις here must mean
addunt. 466 According to him, this "note consists of two parts,
the first dealing with the pronoun (an Origenic addition sub ÷),
and the second (which is to be detached) rectifying the
textual reading αποστραφητε which N shares with a number of
mss." 467 Thus θ', α', and οι ο' have the pronoun υμεις in
their text.
(1) α'ο'; (2) υμεις appears after εαν in bcoqxz(mg)𝕭𝕾(sub
÷). αποστραφητε is found in dfjrstvz(txt).468

     The reading of Th., with its pronoun corresponding to
Hebrew אתם, is a correction to the MT. A note in *BH*^{3},
presented far more cautiously in *BH*^{4}, raises the possibility
that the OG read אם in its Hebrew *Vorlage* rather than אתם as
in the MT. This is a reasonable suggestion. We can even see
how an original אם may have been corrupted into אתם in the
tradition underlying the MT, especially through the appearance
of this same pronoun earlier in v 18. We note, however, that
a 'rendering' of אם is found everywhere outside of the MT,
even in those manuscripts that add the pronoun. Thus it is
likely that the conjunction is used here simply to facilitate
understanding, as in the English translations of this passage,
and does not reflect any particular word in the Hebrew.

158. (22:28)

    OG: και ερουσιν
    Th.:   και ερουμεν
    MT: ואמרנו

(1) ο'α'σ'; (2) the change from third to first person
plural is also found in abcoqx𝕾.

     The first person plural verb of Th. is a correction of the
OG to MT ואמרנו. The OG translator apparently found ואמרו in
his Hebrew *Vorlage*. Since there is but one letter's difference

between the first and third person plural form, ואמרו may
be the result of nothing more than a simple scribal error.
Nevertheless, it is possible to detect a conscious correction
in the change from first to third person plural. Within the
context of this passage the first person does not yield the
best sense, for *we* would not speak of "the copy of the
altar ... which *our fathers* made ..." Rather, that statement
would more logically come from *they* (sc. "our descendants"),
who could speak of an action undertaken by "our fathers."
This slight difficulty occasioned by the first person ואמרנו
is perhaps the best indication of its originality here; on
the basis of our observations above, the third person, read in
the *Vorlage* of the OG, gives the appearance of a 'correction.'

161. (23:4[b])

OG: εθνη εξωλεθρευσα[469]

Th.: εθνη α εξωλοθρευσα

MT: הגוים אשר הכרתי

(1) ο'α'; (2) as recorded in B-McL, v(mg) preserves the
following reading for σ':... οσα εξηρα. εθνη α εξω-, as in Th.,
is also found in AMNθ(τα)achklosuwa₂b₂ A𝒞ℰᶜ𝓢. εθνη και εξω-
is the reading of Bqr. OG εθνη εξω- appears in bdefgijmnpqr
tvxyzℬℰᶠℤ. The verb εξολεθρευω (εξολοθρ-)[470] appears in other
than the first person singular in *exterminabis* (ℤ),
exterminaverunt (𝒜), εξολεθρευσατε (dgnpt), εξωλοθρευσαμεν (k).

The Hebrew *Vorlage* of the OG lacked the relative pronoun
אשר between הגוים and הכרתי. An analogous loss of אשר occurs
in the usually full text at Qumran in 8:35 (LXX 9:8): מכל צרה
(MT: מכל אשר צרה). The reading of Th., with α corresponding
to Hebrew אשר, is a correction to the MT. The και found in
the Egyptian recension is possibly related to the conjunction
ו(כל הגוים), which is (otherwise) lacking in all traditions of
the Greek.[471]

162. (23:10)

OG: εξεπολεμει ημιν

Th.: [ουτος] εξεπολεμει μεθ υμων[472]

MT: הוא הנלחם לכם

(1) ο'; (2) the second person pronoun appears in MNclqr𝒜ℰᶜ𝓢

(υμιν) and gkptw[a?](μεθ υμων). μεθ ημων is the reading of
dfmnw*; elsewhere ημιν, as in LXX[B], is found.

It is not difficult to determine the underlying forms of
the various recensions for the first part of this reading:
E̲, εξεπολεμει; P̲, αυτος εξεπολεμει; S̲, αυτος εξεπολεμησεν
αυτους; C̲, ουτος εξεπολεμει. Th. provided an explicit translation, either ουτος or αυτος, for Hebrew הוא and to this
extent represents a correction of the OG, preserved here in the
E̲ recension.

There is far greater difficulty in determining whether
the underlying forms for the second part of the reading contain
the pronoun in the first or second person. As the manuscript
evidence cited above indicates, good manuscripts in each
recension are divided on this point. The two witnesses to
the text of Th. show the same division: first person in v(mg);
second person in z(mg). The fact that these forms (whether
ημιν/μηων, υμιν/υμων) are so similar in the Greek was un-
doubtedly the source for much confusion in the transmission
of this reading. Thus our determination of the OG here must
take into account the context in which this verse appears.[473]

We note that "your" God of the MT becomes "our" God in
the LXX throughout most of chapter 23. Pronouns referring to
the people of Israel are in the second person in the MT; these
pronouns are generally found in the first person in the LXX
for this section. These two differences, which we suggest are
not unrelated, go back to two different Hebrew texts; that is,
the OG translator reproduced what he found in his *Vorlage*.
Joshua 23 is composed as a speech of Joshua himself.[474]
While we do not doubt that the MT is original here, it is
possible that in some tradition "our" God and "us" were
judged more appropriate in an address of Joshua.[475] With
these considerations in mind, we can state with some confidence
that first person ημιν was the reading of the OG.

In determining the original reading of Th., we cannot rely
on context in the same way. We do know, however, that in a
similar circumstance (no. 165, see below) Th. changed a first
person pronoun in the OG to the second person found in the MT.
That specific example and the procedure of Th. in general
lead us to accept υμων as the authentic reading of Th. here.

The use of μετα by Th. is in agreement with classical Attic usage: πολεμειν/μαχεσθαι συν τινι/μετα τινος means "to wage war *in conjunction with* someone"; the dative alone would imply a hostile association.[476] Not surprisingly, μετα is found elsewhere primarily in manuscripts of the Lucianic recension (as also in v 3).

165. (24:10)

    OG: και ευλογιαν ευλογησεν ημας

    Th.:   και ευλογιαις ευλογησεν υμας

    MT: ויברך בָּרוֹךְ אתכם

(1) ο'; (2) readings for σ' and α' are also recorded in v(mg):

σ' αλλα ευλογησεν ευλογων υμας

α' και ευλογων ευλογησεν υμας. [477]

ευλογιαις, as in Th., is found in abgnptwx𝔖; these are manuscripts of the P and S recensions. ευλογια is the reading of hkm𝔏(vid); c has ευλογησας. The second person pronoun υμας, as in θ', ο', σ', and α', appears in AMNθabdf-mosuv (txt)xyzb₂𝔄𝔏𝔖.

    There is no reason to doubt that OG και ευλογιαν ευλογησεν is a rendering of MT ויברך ברוך. However, here the translator did not choose to use one of the standard methods for rendering the infinitive absolute construction. H. St. J. Thackeray, in his grammar and in a separate study, dealt with the ways in which this construction was handled by various Greek translators.[478] He notes, for example, that at Joshua 17:13 (B text) "a solitary instance occurs of an attempt to render the infinitive absolute quite literally." Elsewhere two principal methods of representing this construction can be described: (1) the finite verb with dative of the cognate noun (this is particularly characteristic of the Pentateuch); (2) finite verb with participle of the same verb or one of similar meaning (this is used almost exclusively in the later historical books). Th., who tended to retain as much of the OG as possible when fashioning his revision, included the noun, as in the OG, in his text. He placed the noun in the dative, in conformity with one of the two principal methods discussed above. Thackeray suggests that where the participle

predominates, it was probably considered "a nearer approach
to the Hebrew infinitive." This might well explain the shift
to the participle in Aq.

With the exception of Sym., the word rendering the Hebrew
infinitive comes before the finite verb; in the MT the infinitive follows the finite verb.[479] The word order of the Greek
does not, however, reflect a Hebrew *Vorlage* in which, unlike
the MT, the infinitive absolute appeared first. As the
following examples demonstrate, the Greek translators did not
feel bound by the Hebrew order when rendering this construction:

Nu	23:11	MT	ברכת ברך
		LXX	ευλογηκας ευλογιαν;[480]
Nu	24:10	MT	ברכת ברך
		LXX	ευλογων ευλογησας.[481]
Also Is 6:9		MT	שמעו שמוע
		LXX	ακοη ακουσετε
		MT	ראו רָאוֹ
		LXX	βλεποντες βλεψετε
Gen 19:9		MT	וישפט שפוט
		LXX	κρισιν κριναι.

At first glance, the variation between ημας and υμας
would appear to be nothing more than an inner-Greek confusion.
While this may well be true in any isolated instance, we
feel that here OG ημας does indeed represent a Hebrew *Vorlage*
in which the first person pronoun appeared. If this is so,
then the reading of Th. is a correction to the second person
found in the MT. The first part of Joshua 24, containing the
"antecedent history," is a first person speech of Yahweh.[482]
The alternation between first and third persons, as in the MT,
is adjudged an "authentic feature" in this context by Klaus
Baltzer.[483] Pronouns referring to the people of Israel are
in the second person. For much of this section a process of
leveling appears to have been carried out in the *Vorlage*
of the OG. The result of this process is that the original
alternation is obscured and the activities of Yahweh are
expressed consistently in the third person. The change from
second to first person pronouns took place at the same time.[484]

At the beginning of this verse there is a considerable difference between the MT and LXX:

MT   ולא אביתי לשמע לבלעם

LXX   και ουκ ηθελησεν κυριος ο θεος σου απολεσαι σε.[485]

Hollenberg suggests that לבלעם was taken for the infinitive of בלע "to destroy." לשמע would then be omitted as unnecessary.[486] This suggestion does not seem to explain adequately all of the features of the Greek here. For example, would we not expect the third person plural pronoun rather than the second singular after the infinitive? In any case, in the OG it is the Lord who does the blessing; in the MT, Balaam carries out such activity.[487]

168. (24:26[a])

OG: ιησους

Th.:   εκει

MT: שם

(1) α'σ'; (2) εκει alone, as in the reading of Th., is found in gnxz(mg) Cyp; εκει ιησους appears in cpt; ιησους εκει is the reading of abdefjwa₂ (ιησους sub ⸓). ιησους is omitted in y𝐴𝐵𝐶.

In the earliest form of this passage there was no word between ויקימה and חחh/και εστησεν αυτον and υπο. In the tradition underlying the MT this clause was filled out by the insertion of the adverb שם. The Hebrew *Vorlage* of the OG lacked יהושע (ιησους) at the beginning of the verse (MT: ויכחב יהושע) and, as it were, made good the omission by the explicit mention of Joshua at this point.[488]

Category 5:   Introduction

Th. ≠ MT and Th. ≠ OG (whether or not OG = MT). If there is
evidence to show that Th. revised something other than the OG
to something other than the MT, it should appear especially in
the readings collected in category 5. Here non-MT features
are visible, as in category 2; however, unlike the examples
in the earlier category, the non-MT features contained in these
readings of Th. are not reproduced from the OG.

Nevertheless, the phenomenon evident in several of these
readings is precisely the same we noted in category 2; namely,
Th.'s high regard for the Greek text with which he worked
sometimes led him to retain non-MT elements that he found there.
In these cases it was not the OG that Th. had before him, but
a text into which a few, relatively insignificant corruptions
had entered. Th. apparently overlooked some of these, as he
did with respect to the readings gathered in category 2. For
our purposes it is useful to distinguish THE Old Greek (as
best as we can reconstruct it) from AN Old Greek (for example,
the text with which Th. worked). Of course, Th. made no such
distinction. It is interesting to note, on the basis of
several readings included here and elsewhere, that LXX^B contains a high percentage of the corrupt forms taken up by Th.
into his recension.

Not all readings in this category can be explained in
the above manner. In a very few cases the non-MT element in
Th.'s text was not found in the Greek that Th. was in the
process of revising. Here, we suggest, Th. either misread a
Hebrew text identical to the MT or correctly reflected a
Hebrew text that differed in the matter of a letter or two
from the MT. This is true in some readings outside of
category 5 as well. Only at no. 56 is there evidence from
category 5 of a more extensive difference in the Hebrew text
to which Th. corrected; a reason for that difference is
supplied. Thus the conclusions we reached on the basis of
previous examples are corroborated by the evidence from
category 5.

The general pattern for presentation of material in this category is as follows: First we give the readings of the OG, Th., and the MT. Then (1) whenever the reading of Th. also appears in ο´, Aq., or Sym., this is noted, with the word "none" indicating that the reading of Th. is not found in any of these three texts; (2) additional readings, including (a) those that support Th., (b) those containing the OG, (c) others. Of primary importance in the discussions that follow is the establishment of the Greek text (corrupt or not) with which Th. worked and the form he read or misread in the Hebrew text to which he corrected.

<u>5</u>

47. (6:24[b])

OG: και χαλκου

Th.:   και παντος χαλκου

MT: ורכלי הנחשת

(1) o'; (2) παντος χαλκου is also found in abchikmpqtxz(mg) a₂𝒸𝒻𝒻𝒔ᵐ; ⁴⁸⁹ παντα χαλκον is the reading of gnw. M(mg)(sine nom) records παντος before σιδηρου; as Margolis states, this note actually refers to παντος before χαλκου.⁴⁹⁰ Thus manuscripts of the Palestinian and Lucianic recensions have a form of πας before "bronze" and "iron": παντος χαλκου και σιδηρου (P), παντα χαλκον και σιδηρον (S).

A similar phrase appears at 6:19:

OG   η χαλκος η σιδηρος

MT   וכלי נחשת וברזל. Here manuscripts of the Palestinian and Constantinople recensions read πας χαλκος ... σιδηρος; Lucianic manuscripts have παντα χαλκον σιδηρον.

Only the Egyptian recension has preserved the shorter reading of the OG in both verses. Not only is the shorter reading (*lectio brevior*) that of the OG, but it is also original in the context of these two verses. In the tradition behind the MT נחשת (ה)ו ברזל (ה)ו was expanded by the introduction of כלי. No such expansion occurred in the Hebrew *Vorlage* of the OG.

All corrections in vv 19, 24 seem to reflect Hebrew כל, rather than כלי of the MT. This is true at v 24, where a reading is recorded for Th., as well as at v 19, where none is (although it is likely that the text of Th. at v 19 also included a form of πας). While the meanings of כל and כלי are of course very different, their similar spelling could easily lead one to (mis)read the familiar כל instead of כלי that actually appeared in one's text. This would be particularly true in chapter 6 of Joshua for two reasons: (1) outside of vv 19, 24, כלי occurs in Joshua only in 7:11. Thus 6:19 is the first appearance of כלי in Joshua. If כלי were misread as כל there, it is not unlikely that the same error would be duplicated in the parallel expression five verses later. (2) The occurrence of a form of πας at the beginning of v 19 may also have led the correctors astray. It is quite possible

that the use of πας in Th. was decisive for its spread to
various manuscript traditions.

The reading of Th. seemingly reflects a Hebrew text
different from that preserved in the MT. If this is so, the
difference is but one letter (a final י-). On the other hand,
we have presented the argument that the "reading" of Th. is
the result of a "misreading" of a Hebrew identical to the MT.

56. (8:12-13)

Origen added sub ※ a translation for the end of v 11 and
all of vv 12-13. Masius ascribes vv 12-13 of this translation
to Th. Although it is difficult to determine what stood in
the Hebrew *Vorlage* of the OG at this point,[491] Holmes was
surely correct when he wrote (concerning the problems, including vv 11-13, in chapter 8): "The original Hebrew text
may have been the same as the present LXX text; or it may have
been longer than the LXX but shorter than our present Hebrew
text. But it is hardly possible that the Hebrew before the
LXX was the same as ours."[492] For the most part, the material
ascribed to Th. is a translation of a Hebrew identical to the
MT. At least twice this is not so, and for this reason no. 56
is placed in category 5. 𝔊 and x are our best witnesses to the
original text of Th. here.
(1) none; (2) the reading ascribed to Th. is found in M(mg)
bcfgnqv(mg)xz(mg)𝐴𝐸𝑆(sub ※ M[mg]𝔊: Sub ϑ' 𝔊^m); significant
variations are discussed below.

We deal first with two apparent variations. At the beginning of v 13 𝔊 reads וסמר לעמא (MT: וישימו העם). However,
as Margolis indicates, לעמא is an error for עמא.[493] The plural
סמו, in agreement with MT, is confirmed by εταξαν in x. Later
in the same verse 𝔊 has וחרתא דילהון (𝔊^m: και τα εσχατα αυτων;
MT: ואח עקבו). The plural pronoun is not found elsewhere,
nor does it suggest a different Hebrew *Vorlage*.[494] In any
case, it seems unnecessary to burden Th. with this reading.

The following two variations are far more significant:
v 12   Th. βηϑαυν (x) (𝔊: <u>בית און</u>)
          MT   בית אל

v 12 (end)   Th.   θαλασσαν της γαι (ℒ: מן ימא דעי) [495]
             MT   מים לעיר.

This second variation is the subject of a separate study by
Margolis, in which he points out that the problem of "Ai or
the City?" is not limited to this passage.[496] For example,
in v 16 we find the following:

MT   כל העם אשר בעיר

ℒ (sub ※) כולה עמא דעי (x: πας ο λαος της γαι).

Margolis suggests that Th. was the source of this translation
at v 16 also. At 15:9 (see no. 123 in category 2) the OG
translator apparently read עי in his Hebrew *Vorlage* (MT: ערי);
Th. retained the OG. In three places in Joshua the OG
translates העיר where the MT has העי (7:3; 8:18, 28). The
similarity of עיר and עי makes such confusion almost unavoidable
in the transmission of a Hebrew text. It appears that at
8:12 Th. read לעי, rather than לעיר of the MT, in the Hebrew
text to which he was correcting -- a difference of only one
letter. Margolis shows that the reading לעי, as in Th., was
attributed by certain authorities to the Orientals. He notes
that Origen generally supports the Occidental text.

Another exception to this general rule is found earlier
in v 12, where "Origen [on the basis of his source, Th.]
again ranges himself on the side of the Orientals (*ketib*)
with his βηθαυν בית און against בית אל of the Occidentals."[497]
It is clear that here Th. read in his Hebrew text something
other than what appears in the MT. Elsewhere we generally
argue that apparent cases of difference between the MT and the
Hebrew text used by Th. were due to his inclusion of forms,
corrupt or otherwise, that he found in the Greek (whether OG
or not) with which he was working. Here such an explanation
is not possible, since we assume that he made a translation
directly from the Hebrew when he found a word or passage missing
in his Greek. It is not surprising that בית און replaced
בית אל in this context, since after a certain time the two
places came to be regarded as identical. In this regard, Soggin
notes that during the rabbinic period the word מקדם in the
phrase עם בית און מקדם לבית אל (Joshua 7:2) was translated "in
the past" rather than "east of."[498]

58.   (9:4[9:10])

    OG: επι των ονων αυτων[499]

    Th.:   ωμων

    MT: לחמוריהם

The ascription of this reading to ϑ' and o' is preserved in
v(txt); in v(mg) it is ονων that is attributed to o'.
(1) o' (see above);   (2) v(mg) attributes the reading επι των
ονων αυτων to α'σ'o'; ονων also appears in AM(txt)N϶agi[a?]1mox
yz(mg)b₂. 𝕷 has *in dorsum asinorū*.[500] ωμων is found elsewhere, including LXX[B].

    As Margolis states, "the OG manifestly wrote ονων."[501]
While it is possible that a word appeared in the Hebrew *Vorlage*
of the OG which could be translated with ωμος (כתף, צד, שכם),
it is far more likely that ωμων is a corruption of OG ονων.
Several factors would account for the appearance quite early
of ωμων: (1) ονων and ωμων look very much alike; in particular, we note that in the Greek of this period the leveling of
quantitative distinctions resulted in the interchange of ω and
o.[502]   (2) Either of the two words yields good sense in the
context. Thus, once the corruption occurred as a scribal
error, even a usually careful corrector might let it slip
into his text. This is precisely what we think happened
with Th. He did not 'correct' ονων to ωμων on the basis of
a Hebrew different from that of the MT, but rather neglected
to correct the corrupt ωμων in the Greek text with which he
was working. An alternate suggestion is that the original
text of Th. did contain ονων, which was corrupted during the
transmission of the text.

    We have placed no. 58 in category 5 because ωμων, re-
corded as the reading of Th., is different from the MT and the
OG. Our judgment, however, is that this difference is the
result of Th.'s retention of a corrupt form, rather than a
reflection of a Hebrew different from that preserved in the MT.

81. (10:33)

    OG: τοτε ανεβη αιραμ βασιλευς γαζηρ βοηθησων τη λαχεις

    Th.: τοτε εξηλθεν αιλαμ βασιλευς γαζειρ βοηθησων τη λαχεις [503]

    MT: אז עלה הרם מלך גזר לעזר את לכיש

In V(txt) the following reading is attributed to ϑ':
τοτε εξηλθεν αιλαμ βασιλευς γαζης βοηθησων τη λαχεις. Also
attributed to ϑ' are αγαζειρ in v(mg) and

                         αγαζειρ βασιλευς λαχεις in z(mg). Support
for our determination of the authentic reading of Th., listed
above, is given in the discussion that follows.
(1) none; (2) v(mg) records this reading for o'α'σ': τοτε
ανεβη ωραμ βασιλευς γαζερ βοηθησαι τη λαχεις; the spelling
γεζερ is also attributed to σ' in v(mg). εξηλθεν is found in
all six manuscripts of the N-group (efjsvz); ηλθεν appears in
gn(+εις λαχεις) 𝔊(mg: אתא). ωραμ, as in o'α'σ', is the
reading of akx. γαζηρ, included by Margolis in his text of
the OG, is found in mr; AF^bGNϑa-diklnopqtwxya₂b₂𝔄𝔏 have γαζερ
(k: της γαζερ; in n the preceding βασιλευς is omitted, see
below). The infinitive βοηθησαι appears in F^bGa-dgnptwx𝔄𝔖.

    The reading of LXX^B, τοτε ανεβη αιλαμ βασιλευς γαζης
βοηθησων τη λαχεις, is the underlying form for the E recension.
The underlying forms for the other recensions are as follows:

S   τοτε ηλθεν ηιραμ βασιλευς γαζερ βοηθησαι τη λαχεις

P   τοτε αωεβη αιλαμ / ωραμ P,P-1,P-2 βασιλευς γαζερ βοηθησαι τη λαχεις

C   τοτε ανεβη αιλαμ βασιλευς γαζερ βοηθησων τη λαχεις.[504]

    Individual elements in the readings attributed to Th.
here present considerable difficulty. While we do not claim
that the authentic text of Th. contained none of the distinctive readings of v(txt), it seems unlikely to us that his
text included all of them.[505] It is not easy to understand
a change from αναβαινω to εξερχομαι on the part of Th.
εξερχομαι as a rendering of עלה is exceedingly rare in the LXX;
the OG of Joshua provides two examples at 18:11 and 19:10,
although in a very different context.[506] Margolis correctly
placed in his text of the OG the form αιραμ, the inner-Greek
corruption of which to αιλαμ is easy.[507] It was apparently

this latter form, with l, that Th. found in the text with
which he was working. His failure to make a correction to
a form with r, as in the MT, may in some way be associated
with the (corrupt?) αιλαμ that is widely attested at v 3
(for Hebrew הרהם).[508]   In any case, it is clear that this
retention of the corrupt αιλαμ at v 33 in no way suggests
that Th. was correcting the OG on the basis of a Hebrew text
different from the MT.

In what form did the next proper name appear in the
original text of Th.? It appears that contradictory readings
are presented in v(txt) and v(mg)(z[mg]). This seeming con-
tradiction is best explained by interpreting the notation in
v(mg) as a correction of the attribution of the entire clause
in v(txt) to Th. Although Th. may have carried over into his
revision γαζης, a corruption of γαζηρ after βασιλευς, the
note in v(mg) indicates that Th. differed from v(txt) in the
form of this proper name.[509]   γαζειρ is essentially the
same form as that found in the reading of ο'α'σ' and elsewhere.[510]   Margolis raises the possibility that initial α
(v[mg]z[mg]) is from βα=βασιλευς. Another remnant of this
same abbreviation may be seen in the following reading of g:
ηιραμαχαζερ. According to Margolis, ηιραμα = ηιρα̅ βα = ηιραμ
βασιλευς (cf. n). However this initial α is to be explained,
neither (α)γαζειρ nor γαζης suggests a Hebrew different from
the MT. It is not surprising that Th. retained the OG participle βοηθησων; ο'α'σ', as well as manuscripts of the P and
S recensions, altered this to the infinitive βοηθησαι, a
construction that corresponds more closely to Hebrew לעזר.

Nothing we have discussed thus far leads to the conclusion that the probable text of Th. represents a correction
to a Hebrew different from that preserved in the MT. However,
we have not yet considered the full citation contained in z(mg):
αγαζειρ βασιλευς λαχεις. Field could make "nothing" of this
reading, and Margolis offers no specific comment on it. There
is no doubt in our mind that βασιλευς λαχεις has been wrongly
attached to αγαζειρ in z(mg) (cf. v[mg]). If it is to be taken
as a serious variant, then it appears that גזר was taken as
the name of a king, לעזר was skipped over, and βασιλευς added

on the analogy of βασιλευς after αιρ(/λ)αμ.[511] While such
speculation is admittedly far-fetched, we note that this is
the first occurrence of גזר in the Hebrew Bible and that
Japhia, the (prior) king of Lachish, had already been killed.[512]

132. (16:2)

    OG: εκ βαιθηλ[513]
    Th.:   εις
    MT: מבית אל

The ascription of this reading to Th. is preserved in v(txt).
(1) none; (2) εκ is the reading of gn. εις, with Th.,
appears in Befhjrsza$_2$. v(mg) preserves the following reading
for o'α'σ': απο. απο is also found in AGNΘa-diklmoptxyb$_2$.
As recorded in B-McL, A𝐸^{C}𝑆 have εκ.

    Margolis includes εκ, the reading of the Lucianic recen-
sion, in his text of the OG.[514] The use of this preposition
is in keeping with the usual practice in the Greek of the
book of Joshua.[515] εκ could easily be corrupted by scribal
error into εις.[516] This is especially so in 16:2, since
εις βαιθηλ occurs at the end of the preceding verse. We
suggest that the text with which Th. worked was one into which
the corrupt εις had already entered. In his desire to make
other corrections toward the MT that the OG required in this
passage,[517] Th. inadvertently failed to correct the preposition to εκ or απο.[518] Therefore, although the reading of Th.
is different from the MT, it does not reflect a different
Hebrew, but rather the inclusion into Th.'s text of a corrupt
form.

144. (21:20)

    OG: πολις των οριων αυτων[519]
    Th.:   η πολις των ιερεων αυτων
    MT: ערי גורלם

The ascription of this reading to ϑ' is found only in z(mg);
both v(mg) and z(mg) ascribe η πολις των ιερεων αυτων to o'.
(1) o'; (2) LXX^B has πολις των ιερεων αυτων. abcefjsvxz
place η before πολις, as in Th.; πολεις appears in ghnoruy𝐸.
OG οριων is found in ANΘb$^{a?}$d-gi-lnpqs-vy-b$_2$A𝐿 (υριων in m).

v(mg)z(mg) preserve the following reading for α'σ': πολεις (πολις in z) κληρου αυτων. 𝔖 also ascribes דפטא דילהון (κληρου αυτων) to α'σ'.

These are the underlying forms for the various recensions: πολις των ιερεων αυτων (Egyptian), η πολις των ιερεων αυτων (Palestinian), πολεις των οριων αυτων (Lucianic), πολις των οριων αυτων (Constantinople = OG). It seems that in the *Vorlage* of the OG the construct plural ערי was corrupted into עיר , thus giving rise to singular πολις in the Greek.[520] The letter η before πολις, which one naturally interprets as the article, in origin is nothing more than the duplication of the preceding (εγενωθ)η, a duplication assured of preservation by the fact that η is the correct form before feminine πολις. The first part of Th.'s reading then retains the OG, which was itself the result of a corruption in its Hebrew *Vorlage*.

As pointed out by Holmes, ιερεων is a corruption of OG οριων.[521] In v 20 this corruption was aided by the occurrence of this same των ιερεων in the preceding verse. Th., we suggest, worked with a text like LXX[B] in which the corrupt των ιερεων already appeared. Since this phrase had just occurred, Th. overlooked its inappropriateness here. Thus, there is no compelling reason to see in the reading attributed to Th. a correction to a Hebrew different from that preserved in the MT. It is noteworthy that the reading of Th. was included in manuscripts of the Palestinian recension.

Despite general agreement that the reading of the OG here and at 15:1, 16:1, 17:1, 21:40 represents גב(ו)ל instead of MT ג(ו)רל,[522] we are not convinced that such a difference existed. גבול, we note, means both "frontier" and "territory,"[523] and the Greek uses οριον to translate גבול in both meanings. Since this is so, there is no reason why the Greek translator could not also have used οριον to translate גורל, where it means "*territory* assigned (by lot)." In all of the passages listed above Hebrew גורל has just such a meaning, and the use of οριον for גורל in these passages, while perhaps imprecise, is nonetheless quite possible.[524] At 21:20 an expected equivalent for גורל appears in α'σ'.

145. (21:26)

    OG: πασαι πολεις

    Th.:   πασαι αι πολεις

    MT: כל ערים

(1) o'α'σ'; (2) the reading of Th. is also found in lo*(vid); ANϑdefijkmpsuyzb₂ have αι πασαι πολεις; αι πασαι αι πολεις is the reading of tv. και πασαι πολεις appears in gnℤ.

It would appear that the reading of Th. reflects a Hebrew text that contained the article. We cannot, however, exclude the possibility of dittography, with αι duplicated from the preceding (πασ)αι. Margolis notes the probable occurrence of this phenomenon in the same phrase at 15:32. There the *Vorlage* of the OG lacked כל. In making good this omission, manuscripts of the Palestinian recension wrote πασαι <u>αι</u> πολεις. Margolis explains that αι was "probably duplicated from πασαι."[525] At 21:26 this duplication may have occurred in the original text of the Theodotionic revision or have been generated during the transmission of the text.

The OG and the MT often differ with respect to the presence or absence of the article. To give just two examples with the phrase "all (the) cities":

21:(37)39   MT   כל ערים

               OG   αι πασαι πολεις

21:(38)40   MT   כל הערים

               OG   πασαι πολεις.

It is doubtful that all such differences represent substantive variants, especially in a phrase like πασαι (αι) πολεις, where the possibility of dittography or haplography must always be considered.

<u>6</u>

At 10:5, 23, 34; 12:12 readings have been preserved for
Th. where the MT is עֶגְלוֹן. The representation by Th. of this
place name is not the same in each case. In order to understand the different ways in which Th. represented עגלון, we
have brought these four examples together in one discussion.

עגלון occurs 8 times in the Hebrew of Joshua (10:3,
5, 23, 34, 36, 37; 12:12; 15:39). It does not occur elsewhere
in the OT as a place name.[526] Below is a chart which lists
for each passage in Joshua the form of the place name in LXX^B
and Margolis' reconstruction of the OG:

	LXX^B		OG (so Margolis)	
10:3	οδολλαμ		εγελαν	
5	οδολλαμ		εγελαν	
23	οδολλαμ		εγελαν	
34	(εις) οδολλαμ	(εις)	εγελαν	
36	-		-	(<u>P</u> ※ απο εγλων:)
37	οδολλαμ		εγελαν	
12:12	αιλαμ		εγλαν	
15:39	ιδεαδαλεα		αγλαν.	

The following is the basis for Margolis' reconstruction of the
OG in chapter 10: "εγελαν inferred from *ογολαν--suggested
by the supernumerary *goggola* Ӿ 12:12 -- which led to οδολαν,
οδολαμ, a more familiar name. Since in chapter 12 the OG
holds עגלון (v 12) and עדלם (v 15) apart, it is difficult to
believe that the confusion in 10(:3, 5, 23, 34, 37) ascends to
the OG....εγελαν = עֶגְלָן, Aramaizing suffix. Unless we go
still further and restore εγελων or εγλων."[527] עֲדֻלָּם occurs
twice in Joshua (12:15; 15:35). In both passages the OG is
οδολλαμ. Outside of Joshua עדלם occurs 9 times.[528] We
believe that Margolis is correct in not including οδολλαμ in
his text of the OG for chapter 10.[529]

We turn now to the readings preserved for ϑ', ο', α',
σ':

65. (10:5[b])   ϑ'ο'α'σ'   αιγλωμ v(mg)
                  ϑ'α'σ'   εγλωμ   z(mg)

77. (10:23)   ϑ'ο'α'σ'   αιγλωμ   v(mg)

α'σ'   דעגלונו ℊ (Field: εγλωμ)

82. (10:34)   ϑ'   οδολλαμ   v(txt)

ο'α'   εγλωμ   v(mg)

ο'α'   αιγλωμ   z(mg)

σ'   לעגלון ℊ (Field: εις εγλων).

At 10:37 לעגלום (Field: την εγλωμ) is attributed to σ' in ℊ.
The interchange of αι and ε is not unusual.[530]   Nor do we
attach great significance to the final consonant (μ or ν).[531]
For Margolis all of the readings of ϑ' (except at 10:34), ο',
α', and σ' go back to an original εγλων. In all of these
passages from chapter 10 οδολλαμ is the underlying form for
the E, S, and C recensions and for the subgroup P₁; εγλων is
the underlying form of P₂. It is clear from 10:34 that Th.
was working with a Greek text in which the substitute οδολλαμ
already appeared. In at least two previous passages (we have
no evidence for 10:3) Th. had corrected this form to one which
accurately reflected Hebrew עגלון; here he failed to do so.

103. (12:12)

At 12:12 οδολλαμ appears only in K(οδολαμ)gnw(οδολαμ και
εγλωμ). These manuscripts omit βασιλεα οδολλαμ (מלך עדלם) in
v 15. Margolis states that the conjectured reading of the OG
(εγλαν) is "presupposed by αιλαμ < αιγλαμ."[532]   There is no
difficulty in accepting the suggestion that an original -γ-
was lost in the transmission of this form.[533]

v(mg) records the following readings:
ϑ' αιλωμ
ο'α' εγλων.
There are two possible explanations for the reading of Th.
(1) In his original text Th. wrote αιγλωμ/ν (αιγλωμ is found
in aikmptz[mg]; b₂ has αιγλων), which was incorrectly transmitted as αιλωμ.[534] In this regard the appearance of αιγλωμ
in the margin of z, even though sine nom, is significant,
since the close connection between the margins of v and z often
allows for the correction of marginal readings in one manuscript on the basis of the other. (2) Th. worked with a
Greek text in which the corrupt αιλαμ (of LXX[B]) already

appeared. With his main concern being the change of α to ω
in the second syllable, Th. failed to take note of the absence
of -γ- in the first syllable.

The readings of Th. in these four passages do not
present the consistent pattern found in α'σ' and one subgroup
of the P̲ recension. While this lack of consistency does introduce some confusion into Th.'s text, a reflection of the
confusion that existed already in the Greek text with which
he worked, there is nothing to suggest that Th. was
correcting to a Hebrew different from that preserved in the MT.

Notes to Chapter 1

1. On μαχαιρα in Th. and Aq.-Sym. see chapter 3 under no. 50.

2. So Margolis, p. 202.

3. גבול בני ראובן is found in the MT earlier in v 23 and נחלה בני ראובן here. In the former phrase υιων is restored in the P̲ recension and in other manuscripts, including the margins of v and z (both sine nom).

4. 1:6 is the only passage in which διαιρω clearly translates Hebrew נחל, but see Joshua 18:4 and Margolis' reconstruction there (p. 343).

5. Margolis, p. 5.

6. Margolis, p. 6.

7. Margolis, "ΧΩΡΙΣ," p. 91.

8. και appears sub ÷ in $\mathcal{G}^m$ and is omitted in manuscripts of the P̲ and C̲ recensions among others.

9. This is noted in Margolis, p. 10.

10. See Margolis, p. 36.

11. See Margolis' comments there (p. 7).

12. The same reading is preserved sine nom in z(mg).

13. Margolis, p. 39.

14. και ειπεν ιησους, attributed to οι λ in the margins of Mvz, is found in manuscripts of the P̲ and S̲ recensions.

15. Margolis, "ΧΩΡΙΣ," pp. 85-86.

16. The singular is found in the MT and all other textual traditions.

17. Further support for referring the notation of M(mg) to v 10 is provided by the observation that M(txt) reads the singular here.

18. Margolis, p. 57.

19. Margolis, "ΧΩΡΙΣ," p. 85.

20. For the siglum οι ο' see the appendix at the end of this chapter. On the basis of the evidence presented there, it is clear that singular διεβη is the reading characteristic of the textual tradition designated as οι ο'.

21. The OG translator may have found ירא׳ in his Hebrew *Vorlage*, but considered an explicit equivalent unnecessary at this point.

22. Margolis, p. 63.

23. See Margolis, p. 104.

24. According to Margolis (p. 178), "the OG simplifies רימזו רבים אשר מחו by writing και εγενοντο κτλ."

25. Margolis, p. 202. See Field, p. 360, and our discussion below.

26. Emanuel Tov has raised the possibility that in certain cases the practice of transliterating Hebrew words is characteristic of the καιγε recension. The significance of nos. 83 and 126 in this regard is discussed, together with related examples, under no. 94 in chapter 3.

27. 10:40; 11:2, 16; 12:8; 15:1, 2(twice), 3(twice), 4, 7, 8, 19, 21; 17:9, 10; 18:5, 13(twice), 14(twice), 15, 16, 19(twice); 19:34.

28. For the distribution of this transliteration elsewhere in the LXX see Thackeray ¶ 4.

29. Field, p. 362.

30. Field, p. 364.

31. Margolis, p. 234; see also p. 220 on 11:16.

32. In a few places he seems to have found נגד.

33. Max L. Margolis, "The Grouping of the Codices in the Greek Joshua: A Preliminary Notice" *JQR* 1 (1910/11), p. 260.

34. The translation here and in the following passages is generally that of Field.

35. Since Syriac תימנא is used for both νοτος and λιψ, we could be wrong in seeing νοτος behind every תימנא of Aq. and/or Sym. where תימנא (=λιψ) also appears in the text of 𝔖. The clearer evidence from those passages in which the OG contained ναγεβ and the statements and translations of Margolis and Field do support our procedure, however.

36. The OG translator may have deliberately chosen the translation λιψ rather than νοτος to avoid confusion with νωτος/-ον (for the gender see Thackeray ¶ 10, 24; כתף occurs three times in the Hebrew of chapter 15 and five times in chapter 18). Some confusion was still practically unavoidable, especially with the leveling of quantitative distinctions.

37. Field, p. 362. Margolis (p. 213) makes the following notation: οι λ <και> εως του υδατος της θαλασσης Procop.

38. See below on the reading of Sym.

39. Margolis, Field.

40. -ρημ- appears in Kw; gn have -ριμ-; -ρεμ- is found in dpt.

41. The rather complete explanation for the various forms offered by Margolis is superior to that of Soggin (p. 134) or Benjamin (p. 45). Soggin: "LXX has μασερων, i.e. perhaps 'from Sharon,' while it read 'in the east' (miyyām) in the mss." (Soggin of course means 'in the west' miyyam, which is what he writes on the following page.) Benjamin: "משרפות. B μασερων = משרן. Confusion of נ and פ."

42. See chapter 3 under no. 94 for a discussion of the practice of Th., Aq., and Sym. with respect to transliteration.

43. Soggin, p. 150. On the form in LXX[B] see Pretzl, p. 381.

44. See also v 6.

45. See, for example, the statistics for the expression "Moses the servant of the Lord" under no. 61 in chapter 3.

46. Note the apparently unrelated occurrence of the same phenomenon here in A*b*n.

47. Note the following variations: αρωηρ, Comp.; ανωηρ, n; αροηδ, a₂; αορι, m.

48. Margolis, p. 228.

49. αρνων also occurs in v 1.

50. Holmes, p. 54.

51. The verb contained in Aquila's reading is also recorded in z(mg) (sine nom). The omission of the conjunction found at the beginning of v 5 in the MT is not, in our opinion, of text critical significance. Only in 𝕰[C] is this conjunction restored, so it appears.

52. This plus in manuscripts of the N-group originated, we might speculate, as a marginal gloss employing transliteration rather than translation to reflect הרפאים earlier in v 4 (compare, for example, the reading of LXX[B] there with that of the Lucianic manuscripts).

53. Margolis, p. 157 (on the Greek plus at the end of 9:10 [9:16 in the LXX]). See also p. 231 (on 12:4-5).

176

54. Margolis, p. 238.

55. See B-F ¶ 29.

56. Margolis includes the form αραδ in his text of the OG at 15:21. See Soggin, p. 167, on the place name at 15:21.

57. Margolis, p. 246.

58. The underlying forms listed here are taken from Margolis.

59. Margolis, p. 221.

60. Cf. λ > α in LXX^B (γαλγαα). Margolis' listing of variants for this reading (p. 246) is not entirely clear. For example, according to him, k(mg) reads βααλγαδ (lines 11-12) and βαελγαδ (line 18, so also B-McL and Field). Perhaps the reading there is unclear, as B-McL indicates is the case in c.

61. For the identification of Baal-gad with Baalbek, see Soggin, p. 140, and the article by O. Eissfeldt cited there.

62. See Margolis, p. 263.

63. On the significance of Aquila's choice of equivalents for קצה, see our discussion of no. 128 (15:21) in the "Aquila" section of chapter 2.

64. ופניהם is translated by Field (p. 367) as και απεκριθην.

65. Margolis, p. 271.

66. The latter is the reading ascribed to o' in v(mg). No tradition outside of the MT has the first person singular pronominal suffix, which is original in this context. See Soggin, p. 165.

67. Note the series of words all ending in -ν. The reading with the noun in the plural is difficult. It may be the result of the mistaken understanding that all the cities that follow, and not just Hebron, were cities of refuge.

68. For the siglum οι o' see the appendix at the end of this chapter. It is clear from the evidence presented there that the N-group is not part of the textual tradition indicated by this siglum. We are somewhat uncomfortable with the notion that χωρις was employed to mean both *addunt*, in some marginal readings, and *omittunt*, in others. Certainly a less ambiguous system of notation could have been developed. However, Margolis' presentation of the evidence (in his "ΧΩΡΙΣ" article) convinces us that χωρις was in fact used with both meanings. Here, for example, unless χωρις means *addunt*, the siglum οι o' would have a signification out of keeping with its usage elsewhere in v(mg).

69. See H-R and L-S.

70. Outside of the reading of Sym., the conjunction that appears in the MT (ולא עמד) is reflected only in 𝔊.

71. It generally translates a form of קום. See H-R for statistics.

72. The translations of איש (in the indefinite sense) found in the texts of Aquila and Symmachus at this point are discussed, together with related examples, under no. 3 in chapter 3.

73. This is especially so in the absence of any attempt to achieve a more literal translation of the MT.

74. z(mg) (sine nom) has εις τας πτερνας.

75. H-R.

76. On שׁוֹט see Soggin (p. 217), who notes that the traditional translation for this word is "scourge." According to Holmes (p. 78), LXX rightly read the plural לשׁטים (confusion of ט and מ) (so also BDB). But, continues Holmes, the translator did not know the meaning of the word. For MT שׁוֹט LXX has ηλους.

77. On the forms πλευρα, πλευρον, both classical, see Thackeray ¶ 10, 26.

78. H-R.

79. Note that πτερναις is attributed to ο' in v(mg).

[end of category 1 (1.1 and 1.2)]

80. Margolis, p. 11.

81. See Margolis, p. 12, and cf. Holmes, p. 18.

82. In 𝔊 both αυτοις and the following λεγουσα are placed sub ÷ . 𝔊 omits both of these words. Since, as Margolis (p. 19) notes, λεγουσα represents כֹּה of the MT, Masius was correct to state that only the pronoun is to be obelized.

83. The appearance of εκρυψεν αυτους in the LXX of both verses (4 and 6) led to the introduction of material from the latter verse at this point.

84. Margolis, p. 18. For the form ותצפנו see GKC ¶ 60d.

85. So Margolis, p. 40, and Field. Bv(mg) read επι μεσου του υδατος.

86. At v 15, where Th. and Aq. both include εις in their text, neither has the reading attributed to him at v 8. A discussion of readings at 3:15 is found under category 3 in this chapter (3:15[a] is no. 29). On Aquila's use of μερος to translate קצה at 3:8 see our comments on no. 128 (15:21) in the "Aquila" section of chapter 2.

87. In z(mg) ανδρα ενα 2° is omitted. Field (p. 340 fn. 23), to whom manuscript v was unknown, perceived that behind the shorter reading as cited in z(mg) lay the full correction that indeed showed up when v was collated.

88. Margolis, pp. 42f.

89. Note also Aquila's use of του σκηπτρου.

90. We refer again to these three verses, together with related examples, under no. 3 in chapter 3.

91. Cf. 8:33 (LXX 9:6), where the situation is more complex; also 22:7(twice), 30.

92. So Margolis; see also Field, p. 344, and Soggin, p. 69. Cf. now Emanuel Tov, "Midrash-Type Exegesis in the LXX of Joshua," *RB* (1978), p. 53, esp. n. 8.

93. *b* 𝕾 (sine nom: והפוך גזור) confirm the last three words in the reading attributed to Aq.

94. Margolis, p. 66.

95. In this regard, the signs in 𝕾 are not to be relied on. See below for v 3.

96. Here πετρινας appears sub ⸓ in 𝕾, which omits ακροτομους. See above.

97. See Pretzl, p. 392. The different OG translations for שר צבא יהוה in 5:14, 15 are discussed under no. 30 in chapter 3.

98. In many cases this effort produced "characteristics" that have been identified with the καιγε recension. See chapter 3.

99. At 9:5 (LXX 9:11) a word or phrase from Th. again exerted a strong influence on almost all subsequent renderings. There also Th.'s method involved correction of the OG through the substitution of phrasing found in the OG of a parallel passage. 9:5 (no. 59) is discussed later in this category.

100. The defective spelling of the imperative of the root שוב occurs twice in the MT (Ex 4:19 and 1 K 18:43), though in neither place preceded by the conjunction.

101.   The use of the root επιστρεφω in Aq. illustrates a characteristic identified elsewhere with the καιγε recension. Its significance in this regard is discussed, together with the readings of Sym. and Th., under no. 82 in chapter 3. Since the readings preserved at 5:2 cover the word חרבות, they are also brought into our presentation of evidence concerning the חרב = ρομφαια equivalence (no. 50 in chapter 3).

Major differences, not unrelated to the differing readings here (שוב or ישב), separate LXX and MT in the following verses. See Soggin, pp. 68ff; Holmes, pp. 28ff; and other commentaries. In these discussions arguments are also advanced for the superiority of the root ישב or שוב at v 2.

102.   See Margolis, "ΧΩΡΙΣ," pp. 85-86.

103.   Margolis, p. 80.

104.   Although this phrase may well not be original here (see Soggin, p. 81), it crept into the underlying tradition of both the OG and MT. For the Greek translator's method of handling גבורי החיל elsewhere in Joshua, see Margolis, p. 12 and references there.

105.   So Margolis, see below.

106.   The reading of the Lucianic manuscripts is conflate: κυριω σαβαωϑ (<u>E</u>) and τω κυριω των δυναμεων (<u>PC</u>). For the latter see below.

107.   Margolis, p. 92.

108.   See no. 12 in chapter 3.

109.   So Margolis, see below.

110.   Note that both of these readings begin και οι αρτοι.

111.   Margolis, pp. 153f.

112.   Margolis brackets the following words: o (1°), o (2°), και (2°).

113.   In a separate notation v(mg) again attributes the plural οι αρτοι to o'.

114.   Field (p. 356): *desiccatus igne*.

115.   Cf. Holmes, p. 47. לחם is found only in these two verses for Joshua.

116.   Soggin, p. 108; Benjamin, p. 41.

117.   Benjamin offers the same explanation.

118.   See our remarks at no. 42 above.

119. Th. also retained ξηρος in the singular, even though he wrote οι αρτοι (plural).

120. The S͟ recension followed Th. in including αυτων twice.

121. Nowhere is there preserved a text that agrees with the MT in all particulars. It may be that (και) ו, without היה, stood in the original text of v 5. In the tradition underlying the MT היה entered the text (on the basis of v 12) and then replaced ו.

122. This holds true whether or not it is necessary to construct divergent *Vorlagen* for the MT and OG.

123. So Margolis conjectures.

124. Soggin, p. 119: φιδων.

125. Margolis, p. 171.

126. See Soggin and Benjamin, p. 42.

127. See below.

128. The only variant for λιθους is -θοις in cnu, where the case ending of the noun appears to have been corrupted by the preceding αυτοις. This variant is not relevant in explaining v(txt), however.

129. Margolis, p. 177.

130. In an alternative reconstruction the OG, accurately reflecting its *Vorlage*, is identical to the MT, μεγαλους being lost subsequently through homoioteleuton and χαλαζης entering the text as above. The absence of μεγαλους in any of our best witnesses to the OG renders this reconstruction far less likely than the first one. The evidence from Qumran (see below) points in the same direction.

131. We thank Professor Cross for making this material available to us.

132. See below.

133. Margolis, p. 184.

134. Margolis: "It is possible that S͟ [the Lucianic recension], rather than E͟[gyptian recension̄], represents the original reading of the Ḡreek."

135. There the OG has οι υιοι ισραηλ.

136. So Margolis conjectures.

137. Margolis, p. 213.

138. Margolis, p. 209.

139. Noth (p. 62) on v 3: "הַמִּצְפָּה soll gewiss identisch sein mit dem מִצְפֶּה von 8."

140. Again Noth: "ist entweder hier [in v 3] מִצְפָּה(ה) oder in 8 הַמִּצְפָּה zu lesen." In his translation Soggin includes Mizpah twice.

141. See BDB and *The Interpreter's Dictionary of the Bible*.

142. See below.

143. Margolis, p. 217.

144. For the siglum οι ο΄ see the appendix at the end of this chapter.

145. In g επι is to be read instead of εκ (so Margolis).

146. Holmes, p. 53.

147. It does occur, though without this precise meaning, in two other sources--one of the second century B.C., the other of the first century A.D. (so L-S).

148. So 10:20; 14:12; 19:29 (at least for PC); cf. 6:1 and H-R under οχυρουν.

149. On Aquila's relationship to the OG in general, see the "Aquila" section of chapter 2.

150. The underlying forms listed here are taken from Margolis.

151. Margolis, p. 225.

152. Margolis, p. 311.

153. The same corruption may have occurred in manuscripts of the S recension at 15:50.

154. Pretzl (p. 385) makes the following comment about the reading of the S recension at 15:50: "viell. hebr. Wechsel ב u. כ!"

155. This is so even though a clear correction to such vocalization is found only at 15:50.

156. So Margolis, see below.

157. For the interchange of *ai* and *e* see Thackeray ¶ 6, 11.

158. See Margolis, p. 261.

159. The preceding τῶν ορ<u>ιων</u> brought about the corruption of -βωρ into -βων in manuscripts of the E and S recensions.

160. Noth (p. 76) vocalizes the form as לִדְבָר and makes reference to 2 S 9:4, 5 (לִו דְבָר) and 2 S 17:27 (לֹא דְבָר). See also Amos 6:13 (לֹא דְבָר). Soggin (pp. 148, 151) includes "Lo-debar" in his translation. The RSV appears to regard "Debir" as the original form here. Support for an original Hebrew text without -ל is supplied by Holmes (p. 58): "ל is a dottograph." Note that ל is the final letter of the preceding word, גבול.

161. Here the OG neither contained a translation of ל as *nota dativi* nor included it as part of the proper name. See above.

162. For the Th.-Aq. relationship in general see the "Aquila" section of chapter 2.

163. On the text of the OG here see below. The OG translator wrote διεκβαλλει and that is the form Th. included in his text. So z(mg); v(mg): εκβαλλει.

164. See v 14 and our discussion of 18:28 (no. 139) under category 4 below.

165. The address was delivered on January 8, 1925, and is published in *JPOS* (1925), pp. 61-63.

166. Margolis, "Presidential Address," p. 62.

167. Since Th. stands in a different relation to the OG in the two passages (at 15:9 he retains the OG; at 18:15 he corrects the OG to the MT), we are not able to discuss nos. 123 and 138 together. The above remarks, however, serve as an introduction to our discussion of both passages.

168. Margolis, "Presidential Address," p. 63. Peter Walters, *The Text of the Septuagint: Its Corruptions and Their Emendation*, ed. D.W. Gooding (Cambridge: University Press, 1973), p. 332, agrees that we should read εις γαι ορος for B εις το ορος.

169. See our discussion of no. 56 under category 5.

170. The first quote is that of Holmes (p. 61); the second comes from Soggin (p. 166).

171. So Margolis conjectures.

172. Margolis' conjectured OG in these two places is γωλαθ μαειν, as above.

173. So Holmes (p. 61): "...in B there must have been considerable corruption before την βοϑϑανεις and την γοναιϑλαν could represent the same word." Also Margolis (p. 291): "While γοναιϑλαν is easily mended, the error in βοϑϑανεις is deep-seated."

174. Cf. Pretzl, pp. 382f. The transliterations here strongly suggest an understanding of Hebrew מים גלת as a proper name.

175. Although γολοϑ- in 77 appears to be an exception, the -o- vowel of the second syllable is but the result of assimilation to the vowel of the first syllable.

176. An anonymous reading is preserved in ℊ at this point: קגירותא דרומא וקנירותא דעומקא (Field, p. 370: κτησιν μετεωρων, και κτησιν ταπεινων). On the basis of its probable use of κτησις, it should be attributed to Sym.

177. See BH^4 at Judges 1:15 and H-R.

178. It is not without significance that λυτρωσιν υδατος is found in the Greek (both A and B) at Judges 1:15. Holmes (p. 61) refers to Moore's suggestion that in the Judges passage the true reading is *Gullath maim, Gullath illith*, and *Gullath tahtith*.

179. Noth (p. 86) translates גלת מים as "Wasserbecken" and adds the following comment: "Hier ist mit גֻּלָּה offenbar ein Quellbecken gemeint." In Noth's opinion the derivation of גֻּלָּה from the root גלל is very uncertain. See BDB.

Soggin (p. 176) notes that these "springs" have been identified "with the place where at the present day the road for heavy goods from Hebron to the south crosses the *sēl eddilbe*, about 9 km from Hebron."

180. In order to discuss the reading attributed to Th., it is necessary for us to reproduce all of v 34a in the OG and MT.

181. The preceding list of variants is not complete. Among other omissions, no attempt is made to include alternate spellings for the proper names.

182. See, for example, Holmes, p. 77.

183. Robert Gordis, "A Note on Joshua 22:34," *AJSL* 47 (1931), pp. 287-288.

184. For further comments on no. 159 see our discussion in the "Aquila" section of chapter 2.

185. σηλω is found in ℊ^m mg.

186. Harry M. Orlinsky, quoted in G. Ernest Wright, *Shechem: The Biography of a Biblical City* (New York: McGraw-Hill, 1965), p. 256. For further discussion and bibliographical references see Soggin, p. 223.

187. See the retroversion by Holmes, p. 80.

[end of category 2]

188. The translation of the Syriac here is that of Field.

189. See Margolis, p. 8.

190. Margolis, pp. 7 f.

191. Holmes, p. 18; Benjamin, p. 24.

192. Margolis may be right in his judgment that συνης, found in manuscripts of the Palestinian and Constantinople recensions, is adjusted to v 7, where συνιημι renders Hebrew שכל (see Holmes p. 18).

193. Soggin's *b* should be *k* (p. 27).

194. For the use of the adverb πλην as a conjunction "often almost = αλλα," see Smyth 2966.

195. See under no. 2 in chapter 3.

196. See H-R.

197. Margolis, p. 20.

198. According to Soggin (p. 36), this "translation follows the versions, assuming it is possible to regard the expression as a 'reverse' construct; but cf. Baldi and Noth, *ad loc.* [for Noth, p. 24 of 1971 edition]."

199. Th.'s participle in the singular may be a retention of the OG construction, rather than a reflection of the MT (where the participle, although agreeing with the word meaning "flax," is in the plural).
       No. 17 is important in determining the nature of the Th.-Aq. relationship, since it would seem to indicate that Aq. knew the OG independently of Th. On this see our discussion at the end of the "Aquila" section in chapter 2.

200. There are several attempts to harmonize the renderings of this construction in v 12. Thus o$Z\beta^m$ place the preposition εν before υμιν. N and E, both of which apparently have the preposition μετα before οικος, show the same preposition before υμιν earlier in the verse. One can view the omission of εν in g and A as an effort in the same direction.

201. Cf. v 14.

202. For the Th.-Aq. relationship in general, see the "Aquila" section of chapter 2.

203. As our placement of no. 29 in this category shows, we favor the view that εις does represent a Hebrew *Vorlage* identical to the MT (עד) in these two verses. It seems that the OG translator allowed himself a limited degree of freedom in rendering Hebrew prepositions. In addition to other examples that can be cited (for example no. 20 just above), we note that later in v 15 the OG reads εις μερος του υδατος, where the MT is בקצה המים. Only in manuscript u is there found a more literal rendering of the Hebrew preposition: εν τω υδατι.

204. As recorded in B-McL.

205. Margolis, p. 45.

206. The use of the imperfect in all Greek traditions tends to support Soggin's understanding of Hebrew מלא as a participle. He states (p. 48) that here it is a question "of a recurrent seasonal phenomenon." Soggin adds that his position is in opposition to that taken by Noth.

207. For the siglum (οι) o´ see the appendix at the end of this chapter; Margolis (p. 47) notes that διεβησαν is the characteristic reading of the Palestinian recension.

208. These seven passages are 3:7; 6:2; 7:10; 8:1; 18; 10:8; 11:6. Beginning with 6:2 the prepositional phrase προς ιησουν becomes the exclusive representation of Hebrew אל יהושע in this clause.

209. With 4:1, τω ιησοι appears a total of five times in this clause, all in the first five chapters of the book of Joshua.

210. In the NT ιησου is the form of the dative. See B-F ¶ 55(1*f*). Our understanding of ιησοι as the original form of the dative is supported by the following observations of Thackeray (¶11,6): "ιησους...differs from the N.T. name in the dative, which throughout Dt. and Jos. is consistently written ιησοι, the N.T. form ιησου appearing as an occasional variant." He offers "the analogy of datives of feminine nouns in -ω, which in the papyri were declined (e.g.)...-οι." Cf. John W. Wevers, *Text History of the Greek Deuteronomy*, Mitteilungen des Septuaginta-Unternehmens (MSU) XIII (Göttingen: Vandenhoeck & Ruprecht, 1978), p. 62.

211. Where τω ιησοι or τω ιησου occurs, the definite article represents the Hebrew preposition.

186

212. The significance of 4:10(a) in this regard is discussed, together with related examples, under no. 45 in chapter
3.

213. See Margolis, "ΧΩΡΙΣ," p. 88. For the siglum οι ο'
see the appendix at the end of this chapter.

214. Smyth 1158-59; cf. B-F ¶ 270.

215. Here we are concerned solely with the construction
at v 7 and not with the number of the verb or other matters.

216. We might have expected the restoration of καὶ (ו) at
the head of v 22; this we don't find. LXX and MT present
different texts in vv 7 and 22 with respect to the word לאמר/
λεγων (λεγοντες):

	MT	LXX
v 7	-	+
v 22	+	(οτι) (?) (see Margolis, p. 62; cf.

Holmes, p. 28).

217. For both the OG and Th. see below.

218. Margolis and Field accept the plural, while B-McL
records the singular. For details see Field, p. 345 note 30.

219. Thus in note 30 referred to just above he states that
z has καρπωματων for καρπων.

220. In a plus earlier in this verse q has (σιτου +) απο
των καρπων (MT: [מ]עבור [האָרץ]). פרי generally stands
behind καρπος (cf. the reading of ﭪ here: פְּאָרֵא).

221. See H-R.

222. γης was lost by haplography in the marginal citation
in vz.

223. So Margolis; see Aq.-Sym.

224. Margolis, p. 76. So Field. See also Holmes, p. 31;
Benjamin, p. 34. Elsewhere κουρα translates גז (shearing)
twice.

225. In Prov 8:19 this verb reflects MT פרי. See Holmes
and Benjamin.

226. On γενημα (Aq.-Sym.) see Thackeray ¶ 7, 38. His
discussion calls into question H-R's procedure in combining
under one heading γεννημα and γενημα.

227. On the "intermediary position" that Th. occupies
between the OG and Aq. (and Sym.) see chapter 2.

228. Cf. the reading of οι λ preserved in 𝔖.

229. So B-McL (in listing the reading of LXX[B]), but see below.

230. Margolis, p. 98; Field, p. 349.

231. See H-R. Elsewhere it translates nouns from the verbal roots שרף, שדף, and בער.

232. So H-R; see also Field.

233. B-McL lists ενπ- as the reading of LXX[B] and indicates that εμπ- is a correction by two later scribes (thus B[ab]). Margolis lists only the form εμπ-.

234. Were εν πυρι the OG, it would be difficult to explain its replacement by such a rare word.

235. The verb εμπιπρημι/εμπρηθω translates שרף four times (five including 6:24[a]), יצת once; it also occurs at 16:10 (translating שרף?). εμπυριζω translates שרף at 8:28.

236. For example, this substitution does not result in greater consistency in translation. See the statistics for Joshua given in the previous note.

237. What we might term the most 'elegant' form would be ενεπυρισθη ενπυρισμω, which is indeed found in the best Lucianic manuscripts, where stylistic 'elegance' is achieved without step 2. The same interest in 'elegance' we outlined above can be viewed in e*j, where the text reads ενεπρησθη ενπρησμω. At 8:19; 11:9, 11; 16:10 the OG is identical to our step 2 (cf. the Lucianic manuscripts at 11:9, 11).

238. In Joshua 24:19, for example, ανομημα renders חטאה. On this passage see further under no. 33 in chapter 3.

239. For the OG in Judges see Bodine.

240. See H-R.

241. See fn. 238 above for the reference to Joshua 24:19 and to our discussion in chapter 3.

242. We discuss the texts of Aq. and Sym. in another context under no. 78 in chapter 3.

243. See Field, pp. 351f, and Margolis, p. 115.

244. Field, who did not have access to v(mg), translated the Syriac ascribed to Sym. as ιματιον. This same Syriac word נחתא, apparently a rather general designation, is also found in 𝔖(txt).

245. אדרת appears five times in 1 Kings 19 and 2 Kings 2. In all five places it is translated as μηλωτη, a word which occurs only there in the Septuagint.

246. At 7:24 the OG lacks a passage in which אדרת again occurs. Origen seems to have taken his translation at this point from Aq., since in it στολη renders אדרת (as in the text of Aq. at v 21).

247. See 7:6, and especially 9:5, 13. Does ιματιον in cq at 7:24 point to Th., as στολη there does to Aq. (see preceding fn.)?

248. The reading of Th.-Aq. is preserved in both Greek (in b, where the form is επεθυμισα according to B-McL) and Syriac (in 𝔖: ורגת).

249. So BH⁴; see also Margolis, p. 93; Soggin, p. 82, where ευ- should be εν-; Holmes, p. 36; Benjamin, p. 36.

250. Cf. M(mg)(sine nom) at 6:18: εν επιθυμια γενομενοι.

251. See below.

252. B-McL (p. viii): "...at the end of an incomplete word or phrase indicates that the completion is wanting or cannot be read."

253. Field alone records κοιλαδα in z(mg)(sine nom).

254. B-McL includes 𝔖 as a witness to this reading. Max L. Margolis, "Corrections in the Apparatus of the Book of Joshua in the Larger Cambridge Septuagint," JBL 49 (1930), p. 239, advises that 𝔖 is to be omitted from this listing in B-McL, since "עומקק is the equivalent of εμεκ."

255. φαραγγα is drawn from earlier in this verse. See below.

256. The retroversion is that of Margolis, p. 118. Margolis includes this clause in his text of the OG, but excises και...εις εμεκαχωρ at the end of the verse on the grounds that it is an interpolation. We see no justification for this procedure. Another explanation is offered by Holmes (p. 41), who terms και...φαραγγα αχωρ "a doublet due to a LXX reviser." Although some support for this suggestion is offered in the following fn., our feeling is that both clauses appeared in the Hebrew Vorlage of the OG.

257. The fact that the OG translator twice used εμεκ to represent (עכור) עמק may indicate that the clause in v 24 containing the translation φαραγγα did not form part of the text of the OG. But see 15:7 and the preceding fn.

258. See Margolis' comments on the OG rendering of this root at v 25: "Did the OG combine עכר with עקר?" Cf. the OG at 6:18.

259. Thus the "Valley of Achor" appears in English translations. This use of transliteration has the added benefit of highlighting the play on words.

260. See below.

261. The fact that the readings of Aq. and Th. both contain στηκετε may have led to the mistaken attribution to Th. in z(mg).

262. Margolis, p. 183.

263. Thackeray ¶ 23, 7.

264. Thackeray ¶ 19, 1. στηκω is better attested in the NT (see B-F ¶ 73) than in the Greek translations of the OT, where it occurs as a variant in only a few passages. See Thackeray.

265. See also B-F ¶ 73.

266. See under no. 29 in chapter 3.

267. See below.

268. Margolis (p. 203f), who explains that "P supplies both the conjunction (so also the Lucianic recension) and την = ואת."

269. Margolis' second sentence refers to πασαν την γην only, and not the form of the proper name.

270. See Margolis' remarks about Origen above.

271. See, e.g., nos. 39 and 43.

272. It is possible that the original text of Th. did contain την γην, as in the OG. Analagous to the process that produced the reading of LXX^B, την could have been lost through haplography during the transmission of his text. In this case no. 85 would more properly belong in category 1.

273. Margolis, p. 215.

274. Margolis, p. 234.

275. In connection with this verse, Margolis (p. 221) states that SPC reproduce [!] the final ה against LXX^B.

276. See also no. 120 (15:3) in the following category.

277. Margolis, p. 232.

278. v(mg) yields [μαχ]ο[θι], so Margolis and B-McL.

279. For the interchange of τ and θ see Thackeray ¶ 7, (11) 13.

280. So Margolis.

281. Margolis, p. 262.

282. For the identification of this site see Soggin, p. 158. Cf. נמרה in Nu 32:3 and also מי נמרים in Is 15:6; Jer 48:34.

283. For the μ > β change in Greek see Thackeray ¶ 7, 19.

284. Margolis, p. 270.

285. ₰ records דגלגל for Aq.-Sym. (Euseb.:εθνων της γελγελ).

286. Here the Lucianic recension has the plural ending.

287. Margolis' further observation that Aq. most probably wrote γαλγαλ here is substantiated at least partially by the reading attributed to Aq. at 12:23 (see fn. 285 above).

288. Margolis, p. 289.

289. Robert G. Boling, *Judges*, The Anchor Bible (Garden City, New York: Doubleday & Company, 1975), p. 56. See also Soggin, pp. 175f.

290. In the MT of Judges כלב is followed by הקטן ממנו, which does not appear in the MT of Joshua. At Judges 1:13 (so also 3:9) both A and B have ο νεωτερος.

291. See the work of Walter Bodine.

292. See our discussion at nos. 42 and 59 in the preceding category.

293. So Margolis conjectures.

294. See below.

295. Since no manuscript designated by the siglum ο´ reads αζωτου (see below and the appendix at the end of this chapter), it is possible that we are to read θ´ instead of ο´ in v(mg).

296. Margolis, p. 309.

297. Cf. the explanation offered by Peter Walters (pp. 90f), who states that ασηδωϑ stood in the OG and represents a confusion with אשדות. Even Walters concedes that at 11:22 "the most ancient evidence...leads to ασεδωδ as the reading of B...." Since interchange of the dentals δ and ϑ is not uncommon (see Thackeray ¶¶ 7, [11] 14, 15) and this would be particularly true at the end of a transliteration, we see no reason to favor the more complicated explanation of Walters over the simpler conjecture of Margolis.

298. Margolis (p. 328) includes εν τω εφραιμ in his text of the OG. The plus in the Lucianic manuscripts is an attempt to harmonize with such passages at 16:4, 5, 8, and 9.

299. Its significance in this regard is discussed, together with related examples, under no. 44 in chapter 3.

300. See H-R. Either the OG translator did not read כתב in his *Vorlage* at this point (the same would hold true for all subsequent correctors, but note the reading of x*[vid]: μετρησατε; cf. Holmes, p. 66: "LXX μερισατε = יחלקו"), or his handling of Hebrew כתב was influenced by the context: (1) the noun μερις is associated with this verb in v 6 and appears above in v 5 (additionally, it occurs three or more times in vv 7-9); (2) the clauses at the beginning of vv 5 and 6 provide close parallels:

v 5   והתחלקו אתה לשבעה חלקים.
v 6 ואתם תכתבו את הארץ שבעה חלקים.

These factors may have led the OG translator to select this rendering of כתב at v 6.

301. This verb is not found elsewhere in LXX. Holmes (pp. 66f) appears to be saying that χωροβατω in v 8 does not translate כתב, but עבר as in v 9. We note, however, that χωροβατω with the general meaning "to write a description or to survey" is paralleled in *PCair.Zen.* 329.11 from the third century B.C. (see L-S and other references there).

302. V 6, for which the text of Th. is not available, remains something of a problem (see fn. 300 above).

303. So Field, see below.

304. See H-R. At Joshua 23:8 προσκολλαω translates דבק.

305. See H-R and, for Joshua, 20:9.

306. For διανοιαν as the OG at 14:8, see Margolis, p. 271.

307. In this regard, cf. 22:5(b) and 23:14, and 2:11 and 5:1.

308. The use of *καρδια by Th. in Exodus, especially at 36:8, indicates that further investigation of this matter might be fruitful.

309. For the siglum (οι) ο' see the appendix at the end of this chapter.

310. For the readings of the OG and Th. see below.

311. See Field, g^m (as recorded in Lagarde). On -ρ-, -ρρ- see Thackeray ¶ 7, 39.

312. See H-R.

313. The use of υποβαλλω, which translates Aramaic עָנָה in some traditions of Dan 3:9, is less satisfactory if the primary purpose is to extend the standard representation ([simple] βαλλω) to this passage.

314. See H-R for statistics.

315. On this see A.V. Billen, "The Classification of the Greek MSS of the Hexateuch," *JTS* 26 (1925), p. 276.

316. In addition to other examples in this chapter, see the καιγε readings listed on pp. 349-351.

317. For τερεμινθος, rather than τερε̱βινθος, as the OG see Thackeray ¶ 7, 19.

318. So Margolis, p. 336; cf. Holmes, p. 65. For a resolution of the difficulties in the Hebrew, see Soggin (p. 168), following Noth.

319. But see below.

[end of category 3]

320. At this point v has the following marginal notation: ο' χω ※ δουλου κυριου. Margolis ("ΧΩΡΙΣ," p. 89) states that "the most natural interpretation" of this notation is "that χω ※ = χωρις αστερισκου, *i.e.* in the text called ο' the plus was to be found, but without the sign." The combined evidence from manuscript M (M[txt] δουλου κυριου sub ※, M[mg] οι ο' χω) points in the same direction.
    For this reading and four others below (nos. 2, 61, 73, 140) Lagarde included the ת siglum in his text. This provides evidence, to which we return at the end of chapter 3, for the extent of Origen's use of Th.

321. We ascribe this reading to Th. on the basis of the following note in Lagarde: "ex M[asius] concluserit aliquis לבניא דאיסראיל ※ex ϑ sumpta esse."

322. Th's choice of κρυβη here is discussed under no. 32 in chapter 3.

323. As recorded in B-McL, the last letter of εγνωσαν is not clear in manuscript g. Margolis (p. 19): εγνωσα (-σαν *vid).

324. For the parallel clause at the end of v 24, which begins ... רגם נמגו כל, the OG has και κατεπτηκεν πας....

325. Margolis, p. 43. See also Field, p. 340.

326. See further Field, p. 341 fn. 34.

327. For an explanation of το ευρεθεν see Margolis, p. 180.

328. With the exception of manuscript f (see above), none of these manuscripts exhibits a correction of the type found in Th. and elsewhere.

[end of category 4.1]

329. The last suffix in v 4, we note, is plural: כם-/υμων.

330. For Aq.'s use of στηλοω to translate יחיצב, see no. 5. The איש = ανηρ equivalence is the subject of no. 3, where Th.'s choice of ουθεις in this passage is also discussed. His use of this word extends to 1:5 the usual representation of איש in the indefinite sense employed by the OG translator of Joshua.

331. Margolis, p. 7.

332. Margolis, p. 25. Other suggestions to explain the reading of the OG are offered by Holmes (p. 21) and repeated by Benjamin (p. 27).

333. See the reading attributed to οι λ above and also those of the Palestinian and Lucianic recensions recorded in B-McL; there is support both for MT חגידו and for חגידי.

334. For πολις here and in v 18 see Holmes and Benjamin. For ארץ and עיר as "a pair of pragmatically synonymous nouns which therefore could be substituted for each other under controlled circumstances," see now Shemaryahu Talmon in *Qumran and the History of the Biblical Text*, ed. Frank Moore Cross and Shemaryahu Talmon (Cambridge: Harvard University Press, 1975), p. 345.

335. See below.

336. In g^m the verb is απηραν. See Field and B-McL.

337. Margolis, p. 44.

338. For the siglum οι ο' see the appendix at the end of this chapter.

339. On the other hand, we cannot be sure what ο' read.

340. In the "Symmachus" section of chapter 2 we raise the possibility that a desire for 'simplification' might explain the reading of Sym. at this point.

341. So Margolis, see below.

342. Margolis, p. 47.

343. Margolis, p. 46.

344. Holmes, p. 23; Benjamin, p. 29.

345. μερος does appear elsewhere as a rendering of Hebrew צד (see H-R).

346. The section of v 16 in which מצד צרחן/εως μερους καριαθαιν appears is difficult and has produced variants in the versions and conjectural emendations among the commentators. See Margolis, Holmes, Benjamin; also Soggin, pp. 48f, 61f and literature referred to there.

347. Margolis, p. 51.

348. The form of the preposition employed by Th. makes such an error less likely.

349. We were also influenced in our decision by an observation of Holmes (p. 26), who characterizes the reading of the Greek as a doublet. According to him, εμπροσθεν μου "shows that לפני יהוה was read as לפני; this could not have been done unless יהוה was abbreviated to י which did not differ in form from ו, לפני ו became by haplography לפני." This process would be possible only in a Hebrew text, here the *Vorlage* of the OG, in which ארון did not appear.

350. For further details, see, e.g., Soggin, pp. 92f.

351. Cf. Margolis (p. 125): "CG om העם."

352. At Est 9:4 the LXX does not have an equivalent for Hebrew שמעו.

353. See Margolis, p. 101, and BH^4. The MT has retained the original reading, which in this case is the *lectio difficilior*. See also Soggin, p. 108.

354. There is, after all, only one letter's difference between these two Hebrew words. Note also that the expression לשם יהוה occurs earlier in 9:9.

355. We have not listed separately other variant spellings of the proper name, all of which retain the β-ζ consonant pattern of the OG (t has αδωνιζεβεκ).

356. Margolis, p. 168.

357. For Noth see Soggin, p. 119. For Wright's discussion of this name see G.E. Wright, "The Literacy and Historical Problem of Joshua 10 and Judges 1," *JNES* 5 (1946), p. 108.

358. The singular also appears in Gx, two manuscripts usually included under the siglum οι ο' (see the appendix at the end of this chapter). For the plural of Th. see below.

359. So Margolis.

360. Margolis, p. 176. Also Holmes, p. 50; Soggin, p. 119.

361. Soggin, p. 119.

362. For βηθ- as the predominant spelling in P(C) see our remarks at no. 113 (13:27[a]) under category 3.

363. Margolis, p. 205.

364. See Soggin, p. 133.

365. μαρων, and not the expected μαδων, appears in xß at this point. As determined by Margolis (pp. 239f), the original text of Origen did contain μαδων, which was subsequently corrupted into μαρων.

366. Soggin, p. 134.

367. The reading characteristic of the N-group, μαρδων, may be termed conflate, in that it reflects both consonants.

368. Margolis includes συμορων in his text of the OG and also calls into question the first vowel of the reading attributed to Th. See below.

369. Margolis, p. 206; Thackeray (¶ 7, 31) supplies but one parallel for the proposed omission of intervocalic -ρ- here.

370. In Gen 46:13; Nu 26:24; 1 Chr 7:1 שמרון is a son of Issachar.

371. Soggin (pp. 133f): various Egyptian texts; El-Amarna no. 225, 1:4; the Hellenistic Onomasticon (Simoniad); the modern Arab semuniye.

372. Soggin, p. 135.

373. Note the appearance of σομ- in manuscripts of the S, P, and C recensions. This need not imply an accomodation to שמרון, but the influence of this well-known location probably was felt here.

374. The interchange of o and e is not uncommon in the LXX (Thackerary ¶ 6, 27).

375. The artificial distinction between this word (-οων) and "Simeon" (-εων) was no longer necessary once Th. restored -ρ-.

376. Holmes p. 54.

377. On αυτ-/ηυτ- see Thackeray ¶ 16, 4.

378. See also 2 Sam 10:19.

379. The use of ου παραδιδωμι to render השלים is paralleled in a difficult passage at Is 38:13. Cf. reference in H-R to 2 Esdras 7:19.

380. The readings of bxF^{b}𝔄𝔔 suggest meanings for השלים other than "to make peace with." See also Is 38:13. Holmes: "παρεδωκεν, an Aramaism."

381. For the Aq.-Th. relationship in general see further in chapter 2.

382. So Margolis conjectures. See our comments under no. 107 below.

383. -ει, so Margolis. This is the form attributed to Th. at 13:11 (no. 107).

384. Margolis, p. 231.

385. See also 1 Sam 27:8.

386. Confusion between ו and י was possible in the Hebrew script of all periods.

387. See no. 101 above.

388. Margolis, pp. 248f.

389. It is likely that this clause did not form part of the original text of 13:8. It may have originated as a marginal gloss, the purpose of which was to supply the oft-used epithet עבד יהוה after the name Moses (see under no. 61 in chapter 3). In an expanded form it subsequently entered the text underlying both the OG and MT traditions.

390. So we conjecture (see below). According to Margolis, the OG was αρχοντας παρα σηων. LXX^B has αρχοντα εναρα σειων.

391. Margolis, p. 258.

392. This reference to Schleusner is taken from Field.

393. Holmes p. 57.

394. So Margolis (p. 257): "και dissociates the נסיכי סיחון from the נשיאי מדין."

395. So Margolis (p. 258): "και as if וישבי (or ואת ישבי), thus connecting with v 22."

396. Cf. נסיך meaning "libation" in Dtn 32:38.

397. For רבע as a number and not a proper name see Soggin, p. 150. On the relationship between this passage and parallels in the book of Numbers see also Soggin, p. 158. For a recent discussion of these names see George E. Mendenhall, *The Tenth Generation: The Origins of the Biblical Tradition* (Baltimore: The Johns Hopkins University Press, 1973), pp. 167-169.

398. The form αρχοντα shows the influence of εναρα.

399. Margolis, p. 272.

400. Cf. the procedure of Soggin (p. 160), who translates "because you have wholly followed the Lord your God." Nowhere does he give his reason for including "your" in his translation.

401. So Margolis.

402. Margolis, pp. 277f.

403. See also Nu 34:4 and the Greek readings recorded there.

404. See, by analogy, the common nouns vocalized צִנָּה, all of which are apparently to be derived from a צנן root (BDB). Or is the doubling on analogy with the directional adverbs שׁמה and הנה? At v 1, where this proper name occurs in the phrase מדבר צן, the OG writes a single -ν-.

405. For both the OG and the reading of Th. see below.

406. For βαιθ- see nos. 67 and 69 in this category. For βηθ- in the text of Th. see no. 113 (13:27[a], included in category 3).

407. Margolis, "ΧΩΡΙΣ," p. 85.

408. Margolis, p. 281.

409. For the identification of this site, see Soggin, p. 173.

410. Margolis, p. 281. At 18:17 the OG reads βεων (so Margolis; LXX^B: βαιων, as here), where the MT again has בֹּהַן.

411. Margolis, p. 288.

412. z(mg) has θυγ-.

413. απο ακρου is confirmed by the reading preserved for σ' in 𝔖: מן רישא דשרבתא דבניא דיהודא (see Field). B-McL errs in attaching the readings of α', σ', and ϑ' to πολεις 2°, even though in this procedure it is following v(mg) (see Margolis). Aq., and probably also Sym. and Th., did not write a form of πολις twice as in the OG. On the other hand, it may be correct to attach the reading of σ' to πολεις 2° (see appendix at the end of this chapter).

414. See Margolis, p. 292.

415. Holmes, p. 62.

416. In the transmission of his text an original της may have dropped out between τελους and φυλης (see the reading ascribed to Aq.).

417. So Margolis conjectures, see below.

418. So Margolis; B-McL records the citation in v(mg) as και ασορ....

419. Margolis, p. 294.

420. Frank M. Cross and G. Ernest Wright, "The Boundary and Province Lists of the Kingdom of Judah," *JBL* 75 (1956), 212, state that "Hazor and Ithnan should be read as one name," and they refer to this city as Hazar-ithnan. So Soggin (p. 167), who notes that only one place (as in the OG) is probably original here. Several other compound place names that include the חצר element are mentioned in Joshua 15 and elsewhere.

421. So Margolis.

422. BH^3 in its first (upper) apparatus indicates that *G omits וחצור. There is, as we have seen, scant evidence to support such a contention. More to the point would be the statement that *G omitted the conjunction. BH^4 has no notation at all on v 23.

423. So Margolis.

424. See Margolis, p. 295.

425. See Holmes, p. 62. The note in BH^3 (not found in BH^4) that the Greek omitted וחצור חדתה is mechanical, for the Greek translator did have these words in some form or other in his *Vorlage*.

426. See BDB.

427. No. 130 is also mentioned under no. 94 in chapter 3.

428. For ε/ο-φερ see below.

429. There is apparently some doubt in his mind concerning this (see p. 331 notes). Margolis follows the same procedure at 12:17.

430. We know from examples such as 101, 107, 122, and 124 that Th. was interested in such matters. In any case, no great significance need be attached to the two spellings here (or to the form of the proper name attributed to Th.), since interchange between *e* and *o* is not infrequent (Thackeray ¶ 6, 27). The distinctive spelling σεχεμ serves to distinguish the Hebrew form שֶׁכֶם from שְׁכֶם found elsewhere in the MT of Joshua.

431. See below.

432. 𝔊(txt) reads דפרזלא (see below).

433. We quote Masius from Lagarde. The translation is ours.

434. Field's translation is confirmed by Ju 4:3, 13.

435. Margolis, p. 340.

436. At v 18 this is the reading of all the recensions; οι λ: מרכבתא דפרזלא, as at v 16.

437. The remarks of Masius, who was referring to a text like that of LXX^B, call attention to the form of σιδηρος. We would expect the adjective (as in Th.; also οι λ and at Ju 4:3, 13) or perhaps the noun in the genitive. Is it possible that σιδηρος in LXX^B and elsewhere, although apparently a noun in the nominative, is the expected adjective? In the LXX the adjective "iron" usually appears in the contracted form σιδηρους (Thackeray ¶ 12, 2). This could perhaps be written σιδηρος; such an interchange of *ou* and *o* is not without parallel (Thackeray ¶ 6, 33).

438. So Margolis, see below.

439. The reading in manuscript a is part of a doublet: τα ορια θαλασσης εις γασειν.

440. Noth (pp. 110f) offers the following explanation for the appearance of ימה in the MT here: "יַמָּה, das sachlich ganz unpassend ist, beruht auf einer falschen Auflösung der Elemente der ursprünglich von O nach W gerichteten und hier also umzukehrenden Grenzfixpunktreihe; nach 15:8 gehörte diese יָמָּה von Hause zu 'dem Berge angesichts des Ben-Hinnom-Tales.'"

441. Cf. Holmes, p. 67.

442. Soggin, p. 187.

443. BH^4 merely notes that the Greek reads εις γα(σ)ιν.

444. Margolis, "Presidential Address," p. 63.

445. Contrast the remarks of Masius: "in Hebraeo...pro, θαλασσης, est εις θαλασσαν. atque ita Symmachus convertit." Th.'s use of the genitive to express direction is paralleled, among other places, in the New Testament (B-F ¶ 166).

446. Margolis includes the definite article in his text of the OG and explains that the loss of τα in manuscripts of the Egyptian and Palestinian recensions was an error induced by the preceding διελευσεται.

447. So Margolis, see below.

448. See below.

449. Margolis, p. 358.

450. Holmes, p. 68.

451. Recent studies on the "Lucianic recension" include Bruce M. Metzger, "The Lucianic Recension of the Greek Bible," *Chapters in the History of New Testament Textual Criticism,* New Testament Tools and Studies, 4 (Leiden: E. J. Brill, 1963), pp. 1-41; D. Barthélemy, "Post-Scriptum: The 'Lucianic Recension,'" *1972 Proceedings IOSCS Pseudepigrapha,* Septuagint and Cognate Studies, 2 (Society of Biblical Literature, 1972), pp. 64-89. See also the literature cited.

452. We are somewhat puzzled that Margolis included πολις, which appears to be in the singular, as the underlying form for the E, C, and P recensions. It seems that, on the basis of πολις in cq𝕶ᶠA̲I̲ma₂b₂𝕶-ed 𝕶ᶜ𝕶 (contra 𝕶ᵐ), Margolis interpreted πολεις in LXXᴮ² and elsewhere as the singular (Thackeray ¶ 6, 25: "πολεις for nom. πολις is common in B)." Holmes, however, speaks of the "LXX mistake of taking קרית‎ᴮ as plural of קרית‎." He makes reference to 15:25, where LXXᴮ reads αι πολεις (MT: קרית‎). There Margolis (p. 295) accepts as the OG πολις "in spite of the spelling πολεις and then the pl. art. (αι)." At 18:28 α̲ι̲ πολεις appears in manuscripts of the N-group.

453. Margolis, p. 357. mẋa₂ read αρειμ (𝕶: דארים‎); αρεμ is found in Nθlub₂𝕶-ed.

454. In certain cases the practice of transliteration may be characteristic of the καιγε recension. The significance of no. 139 in this regard is discussed, together with related examples, under no. 94 in chapter 3.

455. For the location and significance of Kiriath-jearim see Cross-Wright.

456. At least three participles of the verb נחל that
were in use have spellings similar to מנחלחם: piel (מנחלים),
hiphil (מנחילים), hithpael (מתנחלים). Cf. 𝕊(txt) here:
כד ירתיך הון.

457. In spite of the differences between the OG and MT at
13:8, it is clear that τω ρουβην translates הראובני, as in the
MT.

458. The phrase appears 12 times in the Hebrew, 10 times
in the Greek.

459. Holmes, pp. 74f.

460. This plus does accurately reflect a portion of the
MT.

461. This is apparently a mistake for either the present
or aorist imperative.

462. As part of a longer reading 𝕊 attributes to Aq. the
form הפוכו, which Field translates επιστρεψατε.

463. In a plus earlier in the verse the form απελθετε
(=ο′, so v[mg]) appears in manuscript q.

464. For the Th.-Aq. relationship here and in general see
the "Aquila" section of chapter 2.

465. See below.

466. This is also true at no. 143.

467. Margolis, "ΧΩΡΙΣ," p. 88.

468. See above and cf. the first verb in this verse.

469. So we conjecture, see below.

470. See Thackeray ¶ 6, 27 (1).

471. According to many commentators, the clause
וכל הגרים אשר הכרתי is not original either (a) in this location
and/or (b) in this form. See, for example, Soggin, p. 217;
Holmes, p. 77; BH[3],[4].

472. The brackets, taken from B-McL, indicate that this
word cannot be clearly read. v(mg) attributes ημων to θ′. In
z(mg) (sine nom) υμων appears. For our choice of the latter
as the authentic reading of Th. see below.

473. For the importance of such considerations see also
the discussion that follows at no. 165.

474. See Klaus Baltzer, *The Covenant Formulary (in Old Testament, Jewish, and early Christian Writings)*, tr. David E. Green (Philadelphia: Fortress Press, 1971), p. 63.

475. In this way Joshua was including himself. This would be particularly important after the divisive events related in chapter 22.

476. Smyth 1523b and n. 1. In the NT just the opposite is true with respect to μετα: πολεμειν μετα τινος "to fight against somebody" (class. "on the same side with someone"). So B-F ¶ 193(4); see also ¶ 227(2).

477. וּמְבָרְכוּ בְרַכְכוּן, part of a longer reading attributed to α' in ₴, confirms this.

478. In his grammar, pp. 47-50. The separate study is H. St. J. Thackeray, "Renderings of the Infinitive Absolute in the LXX," *JTS* 9 (1907-08), 597-601.

479. According to G*K*C, the infinitive absolute *after the verb* here, as often elsewhere, serves to intensify or strengthen the verbal idea (¶ 113r). The infinitive absolute before the verb can serve the same function.

480. The Greek here apparently influenced the translator at Joshua 24:10.

481. Here ευλογησας is an aorist; at Joshua 24:10 ευλογησας in c is the participle.

482. See Baltzer, p. 63.

483. This judgment is made on the basis of comparisons with statements such as "The great king has ... I have ...." See Baltzer, p. 19 note 4.

484. The first person plural pronoun was inappropriate when Yahweh "spoke" in the first person singular. The verbs וישם and ויבא in v 7 may have been the starting point for the extensive changes that we witness in the Greek. See the remarks of Noth (p. 137) to the effect that vv 6-12 are formulated in the Greek as a speech of Joshua, rather than as a (first person) speech of Yahweh. See also the speech of Joshua in chapter 23 (discussed under no. 162 above).

485. Note the third person verb and the introduction of the divine name.

486. For Hollenberg's comments here see Holmes, p. 79.

487. We have been unable to determine whether the text of the OG (and its *Vorlage*) is the result of changes brought about because of theological concerns. For a recent treatment of the Balaam material see George W. Coats, "Balaam: Sinner or Saint?" *Biblical Research* 18 (1973), pp. 21-29.

488. Cf. the notice in BH^3 (not found in BH^4) that the Greek omitted שם.

[end of category 4.3]

489. Although in the text of Masius the asterisk and metobelus appear with the following εδωκαν, they should be placed at παντος (χαλκου).

490. Margolis, p. 98.

491. See Margolis, pp. 129f, and especially Holmes, pp. 13f, 42f.

492. Holmes, p. 14. Support for the originality of a Hebrew text shorter than the MT, but not necessarily equivalent to the *Vorlage* of the OG, is supplied by one of the Joshua fragments found at Qumran.

493. Margolis, p. 130.

494. This plural pronoun probably shows the influence of the plural verb at the beginning of this verse (see above).

495. 𝔖 preserves the following reading for Sym. here: מן מערבא למדינתא. Field, who associates this note with מים מ לעיר of v 13, translates απο δυσμων τη πολει.

496. Max L. Margolis, "Ai or the City? Joshua 8.12, 16," *JQR* NS 7 (1916/17), pp. 491-497.

497. Margolis, "Ai," p. 496.

498. See Soggin, pp. 93, 99, and the literature referred to there.

499. See below.

500. This represents ωμων των ονων (so Margolis).

501. Margolis, p. 152.

502. See Thackeray ¶ 6, 28ff; B-F ¶ 28.

503. For the texts of the OG and Th. see below.

504. Margolis, p. 195.

505. As indicated above, the notation in the margin of v itself attributes αγαζειρ, not found in v(txt), to Th. See also z(mg).

506. The fact that εξερχομαι is difficult in these two passages does not justify the rather mechanical retroversion contained in *BH*[4]: "G και εξηλθεν = ויצא."

507. See Thackeray ¶ 7, 20.

508. See Margolis, p. 171.

509. Note that v(mg) attributes to σ' both γα̣ζερ and γε̣ζερ, the latter an apparent correction to indicate that σ' parts company with α'ο' in the spelling of this name.

510. See Thackeray ¶¶ 6, 18f.

511. Or perhaps βασιλευς is an interpretive rendering of לעזר: the king is one who "helps" the city.

512. It appears from v 37 that another city, Hebron, had a new king by this time.

513. So Margolis, see below.

514. Margolis, p. 322.

515. For example, at 5:4ff; 8:22 the verb εξερχομαι is followed by the preposition εκ. See also readings at 2:19.

516. This is possible in either an uncial or cursive tradition. See also the comments of Margolis on 2:19 (p. 29).

517. See Margolis; Holmes, p. 63; and especially Soggin, pp. 167, 180f.

518. The choice of απο in manuscripts of the Palestinian and Constantinople recensions may represent a conscious effort to set this preposition off from the preceding (and following [?]) εις.

519. So we determine. See below.

520. Note that the preceding verb is in the singular: ויהי/και εγενηθη. This same corruption probably occurred in a difficult passage at 17:9.

521. Holmes, p. 72.

522. See now A. Graeme Auld, "Textual and Literary Studies in the Book of Joshua," *ZAW* 90 (1978), pp. 416f.

523. For the latter meaning see 12:2 and 13:16.

524. There are further difficulties at 16:1.

525. Margolis, p. 300.

[end of category 5]

526. In Judges 3 עגלון is king of Moab. In the OG Eglon king of Moab also appears in the additional material found at the end of the book of Joshua.

527. Margolis, p. 172; see also pp. 236f (on 12:12).

528. On the identification of these sites see the articles in *The Interpreter's Dictionary of the Bible*; note especially the article on Eglon in the Supplementary Volume.

529. Cf. Benjamin (p. 44) on 10:34: "עגלונה. Β οδολλαμ. Confusion of ג and ד. The error in this name is constant throughout these chapters. Cf. verses 3, 5, 23, 37."

530. See B-F ¶25; Thackeray ¶6, 11.

531. Margolis notes that in Greek *m* and *n* are graphically similar in both uncial and cursive scripts and are also subject to indistinct pronunciation. See Max L. Margolis, "Textual Criticism of the Greek Old Testament," *Proceedings of the American Philosophical Society* 67 (1928), p. 188.

532. Margolis, p. 236.

533. See Thackeray ¶¶ 7, 32, 33.

534. For the loss of -γ- see above.

[end of category 6]

Appendix

To a large extent our evidence for the text of Th. is drawn from one manuscript, v. In its margin and less frequently in its text, readings are attributed to ϑ'. For this reason it is important to determine the accuracy with which citations and ascriptions have been preserved in this manuscript. Sometimes an external check is provided by the survival in another manuscript (or, more rarely, other manuscripts) of a reading and/or ascription that can be compared with the material preserved in v. In general these comparisons show that reliance on manuscript v as a witness to the authentic text of Th. is not misplaced.[1]

Manuscript v provides us with another check, one that we might term internal, on its own accuracy. We have reference to the numerous citations ascribed to (οι) o'; i.e., to Origen's corrected OG column (column 5). From the work of Margolis in particular, it is clear that manuscripts of the P(alestinian) and C(onstantinople) recensions preserve this work of Origen more completely and accurately than manuscripts of the other two major recensions in Joshua (Lucianic and Egyptian).[2] Moreover, Margolis argues persuasively that the text type represented in C was dependent on P.[3] Therefore, it is to manuscripts of the latter recension primarily, and C secondarily, that we look for confirmation that a reading attributed to o' did appear in Origen's Septuagint column. When, as the material below shows, it is determined that v is on the whole an accurate and trustworthy witness to the text tradition designated as (οι) o', we can apply such terms as "accurate" and "trustworthy" to the witness that v bears to the text of Th. as well. Thus external and internal checks converge, and we can continue, with renewed confidence, the practice of employing manuscript v as our primary witness to the authentic and original text of Th.

Of the 171 readings recorded for Th. in Joshua, 136 have partial or complete equivalents ascribed to οι o'. We limit our investigation to these 136, which do constitute a substantial

number of the οι ο′ readings and are representative of them.[4]
Since these 136 readings of οι ο′ are listed and often discussed
at the appropriate point in chapter 1, we do not repeat the
text of ο′ below, except where the lack of repetition would
make our additional remarks unclear.

On the basis of previous research carried out in this area
by Margolis and Pretzl, we see no purpose to be served by
regularly listing manuscripts other than those of the P̲ and C̲
recensions that have a reading attributed to οι ο′.[5] Margolis'
arguments concerning the secondary character of C̲ in this regard
make it unlikely that even the listing of the individual manuscripts in this recension is necessary as a rule.

In the presentation of the relevant material, first we
list those manuscripts of the P̲ recension that have the reading
ascribed to οι ο′. Minor variations are also noted. We include as witnesses to the P̲ recension Gbcx 𝔖.[6] b is bracketed
until 2:18 (middle), since prior to that point its text is
Lucianic. The important uncial manuscript G is available only
for the middle section of Joshua (end of chapter 9 to 19:23).
𝔖, when extant, is cited only if it is clear that its text
reflects the characteristic element(s) of the reading ascribed
in Greek to οι ο′. Through the use of the siglum C̲ or ½ C̲ we
indicate the extent to which the οι ο′ reading appears in
manuscripts of the Constantinople Recension (AMNΘlouyb₂). When
the text attributed to οι ο′ is the OG (as for example in all
examples discussed in category 1.1), this is noted. Although
the appearance of οι ο′ = OG readings is generally less
significant in attempting to isolate the group or subgroup that
has most accurately preserved the ο′ text, these readings ought
not to be omitted. Finally, (1) is placed at the close of
those listings for which reference back to earlier discussions
in this chapter is especially helpful.

1. (1:1)   [b]cx𝔤(sub ※) (1)
7. (1:7[a])   x𝔤 <u>C</u>
9. (1:8)   [b]cx𝔤 <u>C</u>
10. (1:11)   With reference to και (2°) x𝔤^m(sub ⸓) <u>C</u> (1)
11. (1:13)   [b]cx𝔤^m(sub ⸓) <u>C</u> (=OG) (1)
14. (2:2)   [b]cx𝔤 <u>C</u>
15. (2:4[a])   [b]cx𝔤(αυτοις sub ⸓) <u>C</u> (=OG) (1)
17. (2:6)   x <u>C</u> (=OG) (1)
18. (2:7)   [b]cx𝔤 <u>C</u> (=OG)
19. (2:9)   cx𝔤(sub ※) (but see [1])
21. (2:14)   ο': και εσται ως αν παραδω κυριος ημιν την
              πολιν ποιησωμεν μετα σου   cx𝔤^m have και
              εσται (sub ※ 𝔤^m) ως αν παραδω κυριος. For
              the remainder of the citation c has ημιν,
              την πολιν (x𝔤^m[mg]: την γην), και ποιησομεν,
              and μετα σου. (1)
22. (3:4)   bcx𝔤 <u>C</u> (=OG)
23. (3:6)   bx
24. (3:8)   μερος (=ο') ½ <u>C</u>; μερους (=OG) bcx ½ <u>C</u>
25. (3:10)   bcx <u>C</u> (=OG)
26. (3:12)   x <u>C</u> (=OG) (1)
28. (3:14)   ο': και ως απηρεν ο λαος   this reading is
              found in no extant witness to the text. If ο'
              read και εγενετο ως απηρεν ο λαος (with
              εγενετο accidentally lost during the trans-
              mission of this reading?), with α'ϑ', then
              the text attributed to ο' is preserved in bcx.
              𝔤^m reads και ※ εγενετο ως ✕ απηραν. (1)
31. (3:16)   With σαρθαμ/-ν x𝔤𝔤^m also k
33. (4:1)   bcx𝔤 <u>C</u>
36. (4:10[b],
    4:11)   With διεβη bx𝔤 <u>C</u> (1)
37. (4:12)   bcx <u>C</u> (=OG)
38. (4:14)   bcx𝔤 <u>C</u> (=OG)
39. (4:19)   bcx <u>C</u> (=OG)
40. (4:22)   ο': αναγγελειτε   x𝔤 ½ <u>C</u> (cf. b: αναγγελειται)

41. (4:23)   ο': παρηλθομεν   cx C̱ (=OG) (cf. b:
                 παρηλθαμεν)

42. (5:20)   ο': μαχαιρας εκ πετρας ακροτομου   ½ C̱ (Aoy)
                 have exactly this text. bx read μαχαιρας εκ
                 πετρας ακροτομους. ɤ has μαχαιρας÷εκ πετρας
                 ακροτομου ×; according to Margolis, the pro-
                 cedure of Origen was ÷ εκ πετρας: ακροτομους.
                 (1)

44. (6:2)   bxɤ(vid) C̱

45. (6:17)   bxɤ^m(sub ÷) C̱

46. (6:24[a])   ο': ενεπυρισθη εν πυρι   bx C̱. ɤ^m also
                 reads εν πυρι (so Field, who makes no reference
                 to the verb).

47. (6:24[b])   bcxɤ^m(sub ※) (1)

48. (7:1)   bx ½ C̱

49. (7:3)   bcx (=OG)

55. (8:5)   c C̱

57. (8:19)   bcx (om του)ɤ C̱ (=OG)

58. (9:4[9:10]) Two different readings are ascribed to ο' in
                 v: ωμων in v(txt) = bcɤ; ονων in v(mg) = x
                 C̱ (=OG).

59. (9:5[9:11]) ο': και οι αρτοι του επισιτισμου αυτων ξηροι
                 και βεβρωμενοι C̱ has exactly this text.
                 bxɤ read και-ξηροι, then εγενηθησαν (-νοντο b)
                 και βεβρωμενοι (εγενηνθησαν sub ※, και sub ÷
                 ɤ^m). c has και-ξηροι εγενηθησαν και
                 βεβρωμενοι και ευρωτιωντες. (1)

62. (10:1)   x also k

63. (10:3)   Gcx C̱

64. (10:5[a])   ο': βασιλεις του αμορραιου   Gx (cf. c:
                 των αμορραιων)

65. (10:5[b])   ο': αιγλωμ   x has εγλων (similar spellings
                 also found in a k^a q)

66. (10:10[a]) Gbx C̱

67. (10:10[b]) Gbcx C̲
68. (10:10[c]) Gbcx C̲ (=OG)
69. (10:11[a]) Gbx
70. (10:11[b]) o°: λιθους μεγαλους χαλαζης εκ του ουρανου
only akoᵠ have this reading. x has μεγαλους,
but omits χαλαζης (𝔊 is not extant here).
71. (10:11[c]) Gbcx C̲ (=OG)
72. (10:11[d]) Gbcx C̲ (=OG)
74. (10:19) o′: υμεις δε μη εστηκετε καταδιωκοντες οπισω
only x has εστηκετε (x lacks μη); b reads
στηκετε. εστηκατε appears in Gc C̲.
75. (10:20[a]) o′: παντες οι υιοι ισραηλ C̲. Gbx𝔊 have οι
υιοι (om οι x*) ισραηλ; c reads πας υιος
ισραηλ.
76. (10:20[b]) Gbcx𝔊 C̲ (=OG)
77. (10:23) o′: αιγλων x has ελγων (similar spelling
found in a)
78. (10:27) Gbcx𝔊 (μεγαλους sub ※ G𝔊)
79. (10:28) o′: Ϝιϣους Gbcx𝔊 C̲ (for 𝔊 see under no.
50 in chapter 3)
80. (10:30) Gbcx𝔊 C̲ (=OG)
81. (10:33) o′: τοτε ανεβη ω̲ρ̲α̲μ̲ βασιλευς γ̲α̲ζ̲ε̲ρ̲ β̲ο̲η̲θ̲η̲σ̲α̲ι̲ τη
λαχεις only x has exactly this text. For the
three key words (underlined above) ωραμ is
found elsewhere only in ak; γαζερ, in Gbc C̲;
βοηθησαι, in Gbc𝔊.
82. (10:34) o′: αιγλωμ x has εγλων (similar spelling
found in a)
83. (10:40[a]) Gbcx𝔊 C̲ (=OG)
84. (10:40[b]) Gbcx𝔊 C̲ (=OG)
85. (10:41) o′: πασαν γην γοσομ Gb'b*x𝔊 have πασαν γην.
The proper name appears as γοσο̲υ̲ in Gcx (also
in 𝔊 it ends in -ν) and as γοσο̲μ̲ in b.
86. (11:1[a]) Gbcx𝔊 C̲ (=OG)
87. (11:1[b]) Gbcx𝔊 C̲

88. (11:1[c])   o′: συμερων   συμερων is found only in sz(mg).
                Gbx ½ C have σομερων. (1)

89. (11:8[a])   o′: μασρεφωθμαειμ   G(pr των)c∅ C (cf. x:
                μασσεφωθμαιμ; b: μασρεφωθμαιν; b′:
                μαρεφωθμαιν)

90. (11:8[b])   o′: μασσηφα c C (cf. G: μασσηφαθ). Here
                b reads μασιφα, and x has μασφα.

91. (11:10)   o′: επεστρεψεν Gcx C (cf. b: απεστρεψεν)

92. (11:13)   Read θ′ instead of o′ (1)

94. (11:21[a]) Gbcx∅ C (=OG)

95. (11:21[b]) Gbcx∅ C (=OG)

96. (11:23)   Gbcx∅ C (=OG)

97. (12:1)   Gbcx (=OG) (for οι υιοι/υιοι see [1])

98. (12:2[a])   Gbcx∅ C (=OG)

99. (12:2[b])   Gbcx∅ C (=OG)

100. (12:4-5)   Gx∅ (=OG)

101. (12:5)   o′: γεσουρε(-ει) bcx∅ C have γεσουρ-
                (cf. G: γεσσουρε).

102. (12:7)   o′: σεειρα Gbx C (cf. b′: ασσεειρα [for
                OG εις σηειρ])

103. (12:12)   o′: εγλων Gbx∅ C have εγλωμ/-ν (cf. b′c:
                αιγλωμ)

104. (12:14)   Gbcx∅ C

105. (13:5)   o′: Read βασλγαδ c?x (=OG) (cf. Gbc?:
                βαελγαδ) (1)

106. (13:8)   Gbcx ∅

107. (13:11)   o′: γεσουρει bx∅ C have γεσουρ- (cf. G:
                γεσσουρει; c: γεσορει)

108. (13:13)   Gbcx C

109. (13:16)   Gbcx∅ C (=OG)

110. (13:21)   o′: αρχοντας σηων Ga?(for αρχοντας)bcx ½ C

111. (13:23)   Gbcx∅ C (=OG)

112. (13:26)   o′: δεβειρ Gbx (cf. C: δαβειρ; b′: δεβηρ;
                c: δαιβηρ)

113. (13:27[a]) o′ βηθναμρα Gx (cf. b: βηθαναμρα; b′:
                 βηθαναμυρα). According to Margolis, βηθαναμρα
                 is the underlying form for C also. c has
                 βηθναμβρα.

114. (13:27[b])   Gbcx∅ C̲ (=OG)
115. (14:6)   Gbcx∅ C̲
116. (14:7)   ο': και απεκριθησαν αυτω λογον κατα τον νουν
αυτων   Gbcx∅ C̲ have απεκριθησαν. Only ½
C̲ also has αυτων.
117. (14:8)   Gbcx∅ ½ C̲ (=OG)
118. (14:9)   Gbcx∅
119. (14:12)   Gbx C̲
120. (15:3)   ο': σ(ε)ινα   Gbcx   (cf. ½ C̲: σενα). ½ C̲ reads
σεννα.
121. (15:6[a])   ο': Read βαιθαγλα   G*(vid)bc C̲ (cf. G$^{a?}$
[vid]: βαιθαλα; x: βηθαγλα)   (1)
122. (15:6[b])   ο': βοεν   x On-ed
123. (15:9)   ο': και διεκβαλλει επι κωμας ορους   Gb
(διεκβαλει) cx∅ (επι κωμας sub ※ G∅)
124. (15:14)   ο': σησαι   x
125. (15:17)   bcx (∅--so Pretzl)
126. (15:19[a])   x∅
127. (15:19[b])   Gbcx∅ C̲ (=OG)   (cf. b': γολαθμαιμ)
128. (15:21)   ο': πολεις προς τη φυλη   προς τη φυλη is
found in Gbcx (=OG). G places πολεις sub ┬ ,
and x omits it. c reads πολεις (=OG), and b
has πολις. (1)
129. (15:23)   ο': και ασωρ   b'bcx∅ have και ασωρ followed
by various forms (cf. G: ασσωρ) (1)
130. (15:25[15:24])   ο': και ασωρ την καινην   this underlies
the readings in Gbc∅. Here x reads και ασωρ
και αδαθα.
131. (15:46)   ο': αζωτου   none (for the suggestion to
read θ' instead of ο' see [1])
132. (16:2)   Gbcx C̲
133. (16:10)   Gbcx∅ C̲ (=OG)
134. (17:2)   ο' σεχεμ και τοις υιοις εφερ και τοις υιοις
σεμιδαε ουτοι κατα δημους αυτων   x: σεχεμ
και τοις υιοις εφερ και τοις υιοις σεμιδαε
και τοις υιοις μανασση ουτοι υιοι μανασση
υιου ιωσηφ οι αρσενες κατα δημους αυτων;

G: σεχεμ και τοις υιοις σεφερ και τοις υιοις
σεμιδα ουτοι υιοι μανασση υιου ιωσηφ οι
αρσενες κατα δημους αυτων (υιοι-οι sub ※);

b: συχεμ και τοις υιοις εφερ και τοις υιοις
σεμιδαε (b)/σαμιδαε(b') ουτοι-αυτων;

c: εχεμ και τοις υιοις σεφερ και τοις υιοις
σεμιδαε ουτοι-αυτων (note: ουτοι αρσενες
κατα δημους αυτων=OG--so Margolis)

135.	(17:4)	Gbcx𝄐 C̲
136.	(17:16)	Gbcx𝄐 (sub ÷) C̲ (=OG)
138.	(18:15)	ο': ορια θαλασσης 𝄐 also a (cf. x: οκαρια θαλασσης)
141.	(20:9)	bcx𝄐 (=OG)
143.	(21:13)	bcx𝄐 C̲ (=OG) (1)
144.	(21:20)	bcx𝄐
145.	(21:26)	ο': πασαι αι πολεις only lo*(vid), manuscripts of C̲, have πασαι α̲ι̲ πολεις. The rest of C̲ reads α̲ι̲ πασαι πολεις.
146.	(21:44[a])	bx (=OG)
147.	(21:44[b])	bcx𝄐m ½ C̲ (=OG)
148.	(21:44[c])	bcx𝄐 (=OG)
149.	(22:1)	ο': υιους ρουβην bcx (ρουβιν)𝄐 (=OG)
152.	(22:8)	ο': απελθετε only in q, in a plus earlier in the verse. x reads απηλθον.
153.	(22:10[a])	ο': βωμον bcx𝄐 C̲ (=OG)
154.	(22:10[b])	cx
155.	(22:18[a])	With reference to addition of υμεις bcx𝄐 (sub ÷) (1)
156.	(22:18[b])	bcx C̲ (=OG)
157.	(22:25)	ο': Read ανα μεσον ημων και υμων (οι) υιοι ρουβην και (οι) υιοι γαδ τον ιορδανην b(with οι twice)cx (ρουβιν)𝄐(υιοι...γαδ sub ÷) (1)
158.	(22:28)	bcx𝄐
159.	(22:34)	ο': και τω γαδ και ειραν none. bx𝄐 read και τω γαδ τον βωμον και ειραν (και ειπαν sub ÷ in 𝄐). Only bx𝄐 omit OG (γαδ) και του ημισους φυλης μανασση (και ειπ-).

161. (23:4[b])   o': εθνη α εξωλοθρευσα   c⌀ C̲. bx lack α.
162. (23:10)   o': [ουτος] εξεπολεμει μεθ υμων   none. For
                the first part, C̲ reads ουτος εξ-; bcx⌀ have
                αυτος εξ-. υμιν is the reading of c⌀ (so
                B-McL) ½ C̲; ημιν is found in bx ½ C̲.
163. (23:13)   bcx⌀ C̲
164. (24:1)   bcx⌀
165. (24:10)   o': και ευλογιαις ευλογησεν υμας   b(but only
                b has υμας) x⌀
166. (24:15)   bcx C̲
167. (24:25)   o': συχεμ   bcx⌀ (cf. b': συχεν)
169. (24:26[b]) o': τερεμινθον   bx (=OG) (cf. cC̲:
                τερεβινθον)
170. (24:27)   bcx (=OG)
171. (24:33b) bc (=OG) According to a note in B-McL, x⌀
                omit 33a, b. Pretzl, however, includes x as
                a witness to the reading ascribed to o'
                here: και εκυριευσεν.

Manuscripts most frequently containing the text designated as
(οι) o' in v(txt and mg) are those of the P̲ recension. This
is especially so for material found sub ·⁖· in ⌀ and included in
the οι o' citation.[7] Of the manuscripts of the P̲ recension
x is by far the best witness to the text tradition that underlies the readings ascribed to οι o'.[8] While that manuscript
exhibits its own pecularities, the result of corruptions and
other scribal activity, its text type nevertheless shows
unmistakable affinities with the text designated as (οι) o'.
Such agreements, among which one finds some very significant
readings, are in several instances unique. x is also our
best witness to the Greek text that underlies ⌀.

Notes to Appendix

1. Several times earlier in chapter 1 we noted the close relationship between the marginal readings in v and z. This relationship allows us to correct marginal readings in one by reference to similar wording in the other. The connection between marginal citations in v and M is also clear and allows for correction of one on the basis of the other (see also Margolis, "ΧΩΡΙΣ," p. 85). As a rule, it is v that serves as the basis for corrections of wording or ascription in the marginal notations of z and M. The exceptions to this--where v stands in need of correction--are rare.

2. See also Gary Verlan Smith, *An Introduction to the Greek Manuscripts of Joshua: Their Classification, Characteristics and Relationships*, Unpublished Ph.D. dissertation (Philadelphia: The Dropsie University for Hebrew and Cognate Learning, 1973).

3. On this point there is marked disagreement between Margolis and Pretzl. The latter argued that C represents a text type prior to Origen. Pretzl also sought to demonstrate that C was the *Vorlage* of Origen, the κοινη text with which he worked. Thus manuscripts of the C recension are not included in either of the following lists established by Pretzl: "Hss., welche im wesentlichen die Bearbeitung des Origenes bieten," "Von Origenes beeinflusste Hss."

For Margolis, the relationship is completely the opposite: "When all the evidence derived from a critical study of Aϑ [manuscripts of the C recension] throughout the book of Joshua is brought to bear upon the problem the inference is unavoidable that the two uncials have made use of Origen and not the reverse" (Max L. Margolis, "'Man by Man,' Joshua 7, 17," *JQR* NS 3 [1912/13], p. 327). Characteristic of the C recension in this regard, as Margolis states in a number of his articles, is that it passed over asterisked elements and passages. This gives to the recension the appearance of retaining an unrevised text, one not influenced by Origen; however, this appearance, which Pretzl took to be the reality, is only on the surface. As Margolis states (Max L. Margolis, "Hexapla and Hexaplaric," *AJSL* 32 [1916], pp. 137f), a scribe following the procedure outlined above "will betray himself occasionally. A flagrant case" is 15:9. A study of the readings there (15:9 [no. 1]2) is included under category 2 of this chapter) shows that the text of C, και διεκβαλλει ορους εφρων ("with genitive hanging in the air!" [Margolis, "Specimen," p. 310]), is due to the fact "that the archetypal scribe mechanically skipped the asterisked words [επι κωμας] and calmly left the surrounding text intact" (Margolis, "Hexapla," p. 138). For Margolis, "the text which Origen made the basis of his revision" is not A (with Pretzl), but "none other than the famous Vaticanus (B) or a text closely related to it" (Margolis, "Man by Man," p. 327). Our own work confirms the analysis offered by Margolis. On Pretzl's work in the book of Judges see Bodine, especially p. 31 fn. 2.

In this complex and exacting study both Pretzl and Margolis contributed valuable insights. It is to be regretted that they did not engage in the type of fruitful dialogue that accessible international journals and well-attended scholarly meetings make possible today.

4. In order to insure that these examples are representative, we sampled a number of other readings attributed to οι ο'. The results arrived at on the basis of the 136 examples also hold true for the other material.

5. Pretzl (pp. 405ff) includes a section that is similar to our listing below. Ours was prepared independently of his material and then checked against it. Pretzl does list all manuscripts which contain a reading attributed to οι ο', but his results show that it is unnecessary to reproduce all of this evidence. We include readings which he does not have, and our interpretation of readings that we both cover is often different.

6. Margolis divides these manuscripts into two subgroups: P_1, which for him represents the Hexapla, consists of Gbb'c; ɤẋ On, designated P_2, are witnesses to the Tetrapla. On this issue see Harry M. Orlinsky, "Origen's Tetrapla--a Scholarly Fiction?" *Proceedings of the First World Congress of Jewish Studies, 1947* (Jerusalem, 1952), I, 173-182; reprinted in Sidney Jellicoe, ed., *Studies in the Septuagint: Origins, Recensions, and Interpretations* (New York: KTAV, 1974), pp. 382-391. I hope to return to this problem--which, it is true, has not excited much scholarly interest of late. Any future discussions of Hexapla-Tetrapla will benefit substantially from the publication of some of the still-unpublished Margolis material. Also of particular relevance to Joshua is another article by Otto Pretzl: "Der hexaplarische und tetraplarische Septuagintatext des Origenes in den Buchern Josue and Richter," *Byzantinische Zeitschrift* 30 (1929/30), pp. 262-268.

7. See fn. 3 above.

8. Recall that x and ɤ are in subgroup P_2, which for Margolis represents the Tetrapla.

Theodotion and Aquila, Theodotion and Symmachus in Joshua

Kevin O'Connell devoted two chapters (V and VI) of his work to a detailed investigation of the relationship between Theodotion and Aquila in the book of Exodus.[1] He summed up his conclusions on this matter as follows:

> There is a genuine relationship between the versions of Theodotion and Aquila in Exodus that cannot be explained by common familiarity with the OG tradition. There is limited but adequate evidence that Aquila's revision in Exodus was based, not upon the OG directly, but upon a Greek text that had already undergone the revision represented by the Theodotionic material. In other words, Aquila knew and used Theodotion's recension as the basis for his own further revision to the MT.[2]

In the first part of this chapter we look at the relationship between Theodotion and Aquila in the book of Joshua. It is clear from the charts assembled on the following pages that adequate material for this investigation does exist in Joshua. Of the 171 readings recorded for Th. in Joshua, 129 have partial or complete equivalents preserved from Aquila. Using a format similar to that developed by O'Connell, we show that there is "limited but adequate evidence" to allow us to expand the scope of his conclusions to include at least the book of Joshua.

Since 120 readings are available to study the relationship between Theodotion and Symmachus in Joshua, we also conduct an investigation of this material using the format followed for Theodotion-Aquila. Two points emerge from this latter study: (1) There is a genuine relationship between Theodotion and Symmachus independent of the OG. (2) The nature of this relationship differs from that between Theodotion and Aquila. While Symmachus did know and use the work of Theodotion, he also made direct use of the OG. In other words, Symmachus used Theodotion's recension as *a* basis (not *the* basis, as with Aquila) for his own further work.

In the charts immediately following we show category-by-category where the complete or partial equivalents from Aquila and Symmachus occur and then group these equivalents under appropriate headings. The most significant readings receive separate treatment. Wherever possible, reference is made to more complete discussions in chapters 1 and 3.

Of the 171 readings recorded for Th. in Joshua, 129 have complete or partial equivalents preserved for Aquila. The following table breaks down the figures according to the categories and sub-categories established in chapter 1:

	Th.	Aq.
1.1	12	12
1.2	30	20
2	22	18
3	39	28
4.1	15	5
4.2	1	0
4.3	41	37
5	7	5
6 (עגלון)	4	4
	171	129

Of the 171 readings recorded for Th. in Joshua, 120 have complete or partial equivalents preserved for Symmachus. The following table breaks down the figures according to the categories and sub-categories established in chapter 1:

	Th.	Sym.
1.1	12	12
1.2	30	19
2	22	17
3	39	24
4.1	15	5
4.2	1	0
4.3	41	34
5	7	6
6 (עגלון)	4	3
	171	120

Making use of the headings found in chapter V of O'Connell's
work (with slight modifications where appropriate), we list
below the readings of Aq. and Sym. that form complete or
partial equivalents for the readings ascribed to Th. in Joshua.
The number assigned to each reading of Th. in chapter 1 is
retained here, as is the division into categories and sub-
categories (see also the preceding charts). The more significant readings in this regard, for which we also include the
text of Aq. or Sym., are followed by one or more numbers:
(1) see chapter one; (2) see later in this chapter (chapter
two); (3) see chapter three. For the discussions in this
chapter we summarize relevant data found elsewhere and introduce new material where necessary.

Aquila
I. Complete agreement between Aquila and Theodotion (82
readings)
A. Aq.-Th. agree fully with the OG (24 readings)
(1.1 12 readings)
18
57
72
76
80
84
95
96
99
109
111
117

(1.2 10 readings)
41
49
68
71
86

97
98
116
141
163

(2 2 readings)
15 (1) (2) εκρυψεν αυτους και ειπεν αυτοις
94 (1) (2) ανωβ

B. Aq.-Th. agree partially with the OG (17 readings)
(2 2 readings)
75 (1) (2) παντες οι υιοι ισραηλ
159 (1) (2) και τω γαδ και ειπαν

(3 4 readings)
20 (1) (2) μετα του οικου
85 (1) (2) πασαν γην γοσομ
119
133 (2) (3) εν μεσω εφραιμ

(4.1 1 reading)
78

(4.3 9 readings)
21 (1) (2) και εσται ως αν παραδω κυριος ημιν την πολιν
              ποιησωμεν μετα σου
28 (1) (2) και εγενετο ως απηρεν ο λαος
31 (1) (2) μερους σαρθαμ
34 (1) (2) (3) εις προσωπον κιβωτου κυριου
55
106
118
139 (1) (2) (3) καριαθ πολεις
161 (1) (2) εθνη α εξωλοθρευσα

(5 1 reading)
145 (1) (2) πασαι αι πολεις

C. Aq.-Th. have simple expansions of the OG (4 readings)
(4.1 3 readings)
13 (2) (3) κρυβη
27 (1) (2) σωρος εις
135

(4.3 1 reading)
155

D. Aq.-Th. have simple or expanded variants to the OG (37 readings)
(2 1 reading)
112 (1) (2) δεβειρ

(3 16 readings)
12 (2) (3) πλην
29 (1) (2) εις
35 (2) (3) εμμεσω
46 (1) (2) ενεπυρισθη εν πυρι
52 (1) (2) και επεθυμησα
91 (2) (3) επεστρεψεν
102 (1) (2) (εις) σεειρα
108 (1) (2) μαχαθι
125 (1) (2) αδελφος
137 (1) (2) διαγραψαι
150 (1) (2) και κολλασθαι
151 (1) (2) καρδιας
153 (1) (2) (3) θυσιαστηριον
154
166 (1) (2) εκλεξασθε
169 (1) (2) υποκατω της δρυος

(4.3   18 readings)

48
60
62
87
88   (1)   (2)   συμερων
101
107
110
120   (1)   (2)   σ(ε)ινα
121
122   (1)   (2)   βοεν
124
129
130   (1)   (2)   (3)   και ασωρ την καινην
142   (1)   (2)   εκ της κληρονομιας αυτων
149   (1)   (2)   ρουβηνιτας
158
168

(6   2 readings)

65
77

II.   Partial agreement between Aquila and Theodotion (32 readings)

A.   Th. appears closer to the OG or to an earlier revision (or corruption) of the OG than Aquila does (23 readings)

(1.2   5 readings)

23
89
100
105
114

226

2 8 readings)
24
26
37
42 (1) (2) (3) μαχαιρας πετρινας και επιστρεψας περιτεμε
59 (1) (2) και πας ο αρτος ο επισιτισμος αυτων ξηρος εγενηθη
            και εψαθυρωμενος
70 (1) (2) λιθους μεγαλους χαλαζης
90
123

(3 4 readings)
9   (1) (2) οπως φυλασσης του ποιειν κατα παν το γεγραμμενον
43 (1) (2) και εφαγον απο γενηματος της γης χανααν
54 (1) (2) (3) κοιλας ταραχου
74 (1) (2) (3) και υμεις μη στηκετε διωξατε οπισω

(4.3 4 readings)
64 (1) (2) βασιλεις του αμορραιου
128 (1) (2) αι πολεις απο τελευταιου της φυλης
134 (1) (2) σεχεμ και τοις υιοις εφερ και τοις υιοις σεμιδαε
165

(5 2 readings)
81
144

B. Aquila appears closer to the OG than Th. does (1 reading)
(3 1 reading)
17 (1) (2) αυτους εν τη λινοκαλαμη (?)

C. Neither Aquila nor Th. appears closer to the OG than the
other does (8 readings)
(3 1 reading)
160 (1) (2) υπεβαλον

(4.1 1 reading)
157

(4.3 5 readings)
5
67
69
93 (1) (2) η ου παρεδοθη τοις υιοις ισραηλ
152 (1) (2) (3) επιστραφητε

(6 1 reading)
103

III. No significant agreement between Aquila and Theodotion
(15 readings)
A. Th. appears closer to the OG or to an earlier revision
(or corruption) of the OG than Aquila does (13 readings)
(1.2 5 readings)
22
83
104
126
147

(2 5 readings)
63
92 (1) (τας) εστηκυιας επι χωματος
127
164
167

(5 2 readings)
58
132

(6   1 reading)
82

B.   Aquila appears closer to the OG than Th. does (1 reading)
(3   1 reading)
79   (2)   (3)   μαχαιρας

C.   Neither Aquila nor Th. appears closer to the OG than the
other does (1 reading)
(3   1 reading)
51

Symmachus

I. Complete agreement between Symmachus and Theodotion (65 readings)

A. Sym.-Th. agree fully with the OG (23 readings)

(1.1 12 readings)
18
57
72
76
80
84
95
96
99
109
111
117

(1.2 7 readings)
41
68
86
98
105
146
163

(2 4 readings)
15 (1) (2) εκρυψεν αυτους και ειπεν αυτοις
37
90 (1) (2) μασφα
94 (1) (2) ανωβ

B. Sym.-Th. agree partially with the OG (16 readings)

(2 2 readings)
75 (1) (2) παντες οι υιοι ισραηλ
159 (1) (2) και τω γαδ και ειπαν

(3 5 readings)
53 (1) (2) (3) κοιλαδα αχωρ
54 (1) (2) (3) κοιλας αχωρ
85 (1) (2) πασαν γην γοσομ
119
133 (2) (3) εν μεσω εφραιμ

(4.1 2 readings)
78
157 (1) (2) (3) ανα μεσον ημων και υμων (οι) υιοι
ρουβην και (οι) υιοι γαδ τον ιορδανην

(4.3 6 readings)
31 (1) (2) μερους σαρθαμ
34 (1) (2) (3) εις προσωπον κιβωτου κυριου
55
106
118
134 (1) (2) σεχεμ και τοις υιοις οφερ και

(5 1 reading)
145 (1) (2) πασαι αι πολεις

C. Sym.-Th. have simple expansion of the OG (1 reading)
(4.1 1 reading)
140

D. Sym.-Th. have simple or expanded variants to the OG
(25 readings)
(3 8 readings)
46 (1) (2) ενεπυρισθη εν πυρι
91 (2) (3) επεστρεψεν
102 (1) (2) (εις) σεειρα
115 (1) (2) εν γαλγαλοις
137 (1) (2) διαγραψαι
151 (1) (2) καρδιας
153 (1) (2) (3) θυσιαστηριον
154

(4.3 15 readings)
5   (1)   (2)   (3)   ουθεις κατα προσωπον σου
48
60
62
87
88 (1)   (2)   συμερων
101
110
121
124
129
130 (1)   (2)   (3)   και ασωρ την καινην
149 (1)   (2)   ρουβηνιτας
158
168

(6   2 readings)
65
77

II. Partial agreement between Symmachus and Theodotion (35
readings)
A. Th. appears closer to the OG or to an earlier version
(or corruption) of the OG than Symmachus does (22 readings)
(1.2 6 readings)
22
49
89
97
114
141

(2   6 readings)
24
26
42 (1)   (2)   (3)   μαχαιραν εξ ακροτομου και παλιν περιτεμε

59 (1) (2) και πας ο αρτος του επισιτισμου αυτων ξηρος
                εγενετο καπυρος
70 (1) (2) λιθους μεγαλους χαλαζης
123

(3 3 readings)
9   (1) (2) ινα φυλασσης ποιειν κατα παντα τα γεγραμμενα
43 (1) (2) και εφαγον απο γενηματος της γης χανααν
74

(4.3 5 readings)
64 (1) (2) βασιλεις του αμορραιου
93 (1) (2) ητις ειρηνευσε προς τους υιους ισραηλ
107
120 (1) (2) οιν
165

(5 2 readings)
81
144

B. Symmachus appears closer to the OG than Th. does (7
readings)
(3 4 readings)
17 (1) (2) αυτους εν τη λινοκαλαμη (?)
32 (1) (2) διεβαινον
125 (1) (2) αδελφου
169 (1) (2) υπο δρυν

(4.3 3 readings)
28 (1) (2) ως δε απηρεν ο λαος
128 (1) (2) αι πολεις απ ακρου τη φυλη
138

C. Neither Symmachus nor Th. appears closer to the OG than the other does (6 readings)
(3 1 reading)
160 (1) (2) εβαλα or υπεβαλον

(4.1 2 readings)
27 (1) (2) ασκωμα εν
135

(4.3 3 readings)
67
99
122 (1) (2) βοον

III. No significant agreement between Symmachus and Theodotion
(20 readings)
A. Th. appears closer to the OG or to an earlier revision
(or corruption) of the OG than Symmachus does (15 readings)
(1.2 6 readings)
7
23
83
116
126
147

(2 5 readings)
63
92
127
164
167

(4.3 1 reading)
161

234

(5   2 readings)
58
132

(6   1 reading)
82

B.   Symmachus appears closer to the OG than Th. does (2
readings)
(3   2 readings)
79 (2)   (3)   μαχαιρας
166 (1)   (2)   ελεσθε

C.   Neither Symmachus nor Th. appears closer to the OG than
the other does (3 readings)
(3   1 reading)
51

(4.3   1 reading)
152

(5   1 reading)
56

Aquila

In 82 out of 129 places where Aq. has a complete or
partial equivalent for the reading of Th. there is complete
agreement between the two. These are joint α'ϑ' citations.
The large number of such agreements is itself a strong indication that a "genuine relationship" exists between Th. and
Aq. A certain number of these agreements, however, are not
directly relevant in the present context. Thus we must
subtract the 22 agreements that occur in category 1 (22:
12 [1.1] + 10 [1.2]), since in every case Th.-Aq. reproduce
exactly the OG, which in turn is a translation of a Hebrew
identical to the MT. Two of the category 2 readings, nos. 15
and 94, cannot be used as primary evidence for the establishment of a Th.-Aq. relationship independent of the OG, since in
both cases Th.-Aq. = OG. Nevertheless, they may prove
valuable as supplementary examples after we establish a genuine
affinity between Theodotion and Aquila independent of the OG.

There are 36 places (out of the remaining 58) where the
complete agreement between Theodotion and Aquila is significant.
They are (listed in the order in which they appear in the preceding charts) 75, 159, 20, 85, 133, 21, 28, 31, 34, 139, 161,
145, 13, 27, 112, 12, 29, 35, 46, 52, 91, 102, 108, 125, 137,
150, 151, 153, 166, 169, 88, 120, 122, 130, 142, 149. As
O'Connell indicates, the areas of significant agreement are
generally "where Aquila and Theodotion replace an acceptable
OG translation [or transliteration] of the Hebrew with a
different one [our category 3], where they choose one of
several possible equivalents for a Hebrew word or phrase
that is not reflected in the OG [our category 4 (.1 and .3)],
or where they differ from the MT in some way that is not a mere
repetition of the OG [our category 5]."[3] In the following
section we list the reading of the OG and of Th.-Aq., under-
lining the portion of each reading that is especially important for establishing the affinity between Theodotion and
Aquila that O'Connell found in Exodus. We add under each
reading the reference to chapter 1 or 3 given in the preceding
charts. Additional discussion serves mainly to emphasize the
factors that led us to include the reading in this listing.

236

75. (10:20[a])   OG   πας ισραηλ
                            παντες οι υιοι ισραηλ

   (1) The MT here reads בני ישראל.

159. (22:34)   OG   και των γαδ και του ημισους
                          φυλης μανασση και ειπεν οτι

                Th.-Aq.   και τω γαδ και ειπαν

   (1) At this point the MT has כי למזבח גד ובני. The
elimination of the phrase και του ημισους φυλης μανασση, which
is a plus in comparison with the MT, could easily have occurred
in two independent revisions of the OG. On the other hand,
it would be an extraordinary coincidence if each of two revisors, working independently, failed to place an equivalent
for למזבח (θυσιαστηριον?)[4] after גד ובני *and* handled the
additional ειπεν in the same way (that is, making it plural
rather than eliminating it). This agreement between Th. and
Aq. on all three points is significant. Th., as we saw in
Chapter 1, allowed certain (non-MT) elements from the OG to
slip into his text as he corrected the OG to the MT;
Aquila's *dependence* on Th. would explain the presence of such
elements in the recension of Aquila.

20. (2:12)   OG   εν τω οικω
                Th.-Aq.   μετα του οικου

   (1)

85. (10:41)   OG   πασαν την γην γοσον
                Th.-Aq.   πασαν γην γοσομ

   (1)

133. (16:10)   OG   εν τω εφραιμ
                Th.-Aq.   εν μεσω εφραιμ

   (3) εν μεσω is the characteristic καιγε rendering of
Hebrew בקרב.

21. (2:14) OG καιαυτη ειπεν ως αν παραδοι κυριος υμιν την πολιν ποιησετε εις εμε

Th.-Aq. και εσται <u>ως αν παραδω</u> κυριος ημιν <u>την πολιν</u> <u>ποιησωμεν</u> μετα σου

(1) Here Th.-Aq. have OG την πολιν (MT: הארץ; cf. την γην in kx$\not{g}^{m}$[mg]). Although it may be mere coincidence that both Th. and Aq. contain this element, is it not more than chance agreement that both use identical constructions to render the MT (e.g., ως αν παραδω, cf. Br here and Aq. at 6:5; ποιησωμεν, cf. cz [mg]) *and* lack precise representations for the MT in the same places (την πολιν, see above; neither Th. nor Aq. has an equivalent for ו before עשינו, cf. και in c)?

28. (3:14) OG και απηρεν ο λαος

Th.-Aq. <u>και εγενετο</u> ως απηρεν ο λαος

(1) The use of και εγενετο ως to represent the Hebrew construction ויהי ב + infinitive is an important feature of this joint reading; in other places Aq. employed an alternate construction, one that reproduced the preposition of the Hebrew.[5] This agreement between Aq. and Th. may well be the result of Aquila's dependence on Th., a dependence to which other readings in this listing also point. Convincing evidence that this is the nature of the Th.-Aq. relationship, however, can be found only in places where there is significant partial agreement between the two.[6]

31. (3:16) OG εως μερους καριαθαιν

Th.-Aq. <u>μερους</u> σαρθαμ

(1) Many commentators state that OG μερους reflects the presence of קצה in its Hebrew *Vorlage*. Th., in his correction of the OG to the MT, retained μερους, which for him represented MT צד. The appearance of this same comparatively rare rendering of צד in Aq. may be another

indication of his reliance on Th.; here Aq. either saw no
reason to include in his text a more precise translation for
Hebrew צד or neglected to do so.[7]

34. (4:5)   OG   εμπροσθεν μου προ προσωπου
                      κυριου

             Th.-Aq.   εις προσωπον
                      κιβωτου κυριου

    (1) (3)

139. (18:28) OG   και γαβααθ και πολις ιαρειμ
                      πολεις

             Th.-Aq.   καριαθ πολεις

    (1) (3)

161. (23:4[b]) OG   εθνη εξωλεθρευσα
             Th.-Aq. εθνη α εξωλοθρευσα

    (1) Note the reference to Thackeray ¶ 6, 27 (1).

145. (21:26) OG   πασαι πολεις
             Th.-Aq. πασαι αι πολεις

    (1) The MT reads כל ערים here.

13. (2:1)   OG   _____
             Th.-Aq. κρυβη

    (3) חֶרֶשׁ is a *hapax legomenon*.

27. (3:13)   OG   _____
             Th.-Aq. σωρος εις

    (1) σωρος does not translate נד elsewhere. Cf. OG
πηγμα εν for נד אחד at 3:16; also ασκωμα εν, attributed to
Sym. in both verses.

112. (13:26) OG.   εως των οριων δεβωρ
             Th.-Aq.   δεβειρ

    (1) In the MT the name is לִדְבִר.

12. (1:18)   OG   αλλα
                     Th.-Aq.   πλην

(3) The רק = πλην equivalence appears to be characteristic of the καιγε recension in Joshua.

29. (3:15[a])   OG   επι (τον ιορδαηνη)
                     Th.-Aq.   εις

(1) Cf. Th. and Aq. at 3:8 (no. 24), discussed under
category 2 in chapter 1.

35. (4:10[a])   OG   εν τω ιορδανη
                     Th.-Aq.   εμμεσω

(3) εν μεσω is the characteristic καιγε rendering of
Hebrew בתוך.

46. (6:24[a])   OG   ενεπρησθη ενπυρισμω
                     Th.-Aq.   ενεπυρισθη εν πυρι
     (1)

52. (7:21[b])   OG   και ενθυμηθεις
                     Th.-Aq.   και επεθυμησα
     (1)

91. (11:10)   OG   απεστραφη
                     Th.-Aq.   επεστρεψεν

(3) επιστρεφω is the characteristic καιγε translation
of שוב (qal).

102. (12:7)   OG   εις σηειρ
                     Th.-Aq.   (εις) σεειρα
      (1)

108. (13:13)   OG   (τον) μαχατει (1°)
                     Th.-Aq.   μαχαθι
      (1)

125. (15:17)   OG   αδελφου

                     Th.-Aq.   αδελφος

    (1) Sym. has the genitive, as in the OG.

137. (18:8)   OG   χωροβατησαι

                     Th.-Aq.   διαγραψαι

    (1)

150. (22:5[a])   OG   και προσκεισθαι

                     Th.-Aq.   και κολλασθαι

    (1)

151. (22:5[b])   OG   της διανοιας υμων

                     Th.-Aq.   καρδιας

    (1)

153. (22:10[a])   OG   βωμον (1°)

                     Th.-Aq.   θυσιαστηριον

    (1) (3) This is but one example of the systematic use of θυσιαστηριον to translate מזבח in chapter 22 of Joshua.

166. (24:15)   OG   ελεσθε

                     Th.-Aq.   εκλεξασθε

    (1)

169. (24:26[b])   OG   υπο την τερεμινθον

                     Th.-Aq.   υποκατω της δρυος

    (1)

88. (11:1[c])   OG   συμοων

                     Th.-Aq.   συμερων

    (1) Cf. σομορων, the reading of the Lucianic recension, and σομερων, found in manuscripts of the P̲ and C̲ recensions. συμερων is a correction of OG συμοων to MT שִׁמְרוֹן, and as such this form "could easily have arisen in the course of independent revision of the OG toward the MT."[8] When, however, one considers what appears to be the widespread accomodation to

שֹׁמְרוֹן (as in the forms beginning σομ- listed above), the agreement between Th. and Aq. here takes on more importance.

120. (15:3)   OG   σεννα
                      Th.-Aq.   σ(ε)ινα

(1) See remarks at 88 above. Inasmuch as -νν- appears in the underlying forms for the readings of the E, C, and S recensions, it is of some significance that the form present in the text of Th. and Aq. shows only a single -ν-, as in MT צֶנָה.

122. (15:6[b])   OG   βαιων
                      Th.-Aq.   βοεν

(1) See remarks at 88 above. Cf. the reading of Sym., βοον, which also represents בֹּהֶן, the vocalization preserved in the MT.

130. (15:25[15:24]) OG   και αι κωμαι αυτης
                      Th.-Aq.   και ασωρ την καινην

(1) (3) In this correction toward the Hebrew preserved in the MT, חדתה has been interpreted as a form of the adjective "new." It is doubtful that 2 revisors, working independently, would have arrived at the same interpretation of the Hebrew (cf. x: και ασωρ και αδαθα). Is it not more likely that a later revisor (Aq.?) retained the interpretation he found in the text (that of Th.?) he used as the basis (for Sym., who also has this reading, we would say *a* basis) for his own further activity?

142. (21:3)   OG.   εν τω κατακληρονομειν
                      Aq.-Th.   εκ της κληρονομιας αυτων

(1) See remarks at 88 above. This is the only reading preserved in which a clear translation of the Hebrew preposition מן appears. The use of κληρονομια here is not unexpected; however, we can point to at least one passage (18:4) where Aquila employed a different Greek word to render Hebrew נחלה.[9]

242

149.   (22:1)   OG   (τους) υιους ρουβην
                        Th.-Aq.   ρουβηνιτας

   (1) The form used here by Th.-Aq. does not appear
elsewhere. The OG translator of Joshua used ρουβην alone to
represent ראובני in 3 passages.

Finally we turn to the 2 readings from category 2 mentioned
in the introduction to this section:

15.   (2:4[a])   OG-Th.-Aq. εκρυψεν αυτους και ειπεν
                                   αυτοις
94.   (11:21[a])   OG-Th.-Aq. ανωβ
In neither case is this reading an exact rendering of the
Hebrew (no. 15) or the vocalization (no. 94) preserved in the
MT (see chapter 1 for both). Aquila's dependence on Th. would
explain the presence of such non-MT forms in Aquila's recension, although here we cannot exclude the possibility that
it is the OG Aquila failed to correct. Other examples
reviewed thus far, and especially the material we present in
the next section, make the former explanation far more likely
than the latter. At least we can say that nos. 15 and 94 do
not constitute evidence that Aquila knew the OG independently
of Th.

   Taken together, these 38 examples leave no doubt that a
"genuine relationship" exists between Th. and Aq. in Joshua.
A number of these readings show that this affinity is
independent of the OG. Furthermore, many of the readings
exhibit remarkable agreements, all of which surely did not
arise through completely independent textual revisions.
   Relying on the more detailed presentations of chapters 1
and 3, we were repeatedly led to suggest that Th. was the
source from which Aq. drew the wording of his text where there
was complete agreement between the two. In other words, the
evidence pointed to Aquila's dependence on Th. Points of
complete agreement are not, however, sufficient in and of

themselves to prove that this is the relationship between
Th. and Aq. or that we have correctly charted the *direction*
of dependence. This is true even though a number of these
readings fit well into our understanding that Th. sought to
remain close to the OG and retain OG elements, sometimes at
the cost of failing to make fuller corrections to the MT of
the type that characterize the recension of Aq.

In order to present convincing evidence that (1) Th. is
closer to the OG than Aq. in those places where we can
compare and that (2) "Aquila based his version on the Greek
text produced by Theodotion rather than on the OG directly,"[10]
we turn to the places where Th. and Aq. are in partial agreement. Of the 32 readings listed in this section (II) in the
chart above, approximately one half (14) are of particular
significance in this regard. It is especially through these
that we attempt to demonstrate Aquila's dependence on the
text attributed to Th. Such a relationship can be more
easily viewed when Th. is closer to the OG, although one is
also able to speak of dependence when neither Aq. nor Th.
is closer to the OG (as, for example, when they have simple
expansions of the OG). Only at 2:6 (no. 17) is there
evidence recorded contrary to the pattern formed by the other
examples in section II.[11]

The 14 readings to which reference was made above are
(listed in the order in which they appear in the preceding
charts) 42, 59, 70, 9, 43, 54, 74, 64, 128, 134, 17, 160, 93,
152. When we subtract the 5 readings from sub-category 1.2
(where Th.=OG=MT) that appear in section II, it is clear that
more than one half (14 out of 27) of the potentially significant partial agreements are relevant to the topic under
consideration here. In the presentation of evidence from
readings that exhibit partial agreement between Th. and Aq.,
we follow the procedure utilized above for examples of
complete agreement between the two.

42. (5:2)   OG   μαχαιρας εκ πετρας ακροτομου
                            και <u>καθισας</u> περιτεμε
                  Th.   μαχαιρας <u>πετρινας</u> ακροτομους
                            και <u>καθισας</u> περιτεμε
                  Aq.   μαχαιρας <u>πετρινας</u> και
                            <u>επιστρεψας</u> περιτεμε

(1) (3) In Chapter 1 we discuss in some detail the
relationship between Th. and the OG, on the one hand, and
between Th. and Aq., on the other hand. A reading such as
this is significant, as O'Connell states, because "Theodotion's
agreements with the OG against Aquila [here, καθισας] show
that he knew the OG independently of Aquila [while] his
agreements with Aquila against the OG [here, πετρινας] show
that Aquila knew the OG through Theodotion rather than
directly."[12]

59. (9:5[9:11]) OG   και <u>ο αρτος αυτων</u> του
                            επισιτισμου ξηρος <u>και</u>
                            <u>ευρωτιων</u>
                  Th.   και <u>οι αρτοι αυτων ο</u>
                            <u>επισιτισμος</u> αυτων ξηρος
                            <u>και βεβρωμενος</u>
                  Aq.   και πας ο αρτος <u>ο επισιτισμος</u>
                            αυτων ξηρος εγενηθη <u>και</u>
                            <u>εψαθυρωμενος</u>

(1)   Th. retained at least four non-MT features found in
the OG: no translation for כל, αυτων in inverted order, και
rather than a translation for Hebrew היה, the last element in
the singular. The reading of Aq. is a correction *toward* the
MT, which at first glance looks like a revision of either Th.
or the OG; however, the appearance of the expression
ο επισιτισμος (in the nominative in an appositional construction) in Aq. and Th. strongly suggests that Aquila had
before him the text of Th. and not that of the OG. His
reliance on Th. may have led him to include several non-MT
features even as he strove to correct or eliminate others.[13]

70. (10:11[b])   OG   λιθους χαλαζης

                 Th.   λιθους χαλαζης

                 Aq.   λιθους μεγαλους χαλαζης

(1) Since Th.=OG here, no. 70 cannot serve as primary evidence. If, however, Aquila's dependence on Th. is demonstrated on the basis of other readings, then we can include this as another example of Aquila's occasional failure to correct fully the text of Th. as he carried out his further revision to the MT.

9. (1:8)   OG   ινα ειδης ποιειν παντα τα

                        γεγραμμενα

                 Th.   ινα φυλασσης ποιειν παντα

                        τα γεγραμμενα

                 Aq.   οπως φυλασσης του ποιειν

                        κατα παν το γεγραμμενον

(1) See our remarks at 42 above and also the discussion in chapter 1. φυλασσω is such a common translation of שמר that it may not be significant (i.e., indicative of Aquila's dependence on Th.) that this Greek verb appears in both Th. and Aq. Nevertheless, Th. does occupy an "intermediary position between the OG and Aquila."[14]

43. (5:12)   OG   εκαρπισαντο δε την χωραν

                        των φοιωικων

                 Th.   και εφαγον απο των καρπων

                        της γης χανααν

                 Aq.   και εφαγον απο γενηματος

                        της γης χανααν

(1) Th.'s use of καρπων links him with the OG (εκαρπισαντο).[15] While the appearance of εφαγον, απο, and της γης χανααν in both Th. and Aq. is not unexpected (they are standard Greek translations for the Hebrew words involved), Th. does occupy the "intermediary position" of which we spoke above at no. 9. Further revision on the part of Aq. is visible in the use of απο γενηματος, rather than απο των καρπων of Th., to render more precisely Hebrew מתבואת.

54. (7:26)   OG   εμεκαχωρ

                    Th.   κοιλας αχωρ

                    Aq.   κοιλας ταραχου

(1) (3) Th. retained the transliteration of עכור found
in the OG, but provided a translation for עמק. Aq. retained
that translation (cf. OG φαραγγα αχωρ at 7:24), but replaced
the transliteration (αχωρ) that Th. carried over from the OG
with a translation of עכור.[16]

74. (10:19)   OG   υμεις δε μη εστηκατε

                            καταδιωκοντες οπισω

                    Th.   υμεις δε μη στηκετε

                            καταδιωκοντες οπισω

                    Aq.   και υμεις μη στηκετε

                            διωξατε οπισω

(1) (3) This is a clear example of the "intermediary
position" between the OG and Aq. that Th. so often occupies.
Th. included in his text καταδιωκοντες, the "free" OG
representation of the Hebrew imperative. This agreement with
the OG against Aquila shows that Th. knew the OG independently
of Aquila. The appearance of the rare form στηκετε in both
Th. and Aq. is significant in showing that Aquila knew the
OG through Theodotion rather than directly. Aquila's use of
διωξατε eliminated what must have struck him as intolerable
freedom on the part of Th. and introduced into this passage
the characteristic καιγε rendering of רדף (which Th. had
failed to do).

64. (10:5[a])   OG   βασιλεις των ιεβουσαιων

                    Th.   των αμορραιων

                    Aq.   βασιλεις του αμορραιου[17]

(1) In chapter 1 we pointed out that Th.'s retention
of the plural in his correction was in accord with the practice
of the OG translator of Joshua, who regularly used the plural
to translate proper names in the singular (here he read
היבוסי) in expressions such as "king of . . . ." The

rendering in Aq. is a more precise correction in this regard. Thus we can say that Th. occupies "a position midway between the OG and Aquila,"[18] although in this case it cannot be demonstrated that Aquila was dependent on Th. (since Aq. would have corrected either των αμορραιων or των ιεβουσαιων to του αμορραιου).

128. (15:21)   OG   πολεις αυτων πολεις προς τη
                        φυλη
                        πολεις αυτων απο τελους
                        θυλης
                        αι πολεις απο τελευταιου
                        της θυλης

    (1) Th. retained OG πολεις αυτων (cf. Aq. αι πολεις;
MT הערים), but he did eliminate the double representation
(see chapter 1) found in the OG and provide a more literal
rendering of מקצה ל than that employed by the OG translator.
The appearance of της θυλης in Aq. points to his direct
knowledge of the text of Th., the original of which may also
have contained της (for the construction cf. the MT and the
readings of the OG and Sym.). It is less clear that Aquila's
use of τελευταιον also reflects a knowledge of Th.'s text,
for Aq. generally employed this Greek word as the equivalent
of קצה and probably would have done so here regardless of
what he found in Th.'s text.[19] Be that as it may, no. 128 does
provide further evidence that Th. is closer to the OG than is
Aq. and that Th. had independent knowledge of the OG.

134. (17:2)   OG   και τοις υιοις συχεμ και
                       τοις υιοις συμαρε και τοις
                       υιοις ε/ο-φερ
                Th.   σεχεμ και
                       τοις υιοις οφερ και
                Aq.   σεχεμ και
                       τοις υιοις εφερ και τοις
                       υιοις σεμιδαε (ουτοι κατα
                       δημους αυτων)

(1)　The proper names are restored to their MT order
in both Th. and Aq.　One would expect any revisor of the OG
to the MT to make such a correction.　The form of the proper
names in the readings of Th. and Aq., where they overlap,
may prove of more significance.　If οφερ, rather than εφερ,
did appear in the OG (see chapter 1), then Th.'s retention of
this form would be another indication of his tendency to
remain close to the OG even as he revised it toward the MT.
εφερ, the reading of Aq., is then Aquila's correction of Th.'s
text to the vocalization preserved by the Masoretes.　Aq.
could equally well have made such a change on the basis of
the same reading (οφερ) in the OG; however, the fact that Th.
and Aq. share the form σεχεμ,[20] against OG συχεμ, leads us to
conclude that here, as elsewhere, Aquila made use of Th.'s
recension, which retained certain OG forms, as the basis for
his own further corrections.

160.　(23:4[a])　　OG　　　επερ(ρ)ιφα
　　　　　　　　　　　Th.　　　(υπ)εβαλα[21]
　　　　　　　　　　　Aq.　　　υπεβαλον

(1)　In our opinion εβαλα probably appeared in the text
of Th. here.　This use of the verb βαλλω would be in keeping
with Th.'s practice of extending to various passages the usual
Greek representation of a Hebrew word or phrase (here the
causative of נפל, with the specialized meaning "assign,
apportion, by lot").[22]　The reading of Aq., with the verb
υποβαλλω, can be seen as another indication of Aquila's
knowledge of and dependence on the text of Th., although it
is unclear why he substituted the rare verb υποβαλλω for
what appears to be a perfectly acceptabe rendering with βαλλω.
In any case there is nothing to suggest that Aquila knew the
OG independently of Th.

93.　(11:19)　　OG　　　ην ουκ ελαβεν ισραηλ
　　　　　　　　　Th.　　　ητις ου παρεδωκεν τοις υιοις
　　　　　　　　　　　　　　ισραηλ
　　　　　　　　　Aq.　　　η ου παρεδοθη τοις υιοις
　　　　　　　　　　　　　　ισραηλ

(1) The use of ου παραδιδωμι in both Th. and Aq. makes it clear that these two readings are related. Can we determine the nature of that relationship in this instance? Possibly. Since both contain OG ου(κ), add τοις υιοις to correspond to Hebrew אל ב גי, and employ the same non-OG verb (παραδιδωμι), we listed no. 93 under II. C "Neither Aquila nor Th. appears closer to the OG than the other does." If, however, we also bring in several of the other readings discussed in this section, it becomes possible to see in Th.'s ου another example of his retention of an OG element, an element that in this case was also retained when Aq. made his further changes (most notably, παρεδωκεν > παρεδοθη).[23]

152. (22:8)   OG   απηλθοσαν
                     Th.   επιστρεφετε
                     Aq.   επιστραφητε

(1) (3) The verb επιστρεφω, which occurs only in the readings of Th. and Aq. at this point, is the characteristic καιγε rendering of Hebrew שוב (qal). The appearance of a form of επιστρεφω in the texts of both is significant in showing that a relationship between Th. and Aq. does exist; however, there seems to be no way of determining the nature of the relationship in this case. Through his use of επιστραφητε Aq. perhaps aimed at a more precise representation of the underlying Hebrew than he felt Th. had achieved with the form επιστρεφετε.

The 13 examples we present above, when added to the 38 readings in the previous section, leave no doubt that a "genuine relationship" exists between Th. and Aq. A number of the readings here point to the nature of that relationship: Aq. was *dependent* on the text of Th., which he used as the basis for his further revisions. Two factors made such dependence probable: (1) Th. occupies a position midway between the OG and Aq. This can be seen not only in readings presented here, but in the many other places where Th. is closer to the OG than Aq. is.[24] This "midway" position cannot always be demonstrated, but thus far no evidence contrary to this understanding has emerged. (2) Aquila does not seem to have any *independent* knowledge of the OG; no clear, significant examples of the formula Aq.=OG≠Th. are present in the material we have presented. On the other hand, we have established Th.'s independent knowledge of the OG (where Th.=OG≠Aq.). The close relationship between the OG and Th. is all the more apparent because of Th.'s practice of retaining features of the OG in his revision. The exact nature of the Th.-Aq. relationship (bringing in both Th.'s intermediary position and Aquila's dependence on Th.) is most often visible when Th. retains (non-MT) features of the OG which (features) Aq. corrects and corrects (non-MT) features of the OG which (corrections) Aq. retains. Less frequently, Aq. retains (non-MT) features that he found in Th.'s text. Aquila's dependence on Th. is also the best explanation for joint α'θ' readings that exhibit a genuine affinity independent of the OG. This is especially so in those places where the joint reading contains non-MT features, features that in a few cases do not appear in the OG.

Of the 129 readings where a partial or complete equivalent is preserved from Aq., only 2 present evidence at variance with the conclusions we outlined above. One of these is no. 17 (under II. B) and the other is no. 79 (under III. B). We discuss no. 79 first:

79. (10:28)   OG   εν στοματι <u>μαχαιρας</u>

                 Th.   <u>ξιφους</u>

                 Aq.   <u>μαχαιρας</u>

(3) Th. replaced the OG translation of חרב with ξιφος, which we suggest in chapter 3 (under no. 50) is characteristic of the Th.-καιγε recension, as is also the rendering ρομφαια. In many cases Aq. retained Th.'s replacement in his text, in others he modified Th.'s choice of equivalents, while in still others he substituted his own rendering for that

selected by Th. In Exodus, as O'Connell points out, Aq. (and
Sym.) used μαχαιρα to translate חרב, rather than ρομφαια as
in Th.[25] In other words, we have reason to suspect that
Aq. would employ the חרב = μαχαιρα equivalence no matter what
he found in his Greek text.[26] Although in this case it
happens that Aquila's choice of equivalents agrees with the
OG and not Th., there is nothing to suggest that this
anomalous situation, Aq.=OG≠Th., is the result of anything
other than coincidence.[27] We would term the evidence here,
as in so many other places, "neutral"; no. 79 does not point
to Aq.'s independent knowledge of the OG.

17. (2:6)   OG   (αυτους εν) τη λινοκαλαμη
                                  τη εστοιβασμενη
                     Th.   τοις ξυλοις
                                  της λινοκαλαμης της εστοι-
                                  βασμενης
                     Aq. (also (αυτους εν) τη λινοκαλαμη
                     Sym. and o´)

     (1) Both the OG and Th. reflect a Hebrew identical to
the MT.[28] The evidence recorded seems to show that Aquila
knew the OG of this passage independently of Th. If such
direct knowledge on the part of Aq. can be demonstrated in
even this one case, then we must revise our formulation and
speak of Th. as merely one basis for Aquila's revision, with
the OG being another. In our presentation of material
we have used the stronger examples of Aquila's dependence on
Th. to interpret the evidence in those places where the nature
of their relationship is less clear; the lack of Aquila's
independent knowledge of the OG offered a marked contrast to
Th.'s obvious dependence on and knowledge of the OG. What
alternate explanations are there at no. 17 and how probable
do they seem? (1) Least probable is that Aquila's choice of
wording here just happened to agree with the OG (as in no. 79
above), which in this instance is a *hapax legomenon*. If Aq.
had before him the text of Th., why would he eliminate the
element that corresponded to Hebrew העץ (τοις ξυλοις) and

permit τη λινοκαλαμη alone to "answer to" the Hebrew of the
MT? He would most likely have reversed the elements in Th.
(see discussion in chapter 1 and also below) and modified
them to represent more literally the phrase in the MT.
(2) Far more likely is it that there is a mistake in the
attribution of readings. Perhaps, the inclusion of α'
along with σ' and ο' is an error, in which case we simply
do not know the reading of Aq. here. Or is it possible that
we should reverse θ' and α' in the ascriptions, so that Th.
then agrees with the OG? The attribution of τοις ξυλοις. . .
to Aq. constitutes a serious objection to the latter solution,
for even this wording represents translation *ad sensum*, which
does not characterize the revision of Aq. A far more
attractive solution is to reverse θ' and σ', so that Th.
retained the OG (as above) and it was Sym. who introduced
a translation *ad sensum* fully in keeping with his procedure
elsewhere.[29] (3) There is another explanation, one that
leaves all ascriptions intact. The reading attributed to
θ' in our sources may be the result of a "secondary revision
of the Theodotionic material in" Joshua "independently of or
after Aquila."[30] This explanation allows us to reconstruct
an 'original' text of Th. that read τη λινοκαλαμη with the
OG.[31] Aquila, perhaps struck by this wording, retained the
construction he found in Th. A later revisor (Theodotion of
Ephesus?) would then have been responsible for the effort
toward the more literal representation now attributed to θ'.
If similar activity took place in Exodus, O'Connell concluded,
such "secondary revision was neither extensive nor significant."[32] If such activity did take place in Joshua, we must
conclude, this is the only evidence of it we have discerned.

Aware of the dangers of attempting to explain away any
contrary evidence through solutions that are *ad hoc* or
overly ingenious, we point out that the ideas of "secondary
revision" and mistaken attribution have not been developed
solely to account for this one example and that there is
nothing improbable about several of the alternate explanations

offered. It is most likely that the 'original' text of Th.
at this point contained wording identical to the OG. We are
not sure whether Aquila retained that wording, altered it to
τοις ξυλοις. . . , or modified it in some other way that has
not been preserved. Through this discussion we feel that we
have established reasonable doubt that the readings and
attributions as preserved in v(txt) and (mg) represent the
original texts of Th., Aq., and Sym. The unclear and
ambiguous nature of the evidence at no. 17 prohibits any
attempt to use it as proof that Aquila had independent
knowledge of the OG.

The evidence presented in this section demonstrates,
we believe, that in the book of Joshua (1) a genuine relationship exists between Th. and Aq. that is independent of
the OG, and (2) Aquila used Th. as *the* basis for his further
revision and did not know the OG independently of Th.
Our evidence, taken by itself, may in some respects be only
"limited but adequate" (see above); nevertheless, the combined
evidence from Exodus and Joshua does seem less limited and
more than adequate to make the statements we have.

Symmachus

In 65 out of 120 places where Sym. has a complete or partial equivalent for the reading of Th. there is complete agreement between the two. Although the percentage of complete agreements is smaller in this case than was true for Th. and Aq. (82 out of 129), it is nevertheless large enough to suggest that a "genuine relationship" also existed between Th. and Sym. As we indicated in the discussion of Aq., certain of these agreements are not directly relevant in the present context. For the reasons given in that discussion we substract the 19 Th.-Sym. agreements that occur in category 1 (19: 12 [1.1]+ 7 [1.2]). This leaves us with 49 potentially significant examples of complete agreement between Th. and Sym. Of these 49, 25 are particularly valuable for the topic under consideration. In 18 of these cases there is complete agreement not only between Th. and Sym., but also between Th. and Aq. These joint α'σ'ϑ' citations, all of which we dealt with in the first part of this chapter, are 75, 159, 85, 133, 31, 34, 145, 46, 91, 102, 137, 151, 153, 88, 130, 149, 15, 94.[33] Since both Aq. and Sym. show direct, independent knowledge of Th. through their complete agreements with him where the text of the other contains a different reading, we interpret these joint agreements with Th. as the result of this same direct knowledge on the part of each and not the result of their mutual dependence to the exclusion of Th.. The 7 additional cases of significant Th.-Sym. complete agreement are 90, 53, 54, 157, 134, 115, 5.

90. (11:8[b])   OG   μασεφα
         Th.-Sym.   μασφα
     (1) Since no. 90 is included under category 2, it cannot be used as primary evidence to establish a Th.-Sym. relationship independent of the OG. A direct knowledge of Th's text on the part of Sym. could, however, account for the appearance of this same non-MT vocalization in Symmachus' revision (cf. MT מִצְפֶּה).

53. (7:24)   OG   εις <u>εμεκαχωρ</u>

                 Th.-Sym.   <u>κοιλαδα αχωρ</u>

    (1) (3)

54. (7:25)   OG   <u>εμεκαχωρ</u>

                 Th.-Sym. <u>κοιλας αχωρ</u>

    (1) (3) In both examples Th. and Sym. handled the expression עמק עכור in the same way: a translation for עמק (cf. OG φαραγγα αχωρ earlier in v 24) and a transliteration for עכור.[34] This procedure seems more in line with the practice of Th. than of Sym., who generally provided a translation (sometimes no more than a translation guess) for every element in a proper name.[35] In our opinion this makes the complete agreement between Th. and Sym. in these two verses all the more significant and suggests that, for whatever reason, Sym. was content to retain the procedure employed by Th.

157. (22:25)   OG   _____

                 Th.-Sym. <u>ανα μεσον ημων και υμων</u>

                          <u>(οι) υιοι ρουβην και (οι)</u>

                          <u>υιοι γαδ τον ιορδανην</u>

    (1) (3) Cf. Aq. and manuscripts of the <u>N</u>-group; we discuss these and other readings in chapter 1.

134. (17:2)   OG   και τοις υιοις <u>συχεμ</u> και τοις

                          υιοις συμαρε και τοις υιοις

                          ε/ο-φερ

                 Th.-Sym.   <u>σεχεμ</u> και

                          τοις υιοις <u>οφερ</u> και

    (1) It is possible to explain this complete agreement, including the form σεχεμ, as the result of independent revision of the OG toward the MT *and* independent retention of an OG form (οφερ) that prompted correction in Aq. and elsewhere.[36] Is it not more likely, however, that we are correct to view this agreement in all particulars as further evidence of a genuine relationship between Th. and Sym.?

115. (14:6)   OG   εν γαλγαλ

        Th.-Sym.   εν γαλγαλοις

(1) The change from γαλγαλ to γαλγαλοις, which extends
to this passage the usual representations of גלגל in the
OG translation of Joshua, is in keeping with the practice of
Th. Thus it is probable that the appearance of the form
γαλγαλοις in the recension of Symmachus is the result of his
knowledge of Th.'s text.

5. (1:5)   OG   ουκ αντιστησεται ανθρωπος
                      κατενωπιον υμων

        Th.-Sym.   ουθεις

                      κατα προσωπον σου

(1) (3) The most significant feature of this agreement
is the appearance of ουθεις in the text of Th. and Sym. It is
Th. who is responsible for the introduction of ουθεις, a form
that extends to 1:5 the usual representation of this construction in the OG of Joshua (see chapter 3 and our remarks
at 115 above). In at least one other passage in Joshua
Sym. wrote ουθεις (21:42[44]: cf. OG ουθεις and Aq. ανηρ)
where איש again occurred in the indefinite sense. Both
ουθεις and κατα προσωπον are indicative of the genuine
relationship that exists between Th. and Sym. ουθεις has
further significance, for it points to the nature of this
relationship -- Symmachus' dependence on the revision of Th.

If we combine these 7 examples with the 18 examples
discussed earlier in this chapter, there can be no doubt that
there is a genuine affinity between Th. and Sym. independent
of the OG. That Sym. knew and used the text of Th. also
seems beyond doubt. The relatively smaller percentage of
such complete agreements between Th. and Sym., as compared to
Th. and Aq., suggests that Symmachus either altered the text
of Th. quite often (because many of his concerns were
different from those of Th.?) and/or that Th. was but one
basis for his recension.

Further substantiation for the statement that Sym. knew
and used Th. is provided by readings in which Th. and Sym.
are in partial agreement. From these readings it becomes clear
that Th. was a basis for the further activity of Symmachus.
There is, moreover, adequate evidence to demonstrate that
Sym. had independent knowledge of the OG. It is this latter
evidence that points to the fundamental difference between
the Th.-Aq. and Th.-Sym. relationships: in the case of
Symmachus the text of Th. was *a* (not unimportant) basis for
further revision; for Aq., it was *the* basis.

We turn now to the 35 readings which show partial
agreement between Symmachus and Theodotion.[37] There are 8
readings in this section that contain complete agreements
between Sym. and Aq. and 27 that do not. When we subtract
the 6 readings from sub-category 1.2 (see above) so as to
arrive at the number of potentially significant readings, the
statistics are Sym.=Aq. 8 times and Sym.≠Aq. 21 times.
Of the 8 complete agreements between Sym. and Aq., the
following are particularly valuable:[38] 70 (though here
Th.=OG), 43 (Th. occupies a position midway between the OG
and Sym.), 64 (Th. occupies the "intermediary position"), 160
(although we cannot determine with certainty whether Sym.
used the verb βαλλω or υποβαλλω, it is likely that Sym.
knew and used the revision of Th. at this point). As for 17,
we concluded above that "the unclear and ambiguous nature of
the evidence prohibits any attempt to use it as proof that
Aquila had independent knowledge of the OG." The same holds
true for Sym.; this one example cannot *prove* that he had
independent knowledge of the OG, although other evidence may
make such a suggestion very attractive. Moreover, if one of
our alternate explanations is accepted, it was Sym., and not
Th., who introduced the translation *ad sensum* τοις ξυλοις
της λινοκαλαμης της εστοιβασμενης.

A number of readings that contain partial agreements
between Sym. and Aq. begin to reveal both the similarities
and differences between the Th.-Sym. and Th.-Aq. relationships.

We list below the reading of Sym. in each case. We presented
the texts of the OG, Th. and Aq. in the earlier part of this
chapter; the additional discussion here centers on the Sym.-
Th. relationship.

42. (5:2)   Sym.   μαχαιραν εξ ακροτομου και
                                   παλιν περιτεμε

(1) (3) There remains the same agreement of Th. with
the OG (καθισας) against both Sym. and Aq. μαχαιραν is not
found elsewhere; it probably did not form part of Sym.'s
original text, but arose during the transmission of this
reading. There is nothing to suggest that Sym. used the
text of Th. here. Not only does Sym. lack πετρινας found in
Th. (and Aq.), but the appearance of εξ ακροτομου in his text
points to a *direct* acquaintance with the OG (OG: εκ πετρας
ακροτομου).

59. (9:5[9:11])   Sym.   και πας ο αρτος του
                                   επισιτισμου αυτων ξηρος
                                   εγενετο καπυρος

(1) Both the OG and Sym. employ the genitive του
επισιτισμου. This stands in contrast to the appositional
construction in the nominative shared by Th. and Aq.: ο
επισιτισμος. This OG-Sym. agreement strongly suggests
that here Sym., whose knowledge of Th. we have illustrated
through other examples, preferred to follow the OG formulation instead of the revision contained in Th.

9. (1:8)   Sym.   ινα φυλασσης ποιειν κατα
                                   παντα τα γεγραμμενα

(1) φυλασσης, which links the individual readings of
Th., Sym., and Aq., may be indicative of Sym.'s dependence
on Th. More clear is the "intermediary position" that Th.
occupies between the OG and both Sym. and Aq. With its
κατα παντα τα γεγραμμενα, the text of Sym. reflects MT
ככל הכתוב, as does Aq., who wrote κατα παν το γεγραμμενον.

120. (15:3)   Sym.   σιν

(1) This form shows only a single -ν-, as does the reading of Th.-Aq. σ(ε)ινα (MT: הַנָּצ; cf. OG σεννα).

We include the readings listed above, with the exception of nos. 17 and 160, under II. A, "Th. appears closer to the OG. . .than Symmachus does." That formulation remains true even where Sym. reveals direct knowledge of the OG. The next 5 examples come from II. B (where no. 17 is also placed), "Symmachus appears closer to the OG than Th. does." In each of these readings Sym. reproduces an important feature of the OG not found in material attributed ϑ´ or ϑ´α´. From category 3 are the following:

32. (3:17)   OG   διεβαινον
                  Th.   διεβησαν
                  Sym.   διεβαινον

(1)

125. (15:17)   OG   αδελφου
                 Th.-Aq.   αδελφος
                 Sym.   αδελφου

(1) These Sym.-OG agreements may be evidence of Sym.'s retention of the OG or the result of his independent choice of equivalents that just happen to agree with the OG. In view of the previous discussion, the latter explanation is decidedly more attractive.[39]

169. (24:26 b)   OG   υπο την τερεμινϑον
                 Th.-Aq.   υποκατω της δρυος
                 Sym.   υπο δρυν

(1) In our opinion both Sym. and Aq. were dependent on Th. for their use of δρυς in this passage. Aq. also included the equivalent for תחת that precedes δρυς in Th.'s text; Sym., however, preferred to retain the more common υπο that appeared in the OG.[40]

Also under II. B are 2 readings from category 4.3:

28. (3:14)   OG   και απηρεν ο λαος
               Th.-Aq. και εγενετο ως απηρεν ο λαος
               Sym.   ως δε απηρεν ο λαος

(1) Perhaps Sym. (mis)read ובנסע in his Hebrew text
(see v 15: MT וכבוא; OG ως δε εισεπορευοντο). Or he may
have desired to simplify "the unwieldy construction" of this
passage.[41] In any case Sym. did not follow the procedure of
Th., but remained closer to the construction of the OG.

128. (15:21)   Sym.   αι πολεις απ ακρου τη φυλη

(1) The formulation in Sym. shows no trace of dependence
on Th. (cf. Aq.); on the other hand, τη φυλη in Sym. does
suggest his direct knowledge of the OG (where τη φυλη also
appears).

Several other readings listed under II should be brought
into this discussion. They are 93, 27, 122.

93. (11:19)   OG   ην ουκ ελαβεν ισραηλ
               Th.   ητις ου παρεδωκεν τοις υιοις
                       ισραηλ
               Sym.   ητις ειρηνευσε προς τους
                       υιους ισραηλ

(1) There is little to suggest that Sym. made use of
Th. or the OG in his literal translation of the MT (cf. the
reading of Aq. above).

27. (3:13)   OG   _____
               Th.-Aq. σωρος εις
               Sym.   ασκωμα εν

(1) According to Margolis, ασκωμα, also attributed to
Sym. at 3:16, reflects נד instead of MT נב.[42] Did Sym.
reject the wording of Th. in favor of his own interpretation?

122.   (15:6[b])   OG   βαιων
                        Th.-Aq.   βοεν
                        Sym.   βοον

(1)   See the discussion of this reading earlier in the chapter.

Finally, we turn to the 2 readings under III. B: 79 and 166. No. 79 (10:28) does not prove that Aq. knew the OG independently of Th. The same conclusion may be reached for Sym. also, for in Exodus μαχαιρα is the translation of חרב in both Aq. and Sym.[43] Since, however, we have been able to demonstrate Sym.'s direct knowledge of the OG in other passages, retention of the OG by Sym. cannot be ruled out here.

No. 166 presents much clearer evidence of Sym.'s direct knowledge of the OG, independent of Th.:

166.   (24:15)   OG   ελεσθε
                        Th.-Aq.   εκλεξασθε
                        Sym.   ελεσθε

(1)

The evidence presented in this section is, in our opinion, "adequate" to establish that in Joshua (1) there is a genuine relationship between Th. and Sym. independent of the OG; (2) Symmachus used Th. as a basis for his further work, and also knew and used the OG independently of Th. (for this latter point see especially nos. 42, 59, 32, 125, 169, 28, 128, 166 above). At times this direct knowledge of the OG led Sym. to retain elements not carried over by Th. into his text. On other occasions this direct knowledge led to revisions and interpretations different from those found in Th. and often included in Aq.

It is now clear that "ϑ" was prior to α' and σ', and known and used by both. The degree to which Th. served as a basis for the work of Sym. is difficult to determine. Weaker examples of Aquila's dependence on Th. were strengthened by our ability to show that Aq. did not know the OG independently of Th. In the case of Sym., who knew Th. and the OG (and perhaps other sources as well), no general rule can apply in doubtful cases, such as when Th. is in complete or partial agreement with the OG. Further refinements of methodology will allow us to unravel in more detail the complex relationships between Sym. and his predecessors, including Th.

Note: It is interesting to compare our conclusions in this chapter with those reached by Barthélemy. We can discern the thrust of Barthélemy's discussion concerning the Th.-Aq. relationship in the titles he gave to the second and third subdivisionsof chapter VIII: "Aquila ignore la Septante non recensée" and "Intimité de la dépendance qui lie Aquila à 'R.'" In his remarks concerning Symmachus Barthélemy leaves no room for doubt that Symmachus knew "R" and the Hebrew. On two other points, however, the very titles of his subdivisions (in chapter X) indicate the tentative nature of Barthélemy's conclusions: "Symmaque semble ignorer la Septante non recensée" and "Symmaque semble ignorer Aquila."

Notes to Chapter 2

1. O'Connell, pp. 201-273.

2. O'Connell, p. 292.

3. O'Connell, p. 250. Three category 2 readings -- nos. 75, 159, and 112 -- also provide examples of significant agreement between Th. and Aq.

4. See under no. 28 in chapter 3.

5. For a probable example see the reading at 6:5 discussed under no. 6 in chapter 3: και εσται εν σεισμω (Field, p. 346).

6. That evidence is presented in the next grouping, which contains readings from II in the preceding chart.

7. See the remarks of O'Connell in the first paragraph of his "Evaluation" section on p. 248.

8. O'Connell, p. 249.

9. κληροδοσια; so Field, p. 376 and note 11 on the same page.

10. O'Connell, p. 252.

11. See below.

12. O'Connell, p. 261.

13. Aq. would write αρτος for Hebrew לחם, regardless of what he found in Th. See chapter 1 for the procedure of Th. in this matter.

14. O'Connell, p. 291.

15. See chapter 1.

16. See further no. 94 in chapter 3 on the procedures of Th. and Aq. here.

17. So v(mg); see chapter 1.

18. O'Connell, p. 256.

19. See, for example, 13:27(b) (no. 114).

20. See chapter 1 fn. 430.

21. See chapter 1.

22.   This practice on the part of Th. sometimes led to
equivalents that are now considered characteristic of the
καιγε recension.

23.   In several examples presented in the previous section,
where there was complete agreement between Th. and Aq., Aquila's
dependence on Th. could explain the presence in Aq. of certain
features (among them some we categorized as non-MT) that Th.
had carried over from the OG or an earlier revision (or
corruption) of the OG with which he was working.

24.   This is often true even when there is no significant
agreement between the two. See the 13 readings listed under
III. A.

25.   O'Connell, p. 288.

26.   See also Joshua 5:2; 10:11, and our comments in chapter
3.

27.   Bodine, p. 26, notes that ρομφαια and μαχαιρα are
among the common OG renderings of חרב.

28.   For the procedure of each see chapter 1.

29.   These suggestions do not exhaust the possibilities,
but do point to alternate explanations related to ascriptions.

30.   O'Connell, p. 292.

31.   See also above.

32.   O'Connell, p. 292.

33.   The last two, 15 and 94, are from category 2.

34.   For the reading of Aq. at 7:26, see the first part
of this chapter.

35.   See under no. 94 in chapter 3.

36.   See the discussion above in connection with Aquila's
reading at this point.

37.   These readings are listed under II in the chart
above. There are 32 places where Th. and Aq. are in partial
agreement.

38.   We discuss each earlier in this chapter.

39.   Cf. no. 79 discussed above and referred to below.

40. The absence of the definite article in Sym. may not be original.

41. See Margolis (p. 44), who attempted to interpret the OG in this manner. Note also the reading of Sym. at 6:5 discussed under no. 6 in chapter 3.

42. Margolis, p. 43.

43. O'Connell, p. 288.

The καιγε Recension in Joshua

Below is a list of 96 characteristics identified with the
καιγε recension. For the most part they are listed in the
chronological order in which they were brought into the discussion of this recension.[1] Items marked with an asterisk
(for example, *2) are characteristics that we bring into this
discussion for the first time. In addition, some previously
established characteristics receive "peculiar" treatment in
the καιγε material of the book of Joshua.[2] Our treatment of
such "peculiarities" remains within the framework outlined
above. This listing contains only a brief description of each
characteristic, followed by page references to previous discussions.

Barthélemy, Dominique. *Les Devanciers d'Aquila*. Supplements
    to *Vetus Testamentum*, 10. Leiden: E.J. Brill, 1963.

Smith, Michael (see no. 25 below).

Shenkel, James Donald. *Chronology and Recensional Development
    in the Greek Text of Kings*. Harvard Semitic Monographs,
    1. Cambridge: Harvard University Press, 1968.

Grindel, John A. (see no. 36 below).

O'Connell, Kevin G. *The Theodotionic Revision of the Book of
    Exodus*. Harvard Semitic Monographs, 3. Cambridge:
    Harvard University Press, 1972.[3]

Bodine, Walter Ray. *The Greek Text of Judges: Recensional
    Developments*. Harvard Semitic Monographs, 23. Chico:
    Scholar's Press, 1980.

Tov, Emanuel (see no. 94 below).

1.   רגם/נגם = καιγε (Barthélemy, 31-47; O'Connell, 275;
                 Bodine, 11f)
*2.   רק = πλην
3.   איש = ανηρ (Barthélemy, 48-54; O'Connell, 275-278;
                 Bodine, 12)
4.   מעל = επανωθεν (απανωθεν) (Barthélemy, 54-59;
                 O'Connell, 278; Bodine, 12f)
5.   נצב/יצב = στηλοω (Barthélemy, 59f; O'Connell, 279;
                 Bodine, 13f)
6.   שופר = κεπατινη
         חצצרה = σαλπιγξ (Barthélemy, 60-63; O'Connell,
                              279; Bodine, 14)
7. Elimination of the historical present (Barthélemy, 63-65;
    O'Connell, 280; Bodine, 14)
8.   אין = ουκ εστιν (in a series of aorist verbs)
                 (Barthélemy, 65-68; O'Connell, 280f;
                 Bodine, 14f)
9.   אנכי = εγω ειμι (Barthélemy, 69-78; O'Connell, 281;
                 Bodine, 15f)
10.   לקראת = εις συναντησιν/εις απαντην (Barthélemy,
                 78-80; O'Connell, 281f; Bodine, 16, 74f)
11.   גדוד = μονοζωνος (Barthélemy, 81f)
12. יהוה צבאות = κυριος των δυναμεων (Barthélemy, 82f;
                 O'Connell, 282f)
13.   אל = ισχυρος (Barthélemy, 83)
14.   נגד = forms of εναντι (Barthélemy, 84; Bodine, 16)
15.   לפני = ενωπιον (Barthélemy, 84; Bodine, 16f)
16. על זאת and על כן = δια τουτο (Barthélemy, 84f; Bodine, 17)
17.   לעלם = εις τον αιωνα (Barthélemy, 85; Bodine, 17)
18.   הוי = ουαι (Barthelémy, 85)
19.   אסף = συναγω (Barthélemy, 86; Bodine, 17f)
20.   כמר = χωμαρειμ (Barthélemy, 86)
21.   אפלה = σκοτια
         ערפל = γνοφος (Barthélemy, 86f)
22.   חוץ = εξοδος (Barthélemy, 87)

23. הדר and הדרה = ευπρεπεια (Barthélemy, 87)
24.   מהר = ταχυνω (Barthélemy, 184; Shenkel, 115; Bodine, 18)
25.   הורה = φωτιζω (Smith, Michael. "Another Criterion for the καιγε Recension," *Bibl* 48 [1967], 443-445; Bodine, 19f)
26.   בעיני = εν οφθαλμοις (Shenkel, 13-17; O'Connell, 283f; Bodine, 20f, 70)
*27.   פה = στομα
28.   זבח = θυσιαζω (Shenkel, 17f; O'Connell, 285; Bodine, 21f)
29.   רדף = διωκω (Shenkel, 113; Bodine, 22)
30.   שר (ה)צבא = αρχων (της) δυναμεως (Shenkel, 114; Bodine, 22)
31.   חכם = σοφ- (Shenkel, 114; Bodine, 22f)
32.   חרש = κωφευω
               חשה = σιωπαω (Shenkel, 114f; Bodine, 23)
33.   עון = ανομια (Shenkel, 115)
34.   הרה = εν γαστρι εχω/λαμβανω (Shenkel, 116; Bodine, 23-25)
35.   לא אבה = (ε)θελω (Shenkel, 116; Bodine, 68)
36.   נצח = νικος (Grindel, John A. "Another characteristic of the *Kaige* recension: נצח/νικος," *CBQ* 31 [1969], 499-513)
37. אדם (pual part.) = πεπυρ(ρ)ωμενος (O'Connell, 286)
38.   אהל = *σκεπη (O'Connell, 286)
           משכן = σκηνη
39.   אורים = *φωτισμοι ? (O'Connell, 287)
40.   אליה = κερκιον (O'Connell, 287)
41.   אלם = μογιλαλον (O'Connell, 287)
42.   אשה = πυρ(ρ)ον (O'Connell, 287)
43.   בין = *ανα μεσον (O'Connell, 287; Bodine, 25)
44.   בקרב = *εν μεσω? (O'Connell, 287; Bodine 25f)
*45.   בתוך = εν μεσω

272

46.   במימים = αρωματα (O'Connell, 288)

47.   בחים = ϑηϰαι (O'Connell, 288)

48.   ורים = * ϰοσμοι?(O'Connell, 288)

49. חזק (piel) = ενισχυω (O'Connell, 288; Bodine, 26)

50.   חרב = ρομφαια (O'Connell, 288; Bodine, 26)

51. חשב (noun) = *μη χανωματος or *μηχανηματος (O'Connell, 288)

52.   חשן = λογιον (O'Connell, 288)

53.   חֹתֵן = γαμβρος

       חָתָן = νυμφιος (O'Connell, 288; Bodine, 26f)

54.   ילדים = παιδαρια, παιδια (O'Connell, 289)

55.   ירה = τοξευομαι (O'Connell, 289)

56.   יתרת = περιττον (O'Connell, 289)

57.   כפרים = εξιλασμος (O'Connell, 289)

58.   מעיל = επενδυτης or επιδυτης (O'Connell, 289)

59. משבצ(ו)ת = συνεσφιγμενοι or συνεσφραγισμενοι, *σφιγϰτοι ?
            (O'Connell, 289)

60.   ניחוח = ευαρεστησις (O'Connell, 289)

61.   עבד = δουλ- (O'Connell, 289; Bodine, 27-29)

62.עבה and עבחת = *αλυσιδωτα and/or *αλυσεις, χαλαστα (?)
            (O'Connell, 289)

63. ערף (verb) = νωτοϰοπω (O'Connell, 289)

64.   פרע = διασϰεδαζω or διασωζω (O'Connell, 290)

65.   קרסים = περοναι (O'Connell, 290)

66.   קרש = σανις (O'Connell, 290)

67.   שהם = ονυξ (O'Connell, 290)

68.   שולים = *προς ποδων (O'Connell, 290)

69. שלם (piel) = *αποτιννυω (O'Connell, 290)

70.   שרץ = εξερπω (O'Connell, 290)

71. שרשה/שרשרת = χαλαστα (O'Connell, 290)

72.   תמים = *τελειοτητες ? (O'Connell, 290)

73.   תרומה = *απαρχη (O'Connell, 290)

74.   יען אשר = ανϑ ων οσα (Bodine, 18f)

75.   Misc. = ηνιϰα (Bodine, 19)

76.   אחז = ϰρατεω (Bodine)[4]

77. גלה (and cognates) = αποικιζω (and cognates) (Bodine, 48)
78. טוב (all forms of the root) = αγαθος (and cognates)
                                    (Bodine, 48-52)
79. ישר (all forms of the root) = ευθυς (and cognates)
                                    (Bodine, 52)
80.   לין = αυλιζω (Bodine, 52f)
81.   נצל = ρυομαι (Bodine, 53f) [5]
82. שוב (qal) = επιστρεφω (Bodine, 54-56)
83.   אור = διαφαυσκω (Bodine, 69)
84.   הביא = φερω/εισφερω (Bodine, 69f)
85.   צעק/זעק = βοαω (Bodine, 71)
86.   חרה אף = οργιζομαι θυμω (Bodine, 71f)
87.   נלחם = παρατασσομαι (Bodine, 72f)
88.   מלחמה = παραταξις (Bodine, 73f)
89.   נתץ = καθαιρεω (Bodine, 75)
90.   סרן = αρχων (Bodine, 75f)
91.   פגע = συνανταω/απανταω (Bodine, 76)
92.   קצין = αρχηγος (Bodine, 76)
93.   רעה = πονηρια (Bodine, 76f)
94. The practice of leaving unknown words untranslated (Tov,
    Emanuel. "Transliterations of Hebrew Words in the Greek
    Versions of the Old Testament: A Further Characteristic
    of the *kaige*-Th. Revision?" *Textus* 8. Annual of the
    Hebrew University Bible Project, ed. S. Talmon.
    Jerusalem: Magnes Press, 1973, 78-92)
*95. (איש) גדול = αδρος
*96.   אבל = και μαλα

We discuss below each of these items, except for those in
which the characteristic Hebrew word or a related word from
the same root fails to appear in the book of Joshua. Thus we
eliminate from further mention the following characteristics:
11, 18, 20, 23, 25, 31, 34, 36, 37, 39, 40, 41, 46, 47, 48,
51, 52, 53, 56, 57, 58, 59, 60, 62, 64, 65, 66, 67, 68, 69,
70, 71, 72, 73, 77, 83, 89 (37 in all).[6] We have made every
effort to bring into the discussion all evidence, even material
that would appear to have little or no significance in relation
to the καιγε recension. Only in this way, we feel, is it
possible to determine what texts and/or traditions in Joshua
are to be identified with the καιγε recension, how these
texts are related to each other in Joshua, and how these texts
differ from other witnesses to the recension outside of Joshua.

In Joshua characteristics identified with the καιγε
recension appear most often in the additions of Origen
(generally marked with an asterisk [※] and almost always
anonymous);[7] in other, "qualitative" changes made by Origen;
and in the texts of Th., Aq., Sym. We summarize the results in
charts showing the degree of consistency with which καιγε
characteristics appear in these texts and also a selection of
καιγε readings in other witnesses.

1. וגם/גם = καιγε. This is the eponymous characteristic
of the recension. In the MT of Joshua גם occurs 5 times
(1:15; 2:12; 9:4 [LXX 9:10]; 10:30; 24:18) and וגם 7 times
(2:24; 7:11 [5 times]; 22:7). At 1:15 OG και appears as γε
και in s and καιγε in f (both s and f are manuscripts of the
N-group). At 2:12 OG και occurs everywhere. At 9:4(9:10)
the OG apparently read και γε; και is found in the best
Lucianic manuscripts (gnℒ). Is it possible that these
manuscripts alone have preserved the OG and that και γε in
LXX^B and elsewhere is the result of "καιγε" revision?

The evidence at 10:30 requires a fuller presentation:

יהוה גם אותה   MT
αυτην κυριος   OG
κυριος και αυτην Gabcxℓ (και sub ※ Gℓ), manuscripts of the
P recension.
Even a "καιγε" revisor, primarily concerned with rectifying
the word order, might have failed to introduce the expected
equivalence at this point. OG αλλα και, found in all
recensions at 24:18, is the most common translation for גם
found in Sym. [8]

At 2:24 Hebrew וגם is rendered και in the OG and elsewhere.
At 7:11 וגם is in the MT 5 times; both καιγε and και appear
in asterisked additions:

1° OG και
2° OG omits; καιγε bckqv (mg sub ※) xz(mg)ℤℓ^m(sub ※), [9]
    also gn
3° OG και [10]
4° OG omits; not restored anywhere
5° OG omits; και bcdgknptwxℤℓ^m (sub ※).
At 22:7 OG και is found everywhere except in a reading
attributed to Sym. in ℓ: MT   וגם כי
                         Sym. כד מן הכיל (οτε μεν ουν).[11]

On the basis of this one characteristic there is no firm
evidence for the existence of a καιγε revision for the book
of Joshua. No recension or tradition shows the consistent
use of καιγε to translate Hebrew גם. The lack of a consistent
rendering for גם is, however, no reason to exclude the
possibility of a καιγε revision for Joshua; surely, no one

characteristic can be termed most important or decisive in
every case. It is a matter of chance, for example, that we
have no readings preserved for Th. and Aq. here and that גם
does not occur as often in Joshua as it does in books of
comparable length.

2. רק = πλην.   רק occurs 15 times in the MT of Joshua.[12]
The OG represents Hebrew רק in the following ways:

αλλα   5 times (1:18; 6:18; 11:13; 13:6; 22:5)
πλην   5 times (1:17; 6:17; 24; 8:27; 13:14)
αλλα πλην 1 time (11:22)
ουν   1 time (1:7)
δε   1 time (11:14)
και   1 time (8:2)

At 6:15 the OG has no translation for רק and the following
words.

Our attention was first drawn to this characteristic by
the reading preserved for ϑ'α' at 1:18. [13]   In the text of Th.
and Aq. πλην replaces OG αλλα.   πλην also appears in the
asterisked addition at 6:15: πλην εν τη ημερα εκεινη
εκυκλωσαν την πολιν επτακις in M(mg) bcgnv(mg)xz(mg)ℤℤ(sub ※
v[mg]ℤ).   At 8:2 an anonymous reading recorded in ℤ begins
with ברם (πλην). [14]   Since this is the only reading that
represents the MT expression חבזו לכם in the plural (note
also αυτης twice), it should probably be attributed to Aq.
and/or Th.

In 2 places manuscripts of the S recension exhibit this
characteristic. In 11:22 (F^{b?}) gnwℤ have πλην alone (OG
αλλα πλην). What makes this particularly interesting is
the fact that in the preceding prepositional phrase only
manuscripts of the S recension have the correction to the MT.
This raises the possibility that πλην (alone; cf. OG) was
drawn from the same source (Aq.?Th.?) as the prepositional
phrase. At 11:13 the S recension has πλην rather than OG
αλλα as the translation for רק. Later in the same verse,
where the OG has πλην for Hebrew זולתי, these manuscripts
have αλλα. Is this part of an effort to restrict the usage

of πλην, so that it consistently renders רק and no other word? Finally, at 6:18 OG αλλα is replaced by πλην in manuscripts of the N-group.

αλλα and πλην are both common in the OG of Joshua as translations for רק. The evidence we have presented suggests that in some tradition, perhaps the καιγε recension, πλην was the preferred translation of this Hebrew word.

In Judges רק appears 7 times in the Hebrew. In 6 places the practice of A and B is the same: both have πλην 4 times and no specific representation of רק twice. Once, at 14:16, B reads πλην, where A apparently has no translation for רק. R-T, overlooking Joshua 1:18, lists no examples of πλην = רק in Aq. Outside of Joshua, so it appears, Aq. used πλην as a consistent representation of אך (the two occurrences of אך in Joshua show no significant revision of the OG).

Perhaps we are not dealing with a characteristic, but only with a tendency. In any case, it is interesting to note that, while considerable attention has been paid to את and גם "les particules incluantes," very little, if anything, has been written about characteristic representations of אך and רק "les particules excluantes."[15]

3. איש = ανηρ. איש occurs 39 times in the Hebrew of Joshua. In our discussion of this characteristic we employ the categories found in O'Connell (plus another, "איש with a number"). In light of Barthelemy's comments,[16] we cannot limit ourselves to those cases where ανηρ replaces εκαστος:

Uses of איש in Hebrew of Joshua

a) In distributive sense (= "each")   5 times
b) In indefinite sense, with negative   7 times
    (= "no one, not anyone")
c) With כל (= "everyone")   2 times
d) With a number (e.g., "twelve men")   16 times
e) Various other uses   9 times

a) 4:5; 6:5; 6:20; 22:14; 24:28. At 4:5, 6:5; 24:28 the OG
reads εκαστος. At 4:5 only q presents a reading in which OG
εκαστος is not found. In a plus that precedes εκειθεν
εκαστος λιθον ενα αρατω (OG: εκειθεν εκαστος λιθον αρατω),
this manuscript has ανηρ λιθον ενα. εκειθεν εκαστος λιθον
ενα αρατω, found in q and, with αρατω first, in manuscripts of
the P̲ and C̲ recensions, is a correction to the MT. The source
(Aq.? Th.?) of the plus ανηρ λιθον ενα went beyond this
correction with the introduction of ανηρ for Hebrew איש. [17]
At 6:5 OG εκαστος is found everywhere. A form of εκαστος
also appears everywhere at 24:28. [18] In the OG of 6:20 there
is no representation of Hebrew איש נגדו וילכדו את העיר. [19]
εκαστος is found in all renderings of the Hebrew, including
the asterisked addition of Origen: εκαστος εξ εναντιας αυτου
και κατελαβοντο την πολιν (g^m sub ÷). The same or similar
wording appears in FΔ₈b-knpqstvwxza₂Αℂ𝐸𝐿 Luc (manuscripts of
the P̲ and S̲ recensions and the N̲-group). At 22:14 the OG is
αρχοντες (MT: איש ראש). In abcoqx𝐸𝐵 ανδρες precedes αρχοντες.
In this case no asterisk marks ανδρες as an addition of Origen,
although it seems to be one. [20] At least one correction to the
MT at 22:14 does not use ανδρες to render איש in the
distributive sense: 𝐵 attributes to Sym. a reading which
begins כל חד דין (εκαστος δε). [21]

b) 1:5; 2:11; 8:17; 10:8, 21; 21:42(44); 23:9. In the Hebrew
of Joshua איש in the indefinite sense is always found with
the negative. The OG uses ουθεις in five of these passages
(8:17; 10:8, 21; 21:42 [44]; 23:9). In each of these five
passages ουθεις is the reading of most manuscripts outside
of the E̲ recension. [22] At 2:11 ουθεις (ουθενι) is found in
the OG; at 1:5 the OG reads ουκ . . . ανθρωπος. In this
last passage Aq. has ανηρ, the rendering characteristic of
the καιγε recension. The reading of Th.-Sym., which contains
ουθεις, extends to 1:5 the usual representation of this construction in the OG of Joshua. [23] At 21:42(44) readings have
also been preserved for Aq. and Sym. As at 1:5 Aq. has the
καιγε rendering and Sym. does not:

OG   ουκ ανεστη ουθεις

Aq.   ουκ εστη ανηρ

Sym.   και ουκ απεστη ουδεις.

Barthélemy notes that it is characteristic of the καιγε recension to replace words such as ουδεις and ανθρωπος, and not only εκαστος, with ανηρ.[24]

c) 1:18; 10:24. At 1:18 OG ο δε ανθρωπος (MT: כל איש) is not corrected in any extant witness to the text. At 10:24 the MT reads אל כל איש ישראל. The OG translator, who probably did not read איש in his Hebrew *Vorlage* at this point, wrote παντα ισραηλ. Gbcxɢ^m have παντα ανδρα ισραηλ (ανδρα sub ※ Gɢ^m).[25]

d) 3:12(a)(b)(c); 4:2(a)(b), 4(a)(b)(c); 7:3(a)(b), 4, 5; 8:3, 12; 22:20; 23:10. In this category there are numerous examples of the introduction of ανηρ or ανδρες where the OG lacks a specific translation for Hebrew איש. In order to present all the evidence, we list such examples, even though most are of no apparent significance as a καιγε characteristic.[26] 3:12 (b)(c); 4:2(a)(b), 4(b)(c) are discussed under category 2 in chapter 1 (3:12 is no. 26). The OG reads ενα αφ εκαστης φυλης in all three verses. Th. and ο' retain the OG at 3:12; the readings of Aq. and Sym. in that verse are as follows:

Aq.   ισραηλ ανδρα ενα ανδρα ενα του σκηπτρου . . .

Sym.   ισραηλ ανδρα ενα καθ εκαστην φυλην . . . .

In all three passages ανδρα precedes ενα . . . φυλης in manuscripts of the P recension; it is an asterisked addition in 3:12 (ɢ^m) and 4:2, 4 (ɢ). At 3:12 ανδρα is attributed to οι λ in M(mg)v(mg sub ※). The OG lacks a specific representation for the first איש in 7:3. ανδρες is supplied in xɢ(sub ※). The OG lacks the passage in which איש appears in the MT of 8:12. A reading attributed to Th. in ɢ^m contains ανδρων.[27] At 22:20 a literal rendering of איש appears only in ₵: *Achar vir unus erat* (so B-McL). At 23:10 ανηρ precedes OG εις (MT: איש אחד) in bckoqx𝔄-codd ₱ɢ(sub ※).

e)   5:13; 6:21, 26; 8:25; 9:6 (12), 7(13); 10:14; 14:6; 17:1.
At 5:13 the OG has ανθρωπον. In q alone there is a reading
with ανηρ: και ιδου ανηρ εστως. According to Margolis,
this reading of q, which also is unique in restoring (הנה)ו
of the MT, apparently comes from Aq.[28]   At 6:21 and 8:25 the
OG has απο ανδρος for Hebrew מאיש. In the first passage gn,
manuscripts of the Lucianic recension, have απο ανθρωπου. At
6:26 OG ανθρωπος is found everywhere. At 9:6, 7 no extant
witness to the text provides a literal translation of the MT:

9:6	MT	אל איש ישראל	9:7	MT	איש ישראל
	OG	ισραηλ		OG	οι υιοι ισραηλ.
	SPC	προς παντα ισραηλ			

In the remaining passages the reading of the OG (ανθρωπος
in 10:14; 14:6; ανηρ in 17:1) appears everywhere. εκαστος
appears in the Greek at 24:33b (cf. 24:28 and Judges 2:6 A
and B).

Aq. is an important witness for this characteristic in
Joshua; 1:5 and 21:42(44) are especially significant in this
regard. Th. extended the use of ουδεις to 1:5 and retained
the OG construction at 3:12. This may explain why he did not
include ανηρ in his text of these 2 passages. Sym. follows
the text of Th. at 1:5, has ουδεις at 21:42(44), and reads
εκαστος at 22:14. The asterisked (and non-asterisked?)
additions of Origen read ανηρ in most cases, but at 6:20 the
appearance of εκαστος means that the καιγε characteristic
did not appear in Origen's source at this point.

4. מעל = επανωθεν (απανωθεν). מעל occurs 7 times in the
Hebrew of Joshua.[29]   The OG uses εκ twice (5:15, 15:18) and
απο 4 times (5:9, 10:27; 23:13, 15). In no case is there
a revision to επανωθεν (απανωθεν). At 23:16 the OG lacks the
passage in which מעל appears. απο is the reading of all
manuscripts that contain a rendering of the Hebrew: θb-hjkm-
qstvxy[a?]zb₂AEℤ(sub ⁒ vzℤ). Thus επανωθεν is not used in
Joshua to represent Hebrew מעל.[30] Commenting on similar
findings for Exodus, O'Connell writes the following: "Since
it is really a tendency rather than a genuine characteristic,

it is not surprising that there is no evidence of its use in Exodus by Theodotion or by anyone else."[31]

5. נצב/יצב = στηλοω. After a careful re-examination of the evidence for this characteristic, Bodine concluded that "the rendering is not consistent in any of the καιγε material and possibly that it is not a true characteristic at all."[32] Nevertheless, we note that at 1:5 a reading attributed to Aq. contains στηλοω as the translation of Hebrew יחיצב:

OG   αντιστησεται

Aq.   στηλωθησεται.

This is particularly significant because here the verb does have reference to a human; the full reading of Aq. is ου στηλωθησεται ανηρ εις προσωπον σου.[33]

At 24:1 the root יצב occurs again:

MT   ויתיצבו

OG   και εστησεν αυτους. The correction to the MT found in manuscripts of the P and C recensions retains the verb of the OG. The root נצב occurs at 6:26; OG επεστησεν (απεστησεν in Θjos) appears everywhere.

The noun מצב appears in 4:3, 9. At 4:3 the OG lacks a translation of ממצב רגלי הכהנים, which did not form part of its Hebrew *Vorlage*. The translation απο στασεως ποδων των ιερεων is found in Fbcdghknpqtxz(mg)𝔸𝔼𝕾(sub ⁜). This reading is attributed to οι λ in M(mg) v(mg). At 4:9 the MT reads תחת מצב רגלי הכהנים. As Margolis states, the OG labors to express the Hebrew (υπο τους ποδας των ιερεων), and manuscripts of the S recension paraphrase (ου εστησαν οι ποδες των ιερεων).[34] In neither passage is there any evidence of a revision to στηλοω or a noun such as στηλωσις.

6. שופר = κερατινη. חצצרה = σαλπιγξ. The noun חצצרה does
not appear in the MT of Joshua. שופר occurs 14 times in the
Hebrew text of Joshua, all in chapter 6 (6:4[a][b], 5, 6,
8[a][b], 9[a][b], 13[a][b][c], 16, 20[a][b]). In 9 cases the
OG lacks any clear representation of this word (6:4[a][b],
5, 6, 8[b], 9[a][b], 13[c], 16).

We look first at the 5 places in which the OG does
translate שופר. In each case (6:8[a], 13[a][b], 20[a][b])
σαλπιγξ appears in the OG (שיפורא in ʃ in the first 3 passages;
ʃ not extant at 6:20).[35] The OG word is retained everywhere;
at 6:13(b) κερατινες precedes σαλπιγξι in manuscript q.[36]
σαλπιγξ also appears in the OG of chapter 6 as a translation
for קרן (in v 5; ʃ[txt] has the expected שיפורא). The
following reading is preserved for Sym. at this point:
אמתי דין דנורך בקרנא דדכרא. Field translates קרנא as
κερατι.[37] An anonymous reading is also preserved in ʃ here:
רנהוא באועתא בקרנא דירובל (Field: και εσται εν σεισμω εν
κερατινη του ιωβηλ). Field is probably correct to ascribe
this reading to Aq.[38] It seems that here the καιγε
recension (or only Aq.?) replaced σαλπιγξ with κερατινη,
even though the Hebrew reads קרן and not שופר.

We turn now to the 9 places where the OG lacks any clear
representation of Hebrew שופר. At 6:8(b) no extant witness to
the text provides a literal rendering of Hebrew בשופרות.[39]
In the remaining 8 places a literal translation of שופר is
supplied in manuscripts of Margolis' P recension among
others. Even before we began our investigation of this
characteristic, it was clear from the following statement
of Barthélemy that we could expect to uncover significant
evidence: "En ce livre [Joshua] la Septante a très souvent
omis de traduire ce mot [שופר]. Dans ces cas la recension
désignée comme 'palestinienne' par M.L. MARGOLIS...rétablit
κερατινη."[40] Our study of these passages confirms
Barthélemy's observations and at the same time offers more
detailed information about the occurrences of κερατινη in
chapter 6 of Joshua.

At 6:4 κερατινη appears twice in Fbcgknqx𝐸𝑆(sub ÷ 𝑆):
(a) επτα κερατινας, (b) εν ταις κερατιναις. In q σαλπιγγας
follow κερατινας.[41] The same conflate reading, κερατινας
σαλπιγγας τω ιωβηλ, is attributed to οι λ (sub ÷) in v(mg).[42]
According to a (misplaced) notation in M(mg), however, the
correct and full reading of οι λ is επτα κερατινας του ιωβηλ
at 6:4(a) and εν ταις κερατιναις at v 4(b).[43] At 6:5
την φωνην της κερατινης translates קול השופר in FM(mg)bcgkqv
(mg)xz(mg)a₂𝐸𝑆(sub ÷ v[mg]𝑆).[44] At 6:6 the OG lacks the
passage in which שופר occurs. As part of a longer reading
επτα κερατινας is found in Fbcgknqxz(mg)𝐴𝐸𝑆(sub ÷). επτα
κερατινας is also attributed to οι λ in v(mg; + ου ÷) and
M(mg). The OG lacks a clear translation of both occurrences
of שופר in v 9: (a) חקעו השופרות; (b) בשופרות.[45] Again,
manuscripts of the P recension, and a few others, use
κερατινη to supply the clear rendering lacking in the OG:
(a) σαλπιζοντες ταις κερατιναις in Fb (om ταις b')ckqxz
(mg)𝐸𝑆(sub ÷); (b) πορευομενοι και σαλπιζοντες ταις
κερατιναις in Fbkxz(mg)𝐸𝑆. ταις κερατιναις (a) and (b) are
ascribed to οι λ.[46] At 6:13(c) ταις κερατιναις translates
בשופרות in bx𝑆(sub ÷) (also in cq) as part of a longer
reading.

In the 7 examples above there is a consistent pattern
of usage: שופר = κερατινη. At 6:16 the consistency of this
pattern is apparently broken. Part of this verse reads
חקעו הכהנים בשופרות in the Hebrew. At this point the OG,
as preserved in BAM(txt)NӘloywb₂𝒞, has εσαλπισαν οι ιερεις.
In other manuscripts, including those of the P recension,[47]
this is followed by ταις σαλπιγξιν. This is the only place
(with the possible exception of v 9[b])[48] where the
translation of שופר does not appear as part of the rendering
of a longer phrase or clause lacking in the OG. Thus it is
likely that Origen supplied his own translation here on
the basis of the consistent OG rendering, σαλπιγξ.[49]

In the 7 examples discussed prior to 6:16 it is clear
that Origen drew his material from a source that contained
the characteristic καιγε equivalence שופר = κερατινη.

Furthermore, this rendering stands in marked contrast to the
practice of the OG translator, who always employed σαλπιγξ
to translate שופר. In five cases (6:4[a] and [b], 6, 9[a]
and [b]) the attribution of this rendering to οι λ has been
preserved. Is there any way in which we can identify the
source of Origen's asterisked, and one non-asterisked,
additions more specifically? We think that the evidence is
sufficient to do so.

We note first that the preposition ב, which generally
appears before שופר when this noun is used with the verb תקע,
is reproduced in the source used by Origen only at 6:4. If
Aq. were the source, we would expect in each case a fully
literal rendering of the Hebrew, including the preposition.
This is what we find in the reading of Aq.(?) at 6:5
(Syriac: באועתא בקרנא; Greek [see above]: εν σεισμω εν
κερατινη). [50] Secondly, at 6:4(a) Aq. and Sym. may have
used σαλπιγξ, and not (only?) κερατινη, to render שופר in
their texts. The full evidence for their readings is recorded
in Field: "Masius in Comment. pp. 103, 104: 'Aquilas
interpretatur *tubas remissionis*...Chaldaeus [שופריא דקרן דכריא]
et Symmachus reddiderunt *buccinas arietinas*.' Hinc Montef.:
'Α. σαλπιγγας αφεσεως. Σ. σαλπιγγας κερατινας. Utramque
lectionem suspicioni obnoxiam esse monuit Scharfenb. in
Animadv. T. II, p. 7." [51] Even though doubt is rightly
cast on these readings (cf. both Aq. and Sym. at v 5), they do
serve to alert us to those places in chapter 6, e.g. at v 3,
where Aq. and Sym. rendered some Hebrew expressions in a manner
different from that found in the asterisked addition of Origen. [52]
The fact that the rendering chosen for the expression תקע בשופר
is not fully literal, and yet contains the καιγε characteristic and is an intelligent handling of the Hebrew, together
with the observation that Sym. and Aq. do not agree at all
points with the wording found in the source of Origen at
v 3 (which was also his source at v 4 and perhaps elsewhere
as well), leads us to conclude that Th. was used by Origen to
correct the OG in most, if not all, of the passages we have
been discussing in chapter 6.

7. Elimination of the historical present. O'Connell's statement about Exodus applies with equal validity to the OG of Joshua: "the OG for Exodus does not normally use the historical present for the MT converted imperfect but rather the imperfect or the aorist."[53] Thus it is not surprising that this characteristic does not appear in any reading attributed to Th. for Joshua. We have also not noticed the elimination of the historical present in any other tradition or recension of Joshua.

8. אִין = ουκ εστιν (in a series of aorist verbs). אִין occurs 5 times in the MT of Joshua (6:1[twice]; 18:7; 22:25, 27). At 6:1 the OG reads και ουδεις εξεπορευετο εξ αυτης ουδε εισεπορευετο (MT: אֵין יֹוצֵא וְאֵין בָּא). At 18:7; 22:25, 27 the OG uses the characteristic καιγε translation to render Hebrew אֵין חֵלֶק:

18:7   MT   כִּי אֵין חֵלֶק

        OG   ου γαρ εστιν μερις

22:25   MT   אֵין לָכֶם חֵלֶק

        OG   ουκ εστιν υμιν μερις.

In these two passages manuscript n has the future εσται.

22:27   MT   אֵין לָכֶם חֵלֶק

        OG   ουκ εστιν υμιν μερις.

The renderings of אֵין do not provide any help for isolating the καιγε recension of Joshua.

9. אָנֹכִי = εγω ειμι. אָנֹכִי appears 7 times in the Hebrew of Joshua: 1:2 = יהוה; 7:20 = עָכָן; 11:6 = יהוה; 13:6 = יהוה; 14:7 = כָּלֵב; 14:10 = כָּלֵב; 23:14 = יְהוֹשֻׁעַ. In 4 passages (1:2; 11:6; 13:6; 23:14) OG εγω is found everywhere. At 14:7 no explicit translation of Hebrew אָנֹכִי appears.

At 7:20 the OG lacks a translation for אָנֹכִי:

MT   וַיֹּאמֶר אָמְנָה אָנֹכִי חָטָאתִי

OG   και ειπεν αληθως ημαρτον.

εγω is found in bcdkpqtv(mg)xz(mg)Ӽ-ed 𝔤ᶠ𝔤(sub ※). It is possible that here Origen himself supplied the one Greek word without recourse to Th. or any other source. If this is so,

then we learn nothing of the nature of Origen's usual source(s)
for his (longer) additions from this reading. At 14:10 the
OG rendering of Hebrew ועתה הנה אנכי היום is και νυν ιδου εγω
σημερον. Gabk have εγω ειμι, the characteristic καιγε
representation of אנכי. It is probable that Origen drew on
one of his sources (Th.?Aq.?) for the introduction of εγω ειμι
into his text at this point. [54]

10. לקראת = εις συναντησιν/εις απαντην. Bodine states that
εις συναντησιν is the "standard OG equivalent" for Hebrew
לקראת in the books preceding Judges. This is true for the
book of Joshua, in which לקראת occurs 5 times (8:5, 14,
22; 9:11[LXX 9:17]; 11:20). εις συναητησιν is the OG
translation in the first four passages; at 11:20 the verb
συνανταω appears. In no case is there any evidence for the
replacement of the OG with εις απαντην or another form.

12. יהוה צבאות = κυριος των δυναμεων. Although יהוה צבאות
does not appear in the MT of Joshua, this phrase was
apparently found in the Hebrew *Vorlage* of the OG at 6:17,
where the translator rendered it by κυριος σαβαωθ. [55]
(τω κυριω) των δυναμεων, the reading characteristic of the
καιγε recension, is attributed to Th. and o' at this point. [56]
    In his discussion of this phrase, Barthélemy notes
that Aq. used δυνατος for גבור. The expected equivalent is
found in the reading preserved for Aq. (in v[mg]) at 1:14:
MT   כל גבורי החיל
OG   πας ο ισχυων
Aq.   παντες δυνατοι τη ισχυι. [57]

13. אל = ισχυρος. אל occurs 4 times in the MT of Joshua
(3:10; 22:22[twice]; 24:19). In 3:10 θεος ζων translates אל
חי in the OG. κυριος, in addition to or instead of θεος,
appears in Amdefjlpstv(txt)wyzb₂𝒜𝒮. [58] At 22:22 the MT and
OG read as follows:

MT   אל אלהים יהוה אל אלהים יהוה

OG   ο θεος θεος εστιν κυριος και ο θεος θεος (this may
represent the Hebrew *Vorlage* אל אלהים יהוה [ו]אל אלהים יהוה,
with the first יהוה taken as a form of the verb "to be").
𝒮 preserves the text of Aq. for the first word (Hebrew: אל,
OG: ο θεος): חילתחנא. Field translates this into Greek as
ισχυρος and notes that ισχυρος θεος (=אל אלהים) is attributed
to both Aq. and Sym. by Masius. ισχυρος is the characteristic καιγε rendering of Hebrew אל.

At 24:19 the MT reads אל קנוא הוא. The OG at this point
is και ζηλωσας ουτος. bckx have και θεος ζηλωτης (-τος c)
εστιν ουτος, the reading attributed to Sym. in 𝒮ᵐ. The text
of 𝒮 reads ואלהא דטן הנא ⋗ (και ⋇ θεος ⋖ ζηλωσας ουτος). [59]
The use of θεος to represent אל, in Sym. and manuscripts of
the P recension, is in accord with the OG practice for Joshua,
but is not the translation expected in the καιγε recension.

14. נגד = forms of εναντι. The preposition נגד occurs 7
times in the Hebrew of Joshua (3:16; 5:13; 6:5, 20; 8:11,
33[LXX 9:6], 35[LXX 9:8]). The OG translator rendered נגד
in a variety of ways: απεναντι (3:16; 8:33--the reading
attributed to Sym. at 8:33 apparently also contains
απεναντι); [60] εξ εναντιας (8:11); εναντιον αυτου (MT:
לנגדו; 5:13); εις τα ωτα (8:35); [61] κατα προσωπον (MT: נגדו;
6:5). [62]

At 6:20 the OG lacks the section in which נגדו appears. [63]
εξ εναντιας αυτου is found in FΔ₈b-knpstvwxza₂𝒜-ed𝒞𝒠𝒮ᵐ(sub ⋇)
(also εξω εξ εναντιας αυτου in q). Here Origen drew his
additional material from a source that contained the
characteristic καιγε rendering (a form of εναντι) of נגד.

15. לפני = ενωπιον. Both Barthélemy and Bodine note that this equivalence is especially valuable for determining the καιγε recension of Judges and Samuel-Kings. As the evidence below shows, this characteristic is of no help in isolating the καιγε recension of Joshua. This preposition appears 53 times in the MT of Joshua.[64] In the OG we find 12 different translation options (listed in order of decreasing frequency): εναντιον (found 14 times); απο προσωπου (7 times, including once for -מלפ); εναντι (6 times); εμπροσθεν (5 times); προτερ- (4 times); απεναντι (3 times); κατα προσωρον (twice); απο, ενωπιον, κατενωπιον, προ προσωπου, υπ (once each). In addition, the OG lacks a specific translation for the preposition 8 times.[65]

We next list the translations of לפני in Th., Aq., Sym., οι λ̥, ο', and Origen (manuscripts of the P recension, with or without ※):

Th.

απο προσωπου	(once: 10:10 -- see under cateogry 4.2 in chapter 1 [10:10(a) is no. 66])
εις προσωρον	(once: 4:5 -- see fns. and under category 4.3 in chapter 1 [4:5 is no. 34])
κατα προσωπον	(once: 1:5 -- see under category 4.3 in chapter 1 [1:5 is no. 5])

Aq.

| εις προσωπον | (twice: 1:5; 4:5) |
| (?)προ προσωπου | (once: 4:5) |

Sym.

εις προσωπον	(once: 4:5)
κατα προσωπον	(once: 1:5)
(?)προ προσωπου	(once: 4:5)

οι λ̥

εις προσωπον	(once: 18:1)
εμπροσθεν	(twice: 3:6, 11)
ενωπιον	(once: 6:4)
κατα προσωπον	(once: 6:6)
προτεροι	(once: 4:11)

ο′

απο προσωπου   (once: 10:10)

Origen (manuscripts of the P recension)

απο προσωπου   (twice, both sub ※ : 8:6[b]; 23:5)

εμπροσθεν   (twice, once sub ※ : 3:11; once without ※ :
                    3:6)

ενωπιον   (twice, once sub ※ : 6:4; once without ※:
                    7:12[b])

κατα προσωπον   (3 times, twice sub ※: 6:6; 8:14; once
                    without ※ : 20:6).

In the majority of cases listed above a form of προσωπ- is
used to translate Hebrew לפני. This may be seen as a "literal"
rendering,[66] although it is not the rendering   characteristic of the καιγε recension in Judges and Samuel-Kings.[67]

16. על כן and על זאת = δια τουτο.   על זאת does not appear
in Joshua; על כן appears twice (7:26; 14:14).   In both
passages OG δια τουτο, the rendering characteristic of the
καιγε recension, is found everywhere.   Thus the evidence
here does not help us in our efforts to isolate the καιγε
recension of Joshua.

17. לעלם = εις τον αιωνα.   This phrase does not occur in
the MT of Joshua. עולם does appear in the following related
uses:

4:7   MT   עד עולם
      OG   εως τον αιωνος
8:28 MT   עולם
      OG   εις τον αιωνα
14:9 MT   עד עולם
      OG   εις τον αιωνα
24:2 MT   מעולם
      OG   το απ αρχης.

In no case is there evidence of any substantive revision of
the OG rendering.

19. אסף = συναγω. A form of the verb אסף appears 6 times
in the Hebrew of Joshua (2:18; 10:5; 20:4; 24:1; for 6:9, 13
see below). συναγω is the OG rendering at 2:18 and 24:1;
no revision is recorded.

At 10:5 the OG lacks a translation of Hebrew ויאספו.
A form of συναγω, και συνηχθησαν, is found in GM(mg)b-egh
jknotv(mg)xz(mg)𝔄𝔼ᶜ𝔤ᵐ (sub ※ Gvᵐᵍzᵐᵍ𝔤ᵐ)(in q𝔼ᶠ this form
replaces OG και ανεβησαν). While this is the expected καιγε
translation, its significance is difficult to assess, since
it does not represent revision from εκλειπω or any other OG
rendering. At 20:4 the OG lacks the passage in which Hebrew אסף
appears. The full clause in the MT is ואספו אתו העירה אליהם.
Aabcejqvxyz𝔄𝔼𝔅(not sub ※) have και επιστρεψουσιν αυτον η
συναγωγη προς αυτους. As Field states, η συναγωγη reflects
Hebrew העדה (הֵעֵדָה) rather than העירה as in the MT. επιστρεφω
never represents אסף in the OG.⁶⁸ It is not clear from what
source Origen drew this material; the absence of any signs may
mean that he found it in the κοινη text with which he was
working. Manuscripts of the Lucianic recension (dghnptw 74)
read here και προσαξουσιν αυτον προς εαυτας αι πολεις.⁶⁹
The following reading has been preserved for Sym. in 𝔅:
ונקבלוניהי במדינתא לותהון (και προσδεξονται [s. προσληψονται]
αυτον εις την πολιν προς αυτους).⁷⁰

The piel participle והמאסף appears in a specialized
sense at 6:9, 13. At 6:9 OG οι ουραγουντες is retained in
manuscripts of the P recension. At v 13 the OG is και
λοιπος οχλος. No revision to a form of συναγω is found in
either verse.

21. אפלה = σκοτια. ערפל = γνοφος. אפלה does not appear
in the Hebrew of Joshua, but at 24:7 the related *hapax
legomenon* מאפל is found. LXXᴮ contains the double translation
νεφελην και γνοφον (νεφελην και is placed sub ÷ in 𝔅). Holmes
terms νεφελην και γνοφον "probably an amplification."⁷¹
The two Greek renderings of the single Hebrew term may be due

to the fact that מאפל is a *hapax*. On the other hand, such
a double translation may be derived from formulations such as
Ex 14:20. ערפל does not occur in Joshua.

22. חוץ = εξοδος. A form of חוץ appears twice in the MT of
Joshua (2:19: החוצה; 6:23: ל מחוץ). The OG rendering in
both places is εξω, and no revision of this rendering is
recorded.

24. מהר = ταχυνω. The verb מהר in finite form appears 3
times in the Hebrew of Joshua (4:10; 8:14; 8:19). In all 3
verses the OG translates with a form of σπευδω, and there is
no evidence of revision to ταχυνω or any other verb.

The root מהר is used with the meaning of an adverb in
4 places: 2:5: מהר; 8:19, 10:6, 23:16: מהרה. At 2:5 the OG
lacks a translation of Hebrew מהר. In the text of 𝔖 עגל
appears sub ※ . Both the translation of Field, ταχεως
(cf. ταχεως attributed to οι λ in M[mg]v[mg]), and that of
Masius, εν ταχει, are probably wrong. The Greek underlying
the Syriac here is almost certainly ταχυ -- as in Nckx,
especially x. [72] Margolis observes that "α' will have
written ταχυ and σ'θ' ταχεως....α' uses ταχεως for the longer
מהרה....σ' and θ' are not particular; but α' held מהר and
מהרה apart." [73] Thus it is likely that Origen drew his
reading here from Aq. and that ταχεως (the reading of οι λ,
also Ffgz[mg]) was found in the text of Th. and/or Sym. At
8:19 OG εν ταχει (MT: מהרה) appears as ταχυ in gw; the
reading of 𝔖(txt) here is בעגל. At 10:6 OG το ταχος
(MT: מהרה) occurs everywhere (𝔖 is not extant). At 23:16
the OG lacks the section in which מהרה appears. το ταχος is
found in θbcdefjkmoqsvxy[a?]zb₂(om το) 𝔄𝔅𝔖(sub ※ vz𝔖);[74]
ghnpt have εν ταχει. If Origen had drawn his material from
Aq. at this point, would we not find the form ταχεως (see
above)? [75]

Barthélemy observes that Aq., in addition to translating
מהר with ταχυνω, used σπευδω for חוש and κατασπουδαζω for
בהל. Neither of these latter two Hebrew words occurs in the
MT of Joshua.

26. בעיני = εν οφθαλμοις. בעיני with a noun object referring
to someone other than יהוה appears 3 times in the Hebrew of
Joshua (3:7; 4:14; 22:33). This expression appears 4
additional times with a pronominal suffix referring to someone
other than Yahweh (9:25; 22:30; 23:13; 24:15). We are thus
unable to draw any contrast between renderings when Yahweh
is the object and those when He is not. [76]

The OG translator rendered בעיני in a variety of ways:
εν τοις οφθαλμοις (23:13); εναντιον (4:14); κατενωπιον (3:7);
noun or pronoun in the dative (9:25 [LXX 9:31]; 22:30, 33;
24:15). At 22:30 and 24:15 revision with the literal translation is found:

22:30

MT   וייטב בעיניהם

OG   και ηρεσεν αυτοις

Aq.   וטב בעינא דילהון (και αγαθον εν οφθαλμοις αυτων);[77]

24:15

MT   ואם רע בעיניכם

OG   ει δε μη αρεσκει υμιν

Aq. [78]   ואן בישא בעיניכון (Field: και ει πονηρον εν οφθαλμοις
υμων).

In one case, and possibly in another, the text of Aq. contained the explicit, literal translation εν οφθαλμοις, which
is the rendering characteristic of the καιγε recension. The
two changes listed above are in line with the following
remarks by O'Connell: "Shenkel's criterion may be broadened
to say that the ΚΑΙΓΕ/Theodotionic revision and the Aquilan
revision always use εν οφθαλμοις to translate MT b῾yny [בעיני],
even where the OG would have avoided the literal translation." [79]

Less clear are the results when we expand our investigation to include the related expression לעיני, which occurs
twice in the Hebrew of Joshua (10:12; 24:17). At 10:12 the
OG lacks a translation for לעיני ישראל. κατ οφθαλμους
παντος ισραηλ, found in F^b dghnopqt (oq omit παντος), is
characteristic of the Lucianic recension. Just before לעיני
the MT has ויאמר (the OG is και ειπεν ιησους). At this point
𝔊 attributes to Aq. a difficult text:
ואמרו לות בניא דאיסריל (και ειπον προς υιους ισραηλ).[80]

Margolis eliminates one difficulty by reading singular וַיֹּאמֶר
instead of plural וַיֹּאמְרוּ. Unable to eliminate the other
difficulty, he describes לוּת בְּנִיא as "peculiar."[81]It seems
to us that προς υιους reflects the (mis)reading of לְעֵינַי
as לְבָנַי. It is not clear whether or not we should burden
Aquila with such a reading.[82] At 24:17 the OG lacks the
clause in which לְעֵינֵינוּ appears. In b-ejmoqv(mg)xz(mg)𝕬𝕰𝕾
(sub ÷) ημιν represents the Hebrew expression. It is
unlikely that Origen drew this rendering from Aq. or from
Th.

27. פה = στομα. If, as O'Connell states, "the ΚΑΙΓΕ/
Theodotionic revision and the Aquilan revision always use
εν οφθαλμοις to translate MT *b`yny*, even where the OG would
have avoided the literal translation," might not this also
be true with other anatomical features? Our choice of פה
is based partly on the frequency of its occurrence in the book
of Joshua and partly on the fact that Harry M. Orlinsky brought
this word into his discussion of the ways in which the OG
translator of Joshua handled the anthropomorphisms and
anthropopathisms he found in his Hebrew *Vorlage*.

Outside of the phrase לְפִי חֶרֶב, which is discussed under
חֶרֶב,[83] פה occurs 14 times in the Hebrew of Joshua: 1:8, 18;
6:10; 9:2, 14; 10:18, 22, 27; 15:13; 17:4; 18:4; 19:50; 21:3;
22:9. In five places פה appears in the expression
פִּי יהוה (at 19:50; 22:9) עַל or (at 15:13; 17:4; 21:3) אֶל.
The OG uniformly renders this expression δια προσταγματος
(κυριου/του θεου), which Orlinsky translates "by the decree
of the Lord," and this OG rendering is found in all extant
witnesses to the text.[84]   This example supports Orlinsky's
contention that "from the relatively few anthropomorphisms
and -pathisms present in our Hebrew text, it would seem that
the former, the -morphisms, were avoided, i.e., they were not
left out or distorted, but simply rendered innocuously."
Orlinsky provides other examples, with the word קוֹל, to show
that "we may have here a matter of style rather than of
theology."[85]

As noted above, all extant witnesses to the text, including manuscripts of the P̲ recension, retain the OG
translation προσταγμα. This rendering does at least provide
an explicit element corresponding to פה, something not found
in the OG at 9:14. The OG there (v 20 in the LXX) reads
και κυριον ουκ επηρωτησαν; the MT is ואת פי יהוה לא שאלו.
We feel that the lack of an explicit representation for פה
is due neither to the absence of this word in the *Vorlage* of
the OG nor to a theologically-motivated change on the part
of the translator. Rather, considerations of style provide
an adequate motivation for the wording of the OG at this point.
Be that as it may, manuscripts of the P̲ recension, bcq (om το)
xg^{mg}, provide the literal translation το στομα κυριου;
Margolis judges το στομα to be an asterisked addition of
Origen. [86]

No reading has been preserved for Th. or Aq. here, but
Margolis lists passages outside of Joshua where Th. is recorded
as having substituted στομα for a less literal OG rendering. [87]
In the book of Joshua itself we do have one example for Aq.,
and there the literal rendering also appears:
18:4

MT	לפי נחלתם ויבאו אלי
OG	καθα δεησει διελειν αυτην και ηλθοσαν προς αυτον
Aq.	על פומא דפולג פסא דילהון ונאתון לותי

(Field: κατα στομα κληροδοσιας αυτων και ηξουσι προς με). [88]

This last example, while moving us away from the topic
of anthropomorphisms, does relate directly to the use of "the
literal translation...even where the OG would have avoided"
it. The 3 uses of פה in chapter 10 are also instructive in
this regard. In all 3 places the expression in the MT is
פי המערה, which the OG translator rendered with full literal-
ness at v 18 (το στομα του σπηλαιου), but more freely
(το σπηλαιον) in its other 2 occurrences. We consider it
very likely that the texts of Th. and Aq., were they
available to us, would read (το) στομα του σπηλαιου in all
3 verses. [89] With reference to humans, we find the
literal εκ στοματος υμων for מפיכם as part of a longer reading
in an asterisked addition of Origen at 6:10; the OG translator
used both free and literal representations in similar phrases:

1:18 σοι (פיך), 9:2 αμα παντες (פה אחד); 1:8 εκ του στοματος
σου (מפיך).

A revisor who made use of the בעיני = εν οφθαλμοις
equivalence probably did not restrict his interest to that
bodily feature alone. We have sampled some evidence that
suggests that his interest included the "mouth" as well.
For whatever reason or combination of reasons, the OG translator varied his representations of this word, a variation
that at least in some places and in some uses called forth a
revision to στομα. Although we have not pursued this matter
further, either in terms of καιγε material outside of Joshua
or other anatomical features within the book of Joshua, such
an investigation might well prove fruitful.

28. זבח = θυσιαζω. The verb זבח occurs only once in the MT
of Joshua: 8:31 ויזבחו שלמים. The OG here (9:4 in the LXX),
και θυσιαν σωτηριου, apparently reflects a Hebrew *Vorlage* in
which the noun זבח, rather than the verb ויזבחו, appeared.
A verb, corresponding to the construction of the MT, is found
in k(mg)x, εθυσιασαν ειρηνικα, and ₰(txt). θυσιαζω, the
verb characteristic of the καιγε revision, underlies ודבחו
of ₰(txt) as well. This is clear not only from the
appearance of this verb in x,[90]   but also from the fact
that here ₰(txt) contains the D form of *dbḥ*, which is the
normal Syriac equivalent of θυσιαζω.[91]   The full reading
of ₰(txt) is ודבחו ֜ משׁינגא הֿפורֿקֿנֿא. As Margolis notes,
it is likely that σωτηριου appeared sub ÷ in the text of
Origen (see k[mg]x).[92] He adds that ειρηνικας was borrowed
from α'σ'θ',[93] probably the same source(s) from which
Origen also drew the verb θυσιαζω. Since Origen did not
retain the noun θυσιαν in his text (sub ÷), he would not
have marked the verb εθυσιασαν as "additional" (sub ※).[94]

Bodine alerts us to the possibility that nouns from the
root זבח are also worth investigating. In Joshua this is
true for מזבח in chapter 22, where this noun appears 12
times.[95]   The MT used the same Hebrew noun whether it refers
to the (true) altar "of the Lord our God" or the (false) altar

built by the two and one-half tribes. As we noted in our
discussion of 22:10(a) in chapter 1,   the OG made a
lexical distinction between these two structures: θυσιαστηριον
(for the true altar) and βωμος (for the false altar).[96]
This distinction can be seen, for example, in vv 19 and 28;
in v 29 the OG translator apparently slipped and allowed the
false altar to be called θυσιαστηριον (cf. the correct use of
θυσιαστηριον later in the verse). This distinction was
eliminated by Aq., Sym., and Th. at 22:10(a). One or more of
the above (Aq.-Sym.-Th.) are the source for the reading
θυσιαστηριον preserved in z(mg) for the second occurrence of
βωμον in the OG of this verse. At 22:19 𝔖 ascribes to Aq.
the reading מדבחא, which Field correctly translated as
θυσιαστηριον.[97] It is characteristic of the καιγε recension
to eliminate lexical and stylistic distinctions of the OG (as
in the case of בעיני above), and it is probable that we are
viewing the same process here.

29. רדף = διωκω.   As the evidence below shows, this
characteristic is especially useful in Joshua. The verb רדף
appears 19 times in the Hebrew of Joshua.[98]   In 13 places
the OG translates רדף with a form of καταδιωκω (2:5, 7[a],
16[twice], 22[b]; 7:5; 8:16[b], 17, 24; 10:10, 19; 11:8;
24:6). In 2 places the OG uses a form of διωκω (2:7[b];[99]
23:10). In 4 places the OG lacks a translation for רדף
(2:22[a]; 8:16[a]; 8:20; 20:5).

Let us look first at the 4 places where the OG lacks
a translation. At 2:22 εως επεστρεψαν οι διωκοντες appears
in Nbcgknqx 𝔄𝔈𝔖^m(sub ÷ vid 𝔖^m). This same reading is
attributed to οι λ (sub ÷) in v(mg).[100] διωκω is the
rendering characteristic of the καιγε recension. At 8:16 a
form of διωκω again appears: και ενισχυσεν πας ο λαος της
γαι/γης του διωξαι οπισω αυτων
ויזעקו כל העם אשר בעיר לרדף אחריהם[101]   This is the
reading of M(mg)fkqv(mg)xz(mg)𝔄𝔈𝔖(sub ÷).[102] Both at
2:22(a) and at 8:16(a) διωκω in the additional material
stands in contrast to καταδιωκω found later in the OG of the

same verse.   At 8:20 M(mg)bcgknqv(mg)xz(mg)𝕰𝕾(sub ⁒ v[mg]
𝕾) have και ο λαος ο φευγων εις την ερημον εστραφησαν επι
τους διωκοντας (MT has singular הרודף). Finally, at 20:5,
another passage that the OG lacks, a form of διωκω translates
רדף in Aa-eghjnpqtv-z𝕬𝕰𝕾.

Thus for all 3 certain additions, and a probable
fourth one,[103]   Origen drew his material from a source in
which the καιγε rendering was found. This is in marked contrast to the practice of the OG translator, who employed
διωκω only 2 out of 15 times. διωκω, we recall, is also
attributed specifically to Aq. and Sym. at 10:19.[104]

In 3 other passages interesting variants appear for the
OG rendering. Two of these are αποδιωκω (for καταδιωκω) in
M(mg)v(mg)z(mg) Chr at 7:5 (this verb is found in the LXX
only in Lam 3:43; elsewhere it is ascribed to Sym. at Is 16:3)
and εκδιωκω (for διωκω) in k at 23:10 (εκδιωκω renders רדף in
the text of Sym. at Ec 3:15, where διωκω appears in the LXX).
It is somewhat surprising that most manuscripts, including
those of Margolis' P recension, have καταδιωκοντες at 2:7(b)
in place of OG διωκοντες (preserved only in Bcgnr). It is
likely that Origen found the more common καταδιω- in the
κοινη text with which he was working.[105] However we are to
explain the situation at 2:7(b), it alters in no substantial
way the conclusions to be drawn from the rest of the evidence:
Aq., Sym., and the source used by Origen for his additions
(possibly Th.) employed only διωκω, the characteristic
καιγε rendering of Hebrew רדף; in contrast, καταδιωκω
characterizes the OG translation of Joshua.

30. שׂר (ה)צבא = αρχων (της) δυναμεως. This expression, in
the form שׂר צבא, appears in neighboring verses in chapter 5
(vv 14, 15) of the MT of Joshua. The OG renders this phrase
in a different way in each verse:
5:14 αρχιστρατηγος δυναμεως κυριου
5:15 ο αρχιστρατηγος κυριου.
The only attempts recorded to standardize these two renderings
are the elimination of δυναμεως at 5:14 (in m) and the
insertion of δυναμεως at 5:15 (in d Cyp). It is not surprising

that the OG translator rendered the same Hebrew expression
in a different manner, even in neighboring verses.[106]
Neither in the OG of either verse nor in any extant witness
to the text is the representation characteristic of the καιγε
recension found.[107]

32. חרש = κωφευω. חשה = σιωπαω. The sole use of either
root in the Hebrew of Joshua is at 2:1, where the *hapax
legomenon* חֶרֶשׁ is found. The OG lacks a translation of this
word. M(mg)v(mg) attribute the reading κρυβη to Aq.-Th.[108]
κρυφη is found in Ndkptxz^m (sub ÷). Perhaps because the
predominant idea here is secrecy rather than silence, the
καιγε equivalent is not found in Th., Aq., or the addition
of Origen.[109]

33. עון = ανομια. עון occurs twice in the Hebrew of
Joshua (22:17, 20). In the first case OG το αμαρτημα
appears everywhere. At v 20 OG αμαρτια appears in all extant
witnesses to the text (except for ημερα in c). Neither
ανομια, the characteristic rendering of the καιγε recension,
nor αδικια, listed by Shenkel as the OG rendering for the
material with which he was dealing, occurs in the Hebrew of
Joshua.

While the sole occurrence of αμαρτια is at 22:20,
αμαρτημα appears again at 24:19 in a context that might be
significant. The last part of 24:19 reads as follows in the
MT: לא ישא לפשעכם ולחטאותיכם. The OG is ουκ ανησει υμων
τα αμαρτηματα και τα ανομηματα υμων (thus αμαρτημα
presumably = פשע and ανομημα = חטאת). In a number of
manuscripts, a-gjnsvwxz% Thdt, these two words are reversed,
with the result that αμαρτημα = חטאת. Although Origen may
have found this order already in the κοινη text with which he
was working, it is possible that he himself reversed the
order of the OG on the basis of one of his sources. The
purpose of such a reversal would be to establish the
αμαρτημα = חטאת equivalence. Since both the Hebrew and the
Greek root have as one of their meanings "to miss the mark,"

further investigation may lead to the conclusion that חטאה = αμαρτημα is a characteristic of the καιγε recension.

35. לא אבה = (ε)θελω.¹¹⁰ לא אבה occurs in the MT of Joshua only at 24:10: ולא אביתי. There the OG has και ουκ ηθελησεν. The only revision recorded is that of Aq., in which the OG verb (εθελω) was retained.¹¹¹ Bodine notes that θελω, employed by the καιγε revision of Samuel-Kings, is also common in the OG throughout the Old Testament.¹¹²

38. אהל = *σκεπη. משכן = σκηνη. The OG used σκηνη for both אהל and משכן; in Exodus Th. follows the OG practice when there is no contrast between the two Hebrew terms. When there is such a contrast, Th. restricts σκηνη to משכן and employs σκεπη, which usually renders a form of צל in the LXX, to translate Hebrew אהל. Aq. apparently extended this process by introducing the distinctive rendering of אהל in passages where no contrast is found.

אהל occurs 8 times in the MT of Joshua outside of chapter 22 (3:14; 7:21, 22[twice], 23, 24; 18:1; 19:51; for chapter 22 see below). In all but the first case (3:14) the OG translates אהל with σκηνη.¹¹³ At 3:14 OG σκηνωματων is found everywhere except in Fᵇ(mg), in which τενδ<ων>¹¹⁴ appears.

The four occurrences of אהל in chapter 22 (vv 4, 6, 7, 8) merit extensive discussion both because of the OG representation of the term there and because Hebrew משכן also occurs in this chapter (twice: vv 19, 29). In all of the four places listed above the OG employs the rather general term οικος to represent Hebrew אהל; at 22:19, 29 σκηνη, used previously in the OG of Joshua to translate אהל, renders משכן. Revision attributed to Aq. and/or Sym. has been preserved at vv 4, 7, 8 (in the first group of passages) and at v 29 (in the second). For Aq. and Sym. οικος was not a sufficiently specific representation of Hebrew אהל. At 22:4 v(mg) records the following reading for Aq.-Sym.: εις τα σκηνωματα υμων. The readings at vv 7, 8 have been preserved

in Ꞡ: v 7 Sym. מַשְׁכְּנָא; v 8 Aq. מִשְׁכְּנָא (both of these as part
of longer readings). Field translates Syriac מַשְׁכְּנָא as
σκηνας; on the basis of the marginal reading in manuscript v
at v 4, we prefer σκηνωματα. In either case (σκηνη/σκηνωμα)
Aq. and Sym. extended to chapter 22 one of the common and
specific OG renderings of Hebrew אֹהֶל.

The choice of this procedure by Aq. means that the
characteristic καιγε rendering of אֹהֶל (σκεπη; Syriac סַתְרָא)
does not appear in his text at this point, even though a
contrast might well be drawn between the 4 occurrences of אֹהֶל
and the 2 of מִשְׁכָּן in the same chapter. Aq., so it seems,
did make a contrast here, through a distinctive rendering of
מִשְׁכָּן rather than through a distinctive rendering of אֹהֶל, as
in Exodus. At 22:29 Ꞡ preserves the following reading for
Aq.-Sym.: מַשְׁרְיָא. This is translated by Field as κατασκηνωσεως,
a translation with which we agree.[115] This effort on the
part of Aq. (and Sym.) to hold Hebrew אֹהֶל and מִשְׁכָּן apart is
similar to the phenomenon attributed to Aq. and Th. in
Exodus. Although a different procedure is followed by Aq.
here, the intent remains the same. It may be that the OG
translator himself desired to make a contrast through the use
of οικος for אֹהֶל and then σκηνη for מִשְׁכָּן.[116]

42. אִשֶּׁה = πυρ(ρ)ον. אִשֶּׁה appears in the Hebrew of Joshua
only in the expression אִשֵּׁי יהוה at 13:14. The OG lacks a
translation of this word:

MT   רק לשבט הלוי לא נתן נחלה אשי יהוה אלהי ישראל

OG   πλην της φυλης λευει ουκ εδοθη κληρονομια· κυριος ο θεος ισραηλ.

A clear rendering of Hebrew אִשֵּׁי is found only in the conflate
(see below) text of manuscript k: κληρονομια πυρου· οτι κυριος.
Both Margolis and Field agree, however, that παρα, found
sub ※ in G before κυριος, is a corrupt form of original πυρα.[117]
πυρα, in the corrupt form παρα, also appears in c(παρα κυριου
κυριος) and x (παρα κυριου). Although the OG reading is
retained in Ꞡ, Margolis is probably correct in seeing the
following as Origen's procedure here: ※ πυρα κυριου: ÷ κυριος:[118]

From the readings in G, c, and x it is not possible to
tell whether πυρα is the plural of πυρ or πυρον, for both
have neuter plurals.[119]   It is the πυρου of manuscript k,
which can be the genitive only of πυρον, that makes it clear
that the rendering characteristic of the καιγε recension did
appear in Origen's source here. [120]

43. בין = *ανα μεσον.   In Exodus this rendering on the part
of Th. apparently differs from both the OG and Aq. בין appears
20 times in the MT of Joshua (3:4[twice]; 8:9[twice],
11[twice], 12[twice]; 18:11[twice]; 22:25[twice], 27[3 times],
28[twice], 34; 24:7[twice]). In every place where the OG
has an explicit representation of בין, ανα μεσον is found
(3:4[a]; 8:9[twice]; 18:11[twice]; 22:25[a]; 22:27[a] and [c],
28[twice], [121]   34; 24:7[twice]). At 3:4; 22:25, 27 the OG
lacks an explicit rendering of the second בין. At 22:27
manuscripts of the P̲ recension, among others, introduce an
explicit translation for בין(2°): ανα μεσον, in Nbefkotvxz𝕻f𝕾;
also ανα μεσον ημων, in Aiquyb₂. At 22:25 the reading
attributed to θ'o'σ' retains OG ανα μεσον ημων και υμων
without introducing an explicit translation for בין (2°).[122]

The OG lacks the section in which בין appears at 8:11,
12. At 8:11 και η κοιλας ανα μεσον αυτου και της γαι
(MT: העי ובין בינו ויהגי) appears in M(mg)bcfv(mg)xz(mg)𝕻f𝕾
(sub ÷ M[mg]𝕾). As in the reading of Th.-Sym. at 22:25,
no effort is made to supply an explicit rendering for בין
(2°) This observation holds true for the following verse
(8:12) as well. There ανα μεσον βηθαυν [123]   και της γαι
(MT: העי ובין אל בית בין) is found in M(mg)bcfgnqv(mg)xz(mg)
𝕻f𝕾(sub ÷ M[mg]𝕾). Masius places the addition at vv 12–13
sub θ', indicating that Origen drew this material from Th.

Thus Th., Sym., and the source used by Origen for his
addition at 8:11, which may also be Th., always translated
בין with ανα μεσον where they have an explicit translation
of this Hebrew preposition. ανα μεσον is the rendering
characteristic of the καιγε recension. In Joshua, however,
there is no contrast between Th. and the OG in this regard,

so that the evidence here is of only limited significance.
Further, there does not seem to have been any effort on the
part of Th. to supply an explicit representation for each
בין, specifically for the second בין in a series of two or
more. This is also in line with the practice of the OG
translator of Joshua. [124]

44. בקרב = *εν μεσω?. In Exodus this rendering on the part
of Th. also differs from both the OG and Aq. (see no. 43
above). This preposition appears 18 times in the Hebrew
of Joshua.[125] In its renderings of Hebrew בקרב the OG is
without the μεσ- element 16 times. Only at 1:11 does the OG
include μεσ- in its translation of the Hebrew preposition:
κατα μεσον (Hebrew: בקרב). At 10:1 the OG lacks the clause
in which בקרב occurs. With respect to בקרב the rendering
characteristic of the καιγε recension is definitely not
characteristic of the OG as well (cf. no. 43 above).

In six places εν μεσω or a closely related phrase
translates Hebrew בקרב in Aq., Aq.-Sym.-Th., or an addition
of Origen marked with an asterisk. At 3:2 OG δια is followed
by μεσης in Fbcgknpqtv(mg)xℤ𝒮ᵐ(sub ※); δια μεσου is the
reading of N. The insertion of a form of μεσον was
apparently considered adequate here.[126] At 9:16 (LXX
(9:22) the OG translates בקרבו with εν αυτοις. The reading
of Aq., preserved in 𝒮, is במצעתהון, which Field translates
as εν μεσω αυτων (see below for justification of this translation).[127] At 10:1 εν μεσω αυτων (MT: בקרבם) appears
as part of a longer reading in GM(mg--μεσο instead of
εν μεσω)bcehijkqv(mg)xz(mg)ℤℤ𝒮 (sub ※ v[mg]ɢ𝒮). Thus
Origen drew his material here from a source that contained
the καιγε rendering of Hebrew בקרב. 𝒮(txt) has במצעתא דילהון;
from the Greek manuscripts, especially x,[128] it is clear
that εν μεσω αυτων underlies this Syriac phrase. Since
this same or similar wording appears in the Syriac translations of the Aquilan variants (see 9:16 above; 13:13 and
24:17 below), it is almost certain that Field is correct to
include εν μεσω in the Greek text of Aq. for each of these
places.[129]

At 13:13 the OG again uses εν alone to render בקרב
(MT: בקרב ישראל; OG: εν τοις υιοις ισραηλ). In addition to
eliminating τοις υιοις not found in the MT, Aq. represents
the preposition בקרב in the manner characteristic of the καιγε
recension: במצעת איסריל; εν μεσω ισραηλ.[130] gn, manuscripts
of the Lucianic recension, and Ȧ also translate בקרב
with εν μεσω, although they retain OG τοις υιοις in the form
των υιων. At 16:10 the following reading is recorded in
v(mg) for Aq.-Sym.-Th.: εν μεσω εφραιμ (OG: εν τω εφραιμ;
MT: בקרב אפרים).[131] Finally, at 24:17 Aq. replaces OG
δι αυτων with εν μεσω αυτων (במצעתא דילהון).

At 24:5 the OG failed to use even εν alone to represent
Hebrew בקרב, if Bdmoqa₂ have preserved the OG. It is more
likely, however, that εν αυτοις (rather than simply αυτοις),
as in AMNΘrell ȦϾℤȘ (בהו), appeared in the OG here; see also
בה (εν αυτη) attributed to Sym.

The examples discussed above provide solid evidence for
the appearance of this καιγε characteristic in Aq. and the
asterisked additions of Origen. εν μεσω is also attributed
to Th. and Sym. on one occasion (16:10), although the
reading ascribed to the latter at 24:5 lacks the
characteristic καιγε rendering. It is also significant that
in Joshua Aq. employed the καιγε rendering; in Exodus he
apparently did not.[132] The use of εν μεσω in Aq.-Sym.-Th.
and the additions of Origen stands in marked contrast to the
practice of the OG translator of Joshua. In our opinion
this gives added significance to the evidence presented
above for this characteristic.

45. בתוך = εν μεσω. בתוך, a preposition that is virtually
synonymous with בקרב (no. 44), appears 22 times in the MT of
Joshua.[133] In its renderings of Hebrew בתוך the OG
includes μεσ- 10 times (3:17; 13:9; 15:13; 16:9; 17:4[a], 6,
9; 19:1, 9; 21:41[39] --ανα μεσον at 16:9; 17:9; 19:1, εν μεσω
elsewhere). The OG rendering lacks the μεσ- element an
equal number of times (10: 4:9, 10; 7:21; 13:16; 14:3;
17:4[b]; 19:49; 20:9; 22:19, 31). At 8:9, 13 the OG lacks

the section in which בחוך appears. From the evidence listed
above we see that the OG translator was not concerned with
establishing a uniform rendering of Hebrew בחוך. We might
well expect such a concern in Aq.-Th. and the source of
Origen's additional material, where the בקרב = εν μεσω
equivalence appeared a number of times and in contrast to
the practice of the OG translator. In other words, if it is
characteristic of the καιγε recension to translate בקרב
with εν μεσω, would it not also be characteristic of this
recension to establish the same, uniform Greek rendering for
a synonymous Hebrew preposition?

The evidence from Joshua points to an affirmative answer.
In 5 of the passages listed above εν μεσω appears in contrast to
the OG or where the OG lacks the passage in which בחוך occurs
(4:10; 8:9, 13; 13:16; 22:31). In addition, the reading of
Aq. at 17:9 might represent revision of OG ανα μεσον. At
4:10 the OG translates בחוך הירדך with εν τω ιορδανη. M(mg)
ascribes the reading εμμεσω (εν μεσω) to Aq.-Th. εν μεσω is
also found in bcqv(mg)xz(mg)ÅØŚ(vid)Ś (μεσω sub ※ ; the
full reading of Ś[txt] is בּ\יורדנך הע\מצעמתה*בּ). Thus Origen
drew his reading at this point from a source that contained
what we believe to be the καιγε rendering of בחוך; here that
source is probably Th. or Aq.[134] The OG lacks the clause
that appears at the end of 8:9 in the MT. As part of a
longer reading that translates this clause, εν μεσω (MT: בחוך)
is found in M(mg)b-hjknpqstvxzÅØŚ(sub ※ M[mg]v).[135]
Again εν μεσω was found in the source used by Origen. We do
not have any indication of the identity of this source at
v 9, but we do at v 13. There εν μεσω is part of a longer
reading in M(mg)bcfgnqv(mg)xz(mg)ÅØŚ(sub ※ M[mg]Ś). Masius
places the addition at vv 12-13 sub ϑ', thus indicating that
Origen drew this material from Th.[136]

At 13:16 an anonymous reading is recorded in Ś:
הי דמצעמתא דנחלא (MT: אשר בתוך הנחל; OG: η εν τη φαραγγι
Αρνων).[137] Although Field translates the Syriac as
η αναμεσον της φαραγγος, ד מצעמתא could equally well be
translated εν μεσω. The difficulty of determining the

underlying Greek for a phrase preserved only in Syriac also
arises at 17:9. There the OG translates בתוך with ανα μεσον
in a passage where the OG and the MT exhibit several
differences. The Aquilan revision toward the MT has been
preserved only in Syriac. Although the same expression, במצעה,
is used in ₰(txt), where the underlying Greek is ανα μεσον,
and in the reading attributed to Aq., Field translates
במצעה in the reading of Aq. as εν μεσω. While such a
rendering is certainly possible and in keeping with the
practice of Aq. elsewhere (with respect to both בקרב and
בתוך), we cannot be certain that Aq. revised the OG at this
point. Finally, at 22:31 the OG translator used μεθ ημων to
represent Hebrew בתוכנו. Again ₰ preserves a reading, which
in this case is ascribed to οι λ: במצעתא דילן. There can be
little doubt that Field has correctly translated this as
εν μεσω ημων.

A form of μεσ- is also inserted in a number of manuscripts
at 4:18, where the OG translator used εκ alone to represent
Hebrew מתוך. Thus εκ μεσου is found in AFMϑabchi[a?]kloptv
(mg)wxya₂b₂₰-ed₰₰ (q₰-codd have εν μεσω).

It is not surprising to find the בתוך = εν μεσω
equivalence in Th.-Aq. and the asterisked additions of Origen,
where the characteristic καιγε equivalence בקרב = εν μεσω
also appears. On the basis of the examples discussed here,
εν μεσω can definitely be listed as the characteristic καιγε
rendering of Hebrew בתוך, at least for Joshua. For material
outside of Joshua, this equivalence can be clearly shown only
where a similar contrast is established between the practice
of the OG translator and that of the καιγε recension. In
general, so an initial investigation indicates, the translators
responsible for the OG of other books of the Old Testament
were more consistent in their use of εν μεσω for בתוך. If
this is so, then a rendering characteristic of the entire
καιγε recension may surface only in a few places such as Joshua.

49. חזק(piel) = ενισχυω. The piel of this root occurs only
once in the MT of Joshua (11:20). There the OG uses a form
of κατισχυω (κατισχυσαι) to translate Hebrew לחזק. No revision
of this OG is found in any extant witness to the text.

An apparent misreading of the MT provides us with another
example of a Greek rendering of what may well have been interpreted as a piel form of חזק. The beginning of 8:16 reads as
follows in the MT: ויזעקו כל העם אשר בעיר לרדף אחריהם.
The OG lacks this clause, which is supplied in M(mg)fkqv(mg)
xz(mg)ΑΒΣ(sub ⁎ Ϧ) : και ενισχυσεν πας ο λαος της γαι/γης του
διωξαι οπισω αυτων; b, cdpt also have readings that begin
και ενισχυσεν πας ο λαος. As Margolis suggests, the verb
ενισχυσεν presupposes ויחזק rather than ויזעק of the MT.[138]
Since ויחזק could very well have been understood as a piel
form, Margolis' observation leads to the conclusion that here
Origen drew his material from a source in which the
characteristic καιγε rendering of חזק appeared. Although
Masius does not indicate the identity of the source here (as
he does, for example, at vv 12-13 above), Margolis considers
it likely that Th. is the source for the additional material
at v 16 as well.[139]

50. חרב = ρομφαια. This rendering is characteristic of Th.
in Exodus and of the καιγε recension in Judges. O'Connell
points out that in Exodus Aq. and Sym. use μαχαιρα. Both of
these are common translations of חרב in the OG. As one might
expect in a book that contains several descriptions of battles,
this word occurs frequently in Joshua. In the MT חרב appears
20 times.[140] In the OG an equivalent of this noun also
appears 20 times.[141]

The OG translator employed 3 translations for חרב: ξιφος,
9 times, including once where the MT does not have חרב;
μαχαιρας, 7 times, including twice where the MT does not have
חרב; ρομφαια, 4 times. When one examines the uses of these
equivalents in the OG, 2 patterns emerge, which show that the
choice of a representation by the OG translator in a particular
context or construction was not entirely a random matter:

(1) With the exception of 11:11, ξιφος is always used in the OG in the phrase εν στοματι ξιφους (Hebrew לפי חרב).[142] Outside of Joshua, ξιφος is found but 6 times in the LXX (H-R). (2) Wherever reference is made to the knife Joshua used for circumcision, the OG employs μαχαιρα. This is true at 5:2, 3, where חרבות appears in the MT; also at 21:42d and 24:31a, where it does not.

Three readings have been preserved for Aq.-Sym. (at 5:2, 10:11, 28). In each case they included a form of μαχαιρα in their text. While this conforms to their practice in Exodus, we do not believe that all 3 examples are of equal value.

At 5:2, there is no witness to the text, Aq., Sym., and Th. included, that does not have a form of μαχαιρα. The same is true at 10:11, where μαχαιρα (shared by Aq.-Sym.-Th.) has been preserved in v(mg) to contrast with the introduction of the preposition (εν μαχαιρα) (MT בחרב) in v(txt). In both of these passages Th. retained μαχαιρα, the rendering of the OG, which is not the reading characteristic of him in Exodus.[143]

More significant are the readings recorded at 10:28. The OG, as preserved in LXX^B(txt), translates the expression לפי חרב with εν στοματι μαχαιρας. Aq.-Sym. also have this rendering, along with manuscripts of the N-group. Th. replaces this OG with ξιφους, which is also found in manuscripts of the P, S, and C recensions. On the basis of the Greek manuscripts, especially x,[144] it is almost certain that B-McL errs in listing μαχαιρας as the Greek underlying סיפא, the reading of ⅁(txt) at this point.[145] In our judgment revision to ξιφος, as well as to ρομφαια, is characteristic of the καιγε recension. At 10:28 Origen may well have drawn his reading from Th., although he would not have marked it (as he did the following phrase) since it did not constitute a "quantitative" change of the OG vis-à-vis the MT.[146]

In all 3 places where the OG lacks the phrase in which MT חרב appears, Origen drew his asterisked material from a source that contained the rendering already established as characteristic of καιγε-Th. outside of Joshua. At 8:24(a) εν στοματι ρομφαιας (MT: לפי חרב) is found as part of a longer

reading in bckqxⱥⱥ(sub ⁒); in a different location later in
the same verse εν στοματι ρομφαιας is also found in gnv(mg)z
(mg)(sub ⁒v[mg]).[147]   At 11:10 Gbckx(-ναν)ⱥ-coddⱥᶜⱥⱥ(sub ⁒
Gⱥ) Or-lat have απεκτεινεν εν ρομφαια (MT: בחרב הכה). At
13:22 the OG apparently lacks a representation of
בני ישראל בחרב.[148]   At any rate, Origen has supplied a
translation: οι υιοι ισραηλ εν ρομφαια, found in Gbckxⱥⱥ
(sub ⁒ Gⱥ) (εν ρομφαια also appears in a). It is fairly
clear that Origen did not draw his material in these three
passages from Aq. and Sym. On the basis of the evidence from
Exodus and Joshua 10:28 (where there is a contrast between
the renderings of Aq.-Sym. and Th.), it is most likely that
Th. is the source from which Origen drew the material containing ρομφαια at 8:24(a), 11:10, 13:22.

We have already touched upon the question of Syriac
renderings. Bodine states that ρομφαια most likely underlies
saypâ (so also O'Connell) and μαχαιρα underlies sakînâ. We
can both expand on and modify this statement on the basis of
the evidence from Joshua.

First, we note that saypâ translates ξιφος (this is true
in every case in Joshua), as well as ρομφαια (this is true for
the appearance of ρομφαια in the OG at 5:13; 8:24[b]; 24:12
and in the 3 asterisked additions of Origen at 8:24[a]; 11:10;
13:22).[149]   At least in Joshua, saypâ also translates μαχαιρα
(this is true at 10:11 and 19:47).[150]   Elsewhere ⱥ uses
sakînâ (5:2, 3) or sapserâ (21:42d; 24:31a). Thus ⱥ restricts
sakînâ to μαχαιρα, but appears to permit saypâ to translate
μαχαιρα, as well as ρομφαια and ξιφος.

Bodine notes that at Judges 7:22; 8:20; 9:54 ⱥ reads
saypâ, behind which he sees ρομφαια in each case.[151]   If our
observations concerning the practice of ⱥ in Joshua can be
carried over to Judges, we should at least consider the
possibility that Syriac saypâ is translating μαχαιρα in these
3 passages.[152]

Finally, let us return to the text of 𝔊 at 10:28. It is almost certain that *saypâ* there does translate ξιφος, the reading of x. We must, however, allow for a slight bit of uncertainty owing to the practice in 𝔊 of also using *saypâ* to represent μαχαιρα, which is the OG here.

54. ילדים = παιδαρια, παιδια. ילדים does not appear in the MT of Joshua, but 2 adjectives from the root ילד are found: ילוד at 5:5; יליד at 15:14, used as a substantive. At 5:5 the MT reads כל העם הילדים. According to Margolis, Hebrew הילדים is represented by εγενοντο in the OG.[153] Whether this is so or not, Origen placed this section of the OG sub ÷ and added a translation sub ⁕ . This additional material is found in bckx𝔄𝔊(sub ⁕), also M(mg)v(mg, where it is preceded by οι λ ου ο' ⁕)z (mg), and includes πας ο λαος οι γεννηθεντες as the rendering of Hebrew כל העם הילדים. In i(mg) the phrase appears as πας ο λαος ο γεννηθεις. At 15:14 the OG lacks a representation of MT ילידי הענק. γεννηματα του ενακ is the translation in Gbc(γενηματα)x𝔊 Or-lat (sub⁕ G𝔊). In our opinion neither of these 2 examples provides any help for isolating the καιγε recension of Joshua.

55. ירה = τοξευομαι. The verb ירה occurs in the Hebrew of Joshua only at 18:6, where the qal form ויריתי is found. The OG rendering εξοισω (from εκφερω) appears everywhere. This is the only place in the LXX in which this Greek verb translates a form of Hebrew ירה. At 18:8 εκφερω renders the hiphil of שלך, also the only place this equivalence appears in the LXX. It is interesting to note that these 2 Hebrew verbs, each of which receives a unique translation in the OG of Joshua, occur with exactly the same meaning in parallel passages:

18:6   ויריתי לכם גורל

18:8   .אשלוך לכם גורל

61. עבד = δουλ-. As the evidence below shows, this characteristic is particularly useful in Joshua. The noun עבד occurs 27 times in the MT of Joshua.[154] Especially common is

its use in the phrase משה עבד יהוה (either with יהוה or a
pronominal suffix referring to Yahweh). This phrase appears
18 times in the MT of Joshua (1:1, 2, 7, 13, 15; 8:31, 33;
9:24[b]; 11:12, 15; 12:6[twice]; 13:8; 14:7; 18:7; 22:2, 4, 5).
In 4 places (1:1, 15; 12:6[b]; 22:4) the OG lacks a
representation of עבד יהוה after משה. We are in full agreement with Orlinsky's statement that "if the LXX read μωυσης,
as against משה עבד יהוה in our preserved Hebrew text, it was
because the LXX *Vorlage* read משה, without עבד יהוה."[155]
Where the OG translator did find the full phrase משה עבד יהוה
in his Hebrew *Vorlage*, he employed either παις (11 times) or
far less frequently θεραπων (only at 1:2; 8:31, 33) to render
עבד.

The OG never uses the characteristic καιγε rendering in
its translations of the phrase משה עבד יהוה; in contrast, the
source(s) of Origen's asterisked additions contained a form of
δουλος 3 out of 4 times. At 1:1 δουλου κυριου is found in
FM𝕍b̲abcghinqrxz(mg)𝒜𝒞𝒟𝓁𝒮(sub ※ M𝒮) Thdt; also δουλου του θεου
in m and δουλου θεου κυριου in a₂.[156] Masius places δουλου
κυριου sub θ', thus indicating that Origen drew this material
from Th. At 1:15 ο δουλος κυριου follows OG μωυσης in F(om o)
cdejptx(μωσης)z(mg)𝒜𝓔𝒮ᵐ (sub ※); M(mg)v(mg) attribute o
δουλος κυριου to οι λ (M[mg] om o). At 22:4 δουλος κυριου,
not found in the OG, does appear in θbcfkov(mg)xz(mg)𝒜𝓔𝒮(sub
※). q alone has ο παις κυριου, used so frequently in the OG
of Joshua in connection with Moses. This same OG rendering
was in Origen's source at 12:6(b); there the wording ο παις
κυριου appears in Gabcx𝒜𝒮(sub ※). It is probable that in
this case Origen's "source" was nothing other than the OG
earlier in the same verse (12:6[a]), where we find μωυσης ο
παις κυριου as the translation for משה עבד יהוה. Even if
Origen did draw his material in all 4 passages from the same
source (on the basis of Masius' note at 1:1 that source would
be Th.), the practice of that source still presents a sharp
contrast to the practice of the OG translator.[157]

Twice in chapter 8 the OG employs θεραπων to represent
עבד in the phrase משה עבד יהוה. In both of these places δουλος,
the characteristic καιγε rendering, appears in gnw, which are

generally the best witnesses to the Lucianic recension. δουλος κυριου replaces OG ο παις του θεου at 14:7 in ANailp txyz(mg)a₂b₂Å. Although Origen may have found δουλος in the κοινη text with which he was working, it is also possible that he introduced the καιγε rendering here on the basis of one or more of his sources (Th.?).

The noun עבד is used 9 other times in Joshua: 6 times in connection with the Gibeonites (9:8, 9, 11, 23, 24[a]; 10:6); twice in connection with Joshua (5:14; 24:29); once in the phrase בית עבדים (24:17). The OG lacks a translation for לעבדיך at 9:24(a) (not supplied anywhere) and 24:17. Elsewhere, the OG translator employed οικετης 3 times (twice with the Gibeonites, once with Joshua), παις twice (with the Gibeonites), and δουλος twice (once with the Gibeonites, once with Joshua -- in the phrase יהושע בן נון עבד יהוה at 24:29 [30]). We are unable to discern a pattern in the translator's choice of representations in these 7 cases; this is also true in connection with his renderings of משה עבד יהוה.[158] Below is a table of the various representations employed by the OG translator for עבד:

παις	13 times	(Moses and Gibeonites)
θεραπων	3 times	(only Moses)
οικετης	3 times	(Joshua and Gibeonites)
δουλος	2 times	(Joshua and Gibeonites)

21 times (+ 6 times the OG lacks a translation for עבד = 27).[159]

This lack of any overall pattern in the OG contrasts with the evidence we discussed above from Origen's asterisked additions and elsewhere. One further piece of evidence completes this picture. At 24:17 the OG does not have the section in which MT מבית עבדים occurs. The translation εξ οικου δουλων appears as part of a longer reading in cejv (mg)xz(mg)Å(sub ※) (also εξ οικου δουλειας in bdmoqÅÆ). Again the source used by Origen contained the rendering characteristic of the καιγε recension.

Only one other noun from the root עבד appears in the MT
of Joshua. At 22:27 the Hebrew reads לעבד את עבדת יהוה. The
OG translates this with του λατρευειν λατριαν, and no revision
to any other Greek root, for noun or verb, is recorded.
The qal of עבד (this verb is not found in any form other
than the qal in the Hebrew of Joshua) occurs 21 times.[160]
In the 19 places where the OG represents this Hebrew verb, the
translator employs a form of λατρευω.[161] In no case do we
find revision to another Greek root in any extant witness   to
the text.

  Twice the OG lacks a rendering for this verb (at 24:15[c],
not supplied anywhere, and 16:10). At 16:10 the OG does not
have a translation for the MT clause עֹבֵד למס ריהי.[162]
και εγενοντο υποφοροι δουλοι represents this Hebrew in Gbckx
Ⱥȿ(sub ※).[163] The use of δουλοι for the qal participle עבד
is in keeping with the practice of Origen's source elsewhere.
The rather free way in which the Hebrew is represented here
strongly suggests that Aq. is not the source for this material.

  Although in ȿ(txt) for 23:7 a passage is placed sub ※
that contains the OG translation λατρυω,[164]   it is doubtful
that λατρυω is an Origenic addition to the text of the OG.
The Hebrew here reads ולא תשביעו ולא תעבדום ולא תשתחרו להם.
At this point the OG has ου μη προσκυνησετε αυτοις ουδε μη
λατρευσετε αυτοις. In addition to adding και ουκ ομεισθε
sub ※, Origen also reversed the OG order of the Greek verbs,
with the result that λατρευ- clearly rendered תעבדום and
προσκυν- represented תשחחרו.[165] In the process the metobelus
was incorrectly placed at the end of the verse even though the
last two verbs in Origen's corrected text did not constitute
"additional" material.[166]

  At 24:15 Field ascribes to Aq. a reading that contains
למפלח, which he correctly translates as λατρευειν.[167]   If
Field's ascription here is valid, then we suggest that Aq.
inadvertently retained λατρευω, the representation of עבד
found in the Greek text he was in the process of revising.

63. עָרַף (verb) = νωτοκοπω. This verb does not occur in the
MT of Joshua. The noun עֹרֶף appears twice in the MT of Joshua
(7:8, 12). αυχην, the translation of the OG, is found in all
extant witnesses to the text in both verses.[168]

74. יַעַן אֲשֶׁר = ανθ ων οσα. יַעַן אֲשֶׁר occurs in the Hebrew of
Joshua only at 14:14, in the clause
יַעַן אֲשֶׁר מִלֵּא אַחֲרֵי יְהוָה אֱלֹהֵי יִשְׂרָאֵל. The OG employs δια το
followed by an infinitive and accusative (δια το αυτον
επακολουθησαι) to represent ... יַעַן אֲשֶׁר. No revision of this
OG construction is recorded.[169] Neither ανθ ων οσα nor ανθ
ων οτι (see Bodine) is found in the OG of Joshua.

75. Misc. = ηνικα. Bodine raised questions about the
reliability of this criterion, especially since "it stands as
the translation of no exact Hebrew equivalent."[170] Nevertheless, since Thackeray did find the pattern of distribution
for ηνικα to have some significance for his work on Samuel-
Kings,[171] we should examine, if only briefly, the occurrences
of this word in Joshua.

ηνικα is found 4 times in the OG of Joshua (10:12; 22:7;
24:20, 27). At 10:12 the MT reads
אֵת הָאֱמֹרִי לִפְנֵי בְּנֵי יִשְׂרָאֵל וַיֹּאמֶר. At this point the OG presents
a longer text: τον αμορραιον υποχειριον ισραηλ ηνικα
συνετριψεν αυτους εν γαβαων και συνετριβησαν απο προσωπου υιων
ισραηλ και ειπεν.[172] Margolis, Holmes, and Benjamin each
translate ηνικα with a different Hebrew equivalent:
Margolis: בְּיַד יִשְׂרָאֵל בּ-
Holmes: בְּיַד יִשְׂרָאֵל כִּי
Benjamin: כַּאֲשֶׁר.
At 22:7 και ηνικα is used by the OG translator to render
וְגַם כִּי. It seems that Sym. did not retain the rendering of
the OG.[173] All other witnesses to the text read ηνικα,
with the OG. At 24:20 ηνικα, followed by εαν in Babcorx and
αν in AMNΘ rell Thdt, is found everywhere and translates MT כִּי.
ηνικα also occurs in all extant witnesses to the text at
24:27, followed by εαν in Boqryb₂ and αν in AMNΘ rell.[174]

Although ηνικα εαν/αν apparently represents MT פן at this point, Holmes states that the Greek translator read כי here.[175] If we accept Holmes' suggestions at both 10:12 and 24:27, ηνικα translates only כי in the OG of Joshua.

76. אחז = κρατεω.[176]   In the MT of Joshua אחז does not appear in the qal. Twice in chapter 22 (vv 9, 19) the niphal of this verb does occur. The Greek used to render the verb אחז is κληρονομεω at v 9 (in the OG and in all extant witnesses to the text except K[κατακλη-]) and κατακληρονομεω at v 19 (in the OG and everywhere else).[177]

78. טוב (all forms of the root) = αγαθος (and cognates). The root טוב appears 11 times in the Hebrew of Joshua: the adjective טוב at 7:21; 21:45; 23:13, 14, 15 (twice), 16; the verb ייטב/טוב at 9:25; 22:30, 33; 24:20. As we might expect, the OG translator employed both αγαθος (twice: 23:13, 15[b]) and καλος (3 times: 7:21; 21:45; 23:15[a]) to translate the adjective.[178]   It is interesting that both Aq. (apparently) and Sym. retain OG καλην in their revisions at 7:21.[179]

𝔖 did not maintain consistent equivalents for Greek καλος and αγαθος. Only at 7:21 is שפירא found. Elsewhere, including 23:14 and 16, where the OG lacks a translation for טוב, טבתא appears. Thus we must rely on the Greek manuscripts, especially x, for a determination of the underlying Greek.[180]

At 23:14 the MT reads הדברים הטובים. In the OG no rendering of הטובים is found after των λογων. In bcfmqv(mg) xz(mg)𝔖(sub ※) των αγαθων translates הטובים. It is possible that the OG translation of הטובים was lost after παντων των λογων. If this is so, then we suggest that the OG was retained in manuscripts of the Lucianic recension (gnptw Thdt), which read των καλων.[181]   At 23:16 της αγαθης is found as part of a longer reading in θcdefjkmoqsvxy^{a?}zb₂𝔄𝔖(sub ※ vz𝔖).[182] Thus Origen drew his material in both verses from a source that contained the characteristic καιγε rendering. The OG translator, as we pointed out above, used both καλος and αγαθος.

At 9:25; 22:30, 33 the OG translator employed αρεσκω to represent the verb יטב/טוב. At 24:20 the hiphil of the root יטב appears in the MT: היטיב לכם. Here the OG has ευ εποιησεν υμας. At 22:30 a reading has been preserved for Aq. in 𝔖: ... רטב בעינא. Field was probably correct to translate this as και αγαθον εν οφθαλμοις.... Field adds the following observation: "Pro רטב legendum suspicor וטאב, και ηγαθυνθη."[183] In either case, Aq. most likely did make use of a form of αγαθος to render the Hebrew here. טוב = αγαθος, found also in Origen's 2 asterisked additions, is the equivalence characteristic of the καιγε recension.

79. ישר (all forms of the root) = ευθυς (and cognates). ישר appears twice in the MT of Joshua (9:25; 10:13). At 9:25 the MT reads כטוב וכישר בעיניך. At this point (9:31 in the LXX) the OG has ως αρεσκει υμιν και ως δοκει υμιν.[184]

At 10:13 the following clause, lacking in the OG, appears in the MT: הלא היא כתובה על ספר הישר. A representation of the Hebrew is found in GθbcegjmnoqvΝ(mg)xz(mg)𝔄𝔈𝔖 Thdt (sub ※ Gv[mg] 𝔖). As we noted in our listing of this reading under category 4.1 in chapter 1,[185] this representation is found in two slightly different forms:
ουχι τουτο γεγραμμενον επι βιβλιου του ευθους in Gθbcejmoqv(mg) xz(mg) 𝔄𝔈𝔖 (sub ※ Gv[mg]𝔖);
ουχι αυτο γεγραπται επι βιβλιον το ευρεθεν in gn Thdt, witnesses to the Lucianic recension.[186]
The form of this reading preserved in manuscripts of the P recension makes it clear that here Origen drew his material from a source that contained the characteristic καιγε rendering of Hebrew ישר. Masius places this addition sub θ', thus indicating that Th. was Origen's source for this rendering. Margolis provides further evidence that this translation is characteristic of the καιγε recension when he notes that "ישרון is rendered ευθυς (-ης) α'σ'θ' Is 44:2 σ' Dtn 33:5."[187]

The noun מישור occurs 5 times in the Hebrew of Joshua
(13:9, 16, 17, 21; 20:8). In the 4 passages in chapter 13 the
OG translator employed the transliteration μεισωρ to
represent the Hebrew. At 20:8 the OG rendering is πεδιον. In
2 of the verses in chapter 13 the translation ομαλος is
ascribed to Aq.-Sym.[188]   At 13:9 this ascription is preserved
in v(mg) and Eusebius.[189]   At 13:16, where ομαλην is again
attributed to Aq.-Sym,[190]   ομαλην μισωρ is found in k; x
also has ομαλην (𝕊[txt] contains the transliteration).

Although ομαλος is attributed to both Sym. and Aq., there
are reasons for thinking that it properly belongs only in the
text of Sym. (1) For Aq. ομαλος is an equivalent of ערבה.[191]
(2) In several places outside of Joshua a form of ομαλος
represents MT מישור only in the text of Sym.[192]   Bearing this
in mind, we cannot be certain that Field has correctly
rendered a reading ascribed to Aq. in 𝕊 at 13:21. There he
translates Syriac דשׁוריתא as της ομαλης, adding "cf. at v 9."
There is, however, no reading for Aq. or Sym. preserved in
Syriac at v 9 (see above). In any case, neither the reading
preserved in Syriac for Aq. at v 21 nor that recorded for
Aq.-Sym. at 13:9, 16 is the characteristic καιγε rendering
for a form of the root ישׁר.[193]

Although no other form of ישׁר appears in the MT of
Joshua, the phrase επ ευθειας does occur in LXX[B] and almost
all other manuscripts at 8:14:

MT   לקראת ישראל
LXX[B]   εις συναντησιν αυτοις επ ευθειας. Several explanations
have been offered for the reading of LXX[B] at this point.
According to Margolis, who includes these words in his text
of the OG, αυτοις is a "contraction for ישׁראל" and επ ευθειας
is "prob. free addition."[194] Holmes states that επ ευθειας
represents a misreading of MT ישׁראל as ישׁר. He rejects
Ehrlich's suggested אל מישׁור, on the grounds that the OG of
Joshua always transliterated מישׁור.[195] Benjamin makes the
following notations: αυτοις "explicit addition"; "επ ευθειας =
ישׁר abbreviation for ישׁראל."[196] Finally, Soggin states the
"LXX has επ ευθειας ... in Hebrew $b^e y^e \check{s} ar \bar{a}$, originally no doubt

an abbreviation, later misunderstood, of 'against Israel'
b^e yiśrā'ēl."[197]
In our opinion αυτοις alone represents the original
wording of this passage and is the OG. In the tradition
underlying the MT, ישראל entered the text and supplanted this
original wording. Thus αυτοις επ ευθειας, so widely attested
in the Greek, is an early conflation of the OG (and original)
αυτοις and the MT ישראל (misread or misinterpreted as ישר).
The reading from 4QJoshua at this point is לקראתם. This is
supportive of our line of argument; however, since we do not
know what came immediately before or after לקראתם on the
scroll from Qumran, our reconstruction of the original here
remains tentative.

We close the discussion of this characteristic with a
look at the occurrence of ευθεως at 6:11. Holmes thinks that
this word represents פעם אחת found in the MT: "the translator
does not appear to have known the meaning of פעם."[198] According
to Margolis, the OG probably omitted פעם אחת, with ευθεως a
free addition.[199]

80. לין = αυλιζω. This verb (meaning "to lodge, pass the
night") occurs 4 times in the Hebrew of Joshua (3:1; 4:3;
6:11; 8:9). At 8:9 the OG lacks the clause in which לין
appears. The OG translator used a different Greek verb to
represent לין in each of the other 3 passages. At 3:1 the
OG rendering καταλυω is found in all extant witnesses to the
text except q, where a form of καταβαινω appears. At 4:3
the MT reads במלון אשר תלינו. The OG at this point is
εν τη στρατοπεδια υμων ου εαν παρεμβαλητε.[200] bdgnptwx,
manuscripts of the P and S recensions, read παραβαλητε.[201]
The last part of 6:11 reads as follows in the MT:
ויבאו המחנה וילינו במחנה. The OG here is απηλθεν εις την
παρεμβολην και εκοιμηθη εκει.[202] The imperative of the OG
verb, κοιμηθητω (also απελθατω for OG απηλθεν), appears as an
anonymous reading in v(mg)z(mg). κοιμαω, like καταλυω (the
OG at 3:1), is a common rendering of לין in the OG.[203]

κατεπαυσεν, a representation that Margolis terms "more decorous than εκοιμηθη," is found in gnw, manuscripts of the Lucianic recension. The καιγε rendering is found in q, which reads ηυλισθη.[204] If Field is correct, Sym. is perhaps the source for the use of this verb here. 𝔖 preserves a reading for Sym. at this point. In it the Syriac verb חוב appears, which Field translates as αυλισθησεται. Since this form is from the same root (בוח) as that found in 𝔖(txt) at 8:9, where the underlying Greek is ηυλισθη (see below), it is almost certain that Field is correct to include a form of αυλιζω in the text of Sym.[205]

At 8:9, where the OG lacks the clause in which Hebrew לין occurs, ηυλισθη (MT: וילן) appears as part of a longer reading that translates the MT in M(mg)b-hjknpqstvxz𝐴𝐵𝐸 (sub ⁙ M[mg] v).[206] Here Origen drew his material from a source that contained the translation characteristic of the καιγε recension. The use of αυλιζω in Origen's source stands in contrast to the practice of the OG translator of Joshua, who used the other two common Greek translations of לין, καταλυω and κοιμαω, as well as the rare representation παρεμβαλλω.

81. נצל = ρυομαι. This verb appears 4 times in the MT of Joshua.[207] At 2:13; 9:26 (LXX 9:32); 24:10 the OG translation is εξαιρεω, one of the two common OG renderings. In none of these passages is revision to another Greek verb recorded. At 22:31 the OG translator employed ρυομαι, characteristic of the καιγε recension, but also common in·the OG. Again the verb of the OG is found everywhere. These examples do not provide any help for isolating the καιγε recension of Joshua.

The reading of 𝔖 at 22:31, however, might lead to some modification of the following statement made by Bodine: "The equivalents in 𝔖 are clear .... For ρυομαι, 𝔖 employs *praq*; and for εξαιρεω, *pṣâ*."[208] In accordance with these equivalences 𝔖(txt) does contain *pṣâ* at 9:26 and 24:10, but *pṣâ* also appears in 𝔖 at 22:31, where there is no evidence for a form of εξαιρεω as the underlying Greek.[209]

ρυομαι appears again in the OG at 22:22, where the MT has
חושיענו. Here 𝔊(txt) does use *praq* to render ρυομαι, a form
of which is found in all extant witnesses to the text. These
examples lead us to conclude that while 𝔊 may well have
restricted *praq* to ρυομαι, it permitted *peṣâ* to render ρυομαι,
as well as εξαιρεω. If the practice of 𝔊 in Judges is the
same as that in Joshua, then we cannot be sure of the Greek
underlying Syriac *peṣâ*, unless we check those Greek manuscripts
that stand closest to 𝔊.

82. שוב = επιστρεφω. As the evidence below shows, this is
another of the characteristics that is particularly useful in
Joshua. The qal[210] of this verb occurs 33 times in the MT
of Joshua.[211] The OG translator of Joshua used 12 different
Greek verbs to represent Hebrew שוב (listed in order of
decreasing frequency): αποστρεφω (9 times); αναστρεφω (4
times); απερχομαι (παλιν) (3 times); αφιημι (twice);
επιστρεφω (twice); επερχομαι, καθιζω,[212] μεταβαλλω, ορμαω,
παραγι(γ)νομαι, παυω, υποστρεφω (once each). We are unable
to detect any pattern in the translator's choice of representations.

At 6 places the OG lacks a representation of שוב (2:22;
10:15, 43; 20:6; 22:9; 23:12[a]). At 2:22 εως επεστρεψαν οι
διωκοντες (MT: עד שבו הרדפים) appears in FNbcgqxz(mg)𝒜𝒷𝒸ᵐ
(sub ※ vid 𝒷ᵐ).[213] επεσρεψαν also appears in the reading
attributed to οι λ in v(mg; sub ※) and M(mg).[214] The
rendering characteristic of the καιγε recension occurs again
as part of a longer reading at 10:15. There the OG lacks the
following verse found at this point in the MT:
וישב יהושע וכל ישראל עמו אל המחנה הגלגלה. The translation
found in Bᵇ?ᶜ?Gθbcgiknoqrv(mg)xyᵃ?z(mg)𝒜𝒷ᶠ𝒸 contains the form
επεστρεψεν.[215] This addition is placed sub ※ in
Gv(mg)𝒷-cod.[216] At 20:6, in a passage which the OG lacks,
a form of επιστρεφω, επιστρεψει, translates ישוב in Aa-eghjn
pqtv-z𝒜𝒷𝒸. In these 3 places Origen drew his additional
material, marked with an asterisk except at 20:6, from a source
that contained the characteristic καιγε rendering.

We set against these passages 3 other examples, where
another Greek verb translates שוב in an asterisked addition of
Origen. The first of these, 10:43, is particularly significant, since in the MT 10:43 is identical to 10:15. Thus we
might well expect the same Greek translation as that found at
v 15, and that is what we find--with the exception of the
translation of the first word in the clause, וישב. While
Origen's source used επεστρεψεν at 10:15, his source here
(the same or a different one?) employed ανεστρεψεν, the
reading in Gbcxz(mg)$\not{A}\not{E}^c\not{S}$ (sub ※ G$\not{S}$). Although there is
no reason to expect full consistency even in the same source,
it is somewhat surprising to find different translations
for שוב in otherwise identical renderings.

The lack of a translation for שוב at the beginning of
22:9 may be connected with the OG rendering of v 8.[217] At
any rate, the representation of this word appears in 2 forms:
απεστρεψαν in bckox$\not{A}\not{E}$
επεστρεψαν in qv(mg; sub ※) (επεστρεψαν replaces the
following verb [επορευθησαν] in z[mg]).
The reading of $\not{S}$(txt) is והפכו ※. On the basis of
manuscript x,[218] B-McL is probably correct to translate this
as απεστρεψαν; however, three factors make the determination
of the authentic reading of Origen here difficult. (1) $\not{S}$
employs הפך for επεστρεφω, απεστρεφω, and other verbs as
well. (2) The reading in q and especially v(mg ; sub ※)
must be given some weight. (3) Since the only difference
between the 2 forms under discussion is the first letter,
there is the possibility of corruption either way (from *e>a*
or *a>e*) during the transmission of the reading. The OG does
not represent the infinitive absolute found at the beginning
of 23:12 in the MT: כי אם שוב תשובו; OG, εαν γαρ αποστραφητε.
The translation αποστροφη appears in c (αποστραφη) koqxz(mg)
$\not{A}\not{S}$(sub ※). It is likely that at this point Origen
fashioned his own "addition," using the same root, αποστρεφω,
that he found immediately following in the text before him.

No matter how we explain the renderings at 22:9 and 23:12(a), we are still left with the fact that the source(s) used by Origen was (were) not consistent in its (their) use of the καιγε rendering. Nevertheless, even the use of επιστρεφω 3 out of 6 times stands in contrast to the practice of the OG translation of Joshua, where επιστρεφω renders שוב only 2 out of 27 times.

Readings are preserved for Th., Aq., and Sym. at 5:2; 11:10; 22:8. The evidence from these 3 passages shows that Th. and Aq. consistently employ επιστρεφω to translate שוב.[219] At 5:2 Th. retained OG καθισας, a form that translates the root ישב rather than שוב. Thus from this example we learn nothing of the usual practice of Th. with respect to the root שוב. Both Aq. and Sym. provided translations of the root שוב; Aq. employed the καιγε rendering, Sym. did not: και επιστεψας περιτεμε, Aq.; και παλιν περιτεμε, Sym. At 11:10 επεστρεψεν replaces OG απεστραφη in the texts of Th., Aq., and Sym. This reading is also found in AFGNϑacikmxyz (mg)a₂b₂; K has επεστραφη. The reading of Greek witnesses to the P recension, especially x, makes it almost certain that הפך in Ꝯ(txt) here translates the verb επιστρεφω. At the beginning of 22:8 considerable differences separate the MT and the OG:

MT ויאמר אליהם לאמר בנכסים רבים שובו אל אהליכם

OG και εν χρημασιν πολλοις απηλθοσαν εις τους οικους αυτων.

At this point evidence in Greek for the revisions of Th., Aq., and Sym. is limited to only one word:[220]

Th. επιστρεφετε

Aq. επιστραφητε

Sym. αποστρεψετε.

Thus Th. (twice) and Aq. (3 times) used the translation characteristic of the καιγε recension; Sym., in the manner characteristic of him,[221] varied his representations of שוב. At 6:14 we have another example of this variation of representations in the text of Sym. There the OG uses και απελθεν παλιν to render MT וישבו. Ꝯ(txt) contains ויאזלו חוב, which

is a translation of the plural of this OG verb (see below).
In a reading attributed to Sym. the form וּפֹנֶא appears. While
Field may not be correct to translate this as υπεστρεψεν, he
is correct not to include a form of επιστρεφω in the text of
Sym. here.[222]

At both 11:10 and 2:23, passages mentioned above, manuscripts of the P recension, among others, have the שׁוּב =
επιστρεφω equivalence, in contrast to another reading in the
OG.[223] This is also true at 8:24, where και επεστρεψεν
(MT: וַיָּשָׁב; OG: και απεστρεψεν) appears in AFMNϑa-egjkm-qstv
(mg)w-b₂∦.[224] In these 3 passages Origen apparently
replaced the OG with a form of the characteristic καιγε
rendering. He may well have done so on the basis of one or
more of his sources (see especially at 11:10), although he
would not have marked these forms since they did not constitute "quantitative" changes of the OG vis-à-vis the MT.

In 2 places, so it seems, Origen replaced a non-καιγε
rendering of the OG with another non-καιγε rendering. We
have reference here to 2:16 and 22:29. At 2:16, where OG
αποστρεψωσιν is preserved only in Bcr (N has αποστρεψουσιν),
manuscripts of the P, C, and S recensions have αναστρεψωσιν.[225]
The καιγε rendering does appear here, but in manuscripts of
the N-group and a few others: επιστρεψωσιν, in Feijsv(txt)z.

At the beginning of 22:29 the MT reads as follows:
חלילו לנו ממנו למרד ביהוה ולשוב היום מאחרי יהוה. At this
point the OG is μη γενοιτο ουν ημας αποστραφηναι απο κυριου
εν ταις σημερον ημεραις, αποστησαι απο κυριου. In the
Hebrew *Vorlage* of the OG היום apparently came before לשוב,
rather than after לשוב as in the MT. In his effort to
correct toward the MT Origen rearranged the elements of the OG
in the following manner: μη γενοιτο ουν ημας αποστηναι απο
κυριου ωστε αποστραφηναι εν ταις σμηερον ημεραις απο κυριου.[226]
In the process he retained the rather free OG rendering of היום
and reversed the order of the OG verbs, with the result that
αφιημι rendered מרד and αποστρεφω translated שׁוּב. The effect
of this reversal of order is twofold: first, αποστρεφω now

renders שוב, as it does 9 times in the OG of Joshua, including v 18 of this chapter. [227] Secondly, αφιημι now renders מרד, as at 22:18, 19 in a similar context. [228] In our opinion Origen himself was responsible for these changes from the OG, and thus we learn nothing of the way(s) his source(s) translated שוב from this example. The same is true at 6:14, where Origen replaced the singular of the OG verb, απελθεν, with the plural of the same verb, απηλθον, to agree with the plural number of the Hebrew verb at this point. [229] The examples we have discussed provide solid support for the occurrence of the characteristic καιγε rendering of Hebrew שוב in Th., Aq., and the source used by Origen both for asterisked additions and elsewhere--and this in marked contrast to the practice of the OG translator of Joshua.

To complete our presentation of evidence, we note that the שוב = επιστρεφω equivalence also shows up occasionally in a passage where neither the OG nor manuscripts of the P recension show the characteristic rendering. In addition to 2:16 referred to above, this occurs at 10:21 (OG: απεστραφη; A: επεστραφη); 10:38 (OG: απεστρεψεν; a₂: επεστρεψεν); 22:32 (OG: απεστρεψεν; g: επεστρεψεν). [230]

Nos. 83-93 are contained in Bodine's Chapter III: "Characteristics Peculiar to the Vaticanus Family of Judges." [231] For these proposed characteristics we continue to present the evidence as fully as possible.

84. הביא = φερω/εισφερω. The hiphil of בוא occurs 5 times in the Hebrew of Joshua. [232] The OG employs φερω twice (7:23; 18:6), επαγω twice (23:15; 24:7), and αγω once (24:8). Revision to a verb other than that found in the OG is recorded at 23:15, where p^b has φερη: MT, יביא יהוה עליכם כן; OG, ουτως επαξει κυριος ο θεος εφ υμας; p^b, ουτος φερη ης ημας.

85. קעז/קעצ = βοαω. The hiphal of קעז appears in the first clause of 8:16, a clause that is lacking in the OG. The rendering found at this point in M(mg)bcdfkpqtv(mg)xz(mg)𝕬𝕭𝕾 (sub ÷) begins καὶ ενισχυσεν πας ο λαος. The verb ενισχυσεν presupposes ויחזקו rather than ויזעקו of the MT.[233] Thus, from this reading we learn how Origen's source (Th.?)[234] translated חזק; at the same time we are deprived of any evidence concerning the representation of קעז in this source. The qal of קעצ appears at 24:7. The OG translator used the compound αναβοαω to render this verb (OG: καὶ ανεβοησαμεν; MT: ויצעקו). εβοησαμεν, found in abcx, is probably the result of nothing more than the accidental loss of initial αν-.[235]

86. חרה אף = οργιζομαι θυμω. This expression occurs twice in the MT of Joshua (7:1 and 23:16). At 7:1 the OG translator used the phrase θυμουμαι οργη to render the Hebrew: MT, ויחר אף יהוה; OG, καὶ εθυμωθη οργη κυριος. No revision to the Judges-καιγε rendering is recorded. At 23:16 the OG does not contain a translation of the Hebrew phrase that begins וחרה אף יהוה. A representation of the Hebrew is found in θb-hjkm-qstvxy^{a?}zb₂𝕬𝕭𝕾(sub ÷ vz𝕾). In θbcdefjkmoqsvxy^{a?}zb₂ 𝕬𝕭𝕾 this rendering begins καὶ οργισθησεται θυμω κυριος.[236] Here Origen drew his additional material from a source containing the חרה אף = οργιζομαι θυμω equivalence, which Bodine has shown to be characteristic of the καιγε material in Judges.

Bodine notes that both θυμουμαι οργη, found in the OG at 7:11, and οργιζομαι θυμω, found in Origen's addition at 23:16, occur 14 times as the OG rendering of חרה אף. In Judges the B family uses οργιζομαι θυμω to render חרה אף in all 7 places in which the Hebrew expression occurs. Bodine is, therefore, justified to speak of this as "the consistent choice of the καιγε material in Judges."[237] On the basis of but one example, we ought not to speak of a "consistent choice" of the καιγε material in Joshua; however, we can link the usage at 23:16 with that in Judges and suggest that this equivalence may prove characteristic of the καιγε recension elsewhere as more καιγε material is identified and analyzed.

The expression אף חרן occurs at Joshua 7:26 in the clause וישב יהוה מחרון אפו. The OG is και επαυσατο κυριος του θυμου της οργης. This is in line with the OG rendering εθυμωθη οργη at v 1 of the same chapter. What we might term the καιγε rendering appears in dgnp, manuscripts of the Lucianic recension, and Δ₈: και επαυσατο κυριος απο της οργης του θυμου αυτου (Δ₈ omits απο). This reading also supplies the explicit translation for -מ and ו(אף) lacking in the OG, which suggests that it was drawn from a source similar to, if not the same as, that (those) Origen was accustomed to use for his additional material.[238] Was οργιζομαι θυμω chosen as the καιγε rendering because of a feeling that θυμος is a more literal and precise representation of Hebrew אף?

87. נלחם = παρατασσομαι. This Hebrew verb occurs 17 times in the MT of Joshua (9:2; 10:5, 14, 25, 29, 31, 34, 36, 38, 42; 11:5; 19:47; 23:3, 10; 24:8, 9, 11). The OG translator of Joshua employed a number of Greek verbs to represent Hebrew נלחם (listed in order of decreasing frequency): εκπολεμεω (3 times); πολεμεω (3 times); πολιορκεω (3 times); περικαθιζω (twice--10:36, 38);[239] συμπολεμεω (twice); εκπολιορκεω, καταπολεμεω, παρατασσω (once each, but see below for παρατασσω). With the exception of 24:8 (to be discussed in detail below) the Judges- καιγε rendering occurs only at 24:9, in all witnesses to the text, and at 10:38, in manuscripts of the Lucianic recension.

Origen replaced the OG rendering of נלחם only at 9:2: MT, ויתקבצו יחדו להלחם; OG; συνηλθοσαν επι το αυτο εκπολεμησαι; bcx(𝔊), και συνηλθον επι το αυτο εις το πολεμησαι. At 23:10 Th. retained OG εξεπολεμει in his revision: [ουτος] εξεπολεμει μεθ υμων.[240]

We now turn to 24:8 where the MT reads: ויאבאה אתכם אל ארץ האמרי היושב בעבר הירדן וילחמו אתכם ואתן אותם בידכם. The reading of LXX[B] is και ηγαγεν ημας εις γην αμορραιων των κατοικουντων περαν του ιορδανου και παραδεδωκεν αυτους εις τας χειρας ημων. For the purposes of the present discussion our main concern is whether or not the omission of a translation for וילחמו אתכם, only in Bhr, is original to the OG. This question assumes greater significance when we observe that a form of παρατασσομαι is the rendering found in AMNθ rell 𝐴𝐶𝐸𝐿𝑆: παρεταξατο in Aoq𝐶𝐸, παρεταξαντο elsewhere. παρατασσομαι is the rendering characteristic of the καιγε material in Judges (though definitely not after Judges).

At many places in Joshua LXX[B] alone, or with the support of only a few other manuscripts, preserves the authentic reading of the OG. Nevertheless, several considerations lead to the conclusion that here the text of LXX[B] is probably the result of inner-Greek corruption, rather than the preservation of the OG in its original form. (1) An original και παρεταξαντο υμιν could easily have been lost per homoioarchton between περαν and παραδεδωκεν: περαν του ιορδανου και παρεταξαντο υμιν και παραδεδωκεν. This would have occurred even more easily if παρεδωκεν, rather than παραδεδωκεν (only in Bil), were found in the OG. A similar explanation would not account for the loss of this clause in the Hebrew *Vorlage* of the OG. (2) The fact that παρατασσομαι occurs in the next verse is an argument in favor of the originality of παρατασσομαι in v 8. When the OG translator used a specific representation for נלחם more than once, he tended to place the occurrences of that representation next to each other. [241] If this translator did include a rendering of נלחם in his text at 24:8, on the basis of 24:9 we would not be surprised if that rendering were a form of παρατασσομαι. (3) και παρεταξαντο υμιν is not marked as additional material in 𝔊.

In favor of the originality of the shorter text in (the Hebrew *Vorlage* of) the OG we may make the following observations. (1) The very fact that LXX^B alone often preserves the OG in Joshua should guard against the too-hasty rejection of its text, especially when the alternate text could easily be a correction of LXX^B (=OG) to the MT. (2) While it is not easy to explain the loss of וילחמו אתכם in the Hebrew *Vorlage* of the OG (cf. [1] in the preceding paragraph), one might speculate that this clause did not form part of the Hebrew text used by the OG translator, but entered the tradition underlying the MT at a later time. The basis for the addition of the clause here is found through a comparison with verse 11. The sequence of verbs there, בוא-נלחם-נתן ביד, might have prompted a scribe or editor to include נלחם at v 8 (the original wording of which included only בוא [הביא] and נתן) and thus construct a fully parallel structure between the two verses. In this case LXX^B would be a complete and accurate representation of the Hebrew *Vorlage* of the OG. (3) On a number of occasions the presence or absence of signs in 𝔖 has proved not to be a trustworthy indicator of the procedure of Origen. This may be another of those occasions.

Joshua 24:8 does not provide unambiguous evidence that the נלחם = παρατασσομαι equivalence holds true for καιγε material before Judges as well as in Judges. Solid evidence for this equivalence elsewhere in the καιγε recension (for example, in the Pentateuch) would prompt further consideration of what is now at best an isolated extra-Judges example.[242]

88. מלחמה = παραταξις. מלחמה, like נלחם above, occurs frequently in the Hebrew of Joshua (18 times: 4:3; 5:4, 6; 6:3; 8:1, 3, 11, 14; 10:7, 24; 11:7, 18, 19, 20, 23; 14:11, 15; 17:1). The OG translator used a form of πολεμ- to render Hebrew מלחמה in all of these passages except 5:4, 6; 6:3. There is no significant revision in any of the passages where the מלחמה = πολεμ- equivalence appears in the OG.

The OG lacks a translation for כל אנשי המלחמה and
surrounding material at 5:4. παντες ανδρες πολεμου is the
rendering found in M(mg)bckqv(mg)xz(mg)(sub ※ ✠; sub οι λ̥
ου ο᾽ ※ v[mg]). At 5:6 the MT reads עד תם כל הגוי אנשי המלחמה.
The OG at this point is διο οι απεριτμητοι ησαν οι
πλειστοι(αυτων)των μαχιμων.[243] ✠ has preserved readings
for both Aq. and Sym. The text attributed to Aq. includes
עדמא דספר כלה עמא דגברא דקרבא, which Field translates as
εως εξελιπεν παν το εθνος ανδρων πολεμου. Field translates
the reading of Sym. (עדמא דאחטלק כלה עמא גברא קרבתנא) as
εως αναλωθη πας ο λαος ανδρες πολεμισται.[244] At 6:3 the OG
translator used παντες τους μαχιμους to render כל אנשי המלחמה.
Origen placed the OG of verse 3 sub ⸓ and added sub ·※ in his
text a representation of the MT of verses 3 and 4.[245]
Included in this translation is παντες ανδρες (του) πολεμου,
the reading of Fbcghnqtv(mg)xz(mg)✠(sub ※ ✠; sub οι λ ·※
v[mg]). Th. is Origen's probable source at this point.[246]
    It is not surprising to find πολεμος in the OG of
Joshua, in the asterisked additions of Origen, or in the texts
of Aq., Sym., and Th.(?), since πολεμος or an etymologically
related word is the OG equivalent for מלחמה 213 times outside
of Judges and the καιγε equivalent at least 38 times outside
of Judges.[247] In Judges the מלחמה = παραταξις equivalence
is related to the Judges-καιγε characteristic discussed under
no. 87 above. The fact that we find no evidence for the
Judges-καιγε rendering of מלחמה is perhaps another indication
that the reading at 24:8 (with παρατασσομαι) should not be
taken as evidence that a distinctive rendering of נלחם is
characteristic of the καιγε recension in Joshua.

90. סרן = αρχων. Bodine noted that at 13:3 the OG translator
employed a form of σατραπ(ε)ια to represent Hebrew סרן: MT,
חמשת סרני פלשתים; OG, ταις πεντε σατραπιαις των φυλιστιειμ.[248]
B-McL lists the following as variant readings: quinque regibus
(⅄-ed; +et satrapis codd), quinque satrapis (⅄-codd), σατραπαις
(a₂), αστραπειαις (dp).[249]

91. פגע = συνανταω/απανταω.[250] In the MT of Joshua פגע
occurs 10 times (all in the qal: 2:16; 16:7; 17:10; 19:11
[twice], 22, 26, 27, 34 [twice]). Only at 2:16, where the OG
uses συνανταω, does this verb have its general meaning "to
meet, encounter." Elsewhere פגע appears in the specialized
sense of a boundary "touching, striking" a particular
location.[251]

At 16:7, the first occurrence of פגע with this meaning,
the OG translator apparently labored to arrive at a satisfactory rendering. There he used a form of ερχομαι (MT:
ופגע ביריחו; OG [BGbchrx𝑥(vid)𝑒𝑓𝑠]: και ελευσεται επι [ad
𝑙] ιερειχω).[252] Neither q (with απερχομαι) nor ANϑ rell 𝐴
(with διερχομαι) introduce into this passage one of the two
most frequent LXX translations of פגע, απανταω and συνανταω,
or the rendering used by the OG translator in later passages
of Joshua (see below). At 17:10 the OG translator chose
συναπτω as his rendering of פגע, and he continued to employ
this very appropriate choice throughout the rest of Joshua.
This is true for 17:10 and for all the occurrences of פגע in
chapter 19, except 19:11(b), where the OG lacks a translation
for ופגע.

At 19:11(b) και απαντησει translates ופגע in Gbckx𝐴𝑠(sub
⁜ G𝑠). Origen drew his material here from a source in which
απανταω, rather than (OG) συναπτω, rendered פגע, even in this
specialized sense. απανταω is not the verb employed in the
B family of Judges; however, its occurrences in Ruth (referred
to above) alert us to the possibility that the use of απανταω
here may be significant. This possibility becomes even
stronger when we look at a reading attributed to Aq. at 19:22.
In the beginning of this verse the MT reads ופגע הגבול בחבור.
At this point the OG has και συναψει τα ορια επι θαβωρ.[253] A
reading attributed to Aq. has been preserved in 𝑠:
ונפגע תחומא בתבור.[254] Field translates this as και απαντησει
τον οριον εις θαβωρ. Bodine indicates that in Judges Syriac
פגע translates απανταω,[255] and from 19:11(b) we can be sure
that the practice in Joshua was the same.[256] Therefore, we
have no reason to doubt that Field is correct to include
απαντησει in the text of Aq. at 19:22. The use of απανταω in
Origen's asterisked addition at 19:11 and in the text of Aq.

330

at 19:22 strongly suggests that we should understand the פגע =
απανταω equivalence both here and in Ruth as characteristic of
the καιγε recension.[257] It is important to remember that the
use of απανταω in these two verses of Joshua stands in marked
contrast to the practice of the OG translator throughout
chapter 19.[258]

At 19:26 Sym. read וְאֵתַר עַל כַרְמְלָא (MT: וּפָגַע בַכַרְמֶל; OG:
και συναψει τω καρμηλω). Field translates the reading of Sym.
as και κατηντησεν επι καρμηλον and refers to 16:7. There the
following is ascribed to Aq.: וְאֵתֵא לְאִירִיחֻו. According to
Field, the Greek underlying this is και κατηντησεν εις ιεριχω
("Syriacum אתא commutatur cum κατηντησεν in Hex. ad Job. xxix
13").[259] While the evidence from Job 29:13, which refers
to a reading of Sym., might well be brought in to support
Field's translation at 19:26, such evidence is less helpful
at 16:7. This is especially so inasmuch as (1) the reading
here is attributed to Aq. and (2) the Syriac verb used in
the reading of Aq. is the same as that in 𝔖(txt), where it
represents a form of ερχομαι (see above). If this clause
at 16:7 is to be attributed to Aq., then Aq. most likely
retained a form of the verb ερχομαι, while changing επι to
εις as at 19:22.[260]

We do not feel that the evidence at 16:7, however it is
explained, appreciably weakens our conclusion that the
examples at 19:11(b) and 22 represent a rendering characteristic of the καιγε recension in certain books. συvανταω,
which translated פגע at 2:16, was not employed by the καιγε
recension of Joshua as its equivalent for that word, perhaps
because συvανταω also appeared in the OG of Joshua as a
rendering of קרא (at 11:20) and εις συvαντησιν was the
representation of לקראת (4 times).[261] απανταω, on the other
hand, does not occur at all in the OG of Joshua, and thus
there would be less chance of confusion over Hebrew counter-
parts.[262]

92. קציך = αρχηγος. Bodine indicated that at 10:24 the OG translator used a form of εναρχομαι to represent Hebrew קצין.[263] He also noted that the καιγε word of Judges, αρχηγος, appears in manuscripts of the Lucianic recension. A close examination of 10:24 reveals that this rendering found in the Lucianic recension might bear witness to the קצין = αρχηγος equivalence in καιγε material of Joshua.

In the middle of 10:24 the MT reads ויאמר אל קציני אנשי המלחמה. At this point the OG has και τους εναρχομενους του πολεμου.[264] The reading found in dgnptw, all manuscripts of the Lucianic recension, is και ειπεν προς τους αρχηγους των ανδρων του πολεμου.[265] Only in these manuscripts is there a full correction to the MT. This reading, then, has both a rendering characteristic of Judges-καιγε and a correction of the OG to the MT. This suggests to us that the wording here was incorporated into manuscripts of the Lucianic recension on the basis of a source in which characteristic renderings and corrections to the MT appear with some frequency. Th. and Aq. are certainly two sources that fit that description. If this reading does characterize the source--probably Th. or Aq.--from which it was drawn, then we have evidence that the קצין = αρχηγος equivalence is characteristic of the καιγε recension outside of Judges, as well as in Judges.

93. רעה = πονηρια. רעה does not occur in the MT of Joshua. Bodine expanded his discussion to include related Hebrew words.[266] The noun רע, like רעה, does not appear in Joshua; רע, the adjective, and רעע are found (the adjective at 23:15, 24:15; the verb at 24:20). At 23:15 the OG rendering τα ρηματα τα πονηρα (MT: הדבר הרע) is found in all extant witnesses to the text. At 24:15 the OG translator employed ει δε μη αρεσκει υμιν to represent Hebrew ואם רע בעיניכם.[267] A reading preserved in 𝔊 has the literal translation ואן בישא בעיניכון. Field, who ascribes this reading to Aq., translates the Syriac as και ει πονηρον εν οφθαλμοις υμων.

Bodine notes that the text groups of Judges are all "united
in translating רע by a form of πονηρος, as is the rest of the
Heptateuch and Samuel-Kings."[268]   Thus we attach no significance to the single occurrence of this equivalence in the OG
or to the one example preserved in the text of Aq. At 24:20
a form of κακοω translates the verb רעע; no revision to
another verb is recorded.

94. The practice of leaving unknown words untranslated. Even
before the publication of Tov's article, Bodine and others had
noted the potential usefulness of transliteration, rather than
translation, as an aid toward isolating the καιγε recension.[269]
Tov's study, however, is the first extended treatment of this
subject with a view toward establishing certain types of
transliteration as characteristic of the καιγε recension. His
methodological considerations are well taken, and his classification of transliterations is most helpful. He groups
transliterations in four categories "each of which has a
different *raison d'être*: (1) proper nouns; (2) technical terms;
(3) words probably unknown to the translator, which thus
remained untranslated. . . .; (4) transliterations of common
nouns erroneously transliterated as proper nouns because of
the context."[270]   Focusing his investigation on transltera-
tions of the third group, Tov concluded that

> the practice of leaving unknown words untrans-
> lated has been shown to be characteristic of
> *kaige* in reigns γδ and of Th. . . . Or, to
> phrase our conclusion, with due caution, in a
> different way: we were able to point out a new
> characteristic common to two members of the
> *kaige*-Th. group. When used critically, this
> criterion may also be applied to other members
> of the same group.[271]

He is also careful to point out the appropriateness of such a
practice on the part of the individual(s)[272] responsible for
the καιγε recension.

In his appendix Tov lists examples of group 3 under 2
subgroups: a) unknown (?) words which were left untranslated
(in the LXX and Th. [also in Th.-Dan. and collective

readings]); b) transliterations of unknown or difficult words which were probably understood as proper nouns (in the LXX; no sure examples in Th.). According to Tov, transliterations of subgroup a do not occur in the OG of Joshua. He includes one example of subgroup b for Joshua: "11:2; 12:23; 17:11 נפות, נפה, נפח." The MT is ובנפות דור at 11:2, לנפת דור at 12:23, and שלשת הנפת at 17:11. At 11:2 Soggin translates בנפות דור as "in the dunes of Dor" and makes the following observations:

> the Hebrew term nāpāh, here in the plural with prefixes, has not yet been explained, and until this happens, it is pointless to correct the form found here (as BH^3 and Noth do). It appears in the construct in 1 Kings 4.11, again in a geographical context. The expression we propose is also quite hypothetical, but gives a clear meaning if one considers the configuration of the region.[273]

At 12:23 and 17:11 Soggin employs the transliterations Naphath-dor and Napheth, respectively.

As reconstructed by Margolis, the OG is φενναθ δωρ at 11:2 and 12:23, and της ναφετα at 17:11. It is clear, as Tov states, that the OG translator employed transliteration in these three passages. Exactly what he read in his Hebrew *Vorlage* at these places, especially 11:2 and 12:23, is less clear. Margolis calls attention to the different form of the Hebrew in 11:2 (נפות דור) and 12:23 (נפת דור). He continues his remarks concerning the OG at 11:2 as follows: "Apparently the OG read here likewise the singular. In both places the OG transposes נ and פ as if 'פנח ד. But 17:11 הנפּח ναφετα E goes back to ναφετ."[274] In both the form (at 11:2) and transposition (at 11:2 and 12:23) the OG transliteration may well be reflecting a development that had already taken place in its Hebrew *Vorlage*. Manuscripts of Margolis' P and C recensions read ναφεθ δωρ at 11:2 and ναφεθ/-φαθ δωρ at 12:23.

Although we do not know how Th. or Aq. handled these three passages, a reading is preserved for Sym. in all three verses. At 11:2 𝔖 records the following for Sym.: ולספר ימא דדור מן מערבא. Field, who rejects Masius'

retroversion (την ακτην της θαλασσης της δωρ), translates the
Syriac as και εις την παραλιαν δωρ απο δυσμων.[275] At 12:23
the reading of Sym. is דספר ימא ([δωρ] της παραλιας).[276]
Similarly, at 17:11 the Syriac translation of the reading of
Sym. is ספרי ימא ותלתחיהרך (και αι τρεις παραλιαι).[277] In
this case Sym. does not conform to the practice that Tov has
termed characteristic of the καιγε recension.

On the basis of these passages alone we can draw no
general conclusions about the practice of Sym. in Joshua,
to say nothing of the practice of Th. and Aq., for whom no
readings are preserved. On the other hand, the fuller picture
that emerges from the investigation of other examples does
permit the following specific conclusions here: (1) the procedure of Sym. at 11:2; 12:23; 17:11 is in accord with the
practice of Sym. throughout Joshua; (2) Th. included a transliteration of the Hebrew in these three passages; (3) a translation, although not necessarily that found in Sym., probably
appeared in the text of Aq. As we review the evidence from
Joshua on which we base the three statements above, we will
also offer some expansion and modification of Tov's proposed
characteristic.[278]

At 10:40(a) and 15:19(a) Th. retained the OG transliteration ναγεβ. In these two passages, and also at 11:16 and 12:8,
the OG translator understood נגב preceded by the definite
article as a proper name. We would place the transliteration
of the OG and Th. here under category 1 of Tov. There is no
reason to term these "erroneous" transliterations of common
nouns (Tov's category 4), with the possible exception of 15:19
(a).[279] In any case, for all four of these passages (as well
as for others, where נגב is clearly to be understood as a
common noun), Aq. and Sym. consistently employ the translation
νοτος as their rendering of Hebrew נגב.[280]

At 11:8(a) the transliteration of the OG and Th. reflects
an understanding of Hebrew מישרפות מים as a proper name.[281]
While Aq. and Sym. also include a transliteration of משרפות,
both have a translation for מים.[282] It is possible that Aq.

and Sym. interpreted the Hebrew phrase as a common noun, but were unable to supply even a translation guess for משרפות (although משרפות as a common noun does occur twice in the Hebrew Bible).[283] In that case their transliteration would more correctly be placed under Tov's group 3. It seems to us that the OG transliteration at 15:19 should also be included in Tov's group 3, specifically under subgroup b.[284] At the first of the 3 occurrences of (מים) גלח in 15:19 Th., like the OG, employs transliteration to reflect the Hebrew.[285] As at 11:8(a) both Aq. and Sym. translate מים. Unlike 11:8(a) both Aq. and Sym. also attempt to supply translations for גלה. The reading of Sym. (κτησιν) is nothing more than a translation guess, while the reading of Aq. (λυτρωσιν) may reflect a variant Hebrew text (or an interpretive rendering of MT גלה).[286] Here both Sym. and Aq. apparently felt that the replacement of transliteration with translation resulted in an improved representation of the Hebrew phrase.

At 7:24(end), 26 the OG translator again employed transliteration: OG, εμεκαχωρ; MT, עמק עכור. In both verses Th. and Sym. translate עמק (κοιλας), but retain the trans- literation αχωρ. The OG understood the whole phrase as a proper noun. The procedure of Th. and Sym. is in accordance with the practice of English translations (Valley of Achor) and also reflects an understanding of the phrase as a proper noun. At 7:26 (also v 24?) Aq. wrote κοιλας ταραχου, trans- lating both elements of this phrase. It is not easy to discern what motivated Aq. to supply this full translation. Perhaps he was trying to convey a sense of word play through the use of ταραχου in v 26 and the verb ταρασσω in v 25.[287]

At 15:25(24) Th.-Aq.-Sym. all use την καινην to represent חדתה in the phrase וחצור חדתה; OG, και κωμαι αυτης; Th.-Aq.-Sym., και ασωρ την καινην. This representation suggests an under- standing of the Hebrew as a form of the adjective "new" (cf. the procedure of x: και ασωρ και αδαθα).[288] In our discussion of 18:28 we noted that Th. and Aq. rendered Hebrew קרית ערים intelligently and intelligibly.[289] We had reference to the rendering that resulted from transliterating קרית (καριαϑ) and translating ערים (πολεις). The OG translator's use of transliteration for Hebrew מישׁור (4 times: 13:9, 16, 17, 21) may be placed under Tov's group 4. Although the translation ομαλος is attributed to both Sym. and Aq., we presented evidence that this translation properly belongs only in the text of Sym.[290]

Although the examples cited above do not form a complete catalogue of passages where there is a difference of procedure (transliteration-translation) among the various witnesses to the text,[291] we have seen probable examples of Tov's categories 1, 3, and 4, as well as others that cannot be definitely placed in any one category. In general Th. retained the transliterations he found in the (old) Greek text with which he was working. Departures from this rule can usually be explained by the desire for a more intelligent and intelligible rendering. We do not have many examples where the procedure of Th. differs from that of the OG translator; still, we feel that it is not unreasonable to speak of Th. as the *intelligent* transliterator *par excellence* and to speak of *intelligent* and *intelligible* transliteration as a general characteristic of the καιγε recension.[292] From a not yet complete investigation of the readings attributed to Sym. it is clear that Sym. translated in many cases where the revisor(s) responsible for the καιγε material transliterated (whether that involved a retention of the OG or not). Transliteration (in general and to a certain degree with specific reference to Tov's category 3) does not seem to characterize the work of Aq.

We have attempted to offer "some expansion and modification of Tov's proposed characteristic."[293] Perhaps, however, more than anything else we have discovered that there are nuances and subtleties to be encountered at almost every example of transliteration we have discussed under no. 94. We have no doubt that Tov's characteristic is useful and that future work will result in the refining and sharpening of criteria associated with this characteristic. This in turn will allow researchers to apply the 'transliteration characteristic' with an ever increasing degree of precision.

Bodine noted that four of the ten characteristics isolated by Thackeray had not been brought into the discussion of the καιγε recension at the time he was writing.[294] He included two of them (nos. 74 and 75 in this chapter) in his dissertation.[295] We conclude this section of chapter 3 with the other two characteristics isolated by Thackeray.

95. גדול (איש) = αδρος. Thackeray refers to 4 occurrences of αδρος in Reigns βδ (2 Sam 15:18 B; 1 K 1:9 B; 2K 10:6, 11). Thus at 2 K 10:6 LXX has ουτοι αδροι της πολεως (MT: את) גדלי העיר; at v 11 παντας τους αδρους αυτου renders Hebrew כל גדוליו.[296]

גדול occurs 26 times in the MT of Joshua.[297] αδρος does not appear in the OG of any of these passages, nor is it found in any other witness to the text in those places where the OG clearly lacks a translation for גדול (6 times) or fails to provide a clear translation for גדול (4 additional times). The translations appearing in the additions of Origen are μεγαν (8:29), μεγαλη (10:2[b]), μεγαλους (10:18, 27), μεγαλα (24:17), all sub ※ ; and μεγας (20:6), not sub ※ . At 1:4(b) a clear translation of הגדול (הים) is found in manuscripts of the Lucianic recension: μεγαλης (OG: εσχατης). At 6:5 Sym. (and probably also Aq.) used μεγαν (Syriac רבא) to translate גדולה.[298] At 10:11 μεγαλους is attributed to ο'α'σ'.[299] At 14:15 Aq. has ο ανθρωπος ο μεγας (Syriac ברנשא הר רבא).[300] Finally, at 10:27 μεγαλους, which appears in the asterisked addition of Origen (see above), is also found in Th.-Aq.-Sym. Thus there is absolutely no evidence that this equivalence is characteristic of the καιγε recension (or the OG) of Joshua.

We also find in Joshua 2 occurrences of the verb גדל (3:7; 4:14). At 3:7 the OG translator used υψοω to render the piel

of גדל, and at 4:14 he employed αυξανω. In this latter passage
q reads εμεγαλυνε. For Joshua the verb גדל in no way alters
the picture we derived from our examination of גדל.

96. אבל = και μαλα. אבל does not occur in the MT of Joshua.
και μαλα does not appear in the OG of this book.

καιγε readings in Th.[301]

2.	רק	1:18
3.	איש	8:12 [in 𝔤^m]
12.	יהוה צבאות	6:17
28.	מזבח	22:10(a)(?)
29.	רדף	8:16(a)(?)
43.	בין	8:12 (once) [in 𝔤^m]
		22:25 (once)
44.	בקרב	16:10
45.	בתוך	4:10
		8:13 [in 𝔤^m]
49.	חזק	8:16(a)(?)
50.	חרב	10:28 (ξιφος)
61.	עבד	1:1 [in 𝔤^m]
79.	יׁשר	10:13 [in 𝔤^m]
82.	ׁשוב	11:10
		22:8

non-καιγε readings in Th.

3.	איש	1:15 (ουθεις)
		3:12 (————)(?)

29.	רָדַף	10:19 (καταδιω-)
50.	חרב	5:12 (μαχαιρα)
		10:11 (μαχαιρα)
82.	שׁרב	5:2 (?)

341

καιγε readings in Aq.

2.	רק	1:18
3.	איש	1:5
		3:12
		5:13 (?)
		21:42(44)
5.	יצב	1:5
6.	קרן	6:5 (?)
12.	גבור	1:14
13.	אל	22:22(a)
26.	בעיני	22:30
		24:15 (?)
27.	פה	18:4
28.	מזבח	22:10(a)
		22:19(a)
29.	רדף	2:7(b)/8 (?)
		10:19
35.	לא אבה	24:10
38.	אהל	22:4
		22:8
	משכן	22:29

342

44.   בקרב   9:16(22)
                    13:13
                    16:10
                    24:17

45.   בתוך   4:10
                    17:9 (ανα/εν) (?)

50.   חרב   5:2 μαχαιρα (as in Ex)
                    10:11 μαχαιρα (as in Ex)
                    10:28 μαχαιρα (as in Ex)

78.   טוב   22:30 (?)

82.   שוב   5:2
                    11:10
                    22:8

91.   פגע   19:22 (απ-)

93.   רע   24:15 (?)

non-καιγε readings in Aq.

6.   שופר   6:4(a) σαλπιγξ) (?)

26.   לעיני   10:12 (?)

61.   עבד   24:15 (למפלח) (?)

78.   טוב   7:21 (שפירתא) (?)

79.   מישור   13:9 (ομαλος)
                    13:16 (ομαλος)
                    13:21 (דשוריתא)

91.   פגע   16:7 (ראתא)

καιγε readings in the additions of Origen and in other, "qualitative" changes made by Origen

1. רגם   7:11 (2°) ※

2. רק   6:15 ※

3. איש   3:12 ※
               4:2 ※
               4:4 ※
               7:3(a) ※
               8:12 ※ [attributed to ϑ´]
               10:24 ※
               22:14
               23:10 ※

6. שופר   6:4(a) ※
               6:4(b) ※
               6:5 ※
               6:6 ※
               6:9(a) ※
               6:9(b)
               6:13(c) ※

9. אנכי   14:10

14. נגד   6:20 ※

19. אסף   10:5 ※

27. פה   6:10 ※
               9:14(20)
               11:11

28. זבח   8:31 (9:4)

29.	רדף	2:22(a) ⸓
		8:16(a) ⸓
		8:20 ⸓
		20:5
42.	אשה	13:14 (πυρα ?) ⸓
43.	בין	8:11 (once) ⸓
		8:12 (once) ⸓ [attributed to ϑ']
		22:27 (2°)
44.	בקרב	3:2 ([δια] μεσης) ⸓
		10:1 ⸓
45.	בתוך	4:10 ⸓
		8:9 ⸓
		8:13 ⸓ [attributed to ϑ']
	מתוך	4:18
49.	חזק	8:16 (?) ⸓
50.	חרב	8:24 ⸓
		10:28 (ειφος ?)
		11:10 ⸓
		13:22 ⸓
61.	עבד	1:1 ⸓ [attributed to ϑ']
		1:15 ⸓
		14:7
		16:10 ⸓
		22:4 ⸓
		24:17 ⸓
78.	טוב	23:14 ⸓
		23:16 ⸓

79.	יֵשׁר	10:13 ※ [attributed to ϑ']
80.	לִין	8:9 ※
82.	שׁוב	2:22 ※
		2:23
		8:24
		10:15 ※
		11:10
		20:6
		22:9 (επ/απ-) (?) ※
86.	חרה אף	23:16 ※
87.	נלחם	24:8 (?)
91.	פגע	19:11(b) (απ-) ※

non-καιγε readings in the additions of Origen and in other,
"qualitative" changes made by Origen

1.	רגם	7:11 (5°) (και ※)
	גם	10:30 (και ※)
3.	איש	6:20 (εκαστος ※)
4.	מעל	23:16 (απο ※)
6.	שופר	6:16 (σαλπιγξ ⌿ not extant; cf. v[mg]z[mg])
9.	אנכי	7:20 (εγω ※)
13.	אל	24:19 (ㄚ <u>ואלהא</u> ※)
19.	אסף	20:4 (επιστρεφω)

26.   לְעֵינַי   24:17 (ημιν [alone] ※)

29.   רָדַף   2:7(b)/8

61.   עֶבֶד   12:6(b) (παις ※)
                                23:7 (חִפְלָחוּן※) (?)

78.   טוֹב   7:21 (καλος) (?)

82.   שׁוּב   2:16 (αναστρεφω)
                                10:43 (αναστρεφω ※)
                                22:9 (αποστρεφω [probably] ※)
                                22:29 (αποστρεφω) (?)
                                23:12(a) (αποστροφη ※)

καιγε readings in Sym.

3.	איש	3:12
6.	קרן	6:5 (?)
13.	אל	22:22(a)
14.	נגד	8:33 (9:6)
28.	מזבח	22:10(a)
29.	רדף	10:19
38.	אהל	22:4
		22:7
	משכן	22:29
43.	בין	22:25 (once)
44.	בקרב	16:10
50.	חרב	5:2 μαχαιρα (as in Ex)
		10:11 μαχαιρα (as in Ex)
		10:28 μαχαιρα (as in Ex)
80.	לין	6:11
82.	שוב	11:10

non-καιγε readings in Sym.

1.	רגם	22:7 (כד מן הכיל) [MT: ורגם כי])
3.	איש	1:5 (ουθεις)
		21:42(44) (ουδεις)
		22:14 (εκαστος)

6.	שופר	6:4(a) (σαλπιγξ κερατινη) (?)
13.	אל	24:19 (θεος)
19.	אסף	20:4 (ונקבלוניהי)
38.	אהל	22:16 (οικος) (?)
44.	בקרב	24:5 (εν)
78.	טוב	7:21 (καλος)
79.	מישור	13:9 (ομαλος)
		13:16 (ομαλος)
82.	שרב	5:2 (παλιν)
		6:14 (ופנא)
		22:8 (αποστρεφω)
91.	פגע	19:26 (ראתו)

καιγε readings in other witnesses to the text (other than the
OG) (note: With the exception of material attributed to οι λ,
most readings listed below are not included in earlier charts.)

1.   גם   1:15 in f
                    9:4(10) in manuscripts of the E,
                        P, C recensions (if και
                        of the Lucianic recen-
                        sion represents the OG)

2.   רק   6:18 in manuscripts of the N-
                        group
                    8:2 in an anonymous reading
                        recorded in ᵹ
                    11:13 in manuscripts of the
                        Lucianic recension
                    11:22 in manuscripts of the
                        Lucianic recension

3.   איש   3:12   οι λ
                    4:2 in M(mg)
                    4:5 in q
                    5:13 in q (from Aq. ?)

6.   שופר   6:4(a) οι λ
                    6:4(b) οι λ
                    6:5 (קרן) in F^b
                    6:6   οι λ
                    6:9(a) οι λ
                    6:9(b) οι λ; also in q
                    6:13(b) in q

27.   פה   10:22 in Δ₈
                    10:27 in F^{b}oq

28.   מזבח   22:10(b) in z(mg)

29.	רדף	2:22(a) οι $\frac{\lambda}{2}$
44.	בקרב	13:13 in manuscripts of the Lucianic recension
45.	בתוך	13:16 (αναμεσον or εν μεσω) in an anonymous reading recorded in $\cancel{g}$ 22:31 οι $\frac{\lambda}{2}$
50.	חרב	10:33 (εν στοματι ρομφαιας) in i
61.	עבד	8:31 (9:4) in manuscripts of the Lucianic recension 8:33 (9:6) in manuscripts of the Lucianic recension 14:7 in manuscripts of the C̲ recension
78.	טוב	23:15(a) in p^b
80.	לין	6:11 in q
82.	שוב	2:16 in manuscripts of the N̲-group 22:22 οι $\frac{\lambda}{2}$ 5:2 in i(mg) 10:21 in A 10:38 in a$_2$ 22:32 in g
84.	הביא	23:15 in p^b
86.	חרוק אף	7:26 in manuscripts of the Lucianic recension
87.	נלחם	10:38 in manuscripts of the Lucianic recension (?)

92. קָצִין 10:24 in manuscripts of the
Lucianic recension

The material in the preceding charts must be analyzed on the basis of the discussions that accompany the detailed presentation of evidence earlier in the chapter. This analysis shows that the text of Th. in Joshua does form part of the general καιγε recension. Th.'s application of καιγε translation equivalences was not consistent, however. In some cases, other concerns--such as the desire to include as much as possible of the Greek text with which he was working or an effort to standardize the rendering of a certain word/phrase on the basis of its translation elsewhere in the same book-- apparently took precedence. We must also allow for certain lapses during the long process of preparing his recension.

Aq. applied with greater consistency the characteristics identified with the καιγε recension. This can be seen in passages where the texts of both Th. and Aq. have been preserved. Where only the latter is extant, we can be sure that many of the characteristic renderings found there were originally taken up from the Theodotionic recension. Sym. was acquainted with the text of Th. and included Th.'s renderings, some identified with the καιγε recension, when it suited his purposes. He may also have made use of the text of Aq. Sym.'s interests, however, lay in directions other than the efforts at standardization that were so important within the framework of the καιγε recension. In scattered passages καιγε characteristics appear in manuscripts outside of the Palestinian recension. This is most notably the case with respect to the Lucianic recension.

For Joshua our fullest witness to the καιγε recension is neither the text of Th. nor that of Aq., but rather the text of Origen with its additions and other, "qualitative" changes. A number of καιγε readings appear in the material introduced by Origen into the κοινη text with which he worked. And yet, as with Th., complete consistency is absent. Two explanations for this absence of complete consistency suggest themselves: (1) the source(s) used by Origen to supply this material was (were) not itself (themselves) consistent; (2) Origen himself

supplied much of this material based on his own knowledge or
on the Greek he found already in the text with which he was
working.

Let us deal with the latter point first. It is clear to
us that Origen had no need constantly to seek translations for
common words or for a single word that lacked a representation
in his κοινη text. Thus it makes a difference whether a non-
καιγε reading, or a καιγε one for that matter, appears as the
rendering for a single word that is easily supplied from the
surrounding material or is part of a longer, more complex
addition. This holds true not only for the "quantitative"
changes that Origen is generally acknowledged to have made.
We must reckon also with a number of "qualitative" changes,
which involved the substitution, for whatever reason, of
another translation for the one present in the text with
which Origen worked. Although these were marked in no way,
since they are not "additional," they must nevertheless be
considered important witnesses to changes introduced by
Origen either on his own or on the basis of the rendering he
found in one of his sources.

Our study of the relevant material contained in the fifth
column of Origen makes it probable that Th. and Aq. are the
sources drawn upon by Origen when he was unwilling or unable
to fashion a representation on his own. Sym. is not to be
ruled out altogether, but the evidence does not suggest that
Origen often turned to his text.

In our opinion Th. was the main source used by Origen in
the book of Joshua. We base the above statement on these
factors:

(1) Statements to this effect, for the Greek Old Testament
in general and Joshua in specific, have been made in the past.
An example of the latter is the following quotation from
Montfaucon:

Lectiones libri Josuae magno numero nobis suppeditavit
Codex Basiliensis ille, de quo frequenter supra: illius
item ope plerumque ediscitur, ex quo vel ex quibus
interpretibus prodirent ea quae in editione LXX interpretum hexaplari asteriscis notabantur. Nam etsi ea ut
plurimum ex Theodotione desumerentur, aliquando tamen
ex aliis quoque, Aquila scilicet, vel Symmacho, vel ex
omnibus simul excepta adhibebantur.[302]

That Aq. and Sym. are also listed as sources is in no way
surprising; we consider Th. the *main* source, not the *only*
one. Examples of Origen's use of Aq. do exist, and we must
be wary of any attempts to limit the options Origen had open
to him. Pretzl cites Jerome on the use of Th. by Origen:

[Origenes] quod maioris audaciae est in editione LXX
Theodotionis editionem miscuit, asteriscis designans
quae minus antea fuerant et virgulis quae ex super-
fluo videbantur apposita.[303]

(2) In 9 places in the book of Joshua a specific source for
the asterisked material contained in 𝔊 is given, in each case
on the authority of Masius. Without fail the source named is
Th. In 5 of these passages Lagarde included the ת siglum in
his text. It may well be significant that the first
asterisked additions in Joshua are among the 9 we referred to
above. Is this perhaps suggestive of a pattern for Origen's
procedure, at least so far as Joshua is concerned?

(3) In some passages the text of Sym., less often of Aq.,
does not agree with the wording found in an asterisked
addition of Origen. This is never the case with Th.

(4) Where readings attributed to σ', α', οι λ̥, or ϑ' are
included in Lagarde's edition of the Syro-hexapla, they always
contain a variant to the wording of 𝔊(txt) (with the exception
of the examples listed under [2] above). An examination of
these citations, excluding anonymous ones, is revealing: to
Sym. are attributed 46.8% of the variants; to Aq., 42.2%, to
οι λ̥, 6.3%; to Th., only 4.7%.[304] To us this is indicative
of the fact that the text of Origen's corrected OG column
and that of Th. were markedly more similar than were Origen
and Aq. or Sym. Although this closeness is due in part to
similarities in the Greek text with which first Th. and later

Origen worked,[305]it is also the result of "qualitative," and not merely "quantitative," changes introduced by Origen on the basis of material drawn from Th.[306]

(5) Finally, the observation that the renderings contained in the relevant material of Origen are not fully consistent, and yet do exemplify characteristic concerns of the καιγε recension, points again in the direction of Th.

If we have correctly analyzed the data, we are then in a position to expand the number of readings to be attributed to Th. through the cautious use of material included in the "qualitative" and "quantitative" changes of Origen, when such changes appear to have been drawn from a source and when that source can reasonably be identified with Th. Although we have not included any of these "expanded" readings in our 171 examples, we have noted some places where Margolis attributes such material to Th.

Notes to Chapter 3

1. Characteristics first isolated by Thackeray (H. St. John Thackeray, *The Septuagint and Jewish Worship: A Study in Origins* [London: Oxford Press, 1921]) are introduced under Barthélemy, Bodine, or with an asterisk(for this, see below).

2. See chapter 3 of Bodine, "Characteristics Peculiar to the Vaticanus Family of Judges," pp. 67-91.

3. For an explanation of the asterisk in O'Connell's list (e.g., no. 38: *σκεπη) see p. 305 of his work.

4. Walter Ray Bodine, "*KAIGE* and other Recensional Developments in the Greek Text of Judges," *Bulletin of the International Organization for Septuagint and Cognate Studies* 13 (1980), p. 52, fn. 3: "אחז = κρατεω, which Greenspoon cited from my dissertation, has been removed from the revised *GTJ* [*The Greek Text of Judges*] . . . ."

5. Bodine, "*KAIGE* in Judges," p. 53, fn. 9: "לין = αυλιζω and נצל = ρυομαι [our nos. 80 and 81] have also been discussed in Eugene Charles Ulrich, *The Qumran Text of Samuel and Josephus* (Harvard Semitic Monographs 19; Missoula: Scholars Press, 1978), pp. 100-1 and 111-112. They were included earlier in Ulrich's dissertation of 1975 and in mine of 1973, having been discovered independently in the course of the respective dissertation research."

6. Most of these are technical terms from the list of O'Connell. Although אבל, the characteristic word of no. 96, does not appear in Joshua, we include this proposed equivalence, which is taken from Thackeray, for the sake of completeness.

7. On the source(s) of Origen's additions see examples under 4.1 in chapter 1 and remarks later in this chapter.

8. Barthélemy, p. 45; he adds that Sym. "a pour נס des correspondants d'une infinie variété."

9. So Field, p. 351.

10. So Margolis (p. 108): "The omission of και Bru cannot be original."

11. Field, p. 388.

12. 1:7, 17, 18; 6:15, 17, 18, 24; 8:2, 27; 11:13, 14, 22; 13:6, 14; 22:5.

13. See No. 12, found under category 3 in chapter 1.

14. Field, p. 353; OG: και.

15. See Barthélemy, pp. 10ff.

358

16. See especially p. 54 fn. 2.

17. Max L. Margolis, "Specimen of a New Edition of the Greek Joshua," *Jewish Studies in Memory of Israel Abrahams* (New York: Jewish Institute of Religion, 1927), p. 313, notes that the text of q "embodies all sorts of glosses." The very valuable article in which Margolis made this comment was reprinted in Sidney Jellicoe, ed., *Studies in the Septuagint: Origins, Recensions, and Interpretations* (New York: KTAV, 1974), pp. 434-450.

18. Nominative in the OG; accusative in AMNϑabhluxyb₂$\mathcal{C}^m$𝕫, also k in a plus.

19. Margolis (p. 95) suggests that this clause was absent in the Hebrew *Vorlage* of the OG "per homoioteleuton (העירה written העיר)."

20. Either the asterisk was lost in the transmission of the text or ανδρες, although not in the OG, was present in the κοινη text with which Origen was working.

21. Field, p. 389.

22. For ουϑεις/ουδεις see Thackeray, pp. 58-62 and ¶¶ 7, 1, 14, 15.

23. For further details on the full readings of Th., Sym., and Aq. at 1:5 see no. 5 found under category 4.3 in chapter 1 and nos. 5 and 15 in this chapter. See also the remarks on this passage included in our discussion of Symmachus in chapter 2.

24. For reference see fn. 16 above.

25. The signs in 𝕫 have not been correctly preserved: ⁜. לגברא דאיסראיל֟

26. In passages not listed separately below the OG has ανδρες.

27. See further no. 56, found under category 5 in chapter 1.

28. Margolis, p. 76.

29. 5:9, 15; 10:27; 15:18; 23:13, 15, 16.

30. Nor is it found anywhere else in the Greek texts of Joshua as the translation for another Hebrew word.

31. O'Connell, p. 278.

32. Bodine, p. 14.

33. For further discussion of the reading of Aq. and that of Th.-Sym. see no. 5 found under category 4.3 in chapter 1 and nos. 4 and 15 in this chapter.

34. Margolis, p. 55.

35. As Bodine states (p. 35 fn. 38), in 𝔊(txt) *qarnâ* represents κερατινη; σαλπιγξ is consistently rendered by *šîpûrâ*.

36. At 6:13(b) v(mg) records the reading και οι ιερεις εσαλπισαν ταις σαλπιγξιν sub ※. This is not correct. και... σαλπιγξιν is the OG, which is retained in 𝔊 (οι ιερεις sub ⸓) as elsewhere. The addition of Origen begins later in the verse (after της διαθηκης κυριου) and is marked there with an asterisk in 𝔊.

37. Field, p. 346; see H-R.

38. See the remarks in Lagarde at this point.

39. See Margolis, p. 84.

40. Barthélemy, p. 63 fn. 1.

41. Cf. q at 6:13(b) above.

42. Also in z(mg), sine nom and sine ※ .

43. The reading attributed to οι λ in v(mg) covered 6:4(a), but not (b).

44. της φωνης appears in ck; την φωνην is omitted in Fa₂.

45. See Margolis, pp. 85f.

46. In v(mg) for both (a) and (b); in M(mg) for (b).

47. 𝔊 is not extant here.

48. See Margolis.

49. The reading ταις κερατιναις is preserved in v(mg)z(mg) at this point. Unfortunately, the ascription has been lost.

50. In Judges, where κερατινη translates שופר in both A and B, there is a difference between the two with respect to the use or nonuse of εν to render ב in the construction referred to above. Both A and B use the Greek preposition at 6:34 and 7:20(a). However, at 3:27; 7:18(a) and (b), 19 manuscript B contains εν (=Hebrew ב), while A does not. At 7:22 B also has εν (not found in A), in a place where ב does not appear in the Hebrew.

51. Field, p. 346 fn. 10.

52. See also no. 88 later in this chapter.

53. O'Connell, p. 280.

54. It is unlikely that he used an asterisk to mark ειμι, since it is not a "quantitative" change of the OG vis-à-vis the MT.

55. Barthélemy notes that the Greek translation of Isaiah preferred the transliteration σαβαωθ in its rendering of this phrase.

56. This reading is discussed under category 2 in chapter 1 (6:17 is no. 45).

57. For the Greek translator's method of handling the phrase גבורי החיל elsewhere in Joshua, see 6:2 (discussed under category 2 in chapter 1; 6:2 is no. 44) and Margolis, p. 12.

58. According to Margolis (p. 40), this κυριος shows Christian influence.

59. See Field, p. 393.

60. Field, p. 355. לוקבל appears in both 𝔊(txt) and the reading preserved for Sym. in 𝔊.

61. This is the sole use in the OG of ους to represent נגד (see H-R).

62. Cf. Holmes (pp. 32f), who argues that εις την πολιν is the OG translator's original, free rendering of Hebrew נגד here (cf. the free rendering εις τα ωτα at 8:35). κατα προσωπον, which appears nowhere (else) in the OG as a representation of נגד, would then be a later doublet. We prefer to see in εις την πολιν the translation of an additional element that entered the Hebrew *Vorlage* of the OG on the basis of v 20:

v 5 (MT)   ויעלו העם איש נגדו
v 20 (MT)   וייעל העם העירה איש נגדו. κατα προσωποψ then is the OG translator's rendering of the preposition נגד.

63. The words איש-העיר may have been lost in the Hebrew *Vorlage* of the OG per homoioteleuton. See Margolis, p. 95.

64. 1:5, 14; 3:6(twice), 11, 14; 4:5, 11, 12, 13; 6:4, 6, 7, 8, 9, 13(twice), 26; 7:4, 5, 6, 8, 12(twice), 13, 23; 8:5, 6(twice), 10, 14, 15, 32(LXX 9:5); 10:10, 12, 14; 11:6; 17:4(3 times); 18:1, 6, 8, 10; 19:51; 20:6, 9; 22:27, 29; 23:5, 13; 24:1, 12.

65. This yields a total of 54. The difference between this total and the 53 of the MT is explained by 4:5, where OG εμπροσθεν μου προ προσωπου κυριου points to לְפָנַי? לְפָנַי (לפני לפני) in its Hebrew *Vorlage*. For further details see under category 4.3 in chapter 1 (4:5 is no. 34).

66. According to Barthélemy, Aq. generally used εις προσωπον; so twice in Joshua.

67. Is it at all significant that the OG of Joshua does not use προσωπ- with κυριος (יהוה) (except at 4:5, see fn. 65)? See Harry M. Orlinsky, "Review of Charles T. Fritsch's *The Anti-Anthropomorphisms of the Greek Pentateuch*," *Crozier Quarterly* 21 (1944), p. 158; *idem*, "The Treatment of Anthropomorphisms and Anthropopathisms in the Septuagint of Isaiah," *HUCA* 27 (1956), p. 197.

68. H-R lists 20:4 as the sole occurrence of this equivalence in any tradition.

69. This does reflect some form of עיר; the elements representing העירה and אליהם have been transposed.

70. Field, p. 384.

71. Holmes, p. 79.

72. Margolis, "Specimen," p. 309:

> x is invaluable because it alone, in a consistent manner, brings out adjustments to the Hebrew in the matter of word sequence or the use of the article which the Syriac translator was not able to express, or where he employed certain devices to express these matters it is only with the aid of x that we are in a position to become aware of them. As Field, not to say Masius, had no access to this MS.,it is not [to] be wondered at that their retroversion of the Syriac remained imperfect.

73. Margolis, pp. 19f.

74. The reading of x makes it almost certain that το ταχος underlies Syriac בעגל.

75. Bodine (p. 37 fn. 83) notes the following for Judges: מהר is translated with ταχυ at 2:17 and το ταχος at 2:23; at 9:54 το ταχος (A), ταχυ (B)render מהרה.

76. Both Shenkel and Bodine found it useful to draw such contrasts. Cf. the earlier articles of Harry M. Orlinsky listed in fn. 67 and his more recent "Introductory Essay: On Anthropomorphisms and Anthropopathisms in the Septuagint and Targum," with full literature, in Bernard M. Zlotowitz, *The Septuagint Translation of the Hebrew Terms in Relation to God in the Book of Jeremiah* (New York: KTAV, 1980).

77. Field (p. 390): και αγαθον εν οφθαλμοις αυτου; he surely meant to write αυτων.

362

78. So Field, p. 393. The reading stands without ascription in Lagarde's edition; so also B-McL.

79. O'Connell, p. 284.

80. Field, p. 358.

81. Margolis, p. 179.

82. For Thackeray, MT לעיני ישראל is the corruption of a gloss לבני ישראל (so Aq.) later than the OG translation of Joshua. See H. St. J. Thackeray, "New Light on the Book of Jashar (a study of 3 Regn. viii 53^b LXX)," *JTS* 11 (1910), 526ff. See also Holmes, p. 50.

83. See no. 50 below.

84. Orlinsky, "Joshua," p. 193. The OG translator used προσταγμα to translate דבר at 8:27: MT, כדבר יהוה; OG, κατα προσταγμα κυριου. See also δια το αυτον επακολουθησαι τω προσταγματι κυριου at 14:14 (MT: יען אשר מלא אחרי יהוה) and κατα προσταγμα (δια προσταγματος in some manuscripts) κυριου at 21:42b, in a passage lacking in the MT.

85. Orlinsky, "Joshua," p. 193.

86. Margolis (p. 159): ※ το στομα: κυριου. On 𝔊^mg see the following comment of Masius "pro, και κυριον, monet Syrus, per limniscum esse in quisbusdam libris, και το στομα κυριου." The reading of 𝔊^mg is לפומה דפיפי.

87. Margolis, pp. 159f.

88. For the OG here see Margolis, p. 343. Field (p. 376), followed by Margolis, corrects the reading of Aq. as preserved in 𝔊 to the form given here. Field's translation reflects this corrected form of the Aquilan citation.

89. This literal translation is found at 10:22 in Δ_8 and at 10:27 in F^boq. At 11:11 εν στοματι ξιφους translates לפי חרב in manuscripts of the P and C recensions (OG: εν ξιφει). See no. 50 below.

90. See fn. 72 (to no. 24) above.

91. See Bodine, p. 39 fn. 114.

92. Margolis, p. 146.

93. Margolis' insight in this regard is confirmed by Barthélemy (p. 106), who states that correction to ειρηνη "pour mieux rendre שלום est caractéristique de notre recenseur." Our thanks to Walter Bodine ("*KAIGE* in Judges," p. 52 fn. 3) for calling attention to Barthélemy's comments on ειρηνη.

94. In contrast, for the following word he retained the OG (sub ⊤, so Margolis) and introduced a translation (sub ※) from the source(s) named above. ειρηνικας and σωτηριου both appear in the reading found in manuscripts of the Lucianic recension: θυσιας σωτηριου ειρηνικας.

95. 22:10(twice), 11, 16, 19(twice), 23, 26, 28, 29(twice), 34.

96. See under category 3; 22:10(a) is no. 153.

97. On these and other passages cf. the remarks of Suzanne Daniel in *Recherches sur le vocabulaire du culte dans la Septante* (Paris, 1966).

98. 2:5, 7(twice), 16(twice), 22(twice); 7:5; 8:16(twice), 17, 20, 24; 10:10, 19; 11:8; 20:5; 23:10; 24:6.

99. 2:8 in B-McL.

100. In M(mg) the reading ascribed to οι λ contains only εως επεστρεψαν. καταδιωκοντες is found here in Fz(mg): εως επεστρεψαν οι καταδιωκοντες.

101. For ενισχυσεν see below no. 49. For γαι see our discussion of 8:12-13 under category 5 in chapter 1 (8:12-13 is no. 56), where mention is also made of Margolis' suggestion that Th. is the source for the additional material at 8:16.

102. q omits του before διωξαι. In place of the και κατεδιωξαν that follows in the OG (8:16[b]), b has και ενισχυσεν πας ο λαος της γαι του καταδιωξαι.

103. There are no signs marking the material at 20:5 or surrounding verses as additional.

104. Reading at 10:19 are discussed under category 3 in chapter 1 (10:19 is no. 74); in this passage Th., while revising the OG in one respect, retained OG καταδιωκοντες.

105. At this point a reading attributed to Aq. has been preserved in ℊ. Since, however, the Syriac makes no distinction between καταδιω- and διω- (רדף for both), we cannot be **sure** of the verb employed here (Field, p. 338: διωκοντες). We can be sure that διωκω underlies ℊ(txt) in the first group of passages mentioned above because of the evidence from Greek manuscripts, especially x.

106. See our discussions of 5:2 (no. 42) and 9:5 (no. 59) under category 2 in chapter 1; also the reference to Pretzl at no. 42.₃ We can be thankful that *BH*⁴ did not transmit the note from *BH*³ that the OG omitted צבא in v 15.

107. Shenkel speaks of αρχιστρατηγος as the common OG form; it is clear from H-R that αρχιστρατηγος δυναμεως is found almost as often.

108. κρυβη stands without ascription in z(mg); only Field (p. 337) records "ϑ. κρυφη" as a marginal reading of z.

109. For other readings at 2:1 see under category 4.1 in chapter 1 (2:1 is no. 13).

110. In the καιγε recension of Judges אבה לא = ευδοκεω.

111. The reading of Aq. is preserved in Syriac: ולא צבא; this same verb appears also in 𝔊(txt), where the underlying Greek is ηϑελησεν.

112. For a comparison of the MT and the OG in this section of chapter 24, see our discussion at 24:10 under category 4.3 in chapter 1 (24:10 is no. 165).

113. The only potentially significant variation recorded in these passages is the following reading of k(mg) at 7:21: ... εν τη οικια μου.

114. See Margolis, p. 44.

115. For κατασκηνωσις elsewhere see H-R.

116. An anonymous reading at 22:16, preserved in 𝔊, includes του οικου (Syriac על ביתא), which represents an apparent misreading of MT באלהי as באהלי (בְּאָהֳלֵי) (so Field, p. 389). If Field is correct in attributing this reading to Sym., then the OG equivalence אהל = οικος stood alongside אהל = σκηνη/σκηνωμα in the text of Sym. for Joshua chapter 22.

117. Margolis, p. 253; Field, p. 365.

118. οτι κυριος in dkpt𝐴𝐶𝐸 appears to be the result of the misreading of אש as אמר.

119. For the plural of πυρ see Smyth 285.25. The reading attributed to Aq. at Lev 2:3; 24:9 is probably from πυρον, but that of Th. is from πυρ (cf. O'Connell).

120. There is some question about the originality of the phrase אשי יהוה in this context (cf. v 33). As Soggin (p. 150) writes: "'Offerings by fire' is lacking in LXX, which has 'Yahweh the God of Israel is their heritage....' Noth proposes that the phrase be omitted (no doubt as a gloss) because of the hū̃ that follows (cf. v 33), which clearly refers only to Yahweh; cf. Abel and Baldi, as well as Bright (although the latter is not certain)." In our opinion אשי יהוה, the lectio difficilior, is original here. In the Hebrew Vorlage of the OG יהוה alone appeared (as in the MT at v 33), perhaps the result of concerns such as that expressed by Noth.

121. Actually 3 times--και ανα μεσον των υιων ημων, a phrase lacking in the MT, appears in the OG after ανα μεσον υμων και ανα μεσον ημων.

122. For further details on the readings at 22:25 see under category 4.1 in chapter 1 (22:25 is no. 157).

123. For βηθαυν see our discussion of 8:12-13 under category 5 in chapter 1 (8:12-13 is no. 56).

124. We have no evidence for Aq. In 𝔊(txt) for Joshua both *bmsᵀt* and *by(n)t* translate Greek ανα μεσον (see O'Connell).

125. 1:11; 3:2, 5, 10; 4:6; 6:25; 7:13; 8:35; 9:7, 16, 22; 10:1; 13:13; 16:10; 18:7; 24:5, 17, 23.

126. At any rate, no extant witness to the text has εν μεσω.

127. Note that Aq. retains the plural of the OG.

128. See fn. 72 (to no. 24) above.

129. See also εν μεσω attributed to Aq. in v(mg) at 16:10. O'Connell includes εν μεσω as the most probable Greek equivalent for *bmsᵀt* in Exodus.

130. Field, p. 365.

131. Further details related to readings at 16:10 are discussed under category 3 in chapter 1 (16:10 is no. 133).

132. O'Connell refers to Aquila's use of *bgwᵀ* (εντος ?) there.

133. 3:17; 4:9, 10; 7:21; 8:9, 13; 13:9, 16; 14:3; 15:13; 16:9; 17:4(twice), 6, 9; 19:1, 9, 49; 20:9; 21:41(39); 22:19, 31.

134. Details of the readings at 4:10 are discussed under category 3 in chapter 1 (4:10[a] is no. 35).

135. The correct position of the signs has not been preserved in 𝔊 or 𝔊ᵐ.

136. As noted above, εν μεσω is also attributed to Th. at 4:10. For further discussion of the reading ascribed to Th. at vv 12-13 see our remarks under category 5 in chapter 1 (8:12-13 is no. 56); see also nos. 29 and 43 in this chapter.

137. For details of the OG here, which do not however involve the translation of בחור, see Margolis, p. 254.

138. Margolis, p. 132.

139. See our discussion of 8:12-13 under category 5 in chapter 1 (8:12-13 is no. 56); see also no. 29 above. ενισχυω never occurs in the OG of Joshua; at 14:11 ενισχυων replaces OG ισχυων in manuscript a₂ as a rendering of the adjective חזק.

140. 5:2, 3, 13; 6:21; 8:24(twice); 10:11, 28, 30, 32, 35, 37, 39; 11:10, 11, 12, 14; 13:22; 19:47; 24:12.

141. The OG has no translation for חרב at 8:24(a); 11:10; 13:22. On the other hand, the OG has an equivalent of this noun in three places where it is not found in the MT (10:33; 21:42d; 24:31a).

142. At 11:11 the MT is לפי חרב, which the OG translator probably found in his *Vorlage*, but rendered ("freely," so Margolis, p. 216) εν ξιφει. The OG translator also found this Hebrew phrase in his *Vorlage* at 10:33, at a point where it is absent from the MT.

143. 5:2 and 10:11 are discussed in chapter 1: our remarks concerning readings at 5:2 (no. 42) are found under category 2; 10:11 (10:11[d] is no. 72) is placed under category 1.1.

144. See fn. 72 (to no. 24) above.

145. See below for details concerning Syriac renderings of the Greek words under discussion here.

146. 10:28 is also listed under category 3 in chapter 1 (10:28 is no. 79).

147. In still a different location εν στοματι ρομφαιας appears in M(mg) and τω στοματι ρομφαιας in dpt.

148. So Margolis, p. 259, and Holmes, p. 57, also Soggin, p. 150; cf. the notations in *BH*³.

149. 𝔖 is not extant at 6:21, where the OG reads εν στοματι ρομφαιας. For 10:28 see below.

150. Is it possible that *saypâ* at 10:11 and 19:47 does translate ρομφαια, in which case 𝔖 alone provides evidence for καιγε revision? The absence of any substantial support for ρομφαια in the Greek manuscripts makes this very unlikely.

151. Bodine, p. 43 fn. 155.

152. In these passages solid support for μαχαιρα does exist.

153. Margolis, pp. 67f.

154. 1:1, 2, 7, 13, 15; 5:14; 8:31, 33; 9:8, 9, 11, 23,
24(twice); 10:6; 11:12, 15; 12:6(twice); 13:8; 14:7; 18:7;
22:2, 4, 5; 24:17, 29.

155. Orlinsky, "Joshua," p. 193.

156. For the significance of the marginal readings at this
point in M (οι ο' χω) and ν (ο' χω ※ δουλου κυριου) see
Margolis, "ΧΩΡΙΣ," p. 89.

157. Perhaps we should not expect consistency with respect
to this characteristic, for, as Bodine (p. 27) observes: "A
check of this usage for the verb form throughout the presently
identified καιγε material seems to verify the criterion, though
it is not everywhere consistent." What is true for the verb
forms may also be true for the basal noun. With respect to
forms of the verb, Bodine adds, Aq. carried the characteristic
rendering through to full consistency.

158. The only pattern that we can discern is his re-
striction of the term θεραπων to Moses.

159. At 7:7 OG διεβιβασεν ο παις σου apparently goes
back to עבד העביר (Margolis, p. 107; BH⁴).

160. 16:10; 22:5, 27; 23:7, 16; 24:2, 14(3 times), 15
(4 times), 16, 18, 19, 20, 21, 22, 24, 31.

161. 23:7 presents difficulties that we discuss below.

162. Holmes (pp. 63f) has a lengthy analysis of the
differences between the MT and the OG at the end of 16:10.
This analysis is well worth reading, even if one does not
accept his conclusions concerning the original text at this
point. See also Soggin, p. 168.

163. B-McL notes that και...δουλοι appears sub ÷ in G.
From Field (p. 373 fn. 17) it is clear how this circumstance
arose: G "pingit ÷ εως ανεβη-δουλοι, nullo metobelo, nec
interposito asterisco." The asterisk in 𝔖 is correct.

164. 𝔖(txt) here reads plah. As Bodine points out, the
Greek equivalent for this is λατρευω (see also Masius' remark
at 23:7). The Syriac translation of δουλευω is plah ˙ bduta .

165. These are the expected equivalents. Is it not
likely that the OG order accurately reflects its Hebrew Vorlage,
in which תשחחרו preceded, rather than followed, חעבדום?

166. This (mis)placement of the metobelus need not have
originated with Origen. It could have occurred anytime during
the transmission of his text.

167. This passage is discussed in other contexts under nos. 26 and 93 in this chapter. While 𝔊 holds λατρευω and δουλευω apart, it is less useful in attempting to sort out the various Greek representations of the noun עבד. 𝔊 uses עבדא for παις, οικετης, and δουλος. Only θεραπων receives a distinct translation, מניחנא.

168. This is so except where the clause in which it appears was dropped through haplography at v 12. αυχην appears again in LXX[B] at 13:28: αυχην...κατα δημους αυτων. Margolis (p. 263) does not include these words in his text of the OG. See also Holmes, p. 58. O'Connell observes that νωτος is used for the noun ערף 3 times in the καιγε sections of Samuel-Kings and only 2 other times in the rest of the Greek OT.

169. At Dtn 1:36 the same clause appears in the MT, again with reference to Caleb. There also the OG translator makes use of δια το followed by an infinitive and accusative. For this construction see B-F ¶¶ 402(1), 406(3).

170. Bodine, p. 19. In "*KAIGE* in Judges" he states flatly that misc. = ηνικα "can be definitely ruled out as a *kaige* characteristic."

171. Thackeray, *Septuagint*, p. 115.

172. Holmes (p. 50), followed by Soggin (p. 119), presents arguments for the originality of the OG here: "The omission in M.T. is no doubt due to the resemblance between ביד ישראל [for υποχειριος = ביד see, for example, 11:8] and ישראל בני ישראל." For Origen's procedure here see Margolis, pp. 178f. See also Benjamin, p. 42.

173. The text of Sym. here is preserved in 𝔊: כד מן הכיל (Field: οτε μεν ουν). 𝔊(txt), representing the OG, has וכד at this point. This reading is also discussed under no. 1 in this chapter.

174. ηνικα alone appears in manuscript d.

175. Holmes, p. 80.

176. As noted earlier, Bodine included this equivalence in his dissertation, but not in his book. Since both אחז and κρατεω are found in Joshua, we present the relevant evidence below, if only for the sake of completeness.

177. κρατεω appears in the OG of Joshua at 18:1, where it translates Hebrew כבש.

178. Although we have listed 7:21, it is possible that the OG there did not include a translation for טוב. In the MT 7:21 begins as follows: וארא בשלל אדרת שנער אחת טובה. At this point LXX[B] has ιδον εν τη προνομη ψιλην ποικιλην. If this is the OG, then the translator found neither אחת nor

טובה in his Hebrew *Vorlage*. This omission of a representation
for Hebrew טובה is limited to LXX^B and a few other manuscripts.
Elsewhere καλην is found as the translation of טובה, and
Margolis (p. 115) includes καλην in his text of the OG. 𝔖
places only μιαν (Syriac: חד) sub ※ . As Margolis points out,
the signs in 𝔖 are important in determining the OG here:
"The omission of καλην after ποικιλην in LXX^B ⊄ Cyr and others
apparently a textual error. Unless the metobelus should be
moved so as to include καλην, the latter was found by Origen
in his texts. On the other hand, he did not find μιαν."
Even if Origen did find καλην in the κοινη text with which he
was working, this is no guarantee that καλην also formed part
of the OG. The accidental loss of an original καλην after
(ψι)λην (ποικι)λην does, however, provide a reasonable explanation for the absence of this word in LXX^B and elsewhere.

179.   The readings of Aq. and Sym., as well as that of Th.
(which covers only the word אדרת), are discussed under category
3 in chapter 1 (7:21[a] is no. 51). See also the following fn.

180.   See fn. 72 (to no. 24) above. At 7:21, for example,
καλην is found in all manuscripts, including x, in which a
translation of טובה occurs. There is little doubt that שפירא
in 𝔖 (txt, as well as in the readings of Aq. and Sym. [for
Sym. there is other, Greek evidence]) represents καλην.

181.   Note that the OG uses a form of καλος to render טוב
in similar phrases (i.e., after דבר) at 21:45 and 23:15(a).

182.   της αγαθης does appear in similar phrases in the OG
(after אדמה, not ארץ as at v 16) at 23:13, 15(b).

183.   Field, p. 390 fn. 57. This reading is also discussed
under no. 26 in this chapter.

184.   For the first part of this reading see no. 78 above.
δοκει appears in all extant witnesses to the text (in manuscript w αρεσκει and δοκει are reversed).

185.   10:13 is no. 73.

186.   For an explanation of το ευρεθεν see Margolis, p. 180.

187.   In both verses this rendering represents revision of
the OG. The Book of Jashar is mentioned again in the MT at 2
S 1:18, and in the LXX at 2 S 1:18; 1 K 8:(13)53. In the 2 S
passage επι βιβλιου του ευθους appears, as in the text of Th.
here. In 1 K the rendering is εν βιβλιω της ωδης. For an
extensive discussion of the Book of Jashar see H. St. J.
Thackeray, "New Light on the Book of Jashar (a study of 3 Regn.
viii 53^D LXX)," *JTS* 11 (1910), 518-532 (this article was
referred to earlier under no. 26 in this chapter). See also
Soggin, p. 122 fn 2.

188. ομαλος does not occur anywhere in the OG.

189. την ομαλην stands in z(mg) without ascription.

190. Here also v(mg) has preserved the ascription, while την γην ομαλην stands as an anonymous reading in z(mg).

191. For example, at Joshua 11:2 (on this see Field, p. 361 fn. 5) and Deut 1:1.

192. For example, at Dtn 3:10; Ps 142(143):10. Sym. is the probable source for this equivalence at Ps 25(26):12.

193. At 13:17 and 20:8 there is no revision of the OG recorded (except spelling variants in the former passage).

194. Margolis, p. 130.

195. Holmes, p. 43. Although Holmes may be right to reject Ehrlich's suggestion, he is wrong in stating that the OG always transliterated מישור. See 20:8, referred to above.

196. Benjamin, p. 39.

197. Soggin, p. 95.

198. Holmes, p. 34.

199. Margolis, pp. 87f.

200. In the LXX παρεμβαλλω represents Hebrew ליל only here and at 1 Chr 9:26(27). The noun מלון is used again at 4:8. There OG παρεμβολη is found everywhere.

201. For this use of the verb παραβαλλω see Margolis, p. 50.

202. For an explanation of the singular verbs in the OG see Margolis, p. 88.

203. See Bodine (p. 63 fn. 73) for statistics. Bodine notes that αυλιζω, characteristic of the καιγε recension, is also a common OG translation of ליל.

204. Recall Margolis' observation that manuscript q "embodies all sorts of glosses." (See fn. 17 to no. 3 above.)

205. According to Field (p. 348 fn. 38), the reading of 𝔊(txt) at 6:11 also represents a form of αυλιζω, ηυλισθη (as in q), "cum εκοιμηθη in marg., teste Masio."

206. The correct position of the signs has not been preserved in 𝔊 or 𝔊ᵐ (see also under no. 45 above). For the
Syriac verb used in 𝔊(txt) here see above.

207. 2:13; 9:26; 22:31; 24:10.

208. Bodine, p. 64 fn. 77.

209. 𝔊(txt) is not extant at 2:13 or at 10:6, where OG
εξαιρεω renders Hebrew יש״. At 22:31 manuscript x, which is
unique in reading ερρυσατο, is not a reliable witness to the
precise form of the Greek underlying 𝔊(txt) (פציחתו).

210. See Bodine, p. 64 fn. 85.

211. 1:15; 2:6, 22, 23; 4:18; 5:2; 6:14; 7:3, 26; 8:21,
24; 10:15, 21, 38, 43; 11:10; 18;8; 19:12, 27, 29(twice), 34;
20:6; 22:8, 9, 16, 18, 23, 29, 32; 23:12(twice); 24:20.

212. At 5:2, but see below.

213. υπεστρεψαν is found in manuscript k; manuscript 18
has επανεστρεψαν.

214. In M(mg) the reading ascribed to οι λ contains only
εως επεστρεψαν, not the full εως...διωκοντες as in v(mg).

215. Fᵇ has υπεστρεψεν.

216. In 𝔊-ed the obelus, rather than the asterisk,
mistakenly appears.

217. See the reference below.

218. See fn. 72 (to no. 24) above.

219. The readings of Th., Aq., and Sym. at these 3
places are discussed in chapter 1: 5:2 (no. 42) under category
2; 11:10 (no. 91) under category 3; 22:8 (no. 152) under
category 4.3.

220. Longer readings that also cover portions of this
verse are recorded in Syriac for Aq. and Sym.

221. See, for example, Barthélemy's remarks in this
regard, p. 45 and elsewhere.

222. υποστρεφω occurs in the OG of Joshua only at 2:23,
where 𝔊(txt) is not extant. Even if it were, we would gain
no information concerning the Syriac equivalent for υποστρεφω,
since manuscripts of the P recension, especially x, read
επιστρεφω here. Thus we would expect the form הפך in 𝔊(txt)
at 2:23. See below.

223. The manuscripts reading επεστρεψαν at 2:23 are Nabkoqx.

224. B-McL does not include 𝔖 among the witnesses to this reading. On the basis of our previous observations, however, it is clear that וֹהפך in 𝔖(txt) here does render και επεστρεψεν.

225. This is the same verb used in the asterisked addition at 10:43.

226. Note also the following notation in v(mg)z(mg): ο' απο κυριου ωστε αποστραφηναι εν ταις σημερον ημεραις απο κυριου ωστε.

227. See above for the statistics, which show αποστρεφω to be by far the most common representation of שׁוב in this material.

228. At v 23 the OG does employ αφιημι to render שׁוב, but that is the only other place in which the שׁוב = αφιημι equivalence appears in the OG of Joshua.

229. The notation in v(mg), which places this sub ※ , is mistaken. See further under no. 6 in this chapter.

230. None of these examples, with the exception of 2:16, seems to involve anything more than a confusion of the first letter of the verb.

231. Bodine (p. 67): "The purpose of this chapter is to present another aspect of the B family of Judges. It will deal with peculiarities of that family within the entire καιγε recension." We have placed the discussion of analogous "peculiarities" in Joshua within our overall framework.

232. 7:23; 18:6; 23:15; 24:7, 8. For 24:8 (Q וְנָבִיא, K וְנָבֵאָה [cf. at v 3]) see Soggin, pp. 223f and references to GKC there.

233. See the discussion under no. 49 in this chapter; see also no. 29.

234. See nos. 29 and 49.

235. The reading of 𝔖(txt) here is וַגִּעְיָן. Note that Origen retained the first person plural of the OG against the third person plural of the MT.

236. b₂𝔄 omit θυμω. ghnpt have θυμωθεις κυριος; these same 5 manuscripts, which differ from the other witnesses to this reading in their rendering of מחרה (see no. 24 above), also lack a translation for שׁוב (see no. 78 in this chapter).

237. Bodine, p. 71.

238. Origin included αυτου sub ÷ in his text, but not απο or the expression της οργης του θυμου, both of which he may have overlooked even if they appeared in his source.

239. The נלחם = περικαθιζω "equivalence" occurs only in these two passages in the OG. According to Margolis (pp. 198, 200), this verb represents חנה (as in vv 5, 31, 34 of chapter 10) rather than נלחם of the MT.

240. Origen also retained the OG. The various readings at this point are discussed under category 4.3 in chapter 1 (23:10 is no. 162).

241. Thus πολιορκεω at 10:29, 31, 34; περικαθιζω at 10:38, 42; πολεμεω at 11:15; 19:47 (the distance here is admittedly greater than in the other examples; however, 19:47 is the next occurrence of נלחם after 11:15 in the MT of Joshua); εκπολεμεω at 23:3, 10.

242. For the OG rendering of the sole occurrence of the Hebrew root ערף in Joshua, see Bodine, p. 85 fn. 75.

243. Margolis (pp. 70f) does not include αυτων in his text of the OG.

244. Field, p. 344. For further discussion of these readings see Max L. Margolis, "Additions to Field from the Lyons Codex of the Old Latin," *JAOS* 33 (1913), pp. 254-256. Margolis confirms Field's rendering of Aq.'s and Sym.'s trans-lation for אנשי המלחמה, while correcting him in other, minor respects.

245. See Margolis, p. 80; Field, p. 346 fn. 6.

246. See the evidence presented above at no. 6.

247. Bodine, p. 73.

248. Bodine, p. 89 fn. 110.

249. For a discussion of the title סרך and its translation in the versions, see Soggin, p. 149.

250. Bodine suggests that the two occurrences of the פגע = απανταω equivalence in Ruth possibly represent revision also. It is this latter equivalence that is particularly relevant for Joshua, as the evidence below shows.

251. In this specialized sense, which is found only in Joshua, פגע is used with אל at 19:11(b) and -ב at 16:7 and the other passages in chapter 19. Does this unique usage at 19:11(b) point to the secondary nature of פגע there (see below)?

252. This is the only place in the OG in which ερχομαι represents פגע.

253. So Margolis (p. 373), who terms LXX^B γαιθβωρ "corrupt."

254. B-McL fails to note that this reading is ascribed to Aq.

255. Pp. 86ff fn. 91, p. 90 fn. 117.

256. 𝔖(txt) at 19:11 has ופגעין ⁙.

257. Was Aq. the source utilized by Origen at 19:11(b)? Possibly, although Aq. might well have drawn his reading at v 22 from the revision of Th., which is not extant here.

258. This observation makes it most unlikely that Origen supplied his own translation at 19:11(b). Had he done so, the natural choice would have been συναπτω, a form of which appeared but a few words earlier in the OG.

259. See Field, p. 373 fn. 15.

260. On the basis of 19:22 we would expect Aq. to have written και απαντησει. Should the reading at 16:7 be attributed to Sym. (and Field's translation retained)?

261. See no. 10 in this chapter.

262. Cf. Bodine, p. 90 fn. 117.

263. Bodine, p. 90 fn. 123.

264. According to Holmes (pp. 51f), the MT here is a fuller text than the original and "LXX represents an intermediate state of the text."

265. h has και ειπεν προς τους αρχηγους των ανδρων και τους εναρχομενους του πολεμου.

266. Bodine, p. 91 fn. 133.

267. This is in line with his practice elsewhere for similar expressions. See our discussions under nos. 26 and 78 in this chapter.

268. Bodine, p. 91 fn. 133.

269. See Bodine, p. 188, for relevant statistics in Judges. See also Bodine, p. 189 fn. 10 and p. 148 with accompanying fns. (fn. 152 refers to the early studies of Field, Swete, and Thackeray).

270. Tov, p. 82.

271. Tov, p. 85.

272. See Bodine, p. 67.

273. Soggin, p. 134. Tov includes 1 Kings 4:11 in his list under subgroup b.

274. Margolis, p. 208.

275. Field, p. 361 fn. 7. Eusebius (Σ. εν τη παραλια δωρ) supports the procedure of Field here.

276. Field, p. 364.

277. Field, pp. 374f. Just before ναφετα the OG has και το τριτον. According to Margolis (p. 338), ⁙ישלׁשח‎ (MT: אֶלׁשׁח‎) was read as שְׁלׁשָׁה‎. Cf. Holmes, p. 65.

278. All of the examples mentioned below have been discussed either in chapter 1 or chapter 3. Here we limit ourselves to the specific question of translation-transliteration.

279. See Soggin, pp. 166f.

280. A full presentation of the relevant material is contained in chapter 1 under category 1.2, where 10:40(a) (no. 83) and 15:19(a) (no. 126) are discussed together with other examples.

281. 11:8(a) (no. 89) is discussed under category 1.2 in chapter 1.

282. υδατων, the translation of Aq. at 11:8, is attributed to Sym. at 13:6, where מים משרפה again appears in the MT.

283. Cf. their procedure below.

284. For this reason 15:19 is most instructive in our determination of the differing procedures of Th. and Aq. at 11:2; 12:23; 17:11.

285. Although the text of Th. later in v 19 is not preserved, it is reasonable to suppose that he continued to use transliteration for the other 2 occurrences of גלה‎, as did the OG.

286. See our remarks under category 2 in chapter 1; 15:19 (b) is no. 127.

287. For further details see our discussion under category 3 in chapter 1. 7:24 is no. 53 and 7:26 is no. 54.

288. See also under category 4 in chapter 1; 15:25(24) is no. 130.

289. Cf. certain manuscripts of the P recension. 18:28 (no. 139) is discussed under category 4 in chapter 1.

290. See no. 79 in this chapter.

291. The list is complete with respect to Th. and to those places where any of the preceding καιγε characteristics appear.

292. See Tov, p. 79. On Th. as *doctus hindoctus* see Field, pp. xxxix-xlii.

293. See above.

294. Thackeray, *Septuagint*, pp. 114f.

295. At our suggestion he expanded the relevant discussion in his book by bringing in the verb αδρυνω (see below). See now Bodine, p. 38 fn. 86.

296. At 1 K 1:9 LXX^B reads τους αδρους ιουδα (MT: לכל אנשי יהודה). It is probable, however, that ανδρας, found in A and elsewhere, is the original reading.

297. 1:4(twice); 6:5, 20; 7:9, 26; 8:29; 9:1; 10:2(twice), 10, 11, 18, 20, 27; 14:12, 15; 15:12, 47Q; 17:17; 20:6; 22:10; 23:4, 9; 24:17, 26.

298. See Field, p. 347.

299. 10:11(b) (no. 70) is discussed under category 2 in chapter 1.

300. See Field, p. 368.

301. A question mark after a listing in the following charts indicates uncertainty in attribution, translation, and/or significance.

302. This quotation from Montfaucon is found in Field, p. 333.

303. Pretzl, p. 411. See also Pretzl (p. 403): "Nach dem Zeugnis des Hieronymus war dieser Text aus Theodotion ergänzt und mit Asteriski und Obeli versehen."

304. For Th. this includes 3 readings not cited in Lagarde, but found outside of his edition. If we had conducted a complete search for Aq. and Sym. in this regard, the number to be attributed to them would also have increased.

305. Both of them worked with a text that had affinities
with the tradition preserved in LXX^B and related manuscripts.
See also the appendix at the end of chapter 1.

306. Evidence to support points 4 and 5 (see below) is
supplied by the discussion of individual readings in this
and earlier chapters.

CONCLUSION

In chapter one we established that Th. revised (a form of)
the OG to a Hebrew identical in almost all respects to the MT.
The form of the Greek with which Th. worked had apparently
not undergone any systematic revision prior to his contact
with it, and it is separated from the OG chiefly by corruptions
of no great significance. Th., it is clear, had great respect
for this Greek text, and we share his high assessment in this
regard. The OG translator rendered, to the best of his considerable abilities, the Hebrew text that lay before him. His
knowledge of Hebrew and his fidelity to that Hebrew are to be
rated far higher than the derogatory comments of some previous
scholars would allow. Th.'s respect for this Greek led him on
occasion to take up non-MT elements into his revision; this
respect also provided him with a key to many of the corrections
to the MT that he did make, for he often corrected or modified
the Greek translation in one passage on the basis of similar
wording, which he considered more apt, in another.

The evidence points unmistakably to the fact that Th.
corrected to a Hebrew almost identical to the MT. Non-MT
elements retained from the OG in no way speak against this.
In a few passages Th. did read a Hebrew that differed from the
MT, usually by no more than a letter or two. In some of these
cases this 'reading' is probably the result of nothing more
than a misreading of a text identical to the MT. In this
respect Th. in Joshua is similar to Th. in Exodus.

In chapter two the relationship between Th. and Aq. and
Th. and Sym. was explored. On the basis of the material presented there we were able to demonstrate that the readings
attributed to Th. in the various sources were known and used
by both Aq. and Sym. Further study of the relationship
between Th. and Aq. revealed that Th. was *the* basis for the
latter's own further revision; Aq. had no independent knowledge
of the OG. Sym. also knew and used Th.; however, he had

independent knowledge of the OG as well. No sure or even probable evidence of further activity on the part of second-century Theodotion of Ephesus can be detected.

In chapter three we conducted an investigation of the καιγε recension in Joshua. Evidence for characteristic καιγε equivalences is found in the texts of Th. and Aq., and less often Sym. Most frequently the characteristics identified with the καιγε recension can be located in those "qualitative" and "quantitative" changes introduced by Origen on the basis of his source(s). Th., it appears, was the main source for such changes; if this is so, then we can expand the number of readings to be attributed to Th. by examining the relevant material in Origen. Although Th. did not consistently apply the characteristic equivalences of the καιγε recension, his efforts to establish standard Greek renderings are unmistakable and significant.

The καιγε recension of Joshua, like that of Judges (and, we expect, of every book or connected block of material) exhibits some peculiarities of its own. These "peculiarities" are often brought about by words or phrases, in the Hebrew or Greek, that are unique to Joshua or at least rare outside of this book. These "peculiarities" are often modifications of previously established characteristics and generally serve to standardize renderings in the same way that other καιγε equivalences do.

The accumulated evidence leaves no doubt that Th. in Joshua is to be included in the general καιγε recension. He did revise (a form of) the OG to a Hebrew identical in most respects to the MT; he does occupy a position midway between this form of the OG and Aquila (also Symmachus); and he does share a number of καιγε equivalences, and especially the tendency to standardize the Greek rendering of individual Hebrew words and phrases.

Theodotion, in our opinion, embodies those concerns that a revisor or translator ought to display. First of all, he was faithful to and respectful of the text he was revising.

Secondly, he was knowledgeable of and careful with the text
to which he was correcting. And, perhaps most important,
he took into account the needs of his intended audience and
produced a text in which the flavor of neither the Hebrew (as
with Sym.) nor the Greek (as with Aq.) was lost.

BIBLIOGRAPHY

Albright, W. F. "The List of Levitic Cities," *Louis Ginzberg Jubilee Volume.* New York: American Academy for Jewish Research, 1945, pp. 49-73.

Auld, A. Graeme. "Textual and Literary Studies in the Book of Joshua," *ZAW* 90 (1978), 412-417.

Baldi, Donato. *Giosuè.* La Sacra Bibbia. Roma: Marietti, 1956.

Baltzer, Klaus. *The Covenant Formulary (in Old Testament, Jewish, and early Christian Writings).* Tr. David E. Green. Philadelphia: Fortress Press, 1971.

Barthélemy, Dominique. *Les Devanciers d'Aquila.* Supplements to *Vetus Testamentum,* 10. Leiden: E. J. Brill, 1963.

_____. "Post-Scriptum: The 'Lucianic Recension,'" *1972 Proceedings IOSCS Pseudepigrapha.* Septuagint and Cognate Studies, 2. Society of Biblical Literature, 1972, pp. 64-89.

Benjamin, Charles Dow. *The Variations between the Hebrew and Greek Texts of Joshua: Chapters 1-12.* University of Pennsylvania, 1921.

Billen, A. V. "The Classification of the Greek MSS of the Hexateuch," *JTS* 26 (1925), 262-277.

Blass, F., and A. Debrunner. *A Greek Grammar of the New Testament and Other Early Christian Literature.* Translated and revised by Robert W. Funk. Chicago: The University of Chicago Press, 1961.

Bodine, Walter Ray. *The Greek Text of Judges: Recensional Developments.* Harvard Semitic Monographs, 23. Chico: Scholars Press, 1980.

_____. "*KAIGE* and other Recensional Developments in the Greek Text of Judges," *Bulletin of the International Organization for Septuagint and Cognate Studies* 13 (1980), 45-57.

Boling, Robert G. *Judges.* The Anchor Bible. Garden City, New York: Doubleday & Company, 1975.

383

384

Brooke, Alan England, and Norman McLean, with Henry St. John
Thackeray for Vols. II and III, eds. *The Old Testament
in Greek According to the Text of Codex Vaticanus, Supple-
mented from Other Uncial Manuscripts, with a Critical
Apparatus Containing the Variants of the Chief Ancient
Authorities for the Text of the Septuagint.* Vol. I: *The
Octateuch.* Vol. II: *The Later Historical Books.* Vol. III,
Part 1: *Esther, Judith, Tobit.* Cambridge, 1906-1940.

Brown, Francis, S. R. Driver, and Charles A. Briggs, eds. *A
Hebrew and English Lexicon of the Old Testament with an
Appendix Containing the Biblical Aramaic.* Corrected
reprint of 1907 ed. Oxford: Clarendon Press, 1968.

Chesman, Edward A. "Studies in the Septuagint Text of the
Book of Joshua." Unpublished master's-and-ordination
thesis. New York: Hebrew Union College-Jewish Institute
of Religion, 1967.

Coats, George W. "Balaam: Sinner or Saint?" *Biblical Research*
18 (1973), 21-29.

Cross, Frank Moore. *The Ancient Library of Qumran and Modern
Biblical Studies.* 2nd ed. Garden City, New York:
Doubleday Anchor Books, 1961.

_____. "The Contribution of the Qumrân Discoveries to
the Study of the Biblical Text," *IEJ* 16 (1966), 81-95.

_____. "The Evolution of a Theory of Local Texts,"
Qumran and the History of the Biblical Text. Eds. Frank
Moore Cross and Shemaryahu Talmon. Cambridge: Harvard
University Press, 1975, pp. 306-320.

_____. "The History of the Biblical Text in the
Light of Discoveries in the Judaean Desert," *HTR* 57
(1964), 281-299.

Cross, Frank Moore, and Shemaryahu Talmon, eds. *Qumran and the
History of the Biblical Text.* Cambridge: Harvard University Press, 1975.

Cross, Frank Moore, and G. Ernest Wright. "The Boundary and
Province Lists of the Kingdom of Judah," *JBL* 75 (1956),
202-226.

Cross, Frank Moore, *et al.* "Le Travail d'Édition des Fragments
Manuscrits de Qumrân," *RB* 63 (1956), 49-67.

Eliger, K., W. Rudolph, *et al.*, eds. *Biblia Hebraica
Stuttgartensia.* Stuttgart, 1977.

Field, Frederick, ed. *Origenis Hexaplorum quae supersunt sive veterum interpretum Graecorum in totum Vetus Testamentum fragmenta*. 2 vols. Oxford, 1875.

Gesenius, W. *Hebrew Grammar*. Ed. E. Kautzsch. 2nd Eng. ed., revised in accordance with 28th German edition by A.E. Cowley. Oxford: Clarendon Press, 1966.

Gordis, Robert. "A Note on Joshua 22:34," *AJSL* 47 (1931), 287-288.

Gottstein, M.H. "Neue Syrohexaplafragmente," *Biblica* 37 (1956), 162-183.

Grindel, John A. "Another characteristic of the *Kaige* recension: הצנ/νικος," *CBQ* 31 (1969), 499-513.

Hatch, Edwin, and Henry A. Redpath. *A Concordance to the Septuagint and the Other Greek Versions of the Old Testament (Including the Apocryphal Books)*. Photomechanical reprint of the 1897 Oxford ed. 3 vols. in 2. Graz, Austria, 1954.

Hoenig, Sidney B., ed. *The Book of Joshua: A new English Translation of the Text and Rashi, with a Commentary Digest*. New York: The Judaica Press, Inc., 1969.

Holladay, John S., Jr. "The Day(s) the *Moon* Stood Still," *JBL* 87 (1968), 166-178.

Hollenberg, Johann. *Der Charakter der alexandrinischen Übersetzung des Buches Josua und ihr textkritischer Werth*. Moers, 1876.

Holmes, Samuel. *Joshua: The Hebrew and Greek Texts*. Cambridge: University Press, 1914.

Janzen, J. Gerald. *Studies in the Text of Jeremiah*. Harvard Semitic Monographs, 6. Cambridge: Harvard University Press, 1973.

Jellicoe, Sidney. *The Septuagint and Modern Study*. Oxford, 1968.

_____. "Some Reflections on the ΚΑΙΓΕ recension," *VT* 23 (1973), 15-24.

Jenni, Ernst. "Zwei Jahrzehnte Forschung an den Büchern Josua bis Könige," *Theologische Rundschau* 27 (1961), 1-32, 97-146.

Kittel, Rud., *et al.*, eds. *Biblia Hebraica*. 14th ed., emended printing of 7th ed., a revised and expanded version of 3rd ed. Stuttgart, 1966.

Lagarde, Paul de. *Bibliothecae Syriacae a Paulo de Lagarde collectae quae ad philologiam sacram pertinent*. Ed. Alfred Rahlfs. Göttingen, 1892.

Liddell, H. G., and R. Scott. *A Greek-English Lexicon*. New York, 1878.

Lisowsky, Gerhard. *Konkordanz zum hebräischen Alten Testament nach dem von Paul Kahle in der Biblia Hebraica edidit Rudolf Kittel besorgten Masoretischen Text*. Stuttgart, 1958.

Mandelkern, Solomon. *Veteris Testamenti Concordantiae Hebraicae atque Chaldaicae*. 9th expanded and rev. ed. Tel Aviv: Schocken Publishing House Ltd., 1971.

Margolis, Max L. "Additions to Field from the Lyons Codex of the Old Latin," *JAOS* 33 (1913), 254-258.

_____. "Ai or the City? Joshua 8.12, 16," *JQR* NS 7 (1916/17), 491-497.

_____. *The Book of Joshua in Greek*. Paris: Librairie Orientaliste Paul Geuthner, 1931.

_____. "Complete Induction for the Identification of the Vocabulary in the Greek Versions of the Old Testament with its Semitic Equivalents: Its Necessity and the Means of obtaining it," *JAOS* 30 (1910), 301-312.

_____. "Corrections in the Apparatus of the Book of Joshua in the Larger Cambridge Septuagint," *JBL* 49 (1930), 234-264.

_____. "The Grouping of the Codices in the Greek Joshua: A Preliminary Notice," *JQR* NS 1 (1910/11), 259-263.

_____. "Hexapla and Hexaplaric," *AJSL* 32 (1916), 126-140.

_____. "The K Text of Joshua," *AJSL* 28 (1911), 1-55.

_____. "'Man by Man,' Joshua 7, 17," *JQR* NS 3 (1912/13), 319-336.

_____. "Presidential Address," *Journal of the Palestine Oriental Society* (1925), 61-63.

387

_____. "Specimen of a New Edition of the Greek Joshua," *Jewish Studies in Memory of Israel Abrahams.* New York: Jewish Institute of Religion, 1927, pp. 307-323; reprinted in Jellicoe, Sidney, ed. *Studies in the Septuagint: Origins, Recensions, and Interpretations.* New York: KTAV, 1974, pp. 434-450.

_____. "Textual Criticism of the Greek Old Testament," *Proceedings of the American Philosophical Society* 67 (1928), 187-197.

_____. "Transliterations in the Greek Old Testament," *JQR NS 16* (1925/26), 117-125.

_____. "ΧΩΡΙΣ," *Oriental Studies published in Commemoration of the Fortieth Anniversary of Paul Haupt as Director of the Oriental Seminary of the Johns Hopkins University.* Baltimore: The Johns Hopkins University Press, 1926, pp. 84-92.

Mendenhall, George E. *The Tenth Generation: The Origins of the Biblical Tradition.* Baltimore: The Johns Hopkins University Press, 1973.

Metzger, Bruce M. "The Lucianic Recension of the Greek Bible," *Chapters in the History of New Testament Textual Criticism.* New Testament Tools and Studies, 4. Leiden: E. J. Brill, 1963, pp. 1-41.

Moore, George F. *A Critical and Exegetical Commentary on Judges.* The International Critical Commentary. New York: Charles Scribner's Sons, 1895.

Noth, Martin. *Das Buch Josua.* 3rd ed. HAT 7. Tübingen: J. C. B. Mohr (Paul Siebeck), 1971.

O'Connell, Kevin G. *The Theodotionic Revision of the Book of Exodus.* Harvard Semitic Monographs, 3. Cambridge: Harvard University Press, 1972.

Orlinsky, Harry M. "The Hebrew *Vorlage* of the Septuagint of the Book of Joshua," *Supplements to Vetus Testamentum,* 17 (Rome, 1968). Leiden: E. J. Brill, 1969, 187-195.

_____. "Introductory Essay: On Anthropomorphisms and Anthropopathisms in the Septuagint and Targum" in Zlotowitz, Bernard M. *The Septuagint Translation of the Hebrew Terms in Relation to God in the Book of Jeremiah.* New York: KTAV, 1980, pp. *xv-xxiv.*

_____. "Margolis' Work in the Septuagint," *Max Leopold Margolis: Scholar and Teacher.* Philadelphia, 1952, pp. 34-44 (chapter IV).

_____. "Origen's Tetrapla -- a Scholarly Fiction?" *Proceedings of the First World Congress of Jewish Studies, 1947.* Jerusalem, 1952. I, 173-182; reprinted in Jellicoe, Sidney, ed. *Studies in the Septuagint: Origins, Recensions, and Interpretations.* New York: KTAV, 1974, pp. 382-391.

_____. "Review of Charles T. Fritsch's *The Anti-Anthropomorphisms of the Greek Pentateuch,*" *Crozier Quarterly* 21 (1944), 156-160.

_____. "The Treatment of Anthropomorphisms and Anthropopathisms in the Septuagint of Isaiah," *HUCA* 27 (1956), 193-200.

Pretzl, Otto. "Die griechischen Handschriftengruppen im Buche Josue untersucht nach ihrer Eigenart und ihrem Verhältnis zueinander," *Biblica* 9 (1928), 377-427.

_____. "Der hexaplarische und tetraplarische Septuagintatext des Origenes in den Büchern Josue und Richter," *Byzantinische Zeitschrift* 30 (1929/30), 262-268.

Rahlfs, Alfred, ed. *Septuaginta: Id est Vetus Testamentum graece iuxta LXX interpretes.* 2 vols. 9th ed. Stuttgart, 1971.

Reider, Joseph. *An Index to Aquila, Greek-Hebrew·Hebrew-Greek· Latin-Hebrew, with the Syriac and Armenian Evidence.* Completed and revised by Nigel Turner. Supplements to *Vetus Testamentum,* 12. Leiden: E. J. Brill, 1966.

Shenkel, James Donald. *Chronology and Recensional Development in the Greek Text of Kings.* Harvard Semitic Monographs, 1. Cambridge: Harvard University Press, 1968.

Smith, Gary Verlan. *An Introduction to the Greek Manuscripts of Joshua: Their Classification, Characteristics and Relationships.* Unpublished Ph.D. dissertation. Philadelphia: The Dropsie University for Hebrew and Cognate Learning, 1973.

Smith, Michael. "Another Criterion for the καιγε Recension," *Bibl* 48 (1967), 443-445.

Smyth, Herbert Weir. *Greek Grammar.* Revised by Gordon M. Messing. Cambridge: Harvard University Press, 1966.

Soggin, J. Alberto. *Joshua.* Tr. R. A. Wilson. The Old Testament Library. Philadelphia: Westminster Press, 1972.

Swete, Henry Barclay. *An Introduction to the Old Testament in Greek.* Revised by Richard Rusden Ottley. Cambridge, 1914.

Talmon, Shemaryahu. "The List of Cities of Simeon," *Eretz-Israel* 8. Jerusalem: Israel Exploration Society, 1967, 76*, 265-268.

_____. "The Textual Study of the Bible: A New Outlook," *Qumran and the History of the Biblical Text*. Eds. Frank Moore Cross and Shemaryahu Talmon. Cambridge: Harvard University Press, 1975, pp. 321-400.

Thackeray, H. St. John. *A Grammar of the Old Testament in Greek*. Vol. 1 (Introduction, Orthography and Accidence). Cambridge: University Press, 1909.

_____. "New Light on the Book of Jashar (a study of 3 Regn. viii 53^b LXX)," *JTS* 11 (1910), 518-532.

_____. "Renderings of the Infinitive Absolute in the LXX," *JTS* 9 (1907-08), 597-601.

_____. *The Septuagint and Jewish Worship: A Study in Origins*. London: Oxford Press, 1921.

Tov, Emanuel. "Midrash-Type Exegesis in the LXX of Joshua," *RB* (1978), 50-61.

_____. "Transliterations of Hebrew Words in the Greek Versions of the Old Testament: A Further Characteristic of the *kaige*-Th. Revision?" *Textus* 8. Annual of the Hebrew University Bible Project, ed. S. Talmon. Jerusalem: Magnes Press, 1973, 78-92.

Ulrich, Eugene Charles. *The Qumran Text of Samuel and Josephus*. Harvard Semitic Monographs, 19. Missoula: Scholars Press, 1978.

Walters, Peter. *The Text of the Septuagint: Its Corruptions and Their Emendation*. Ed. D. W. Gooding. Cambridge: University Press, 1973.

Wevers, John, "Proto-Septuagint Studies," *The Seed of Wisdom: Essays in Honour of T. J. Meek*. Ed. W. S. McCullough. Toronto: University of Toronto Press, 1964, pp. 58-77.

_____. *Text History of the Greek Deuteronomy*. Mitteilungen des Septuaginta- Unternehmens (MSU), XIII. Göttingen: Vandenhoeck & Ruprecht, 1978.

Wright, G. Ernest. "The Literary and Historical Problem of Joshua 10 and Judges 1," *Journal of Near Eastern Studies* 5 (1946), 105-114.

_____. *Shechem: The Biography of a Biblical City.*
New York: McGraw-Hill, 1965.

Würthwein, Ernst. *The Text of the Old Testament.* Tr. Peter
R. Ackroyd. Oxford: Basil Blackwell, 1957.

Ziegler, Joseph, ed. *Septuaginta: Vetus Testamentum Graecum
Auctoritate Academiae Litterarum Gottingensis editum.*
Vol. XII, 1: *Sapientia Salomonis.* Vol. XII, 2:
Sapientia Iesu Filii Sirach. Vol. XIII: *Duodecim
Prophetae.* Vol. XIV: *Isaias.* Vol. XV: *Ieremias, Baruch,
Threni, Epistula Ieremiae.* Vol. XVI, 1: *Ezechiel.* Vol.
XVI, 2: *Susanna, Daniel, Bel et Draco.* Göttingen,
1939-1965.

Joshua

	Page		Page
1:1	89, 117, 301	2:23	**322**, 371-372
1:2	117	2:24	275
1:3	117	3:1	317
1:4	337	3:2	302
1:5	123, 257, 278,	3:4	39, 301
	280, 281	3:6	39-40
1:6	38, 173	3:8	60, 87-88, 239
1:7	38, 84-85,	3:10	40, 287
	123-124, 184	3:12	60-61, 279-280
1:8	39, 84-85, 245	3:13	119, 125, 238, 261
	259	3:14	125, 237, 261
1:9	124	3:15	60, 87-88, 125, 178
1:11	38-39		185, 239, 261
1:12	150	3:16	119, 126, 194,
1:13	59		237-238, 261
1:14	286	3:17	88-89, 260
1:15	275, 310	4:1	89
1:18	85-86, 239,	4:2	61, 279
	276-277, 279	4:3	281, 317
2:1	117, 238, 298	4:4	61, 279
2:2	118	4:5	127, 238, 278,
2:4	59-60, 118, 242		360-361
2:5	291	4:7	91, 186, 289
2:6	86-87, 243,	4:8	370
	251-253, 258	4:9	281
2:7	35, 297, 363	4:10	90, 239, 304
2:9	118	4:10-4:11	40-41, 173
2:11	278	4:12	62
2:12	87, 236, 275	4:14	41
2:14	124, 237	4:15	89
2:16	322, 329, 372	4:18	305
2:22	296-297, 319,	4:19	90
	363	4:22	91, 186

	Page		Page
4:23	41	6:21	280
5:2	62-63, 89, 244,	6:24	93-94, 161-162,
	259, 307, 321		187, 239
5:3	62-63, 307	6:26	280, 281
5:4	328	6:27	128-129
5:5	309	7:1	128, 324
5:6	328	7:2	163
5:9	89	7:3	42, 163, 279
5:12	91-93, 186, 245,	7:5	297
	258	7:7	367
5:13	280	7:11	275
5:14	297-298, 309	7:15	94
5:15	297-298, 363	7:20	285-286
6:1	285	7:21	95-97, 239, 314
6:2	63-64, 360		364, 368-369
6:3	284, 328	7:24	97-98, 188, 246,
6:4	283-284		256, 335
6:5	237, 265, 267,	7:25	98, 189, 335
	278, 282-284,	7:26	97-98, 246, 256,
	287, 337, 360		289, 325, 335
6:6	283-284	Chapter 8	162
6:8	282	8:2	276
6:9	283-284, 290	8:5	128
6:10	294	8:9	304, 318
6:11	317-318, 370	8:11	301
6:13	282-283, 290,	8:12-13	162-163, 279, 301, 304
	359	8:14	316-317
6:14	321-322	8:16	163, 296-297, 306
6:15	276		324
6:16	283	8:18	163
6:17	64-65, 286	8:19	35, 291
6:18	96, 277	8:20	297
6:19	161-162	8:24	307-308, 322, 372
6:20	278, 282, 287	8:25	280
	360	8:27	362

	Page		Page
8:28	74, 163, 289	10:15	319-320
8:29	337	10:18	294, 337
8:31 (9:4)	295, 310-311	10:19	98-99, 246, 297
8:33 (9:6)	287, 310-311,	10:20	35, 70-71, 236
	360	10:21	323
8:34 (9:7)	85	10:22	362
8:35 (9:8)	287, 360	10:23	170-172
9:2	325	10:24	279, 331, 374
9:4 (9:10)	164, 275	10:27	120, 337, 362
9:5 (9:11)	65-68, 178,	10:28	100, 250-251, 262,
	244, 259		307-309
9:6 (9:12)	280	10:30	35, 275
9:7 (9:13)	280	10:33	165-167, 204, 366
9:9 (9:15)	128-129	10:34	170-172
9:10 (9:16)	175	10:36	170, 373
9:12 (9:18)	66-67	10:37	170
9:14 (9:20)	294	10:38	323, 325, 373
9:16 (9:22)	302	10:40	36, 42-45, 334
9:21 (9:27)	119	10:41	100-101, 236
10:1	129, 135, 302	10:43	320
10:2	337	11:1	45, 132-134,
10:3	68-69, 166,		240-241
	170	11:2	333-334
10:4	135	11:3	72
10:5	130, 170-172,	11:5	132
	246-247, 258,	11:7	132
	290	11:8	45-46, 71-72, 255,
10:6	291		334-335
10:10	42, 122, 130-131	11:10	101, 239, 308,
10:11	35, 42, 69-70,		321-322
	110-111, 130-131,	11:11	307, 362, 366
	245, 258, 307, 337	11:13	72-74, 276-277
10:12	292-293, 313-314	11:16	43, 334
10:13	119-120, 315	11:17	49, 102, 189
10:14	280	11:19	134-136, 248-249,
			261

	Page		Page
11:20	306	13:23	37, 173
11:21	36, 74-75, 242	13:26	72, 75-76, 238
11:22	106, 191, 276	13:27	50, 103
11:23	36	13:28	368
		13:33	364
		14:6	103-104, 190,
12:1	46-47		257, 280
12:2	36, 47	14:7	50-51, 311
12:4-5	48, 175	14:8	37, 51, 140, 191
12:5	102, 136-137	14:9	140, 289
12:6	150, 310	14:10	286
12:7	49, 101-102,	14:11	366
	141, 239	14:12	104-105
12:8	43-44, 334	14:14	289, 313, 362
12:12	170-172	14:15	337
12:14	48-49	15:1	168, 197
12:15	170-171	15:2	44
12:19	132, 195	15:3	140-141, 241, 260
12:20	132-133	15:6	141-142, 241, 262
12:23	104, 190,	15:7	104
	333-334	15:9	76-78,
13:2	136-137		147-148, 149, 163
13:3	328	15:14	142
13:5	49	15:17	105-106, 190, 240,
13:6	46, 375		260
13:8	137-138, 150,	15:19	42-45, 78-79,
	196		334-335
13:9	316	15:21	48-49, 143-144,
13:11	102, 136-137		176, 247, 261
13:13	102-103, 136-137,	15:23	144, 198
	239, 303	15:25 (15:24)	145, 198, 200, 241,
13:14	300-301, 364		335
13:16	37, 304, 316	15:27	144
13:21	138-140, 316	15:28	144
13:22	308	15:32	169

	Page		Page
15:35	170	18:17	197
15:38	72	18:19	142
15:39	170	18:21	142
15:46	106	18:26	72
15:47	106	18:28	148-149, 238,
15:50	75, 181		335-336
15:60	149	19:1-9	133
16:1	168	19:10	165, 204
16:2	167	19:11	329-330, 373-374
16:7	329-330, 374	19:15	133
16:10	107, 236, 303,	19:22	329-330, 374
	312, 365, 367	19:26	330
17:1	168, 280	19:34	120
17:2	145-146,	20:4	290
	247-248, 256	20:5	297
17:3	146	20:6	319, 337
17:4	120	20:9	51
17:9	112, 204,	21:3	150, 241
	304-305	21:4	133
17:11	333-334, 375	21:9	133
17:13	155	21:13	51-52
17:16	146-147	21:20	167-168
17:18	146, 199	21:26	169, 238
18:4	107, 173, 241,	21:39	169
	265, 294	21:40	168-169
18:6	107, 191, 309	(21:42b)	362
18:7	285	(21:42d)	307
18:8	107, 191,	21:44	52-53, 177, 257,
	240, 309		278-280
18:9	107	22:1	150-151, 242
18:11	165, 204	22:4	299-300, 310
18:13	44	22:5	108, 240
18:14	44, 149	22:7	275, 299-300, 313
18:15	44, 76-77,	22:8	151, 249, 299-300,
	147-148, 149		320-321

	Page		Page
22:9	151, 320	24:2	289
22:10	109, 240, 296	24:5	303
22:14	278, 280	24:7	290-291, 324, 337,
22:16	364		372
22:18	53-54, 152	24:8	325-327, 328, 372
22:19	296	24:9	325-326
22:20	53-54, 279,	24:10	154-157, 299
	287	24:11	327
22:25	121, 256, 285,	24:15	111, 240, 262, 292,
	301		312, 331-332
22:27	285, 301, 312	24:17	293, 303, 311
22:28	152-153, 296,	24:18	275
	365	24:19	187, 287, 298-299
22:29	296, 299-300,	24:20	313
	322-323, 372	24:25	80-81
22:30	292, 315	24:26	112, 157, 240, 260
22:31	305, 318-319	24:27	113, 313-314
22:32	323	24:28	278
22:34	79-80, 236	(24:31a)	307
Chapter 23	154	(24:33b)	81-82, 280
23:4	110-111, 153,	*Outside of Joshua*	
	201, 238, 248,	Gen 19:9	156
	258	Lev 2:3	364
23:7	312	Lev 24:9	364
23:10	153-155, 279,	Nu 13:22	142
	297, 325	Nu 23:11	156, 202
23:12	320	Nu 24:10	156
23:13	54-55	Nu 33:55	54-55
23:14	314	Dtn 1:36	368
23:15	323, 331-332	Dtn 7:25	97
23:16	280-281, 291,	Dtn 11:25	123
	314, 324, 372	Dtn 29:8	123
Joshua 24		Dtn 33:5	315
(1st part)	156, 202	Ju 1:5-7	129
24:1	80-81, 281	Ju 1:10	142

	Page
Ju 1:13	105-106, 190
Ju 1:15	79, 183
Ju 2:17	361
Ju 2:23	361
Ju 3:27	359
Ju 6:34	359
Ju 7:18	359
Ju 7:19	359
Ju 7:20	359
Ju 7:22	308, 359
Ju 8:20	308
Ju 9:54	308, 361
Ju 14:16	277
2 S 1:18	369
1 K 1:9	376
1 K 8:(13)53	369
2 K 10:6	337
2 K 10:11	337
Is 6:9	156
Is 38:13	196
Is 44:2	315